All about COOKERY

All about COOKERY

Norma MacMillan

OCTOPUS

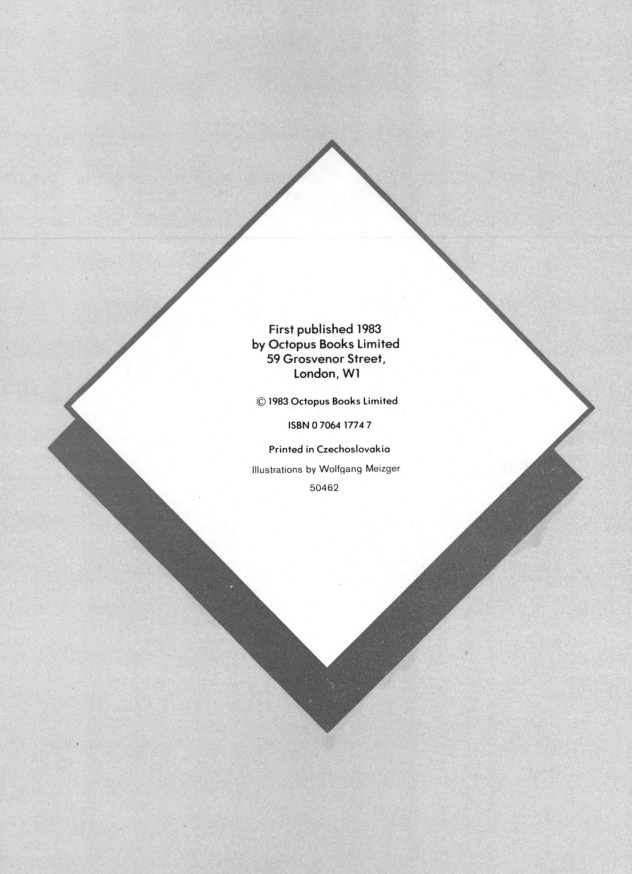

First published 1983
by Octopus Books Limited
59 Grosvenor Street,
London, W1

© 1983 Octopus Books Limited

ISBN 0 7064 1774 7

Printed in Czechoslovakia

Illustrations by Wolfgang Meizger

50462

Contents

Soups

A hearty bowl of soup on a winter's day
can be a meal in itself, or a nourishing
start to a meal. But although soups with
traditional ingredients come to mind, there
is a wealth of more unusual soup recipes,
containing all sorts of meat, fish, fowl and
vegetables, to add to the family favourites.
In this chapter you will find recipes to suit
the seasons and the available ingredients.
Soups hale and hearty, smooth and creamy,
or spicy and refreshing are selected here
for you.

Kidney Soup

If liked, add 3 tablespoons cream before serving.

METRIC	IMPERIAL
225 g ox kidney, skinned, cored and chopped	8 oz ox kidney, skinned, cored and chopped
25 g flour	1 oz flour
40 g butter	1½ oz butter
2 onions, chopped	2 onions, chopped
1.2 litres beef stock	2 pints beef stock
1 bouquet garni	1 bouquet garni
½ teaspoon lemon juice	½ teaspoon lemon juice
salt and pepper	salt and pepper

Coat the kidney pieces with the flour. Melt the butter in a saucepan. Add the kidney and onions and fry until lightly browned. Stir in the stock, bouquet garni, lemon juice and salt and pepper to taste and bring to the boil. Cover and simmer for 1½ hours.

Cool slightly, then skim any fat from the surface of the soup. Discard the bouquet garni. Purée the soup in a blender or food processor, then return to the saucepan. Reheat gently.

Taste and adjust the seasoning before serving.

Serves 4 to 6

Oxtail Soup

METRIC	IMPERIAL
25 g dripping	1 oz dripping
1 large onion, chopped	1 large onion, chopped
1 oxtail, chopped	1 oxtail, chopped
2 carrots, chopped	2 carrots, chopped
2 celery sticks, chopped	2 celery sticks, chopped
1 bay leaf	1 bay leaf
6 peppercorns	6 peppercorns
salt	salt

Melt the dripping in a large saucepan. Add the onion and oxtail and fry until browned. Cover with water and add the remaining ingredients with salt to taste. Bring to the boil, then cover and simmer for 3 to 4 hours or until the oxtail is very tender and the meat is falling from the bones.

Remove the oxtail from the pan. Take the meat from the bones and discard the bones.

Skim all fat from the surface of the soup. Discard the bay leaf and peppercorns, if possible. Return the meat to the soup, then purée.

Reheat the soup, and thin with a little water if it is too thick. Taste and adjust the seasoning.

Serves 4 to 6

Chicken Chowder

A chowder is a thick soup, almost a stew.

METRIC	IMPERIAL
3 streaky bacon rashers, rinded and chopped	3 streaky bacon rashers, rinded and chopped
1 onion, chopped	1 onion, chopped
450 ml chicken stock	¾ pint chicken stock
350 g mixed root vegetables (potato, carrot, parsnip, etc.), diced	12 oz mixed root vegetables (potato, carrot, parsnip, etc.), diced
300 ml milk	½ pint milk
175 g cooked chicken meat, diced	6 oz cooked chicken meat, diced
4 heaped tablespoons fresh, frozen or canned sweetcorn kernels	4 heaped tablespoons fresh, frozen or canned sweetcorn kernels
salt and pepper	salt and pepper

Place the bacon and onion in a saucepan and fry until the onion is softened. Stir in the stock and bring to the boil. Add the root vegetables and simmer until tender.

Add the remaining ingredients, with salt and pepper to taste and mix well. Simmer for a further 10 minutes. Serve hot.

Serves 4 to 6

Beef and Vegetable Soup

If liked, add 50 g/2 oz pasta shapes to the soup 30 minutes before the end of the cooking time.

METRIC	IMPERIAL
2 tablespoons oil	2 tablespoons oil
2 large onions, chopped	2 large onions, chopped
3 streaky bacon rashers, rinded and chopped	3 streaky bacon rashers, rinded and chopped
25 g flour	1 oz flour
1 × 400 g can tomatoes	1 × 14 oz can tomatoes
900 ml beef stock	1½ pints beef stock
225 g chuck steak, diced	8 oz chuck steak, diced
100 g frozen peas	4 oz frozen peas
3 large carrots, diced	3 large carrots, diced
1 bouquet garni	1 bouquet garni
salt and pepper	salt and pepper

Heat the oil in a saucepan. Add the onions and bacon and fry until the onions are softened. Sprinkle over the flour, stir in well and cook for 2 minutes. Add the tomatoes with their juice and the stock. Bring to the boil, stirring.

Add the steak, peas, carrots, bouquet garni and salt and pepper to taste and mix well. Cover and simmer for about 2 hours or until the beef is tender.

Discard the bouquet garni, and taste and adjust the seasoning before serving.

Serves 6

Scots Haddock Chowder

Hot garlic bread is a good accompaniment for this thick and filling soup.

METRIC	IMPERIAL
500 g smoked haddock fillet	1 lb smoked haddock fillet
50 g butter	2 oz butter
2 large onions, chopped	2 large onions, chopped
4 potatoes, sliced	4 potatoes, sliced
2 celery sticks, sliced	2 celery sticks, sliced
1 bay leaf	1 bay leaf
1 tablespoon chopped parsley	1 tablespoon chopped parsley
salt and pepper	salt and pepper
2 tablespoons quick-cooking porridge oats	2 tablespoons quick-cooking porridge oats
450 ml hot milk	¾ pint hot milk
3 tablespoons sherry	3 tablespoons sherry

Place the haddock in a heatproof dish and pour over boiling water to cover. Leave for 3 minutes, then drain, reserving 300 ml/½ pint of the liquid. Remove the skin and flake the fish.

Melt the butter in a saucepan. Add the onions and fry until softened. Add the fish, potatoes, reserved poaching liquid, celery, bay leaf, parsley and salt and pepper to taste. Bring to the boil and simmer for about 20 minutes or until the potatoes are tender.

Stir in the oats and milk and simmer for a further 5 minutes. Discard the bay leaf. Taste and adjust the seasoning, then stir in the sherry and serve.

Serves 4 to 6

Garlic bread
Garlic bread is a popular accompaniment to soups and Italian dishes like spaghetti bolognese. To make garlic bread, crush a clove of garlic and blend in about 50 g/2 oz softened butter. Make cuts in a loaf of French bread, crossways about 5 cm/2 inches apart, not cutting all the way through. Spread the garlic butter in the cuts. Wrap the loaf in foil and heat through in a preheated moderately hot oven (190°C/375°F, Gas Mark 5) for 15 to 20 minutes. The garlic butter will melt and flavour the bread, which can be broken apart at the table.

An alternative to garlic bread is herb bread. This is made in the same way, but the butter is mixed with 1 tablespoon dried mixed herbs and a good squeeze of lemon juice.

Leek and Tomato Soup

Each serving of this soup has only 240 calories, so you can enjoy it as a starter for a slimming meal.

METRIC	IMPERIAL
4 large leeks, finely chopped	4 large leeks, finely chopped
4 large tomatoes, skinned and chopped	4 large tomatoes, skinned and chopped
1 bay leaf	1 bay leaf
1 teaspoon dried mixed herbs	1 teaspoon dried mixed herbs
300 ml water	½ pint water
300 ml plain yogurt	½ pint plain yogurt
salt and pepper	salt and pepper

Place the leeks, tomatoes, bay leaf, herbs and water in a saucepan and bring to the boil. Simmer gently until the leeks are softened.

Discard the bay leaf, then purée the soup in a blender or food processor. Alternatively, sieve the soup. Return to the saucepan and stir in the yogurt and salt and pepper to taste. Heat through gently.

Serves 4

Creamy Fish Soup

For slimmers, add plain yogurt instead of cream.

METRIC	IMPERIAL
225–350 g white fish fillets	8–12 oz white fish fillets
900 ml Court Bouillon★	1½ pints Court Bouillon★
25 g cornflour	1 oz cornflour
25–50 g butter	1–2 oz butter
grated rind of 1 lemon	grated rind of 1 lemon
salt and pepper	salt and pepper
150 ml milk	¼ pint milk
150 ml double cream	¼ pint double cream
chopped parsley or fresh dill to garnish	chopped parsley or fresh dill to garnish

Place the fish in a saucepan and cover with 300 ml/½ pint of the court bouillon. Bring to a simmer and poach until the fish will flake easily when tested with a fork. Drain the fish, reserving the liquid. Flake the fish and keep hot.

Blend the cornflour with the remaining cold stock and place in the cleaned saucepan. Add the strained cooking liquid from the fish, the butter, lemon rind and salt and pepper to taste. Bring to the boil, stirring, and simmer until thickened.

Stir in the milk, cream and flaked fish and heat through gently without boiling. Taste and adjust the seasoning, and garnish with parsley or dill.

Serves 4 to 6

Hearty Bean and Vegetable Soup

METRIC	IMPERIAL
225 g dried haricot beans, soaked overnight	8 oz dried haricot beans, soaked overnight
1.8 litres water	3 pints water
3 tablespoons oil	3 tablespoons oil
1 onion, chopped	1 onion, chopped
1 garlic clove, crushed	1 garlic clove, crushed
1 celery stick, chopped	1 celery stick, chopped
2 leeks, thinly sliced	2 leeks, thinly sliced
500 g green cabbage, finely shredded	1 lb green cabbage, finely shredded
¼ teaspoon dried thyme	¼ teaspoon dried thyme
¼ teaspoon dried rosemary	¼ teaspoon dried rosemary
1 tablespoon tomato purée	1 tablespoon tomato purée
salt and pepper	salt and pepper
2 tablespoons chopped parsley	2 tablespoons chopped parsley

Drain the beans and place in a saucepan. Cover with fresh cold water and bring to the boil. Boil for 5 minutes, then drain the beans and throw away the water. Return the beans to the pan and add the measured water. Bring to the boil, then cover and simmer for about 2 hours or until tender.

About 15 minutes before the beans have finished cooking, heat the oil in another saucepan. Add the onion, garlic, celery and leeks and fry until the vegetables are softened. Stir in the cabbage and cook for a further 3 minutes.

Drain the beans, reserving the cooking liquid. Add the liquid to the vegetables, with the herbs, tomato purée and salt and pepper to taste. Bring to the boil and simmer for 30 minutes.

Stir in the beans and simmer for a further 10 minutes or until all the vegetables are tender. Stir in the parsley. Taste and adjust the seasoning and serve hot.

Serves 6 to 8

Freezing liquids
When freezing any liquid, such as soups, purées or stocks, or food in a liquid or syrup, such as a casserole or fruit in syrup, it is essential to leave **headspace** in the container. This allows for expansion when the liquid freezes. If headspace were not allowed, the container could be cracked as the contents burst through it.

For a 600 ml/1 pint container, leave 2.5 cm/1 inch headspace. Double this amount of headspace for a 1 litre/1¾ pint container.

Curried Lentil Soup

METRIC	IMPERIAL
500 g cooking apples, peeled, cored and chopped	1 lb cooking apples, peeled, cored and chopped
2 celery sticks, chopped	2 celery sticks, chopped
2 large onions, chopped	2 large onions, chopped
4 carrots, chopped	4 carrots, chopped
225 g red lentils	8 oz red lentils
1–2 teaspoons curry powder	1–2 teaspoons curry powder
2 teaspoons tomato purée	2 teaspoons tomato purée
1.8 litres stock or water	3 pints stock or water
salt and pepper	salt and pepper

Place the apples and vegetables in a saucepan and stir in the lentils. Add the remaining ingredients with salt and pepper to taste. Bring to the boil, then cover and simmer for 1 to 1½ hours or until the lentils are soft.

Purée the soup in a blender or food processor, or sieve it. Return to the saucepan and reheat gently. Taste and adjust the seasoning before serving.

Serves 5 to 6

Soups as a meal
A thick soup makes a nutritious meal when served with wholemeal bread and cheese.

Carrot and Kidney Bean Soup

METRIC	IMPERIAL
50 g butter	2 oz butter
500 g carrots, sliced	1 lb carrots, sliced
1 large potato, diced	1 large potato, diced
1 onion, chopped	1 onion, chopped
900 ml water	1½ pints water
1 tablespoon tomato purée	1 tablespoon tomato purée
good pinch of ground coriander	good pinch of ground coriander
salt and pepper	salt and pepper
1 × 425 g can red kidney beans, drained	1 × 15 oz can red kidney beans, drained

Melt the butter in a saucepan. Add the carrots, potato and onion and fry until the onion is softened. Stir in the water, tomato purée, coriander and salt and pepper to taste. Bring to the boil, then cover and simmer for 45 minutes.

Stir in the kidney beans and heat through gently. Taste and adjust the seasoning before serving.

Serves 4

Vegetable Rice Soup

METRIC	IMPERIAL
1 tablespoon oil	1 tablespoon oil
3 tablespoons long-grain rice	3 tablespoons long-grain rice
1.2 litres chicken stock	2 pints chicken stock
1 small carrot, grated	1 small carrot, grated
1 small turnip, grated	1 small turnip, grated
small piece of swede, grated	small piece of swede, grated
2 celery sticks, grated	2 celery sticks, grated
salt and pepper	salt and pepper

Heat the oil in a saucepan. Add the rice and fry, stirring, for about 3 minutes. Stir in the stock and bring to the boil. Cover and simmer for 20 minutes or until the rice is just tender.

Add the vegetables and salt and pepper to taste. Simmer for a further 5 minutes or until the vegetables are just tender but still firm. Serve hot.

Serves 4 to 6

Freezing soups and stews

Soups, stews and casseroles can usually be frozen without difficulty. If they contain wine or vinegar, do not use an aluminium container because the flavour of the dish could be affected, and the container discoloured. Use salt, pepper, garlic, spices and herbs sparingly because seasonings taste stronger after freezing; more can be added when the food is reheated, if necessary. Some ingredients, such as cream and soured cream, should be added after reheating, just before serving.

If a soup has been thickened with egg yolks and cream, it must be reheated in a double boiler and stirred constantly to prevent separation. Sauces, soups, etc., which have been thickened with flour may also separate when thawed and reheated, so use cornflour instead. Dissolve the cornflour in a little water or stock before adding to the sauce, etc. If the flour is added to melted fat, just omit it and add the dissolved cornflour at the end.

Green Minestrone

METRIC	IMPERIAL
100 g dried haricot beans, soaked overnight	4 oz dried haricot beans, soaked overnight
2 tablespoons oil	2 tablespoons oil
2 leeks, sliced	2 leeks, sliced
2 tablespoons chopped parsley	2 tablespoons chopped parsley
2 tablespoons chopped mixed fresh herbs	2 tablespoons chopped mixed fresh herbs
1.8 litres water	3 pints water
2 celery sticks, chopped	2 celery sticks, chopped
4 tomatoes, skinned and chopped	4 tomatoes, skinned and chopped
2 potatoes, diced	2 potatoes, diced
salt and pepper	salt and pepper
50 g small pasta shapes	2 oz small pasta shapes
100 g frozen peas	4 oz frozen peas

Drain the beans and place in a saucepan. Cover with fresh cold water. Bring to the boil and boil for 10 minutes, then simmer for 1½ hours or until tender.

Meanwhile, heat the oil in a large saucepan. Add the leeks and herbs and fry for 10 minutes. Stir in the water, celery, tomatoes, potatoes and salt and pepper to taste. Bring to the boil and simmer for 30 minutes.

Stir in the pasta and peas. Drain the beans and add to the soup. Simmer for a further 15 minutes or until all the vegetables are tender. Adjust the seasoning.

Serves 6 to 8

Lentil Soup

METRIC	IMPERIAL
900 ml water	1½ pints water
1 rounded teaspoon yeast extract	1 rounded teaspoon yeast extract
100 g lentils	4 oz lentils
1 large carrot, chopped	1 large carrot, chopped
1 large onion, chopped	1 large onion, chopped
1 tablespoon tomato purée	1 tablespoon tomato purée
1 tablespoon flour	1 tablespoon flour
300 ml milk	½ pint milk
salt and pepper	salt and pepper
2 slices of wholemeal bread	2 slices of wholemeal bread

Bring the water to the boil in a large saucepan. Spoon a little of the water into a cup and stir in the yeast extract until dissolved. Add this mixture to the remaining water in the pan. Stir in the lentils. Return to the boil, then cover and remove from the heat. Leave to soak overnight.

The next day, bring back to the boil and add the carrot, onion and tomato purée. Simmer, covered, for 1 hour.

Blend the flour with a little of the cold milk. Add to the pan with the remaining milk and simmer, stirring, until thickened. Season to taste with salt and pepper and leave to heat through gently.

Toast the bread, then cut into small cubes. Serve the soup topped with the toast cubes.

Serves 4

> **Garnish after freezing**
> Add garnishes such as chopped parsley and croûtons after reheating a frozen soup.

Creamed Potato and Leek Soup

METRIC	IMPERIAL
50 g butter	2 oz butter
500 g leeks, sliced	1 lb leeks, sliced
225 g potatoes, sliced	8 oz potatoes, sliced
1 parsnip, sliced	1 parsnip, sliced
600 ml chicken stock	1 pint chicken stock
salt and pepper	salt and pepper
150 ml single cream	¼ pint single cream
chopped chives to garnish	chopped chives to garnish

Melt the butter in a large saucepan. Add the leeks, potatoes and parsnip and fry gently until softened. Stir in the stock and bring to the boil. Season to taste with salt and pepper, then cover and simmer for 1 hour.

Cool slightly, then purée in a blender or food processor, or sieve to a smooth purée. Return to the pan and stir in the cream. Heat through gently, but do not allow to boil.

Taste and adjust the seasoning, then serve hot, garnished with chives.

Serves 4

French Onion Soup

For a traditional French topping, pour the soup into four to six flameproof serving bowls and top with slices of French bread or toast and grated Gruyère or Cheddar cheese. Grill until the cheese has melted and the tops are golden brown.

METRIC	IMPERIAL
25 g butter	1 oz butter
2 tablespoons oil	2 tablespoons oil
4 large onions, thinly sliced into rings	4 large onions, thinly sliced into rings
1 garlic clove, crushed	1 garlic clove, crushed
900 ml strong beef stock (homemade if possible)	1½ pints strong beef stock (homemade if possible)
salt and pepper	salt and pepper

Melt the butter with the oil in a saucepan. Add the onions and garlic and cook gently until pale golden. Add the stock and salt and pepper to taste and bring to the boil. Cover and simmer for 30 minutes. Serve hot.

Serves 4 to 6

Cabbage and Apple Soup

If Savoy cabbage is not available, use 500g/1 lb spring greens.

METRIC	IMPERIAL
2 tablespoons oil	2 tablespoons oil
3 onions, sliced	3 onions, sliced
750 g cooking apples, peeled, cored and sliced	1½ lb cooking apples, peeled, cored and sliced
½ large Savoy cabbage, shredded	½ large Savoy cabbage, shredded
1.8 litres stock	3 pints stock
salt and pepper	salt and pepper
chopped parsley to garnish	chopped parsley to garnish

Heat the oil in a large saucepan. Add the onions and fry until softened. Stir in the apples and cabbage and fry until the cabbage is bright green.

Add the stock and salt and pepper to taste and bring to the boil. Simmer for about 20 minutes or until the vegetables and apples are very soft.

Purée the soup in a blender or food processor, or sieve it. Return to the saucepan and reheat gently. Taste and adjust the seasoning, then serve hot sprinkled with parsley.

Serves 5 to 6

Mushroom and Onion Broth

Some of the smaller pasta shapes described on page 80 could be used here.

METRIC	IMPERIAL
500 g onions, thinly sliced	1 lb onions, thinly sliced
1.8 litres chicken stock	3 pints chicken stock
500 g mushrooms, thinly sliced	1 lb mushrooms, thinly sliced
4 teaspoons Dijon mustard	4 teaspoons Dijon mustard
75 g pasta shapes	3 oz pasta shapes
salt and pepper	salt and pepper
chopped parsley to garnish	chopped parsley to garnish

Place the onions and half the stock in a saucepan and bring to the boil. Simmer for 15 to 20 minutes or until the onions are softened. Stir in the mushrooms, mustard and remaining stock and return to the boil. Add the pasta shapes and salt and pepper to taste. Cover and simmer for 10 to 15 minutes or until the pasta is tender.

Sprinkle with parsley and serve hot.

Serves 4

Cheesy Celery Soup

METRIC	IMPERIAL
25 g butter	1 oz butter
1 large onion, chopped	1 large onion, chopped
2 sticks celery, chopped	2 sticks celery, chopped
300 ml water	½ pint water
600 ml milk	1 pint milk
1 tablespoon cornflour	1 tablespoon cornflour
2 tablespoons	2 tablespoons
Worcestershire sauce	Worcestershire sauce
175 g Cheddar cheese,	6 oz Cheddar cheese,
grated	grated
salt and pepper	salt and pepper

Melt the butter in a saucepan. Add the onion and celery and fry until softened. Add the water and milk and bring to the boil. Simmer for 20 minutes.

Blend the cornflour with the Worcestershire sauce. Add to the pan and simmer, stirring, until thickened. Remove from the heat and stir in three-quarters of the cheese. Season to taste with salt and pepper.

Serve hot, topped with the remaining cheese.

Serves 4

Minted Pea Soup

This is a lovely, fresh soup to make when the first mint is available.

METRIC	IMPERIAL
50 g butter	2 oz butter
2 large old potatoes,	2 large old potatoes,
diced	diced
1 large onion, chopped	1 large onion, chopped
900 ml chicken stock	1½ pints chicken stock
225 g shelled fresh or	8 oz shelled fresh or
frozen peas	frozen peas
1 bouquet garni	1 bouquet garni
1 fresh mint sprig	1 fresh mint sprig
salt and pepper	salt and pepper
chopped fresh mint to	chopped fresh mint to
garnish	garnish

Melt the butter in a saucepan. Add the potatoes and onion and fry until the onion is softened. Do not let the vegetables brown. Add the stock and bring to the boil. Simmer for about 15 minutes.

Stir in the peas, bouquet garni, mint sprig and salt and pepper to taste. Cover and simmer for a further 30 minutes.

Discard the bouquet garni, then purée the soup in a blender or food processor, or sieve it. Return to the pan and reheat gently. Taste and adjust the seasoning and serve hot, garnished with chopped mint.

Serves 4 to 6

Creamed Vegetable Herb Soup

If liked, add a few small sprigs of cauliflower with the carrot. Double cream mixed with 2 tablespoons lemon juice may be used instead of soured cream.

METRIC	IMPERIAL
50 g butter	2 oz butter
2 onions, chopped	2 onions, chopped
2 medium potatoes,	2 medium potatoes,
chopped	chopped
600 ml chicken stock	1 pint chicken stock
salt and pepper	salt and pepper
25 g flour	1 oz flour
300 ml milk	½ pint milk
1 large carrot, grated	1 large carrot, grated
2 tablespoons chopped	2 tablespoons chopped
mixed fresh herbs	mixed fresh herbs
300 ml soured cream	½ pint soured cream

Melt the butter in a saucepan. Add the onions and potatoes and fry until softened. Stir in the stock and salt and pepper to taste and bring to the boil. Cover and simmer for 30 minutes.

Purée the mixture in a blender or food processor, or sieve it. Return to the saucepan. Blend the flour with the cold milk and add to the pan. Simmer, stirring, until thickened.

Add the carrot, herbs and half the soured cream. Cook very gently for 10 minutes, stirring occasionally. Do not boil.

Taste and adjust the seasoning, then serve hot, topped with the remaining soured cream.

Serves 6 to 8

Garnishes for soups

Croûtons are an easily-made garnish for soups, and make the soup much more special. Remove the crusts from 2 to 3 slices of stale bread, then cut the bread into small dice. Pour enough oil into a frying pan to make a 2 cm/¾ inch layer and heat it. Add the bread dice and fry until golden brown on all sides; this should take only a few seconds. Drain on paper towels and sprinkle with salt before using. The croûtons may be prepared ahead of time and reheated for 1 to 2 minutes in a preheated hot oven (220°C/425°F, Gas Mark 7). This will make enough croûtons to serve 4.

Potato croûtons may be made in the same way. Cook 2 potatoes in boiling salted water until they are almost tender. Drain well and cut into small dice while still hot. Fry as above and serve hot.

Beurre manié and roux

Beurre manié, or kneaded butter, is a mixture of butter and flour used to thicken soups, gravies, casseroles, stews, etc. just before serving. Twice as much butter as flour are worked together into a paste. This paste may then be added to the liquid to be thickened in two ways. One is to whisk the paste into the hot liquid in small pieces. The other is to blend some of the hot liquid into the paste and then to add this to the remaining liquid. The liquid is then simmered until thickened.

* *

Another mixture of butter and flour used to thicken is called a **roux**. Unlike beurre manié which is added at the end of cooking, a roux forms the basis for a sauce, soup, casserole, etc. in that the butter is melted, the flour stirred in and the liquid added. The cooking may continue just until the sauce has reached the desired consistency or for several hours.

Tomato Soup

Use well-flavoured tomatoes for this soup or substitute two 400 g/14 oz cans of tomatoes, drained.

METRIC	IMPERIAL
50 g butter	2 oz butter
2 streaky bacon rashers, rinded and chopped	2 streaky bacon rashers, rinded and chopped
1 onion, chopped	1 onion, chopped
1 celery stick, chopped	1 celery stick, chopped
750 g tomatoes, chopped	1½ lb tomatoes, chopped
600 ml chicken stock	1 pint chicken stock
½ teaspoon paprika	½ teaspoon paprika
½ teaspoon caster sugar	½ teaspoon caster sugar
1 teaspoon dried chervil	1 teaspoon dried chervil
1 teaspoon dried basil	1 teaspoon dried basil
salt and pepper	salt and pepper
chopped chives to garnish	chopped chives to garnish

Melt the butter in a saucepan. Add the bacon, onion and celery and fry until softened. Stir in the tomatoes and cook for a further 2 minutes, then add the stock, paprika, sugar, herbs and salt and pepper to taste.

Bring to the boil, stirring. Cover and simmer for 20 minutes.

Discard the bacon, then purée the soup in a blender or food processor, or sieve it. If using a blender or food processor, sieve the soup to remove the tomato skins, if liked.

Return the soup to the saucepan and reheat gently. Taste and adjust the seasoning and serve hot, sprinkled with chives.

Serves 4

Cidered Potato Soup

METRIC	IMPERIAL
350 g onions, sliced	12 oz onions, sliced
500 g cooking apples, peeled, cored and sliced	1 lb cooking apples, peeled, cored and sliced
1 kg potatoes, sliced	2 lb potatoes, sliced
300 ml cider	½ pint cider
1.2 litres beef stock	2 pints beef stock
½ teaspoon dried mixed herbs	½ teaspoon dried mixed herbs
½ teaspoon ground coriander	½ teaspoon ground coriander
150 ml plain yogurt	¼ pint plain yogurt
salt and pepper	salt and pepper
chopped chives to garnish	chopped chives to garnish

Place the onions, apples, potatoes and cider in a large saucepan and bring to the boil. Simmer for 10 minutes. Stir in the stock, herbs and coriander. Cover and simmer for about 1 hour or until the vegetables are very tender.

Purée the soup in a blender or food processor, or sieve it. Return to the saucepan and stir in the yogurt and salt and pepper to taste. Reheat gently. Serve hot, sprinkled with chives.

Serves 5 to 6

Cream of Mushroom Soup

For a richer result, you could use single cream instead of the plain yogurt.

METRIC	IMPERIAL
40 g butter	1½ oz butter
1 onion, finely chopped	1 onion, finely chopped
500 g mushrooms, sliced	1 lb mushrooms, sliced
900 ml milk	1½ pints milk
1 chicken stock cube	1 chicken stock cube
salt and pepper	salt and pepper
250 ml plain yogurt	8 fl oz plain yogurt
2 tablespoons chopped parsley	2 tablespoons chopped parsley

Melt the butter in a saucepan. Add the onion and fry until softened. Stir in the mushrooms, then cover and cook very gently for 10 minutes, shaking the pan occasionally to prevent sticking.

Stir in the milk and bring to the boil. Crumble in the stock cube and season to taste with salt and pepper. Simmer, stirring occasionally, for 5 minutes.

Stir in the yogurt and parsley and heat through gently. Serve hot.

Serves 4 to 6

Soups

Oven Soup

If you are roasting a joint, or baking a casserole, make the first course soup in the oven at the same time, and save fuel.

METRIC	IMPERIAL
500 g mixed vegetables (onions, carrots, tomatoes, turnips, etc.), chopped	1 lb mixed vegetables (onions, carrots, tomatoes, turnips, etc.), chopped
900 ml chicken stock	1½ pints chicken stock
1 bouquet garni	1 bouquet garni
1 tablespoon long-grain rice	1 tablespoon long-grain rice
salt and pepper	salt and pepper
chopped parsley to garnish	chopped parsley to garnish

Place the vegetables, stock, bouquet garni, rice and salt and pepper to taste in a deep casserole. Cover and place in a preheated moderate oven (160°C/325°F, Gas Mark 3). Cook for about 1 hour. Remove bouquet garni.

Sprinkle with parsley before serving.

Serves 4

Speedy Beetroot Soup

This soup looks very attractive when topped with a little plain yogurt or soured cream. For an even richer effect, top with a swirl of double cream or a dollop of whipped cream.

METRIC	IMPERIAL
25 g butter	1 oz butter
1 onion, grated	1 onion, grated
900 ml beef stock or canned consommé	1½ pints beef stock or canned consommé
salt and pepper	salt and pepper
1 large beetroot, cooked, peeled and grated	1 large beetroot, cooked, peeled and grated

Melt the butter in a saucepan. Add the onion and fry until softened. Add the stock or consommé and bring to the boil. Season to taste with salt and pepper.

Stir in the beetroot and heat through. Serve piping hot.

Serves 4

Using canned and packet soups

Canned and packet soups are a very useful standby to have on hand in the storecupboard. And for a more special occasion, or just to give them a lift, you can make the soup more interesting with the addition of a few ingredients. Here are some ideas. Stir a few tablespoons of fresh or soured cream into a creamed soup. Top soups with colourful garnishes such as freshly grated or shredded orange or lemon rind, mushroom slices sautéed in butter on mushroom soup, canned asparagus tips on asparaus soup, thin lemon slices, chopped fresh herbs, toasted/flaked almonds, croûtons (bought or homemade), chopped and crisply fried bacon, and avocado slices. A spoonful or two of sherry stirred into canned consommé or oxtail soul gives it a luxurious 'kick'. Sprinkle grated Cheddar or Gruyère cheese over canned French onion soup and pop it under the grill to melt and brown the cheese topping (be sure to use heatproof bowls). Chill canned consommé in the fridge for 3 hours, then chop and garnish with parsley for a very elegant starter.

To make a quick, hearty chicken soup, heat cream of chicken soup with shredded processed cheese until melted, then sprinkle with chopped parsley. Another idea for condensed cream of chicken or mushroom soup is to heat it with 150 ml/¼ pint chicken stock (made with a stock cube) and 1 teaspoon curry powder. Stir in 4 tablespoons cream just before serving.

A delicious cold tomato soup can be made by blending a can of condensed tomato soup with 300 ml/½ pint soured cream, chopped spring onions, a little dried basil and seasoning to taste. Chill well, then serve garnished with chopped hard-boiled egg.

Canned soups can also be used as instant 'sauces' in quick dishes and casseroles. For a tuna curry, fry a chopped onion in butter, then stir in a 200 g/7 oz can of tuna, drained and flaked, a can of cream of mushroom soup, 1–2 teaspoons of curry powder and 4 tablespoons sherry. Heat through, then fold in 4 halved hard-boiled eggs.

An Italian-style casserole can be made by browning minced beef with chopped onion and stirring in a can of cream of tomato soup, dried oregano or basil and seasoning. Fold in cooked pasta shapes, pour into a casserole and top with lots of grated cheese. Grill to brown the top, or bake in a moderate oven (180°C/350°F, Gas Mark 4) for 30 minutes.

Celery soup makes a delicious cooking liquid for a casserole of stewing beef and vegetables, and in any stew or casserole – beef, lamb, pork or chicken – canned consommé is a very superior alternative to beef stock made with a stock cube.

For a speedy chilli con carne, use canned tomato soup with minced beef, canned tomatoes, canned red kidney beans and chilli powder or seasoning.

An interesting starter need not take a lot
of time to prepare and will make any meal
something special. Don't be tied down to
the usual fare; try Hot Curried Eggs, Salmon
Mousse or an exciting dip. A starter should
be an imaginative beginning to a lunch or
dinner, so that the meal commences with
flavours that will whet the appetite and give
an indication of delicious things to follow.
Many of the recipes in this chapter can
also be served as snacks with drinks
or cocktails.

French Pork Pâté

This is a coarse-textured pâté, full of flavour. For a smoother texture, mince the meat. Serve it with hot toast and butter.

METRIC	IMPERIAL
50 g lard or butter	2 oz lard or butter
1 small onion, chopped	1 small onion, chopped
1 garlic clove, crushed	1 garlic clove, crushed
25 g flour	1 oz flour
150 ml beef stock	¼ pint beef stock
2 teaspoons chopped fresh mixed herbs	2 teaspoons chopped fresh mixed herbs
good pinch of grated nutmeg	good pinch of grated nutmeg
salt and pepper	salt and pepper
500 g pig's liver, chopped	1 lb pig's liver, chopped
225 g lean pork, chopped	8 oz lean pork, chopped
225 g fat belly pork, chopped	8 oz fat belly pork, chopped
2–3 sage leaves	2–3 sage leaves
500 g streaky bacon rashers	1 lb streaky bacon rashers

Melt the lard or butter in a frying pan. Add the onion and garlic and fry until softened. Sprinkle over the flour and stir in well. Cook for 2 minutes, then gradually stir in the stock and bring to the boil. Simmer, stirring, until thickened.

Add the herbs, nutmeg and salt and pepper to taste. Mix in the meats.

Place the sage leaves on the bottom of a 1kg/2 lb loaf tin or ovenproof dish, then line the bottom and sides with the bacon rashers. Spoon in the meat mixture and smooth the top.

Cover with greased foil or greaseproof paper and place the tin or dish in a roasting tin. Pour hot water into the roasting tin to come halfway up the sides of the loaf tin or dish.

Bake in a preheated moderate oven (160°C/325°F, Gas Mark 3) for about 1¼ hours. Leave to cool in the tin or dish. Place a weight on top and leave overnight before serving.

Serves 8 to 10

Extracting zest

The zest is the oil in the rind of citrus fruit, and gives the fruit its colour, flavour and scent. To extract the zest from an orange, lemon, etc. to use in a sweet dish, rub a large sugar lump over the rind until it is saturated with the oil. Crush the sugar lump before use.

For a savoury dish, use the finest side of a grater, or a special implement called a zester which scrapes away only the thinnest outer part of the rind.

Prawn and Cream Cheese Pâté

METRIC	IMPERIAL
100 g cream cheese	4 oz cream cheese
2 spring onions, chopped	2 spring onions, chopped
175 g cooked peeled prawns, chopped	6 oz cooked peeled prawns, chopped
juice of ½ lemon	juice of ½ lemon
1 teaspoon dried dill	1 teaspoon dried dill
salt and pepper	salt and pepper

Beat the cream cheese until softened. Beat in the spring onions, then mix in the prawns, lemon juice, dill and salt and pepper to taste.

Divide the pâté between four small serving dishes and chill lightly before serving.

Serves 4

VARIATION
Prawn and garlic cheese rolls: Make as above, omitting the dill and using garlic and herb cream cheese instead of plain cream cheese. Spread over thin slices of brown bread and roll up. Chill.

Smoked Mackerel Pâté

If you don't have a blender or food processor, the ingredients may be mashed together with a wooden spoon.

METRIC	IMPERIAL
500 g smoked mackerel fillets, flaked	1 lb smoked mackerel fillets, flaked
150 ml soured cream	¼ pint soured cream
500 g cottage cheese, sieved	1 lb cottage cheese, sieved
25 g butter, melted	1 oz butter, melted
grated rind and juice of ½ lemon	grated rind and juice of ½ lemon
salt and pepper	salt and pepper

Place the mackerel, soured cream, cottage cheese and butter in the blender goblet or bowl of a food processor and blend until smooth. Pour into a bowl and add the lemon rind and juice and salt and pepper to taste. Cover and chill before serving. Serve with brown bread.

Serves 8

VARIATION
Kipper pâté: Use 225 g/8 oz kipper fillets, cooked and flaked, instead of mackerel. Decrease the cottage cheese to 150 g/5 oz. Omit the butter and add 1 teaspoon made mustard and 1 teaspoon dried mixed herbs. Prepare as above. Serves 4.

Herring Salad

METRIC	IMPERIAL
2 rollmop herrings, diced	2 rollmop herrings, diced
1 dessert apple, peeled, cored and diced	1 dessert apple, peeled, cored and diced
1 small onion, grated	1 small onion, grated
2 medium potatoes, cooked and diced	2 medium potatoes, cooked and diced
2 hard-boiled eggs, chopped	2 hard-boiled eggs, chopped
150 ml soured cream	$\frac{1}{4}$ pint soured cream
salt and pepper	salt and pepper
lettuce leaves	lettuce leaves
diced beetroot to garnish	diced beetroot to garnish

Place the herrings, apple, onion, potatoes, eggs, soured cream and salt and pepper to taste in a bowl and mix together gently but thoroughly. Cover and chill for 2 to 3 hours.

Line a serving plate, or individual plates, with lettuce leaves. Spoon the herring salad on top and garnish with diced beetroot.

Serves 4 to 6

Salmon Mousse

METRIC	IMPERIAL
1 tablespoon powdered gelatine	1 tablespoon powdered gelatine
150 ml water	$\frac{1}{4}$ pint water
50 g butter	2 oz butter
1 hard-boiled egg yolk, sieved	1 hard-boiled egg yolk, sieved
$\frac{1}{2}$ teaspoon made mustard	$\frac{1}{2}$ teaspoon made mustard
2 teaspoons vinegar	2 teaspoons vinegar
pinch of cayenne pepper	pinch of cayenne pepper
salt	salt
1 × 100 g can red salmon, drained and flaked	1 × 4 oz can red salmon, drained and flaked
150 ml milk	$\frac{1}{4}$ pint milk
lemon slices to garnish	lemon slices to garnish

Dissolve the gelatine in the water. Cream the butter with the egg yolk until smooth, then beat in the mustard, vinegar, cayenne and salt to taste. Gradually whisk in the gelatine mixture. Add the salmon and milk and mix well.

Pour into six small ramekins or one serving dish. Cover and chill until set. Garnish with lemon slices and serve with toast or savoury biscuits.

Serves 6

Temperature testing for deep frying

When deep frying, the temperature of the oil or fat is critical, and a deep fat thermometer is the most accurate way of measuring the temperature of the oil or fat to be sure it is correct for the food you are frying. If a thermometer is not available, you can use the following test: drop a small cube of day-old bread into the oil. If it becomes crisp and golden in 30 seconds, the temperature of the oil is about 180°C/360°F, which is suitable for frying chips and doughnuts. But remember that this test will only give an approximate temperature.

A deep pan with a thick base and a frying basket are needed for successful deep frying. Never fill the pan more than half or two-thirds full of cooking oil or solid fat because the oil will rise when the food to be fried is put in. The oil could overflow and catch alight.

The oil or fat for frying should be free from moisture or it will spit when heating.

Should the oil or fat catch alight, turn off the gas or electricity and cover the pan with the lid. The flames will go out without any oxygen to feed them. Never use water to put out the flames: water will only splash the burning oil or fat around.

Fried Whitebait

These tiny fish do not need any preparation other than rinsing in cold water. Serve as a starter with brown bread and butter.

METRIC	IMPERIAL
50 g flour	2 oz flour
salt and pepper	salt and pepper
500 g whitebait, thawed if frozen	1 lb whitebait, thawed if frozen
oil for deep frying	oil for deep frying
lemon wedges to serve	lemon wedges to serve

Season the flour with salt and pepper and place in a polythene bag. Add the well-dried fish and shake the bag to coat all the fish evenly.

Deep fry in oil heated to 180°C/350°F for 2 to 3 minutes or until golden. Do not crowd the pan, and shake the frying basket occasionally to prevent the fish sticking together.

Drain on paper towels and serve hot, with lemon wedges.

Serves 4

Avocado pears

Avocados are a popular starter, the halves filled with French Dressing* or a prawn mixture.

When choosing an avocado in the green-grocer or supermarket, do not judge ripeness by the colour of the skin. Avocados may be a shade of green, a brownish-purple or a purplish-black, and the skins may be thick or thin, smooth or bumpy. The shape may be like a pear or almost round. But whatever the colour, size or shape, the inside will be greenish-gold.

Unlike most fruits, avocados ripen best off the tree, so they are picked and shipped when underripe. When you buy an avocado, it will still probably need a few days to ripen at home, at room temperature. It is ready to eat if it will yield to gentle pressure when cradled between the palms of your hands. Don't pinch an avocado because it will bruise very easily.

To halve an avocado, cut it all round lengthways, then gently twist the halves in opposite directions until they come apart. Flick out the stone with the point of the knife. Be sure to brush the cut surfaces with lemon juice to prevent them turning brown.

Cheese-stuffed Mushrooms

METRIC	IMPERIAL
16 large mushrooms	16 large mushrooms
3 egg yolks	3 egg yolks
3 tablespoons fresh breadcrumbs	3 tablespoons fresh breadcrumbs
3 tablespoons grated Cheddar cheese	3 tablespoons grated Cheddar cheese
salt and pepper	salt and pepper
dry breadcrumbs for coating	dry breadcrumbs for coating
oil for shallow frying	oil for shallow frying
lemon wedges to serve	lemon wedges to serve

Remove the stalks from the mushrooms and chop them. Mix the chopped stalks with two of the egg yolks, the breadcrumbs, cheese and salt and pepper to taste. Spread this mixture over half the mushrooms and place the remaining mushrooms on top, so that the rounded sides are facing out.

Lightly beat the remaining egg yolk with a few drops of water. Dip the mushrooms into the yolk, then coat with dry crumbs.

Shallow fry until golden brown on both sides. Drain on paper towels and serve hot, with lemon wedges.

Serves 4

Avocado with Grapefruit

METRIC	IMPERIAL
2 avocados, peeled, stoned and sliced	2 avocados, peeled, stoned and sliced
1 quantity French Dressing*	1 quantity French Dressing*
lettuce leaves	lettuce leaves
2 grapefruit, peeled and segmented	2 grapefruit, peeled and segmented

Toss the avocado slices in the dressing to prevent discoloration.

Line four serving plates with lettuce leaves. Arrange the avocado slices and grapefruit segments on top and drizzle over any remaining dressing.

Serves 4

Sardine Lemons

Smooth, creamy sardine pâté is served in hollowed-out lemons, making a very attractive appetizer.

METRIC	IMPERIAL
2 large lemons	2 large lemons
1 × 100 g can sardines in oil, drained	1 × 4 oz can sardines in oil, drained
100 g cream cheese	4 oz cream cheese
1 hard-boiled egg, chopped	1 hard-boiled egg, chopped
pepper	pepper
parsley sprigs to garnish	parsley sprigs to garnish

Cut the lemons in half lengthways. Scoop out the flesh. Strain the juice from the flesh and reserve. Cut a small slice from the bottom of each half to make a flat surface.

Mash the sardines with the cream cheese, egg, 2 teaspoons of the reserved lemon juice and pepper to taste. Spoon into the lemon shells and garnish with parsley sprigs. Serve with hot toast.

Serves 4

Cheese straws

Tidbits to serve with drinks can be easily made from Cheese Shortcrust Pastry*. To make cheese straws, roll out the dough on a floured surface to a strip about 10 cm/4 inches wide. Cut the dough into thin strips and place the strips on greased baking sheets. Bake in a pre-heated hot oven (220°C/425°F, Gas Mark 7) for 5 to 7 minutes or until golden brown. Cool on a wire rack.

Tuna and Cucumber Cocktail

METRIC	IMPERIAL
1 × 200 g can tuna fish	1 × 7 oz can tuna fish
½ cucumber, finely diced	½ cucumber, finely diced
2 tablespoons mayonnaise	2 tablespoons mayonnaise
1 tablespoon tomato purée	1 tablespoon tomato purée
salt and pepper	salt and pepper
lemon juice	lemon juice
shredded lettuce	shredded lettuce

Tip the tuna, with its oil, into a bowl and flake. Add the cucumber.

Mix together the mayonnaise, tomato purée and salt and pepper to taste. Sharpen with a little lemon juice. Add to the tuna mixture and fold together.

Put a little shredded lettuce in each of four stemmed glasses and spoon the tuna mixture on top. Serve lightly chilled.

Serves 4

Artichokes

Jerusalem artichokes are not related to globe artichokes, but are in fact a member of the sunflower family. They have a delicate, nutty flavour that is particularly suitable for soups. To prepare them, peel them as you would a potato.

Globe artichokes, from the thistle family, are considerably more fiddly to prepare. First, trim off the stalk level with the bottom, then trim off the thorny points of the outer leaves using scissors. Because artichokes will darken if their cut surfaces are left exposed to the air for too long, drop them into acidulated water as they are cut. (This is water to which vinegar or lemon juice has been added.)

To cook globe artichokes whole, place them in a saucepan of boiling salted water. Put a plate on top to keep the artichokes submerged, then cover the pan and simmer for 15 to 50 minutes (depending on size) or until the stalk end can be pierced easily with a fork. Lift out of the water and drain upside-down. Serve hot or cold.

A whole globe artichoke is eaten by pulling off the leaves one at a time and dipping them into a sauce. Only the tender light green base part of each leaf is eaten by drawing it between the teeth. When you reach the fuzzy centre or choke, scoop it out with a spoon and discard it. The base that remains is the most succulent part.

Asparagus

Asparagus is a very special seasonal treat, and should be handled accordingly. To prepare asparagus for cooking, cut the bottom off each stalk, then peel or scrape the white part that remains. Rinse well. If using an asparagus cooker, or another tall saucepan, tie the asparagus into even bundles. Place the asparagus in boiling salted water, keeping the tips above the water. Alternatively, cook the asparagus lying in a frying pan of water. Simmer for 12 to 15 minutes or until just tender. Drain well, then serve hot with melted butter or Hollandaise Sauce* or cold with French Dressing*.

Here are a few quickly-made sauces to pour over hot, freshly-cooked asparagus:

Melt 50 g/2 oz butter in a saucepan and stir in 1 grated small onion and 1 teaspoon Worcestershire sauce. Cook until the onion is softened, then season to taste with salt and pepper.

Melt 50 g/2 oz butter in a saucepan and stir in 25 g/1 oz chopped salted cashew nuts, 2 teaspoons lemon juice and a pinch of dried marjoram. Heat through for 2 minutes, then season to taste with salt and pepper.

Gently warm 1 × 75 g/3 oz packet of cream cheese with 2 tablespoons single cream in a saucepan. Stir in 2 tablespoons chopped chives or spring onion tops and season to taste with salt and pepper.

Place 300 ml/½ pint soured cream in a saucepan and add 1–2 teaspoons French mustard, 1 tablespoon lemon juice and salt and pepper to taste. Heat through gently.

Corn-on-the-Cob

Special corn-on-the-cob holders, that are inserted into each end of the cob, make this delicious vegetable starter much easier to eat. Do not add salt to the cooking water as this will toughen the corn kernels.

METRIC	IMPERIAL
4 plump corn cobs	4 plump corn cobs
1 teaspoon sugar	1 teaspoon sugar
butter	butter
salt and pepper	salt and pepper

Remove the outside leaves and silky threads from the cobs. Place in a saucepan of boiling water to which the sugar has been added and cook for 4 to 7 minutes, according to size.

Drain well and place on warmed plates or special corn serving dishes. Top each cob with a large knob of butter and sprinkle with salt and pepper. Serve immediately.

Serves 4

Soufflé Eggs

These little starters are simple to make, being a slightly more elaborate version of baked eggs. If preferred, use more grated cheese instead of the ham.

METRIC	IMPERIAL
4 eggs, separated	4 eggs, separated
2 tablespoons single cream	2 tablespoons single cream
salt and pepper	salt and pepper
25 g cooked ham, diced	1 oz cooked ham, diced
25 g cheese, finely grated	1 oz cheese, finely grated

Lightly beat the egg yolks with the cream and salt and pepper to taste. Stir in the ham. Divide the mixture between four shallow ovenproof dishes or ramekin dishes.

Whisk the egg whites with salt and pepper to taste until very stiff. Spoon on top of the egg yolk mixture and sprinkle over the cheese.

Bake in a preheated moderately hot oven (200°C/400°F, Gas Mark 6) for about 10 minutes or until the yolks are just set and the tops are golden brown. Serve immediately.

Serves 4

Hot Curried Eggs

These may also be served cold.

METRIC	IMPERIAL
4 hard-boiled eggs, halved lengthways	4 hard-boiled eggs, halved lengthways
2 tablespoons mayonnaise	2 tablespoons mayonnaise
1 tablespoon chutney	1 tablespoon chutney
1–2 teaspoons curry powder	1–2 teaspoons curry powder
4 teaspoons fine dry breadcrumbs	4 teaspoons fine dry breadcrumbs

Carefully scoop the yolks out of the egg white halves. Mash the yolks with the mayonnaise, chutney and curry powder. Pack back into the egg white halves, doming the mixture.

Sprinkle over the crumbs and grill until lightly browned. Serve hot.

Serves 4

VARIATION

Cheese stuffed eggs: Mix the yolks with 75 g/3 oz grated Cheddar cheese and 1–2 tablespoons double cream. Season to taste with salt and pepper, then pack back into the egg white halves. Sprinkle with crumbs and grill as above. Serve hot.

Storing leftover foods

Leftovers will not keep indefinitely in the refrigerator. Here is a guide to how long foods can be stored:

beef, cooked, tightly wrapped	3–4 days
cheese, hard, tightly wrapped	1–2 weeks
cheese, soft, in sealed container	3–4 days
cream, fresh and soured, covered	3–4 days
egg yolks, covered with water	2–3 days
egg whites, in sealed container	4 days
eggs, hard-boiled, in shells	1 week
fish, cooked, tightly wrapped	1–2 days
lamb, cooked, tightly wrapped	3–4 days
mayonnaise (home-made), covered	5 days
pastry, uncooked, tightly wrapped	1 week
pork, cooked, tightly wrapped	2 days
potatoes, cooked, covered	2–3 days
poultry, cooked, tightly wrapped	3–4 days
rice, boiled, in sealed container	1 week
sausages, cooked, tightly wrapped	2 days
turkey, cooked, tightly wrapped	1 week
vegetables, cooked, covered	2 days

Pâté-stuffed Eggs

METRIC	IMPERIAL
6 hard-boiled eggs	6 hard-boiled eggs
25 g soft liver pâté	1 oz soft liver pâté
1 tablespoon mayonnaise	1 tablespoon mayonnaise
salt and pepper	salt and pepper
sliced stuffed olives to garnish	sliced stuffed olives to garnish

Halve the eggs lengthways and carefully remove the yolks. Sieve the yolks, or mash them with a fork, and beat in the pâté and mayonnaise. Season to taste with salt and pepper.

Fill the egg white halves with the pâté mixture, either spooning or piping it in. Garnish with slices of stuffed olives.

Serves 6

Starters

Piquant Cheese Spread

Use this on savoury scones or for sandwiches. It will keep in the refrigerator for 3 to 4 days.

METRIC	IMPERIAL
225 g cottage cheese, sieved	8 oz cottage cheese, sieved
150 ml soured cream	$\frac{1}{4}$ pint soured cream
2 teaspoons capers	2 teaspoons capers
1 gherkin, chopped	1 gherkin, chopped
1 tablespoon chopped parsley	1 tablespoon chopped parsley
grated rind of $\frac{1}{2}$ lemon	grated rind of $\frac{1}{2}$ lemon
1 teaspoon chopped onion	1 teaspoon chopped onion
salt and pepper	salt and pepper

Place all the ingredients, with salt and pepper to taste, in a blender goblet or bowl of a food processor and blend to a smooth mixture.

Alternatively, finely chop the capers, gherkin and onion and mix with the remaining ingredients.

Use as required.

Serves 6

Devilled Dip

METRIC	IMPERIAL
500 g cottage cheese, sieved	1 lb cottage cheese, sieved
150 ml soured cream	$\frac{1}{4}$ pint soured cream
2–3 tablespoons mayonnaise	2–3 tablespoons mayonnaise
1 tablespoon made mustard	1 tablespoon made mustard
2–3 tablespoons chopped pickled onions	2–3 tablespoons chopped pickled onions
2–3 tablespoons chopped gherkins	2–3 tablespoons chopped gherkins
1–2 teaspoons Worcestershire sauce	1–2 teaspoons Worcestershire sauce
few drops of chilli sauce	few drops of chilli sauce

Mix together all the ingredients and serve with raw vegetables for dipping.

Serves 4 to 6

Anchovy appetizers

For anchovy plaits, cut the dough into strips as for cheese straws (see page 20). Lay two of the strips side by side and place an anchovy fillet in the centre. Plait together, pressing the ends to seal. Bake as for cheese straws.

Stocking your storecupboard

A well-stocked storecupboard is a boon for a busy cook, but remember that foods can deteriorate if not stored correctly or left too long on the shelf.

Cupboards should be cool – no more than 18°C/65°F – and dry. Any food already in the cupboard should be moved to the front when stocks are replenished. Check the manufacturer's 'eat by' or 'best by' date, or label things yourself when you buy them if they are to be stored for a while.

Staples such as flour, salt and sugar are best stored in moistureproof containers, so remove them from their wrappings and decant them when you buy them. Herbs and spices will keep their flavour and scent if stored in dark glass bottles or a cupboard rather than an open spice rack; light is their enemy. Oil, too, should be stored in a dark place, in an airtight container. Breakfast cereals may become soft and lose their flavour once opened, so wrap the packet in foil and store in a cool, dark, dry place.

You might think certain foods could be kept almost forever, but you'd be surprised: dried yeast has a shelf life of only 6 months, wholemeal flour 2 months, dried herbs 6 months, chopped or ground nuts 6 months, and stock cubes 6 months. However, there are some foods that *can* be kept indefinitely: cocoa powder, tins of anchovies, sardines and pilchards, food colourings and essences, powdered gelatine, malt powder and vinegar.

Cheese Dip

This is a good way to use up small bits of cheese, and any combination of cheeses you like may be mixed together. Add chopped onion, or chives or other herbs if liked.

METRIC	IMPERIAL
100 g cheese, grated	4 oz cheese, grated
2 tablespoons plain yogurt	2 tablespoons plain yogurt
100 g cream cheese	4 oz cream cheese
salt and pepper	salt and pepper

Mix together all the ingredients with a fork until well combined. Spoon into a bowl and serve with savoury biscuits or with a selection of raw vegetables for dipping. Suitable vegetables include cucumber, carrot, radishes, celery, red or green pepper, spring onions and cauliflower.

Serves 4 to 6

The choice of fish from in and around
our islands is immense but rarely is this
nourishing food given the chance to excel.
All of us have memories of boiled, bland fish
for school dinners or at seaside hotels, and
it is no wonder that children sometimes
have to be encouraged to eat fish as part
of a balanced diet. But with so many kinds of
fish available, fresh, frozen or even tinned,
the following recipes can offer an exciting
alternative to the usual meat dishes and be
just as, or more, nutritious. Flavours can be
rich and cheesy or light and refreshing.
So enjoy kebabs, curries and casseroles, all
using fish in a new way.

Fluted mushrooms

Fluted mushrooms will give any dish, particularly one made with fish, a very elegant appearance. To make this garnish, use large, firm button mushrooms. Trim the stalks level with the caps. Holding the cap of a mushroom between the finger and thumb of one hand, make shallow grooved cuts in the side with the point of a knife. Slightly turn the mushroom as you cut so that the grooves will have a half-moon shape. (The strips that are cut out may be used in a soup or a casserole.) Then cut a star shape on the top of the mushroom cap where the grooves meet.

Halibut in Herby Orange Sauce

METRIC	IMPERIAL
4 halibut steaks	4 halibut steaks
900 ml Court Bouillon★	1½ pints Court Bouillon★
15 g butter	½ oz butter
2 teaspoons oil	2 teaspoons oil
1 small onion, chopped	1 small onion, chopped
175 ml thawed frozen concentrated orange juice	6 fl oz thawed frozen concentrated orange juice
2 teaspoons chopped parsley	2 teaspoons chopped parsley
2 teaspoons chopped fresh tarragon	2 teaspoons chopped fresh tarragon
salt and pepper	salt and pepper
2 teaspoons cornflour	2 teaspoons cornflour
1 tablespoon water	1 tablespoon water
150 ml soured cream	¼ pint soured cream

Place the fish steaks in a buttered flameproof dish. Pour over the court bouillon and bring to the boil. Poach for 10 minutes or until the fish flakes easily when tested with a fork. Transfer the fish to a warmed serving dish and keep hot. Strain the cooking liquid and reserve 150 ml/¼ pint.

Melt the butter with the oil in a saucepan. Add the onion and fry until softened. Stir in the orange juice, reserved cooking liquid, herbs and salt and pepper to taste. Bring to the boil and simmer for 3 minutes.

Blend the cornflour with the cold water and add to the sauce. Simmer, stirring, until thickened. Stir in the soured cream and heat through gently. Taste and adjust the seasoning.

Pour the sauce over the fish and serve hot.

Serves 4

Stuffed Plaice with Orange

Despite the delicious creamy stuffing, this dish is very low in calories – only 450 per serving!

METRIC	IMPERIAL
4 plaice fillets, skinned	4 plaice fillets, skinned
grated rind and juice of 1 orange	grated rind and juice of 1 orange
Stuffing:	*Stuffing:*
100 g cottage cheese	4 oz cottage cheese
1 small orange, peeled and chopped	1 small orange, peeled and chopped
½ small green pepper, cored, seeded and diced	½ small green pepper, cored, seeded and diced
salt and pepper	salt and pepper

Mix together the ingredients for the stuffing. Divide between the plaice fillets and roll them up. Place in a baking dish and sprinkle over the orange rind and juice.

Cover and bake in a preheated moderately hot oven (190°C/375°F, Gas Mark 5) for 40 minutes or until the fish flakes easily when tested with a fork.

Serves 4

Fish Milan-style

METRIC	IMPERIAL
4 white fish fillets	4 white fish fillets
salt and pepper	salt and pepper
3 tablespoons dry white wine	3 tablespoons dry white wine
50 g butter	2 oz butter
175 g ribbon noodles	6 oz ribbon noodles
100 g button mushrooms	4 oz button mushrooms
25 g peas, cooked	1 oz peas, cooked

Place the fillets on a buttered heatproof plate. Season to taste with salt and pepper, then sprinkle over the wine. Dot with 15 g/½ oz of the butter.

Place the plate over a pan of boiling water, cover with the pan lid or foil and steam for 8 to 15 minutes or until the fish flakes easily when tested with a fork.

Meanwhile, cook the noodles in boiling salted water until tender. Melt the remaining butter in another saucepan, add the mushrooms and fry until lightly browned. Drain the noodles and add to the mushrooms with the peas. Add salt and pepper to taste and heat through well.

Spread out the noodle mixture on a warmed serving plate and top with the fish fillets. Serve hot.

Serves 4

WHITE FISH FOR SPECIAL OCCASIONS

Grilled Fish with Cream

Add a touch of luxury to plain grilled fish – by topping it with lemon-flavoured whipped cream!

METRIC	IMPERIAL
4 white fish steaks or fillets	4 white fish steaks or fillets
lemon juice	lemon juice
melted butter	melted butter
salt and pepper	salt and pepper
150 ml double or whipping cream	¼ pint double or whipping cream
To garnish:	*To garnish:*
chopped parsley	chopped parsley
paprika	paprika

Place the fish on the buttered grill rack and sprinkle with lemon juice. Drizzle over a little melted butter and season to taste with salt and pepper. Grill until nearly tender. If using fish steaks, turn them once; fillets do not need to be turned.

Whip the cream with a squeeze of lemon juice and salt and pepper to taste until thick. Spread the cream over the fish and continue grilling gently until the cream browns lightly and the fish flakes easily when tested with a fork.

Sprinkle with a little chopped parsley and paprika and serve hot.

Serves 4

Fish Kebabs

Any firm-fleshed white fish, such as cod, haddock or hake, may be used for these kebabs. You could also add a few prawns, if liked.

METRIC	IMPERIAL
750 g boneless white fish, cut into 4 cm cubes	1½ lb boneless white fish, cut into 1½ inch cubes
24 large button mushrooms	24 large button mushrooms
1 large red pepper, cored, seeded and cut into squares	1 large red pepper, cored, seeded and cut into squares
100 g butter, melted	4 oz butter, melted
juice of 1 lemon	juice of 1 lemon
few drops of chilli sauce	few drops of chilli sauce
salt and pepper	salt and pepper
1 tablespoon chopped parsley	1 tablespoon chopped parsley

Thread the fish cubes on to skewers alternating with the mushrooms and pepper squares.

Mix together the butter, lemon juice, chilli sauce and salt and pepper to taste. Brush over the kebabs.

Grill for about 10 minutes, turning and brushing with butter mixture frequently, until the fish flakes easily when tested with a fork.

Warm the remaining butter mixture, then stir in the parsley. Serve this separately as a sauce with the kebabs.

Serves 4

Haddock and Mushroom Scallops

These take a little time to prepare, but they are not expensive and look very impressive. The addition of smoked fish makes a tastier dish.

METRIC	IMPERIAL
500 g mashed potato	1 lb mashed potato
225 g haddock fillets	8 oz haddock fillets
225 g smoked haddock fillets	8 oz smoked haddock fillets
600 ml milk	1 pint milk
40 g butter	1½ oz butter
25 g flour	1 oz flour
100 g mushrooms	4 oz mushrooms
salt and pepper	salt and pepper

Put the mashed potato into a piping bag fitted with a 1 cm/½ inch rose nozzle and pipe a border around the edge of six scallop shells or individual heatproof dishes. Place in a preheated moderate oven (160°C/325°F, Gas Mark 3) and leave to heat through and brown lightly while making the filling. Do not leave too long or the potato will dry out.

Put the fish, milk and 15 g/½ oz of the butter in a saucepan and simmer gently until the fish flakes easily when tested with a fork – this will take about 10 minutes.

Drain the fish, reserving the milk. Flake the fish, discarding any skin, and keep hot.

Melt the remaining butter in the saucepan. Stir in the flour and cook for 1 minute, then gradually stir in the reserved strained milk. Bring to the boil, stirring, and simmer until thickened. Add the mushrooms and salt and pepper to taste and simmer gently for 5 minutes.

Fold in the fish, then divide the mixture between the scallop shells or dishes. Serve hot.

Serves 6

VARIATION

Curried seafood scallops: Prepare the potato border as above. To make the filling, mix 1 to 2 teaspoons curry powder into a thick hot White Sauce* (made with 40/g/1½ oz each butter and flour and 300 ml/½ pint milk). Fold in 500 g/1 lb mixed cooked fish (flaked white fish and tuna, chopped shellfish, etc.). Divide between the scallop shells and sprinkle over dry breadcrumbs. Grill until the tops are golden brown.

HERBS

Bouquet garni

A *bouquet garni*, which is the French name for a bunch of fresh herbs, traditionally comprises 2 to 3 parsley stalks, a sprig of thyme and a bay leaf, tied together with string. Other herbs and flavourings such as celery may be added. A convenient form of *bouquet garni* is widely available in supermarkets now. It consists of the dried herbs wrapped in a small muslin sachet or bag. A *bouquet garni* is removed from a dish before serving.

If fresh herbs are called for in a recipe, and they are not available, substitute dried herbs in the proportion of one-third the quantity of fresh. A good substitute for fresh mixed herbs is half the quantity in chopped parsley and one-third the quantity in dried mixed herbs.

Using fresh herbs

Some fresh herbs are chopped before using in a dish or for a garnish. To do this, rinse the herbs and dry well with paper towels. Strip the leaves from the sprig, if necessary, and place on a wooden board. Use a sharp knife and, holding the point of the knife down on the board with the fingers of one hand, raise and lower the handle of the knife with your other hand, moving the knife back and forth across the herbs. This method of chopping will keep the herbs together on the board. (Many other ingredients can be chopped in the same way.)

Herbs such as chives are snipped with scissors rather than chopped. Parsley may be snipped, as well. Place the parsley in a cup to do this.

Chopped fresh herbs for garnishing should be very dry, so squeeze them in a tea towel before sprinkling.

Using herbs and spices

Herbs are the leaves of low-growing plants, some annual and some perennial. Spices, on the other hand, come from the bark, roots, fruit or berries of perennial shrubs and trees.

Herbs and spices can turn an ordinary dish into something really special, but as many of these seasonings are strong and pungent in flavour, they should be used sparingly. And not all herbs and spices go well with every type of food. So here is a chart to guide you in using the most popular herbs and spices.

Herb/Spice	Soups	Fish	Meat
Basil	tomato and most others	white fish; prawns	roast and grilled lamb, pork, veal; beef stews
Marjoram		*	roast and grilled lamb, veal, pork; sausages; most stews
Rosemary	minestrone; most other soups		roast and grilled lamb; most other meat dishes
Sage	fish chowder		stuffing for pork
Thyme	*	stuffings; most fish	stuffings; most stews
Mixed herbs		white fish	stuffings; stews
Cayenne		shellfish	*
Cinnamon			some beef stews
Cloves			ham; meat stews
Curry		shellfish; most other fish	*
Ginger		*	*
Paprika		shellfish; most other fish	roast and grilled lamb, pork, veal; goulash
Mixed spice			

* indicates the herb or spice goes well with most dishes in the category

Fish

Poultry	Vegetables	Eggs	Cheese	Sauces	Baking	Preserves	Other uses
	tomatoes; broad beans; green salads	tomato and herb omelettes		for pasta and rice			
stuffing for goose	tomatoes; most salads	most omelettes	pizza				
	sauté potatoes						
stuffing for most poultry							
stuffings	tomatoes; salads	most cold egg dishes	cream cheese; most other cheese dishes				
*	green salad dressing	omelettes	*				
		*	*	*			
					cakes; pies	pickles	mulled wine
*				bread sauce	fruit cake	sauces; chutney	mulled wine
chicken	*	*		curry sauces			
duck							
chicken; most other poultry		*		cream sauces			rice
					fruit cakes		

Piquant Fish Casserole

METRIC	IMPERIAL
25 g butter	1 oz butter
100 g mushrooms, sliced	4 oz mushrooms, sliced
2 spring onions, chopped	2 spring onions, chopped
1 tablespoon chopped parsley	1 tablespoon chopped parsley
150 ml single cream or top of milk	¼ pint single cream or top of milk
2 teaspoons Angostura bitters	2 teaspoons Angostura bitters
4 white fish steaks	4 white fish steaks
salt and pepper	salt and pepper

Melt the butter in a frying pan. Add the mushrooms and spring onions and fry for 3 to 4 minutes. Stir in the parsley, cream or milk and bitters and remove from the heat.

Arrange the fish steaks in a buttered baking dish. Season to taste with salt and pepper, then pour over the cream mixture.

Cover and bake in a preheated moderately hot oven (190°C/375°F, Gas Mark 5) for 40 minutes or until the fish flakes easily when tested with a fork.

Serves 4

Cod Parcels

Any white fish steaks may be cooked in this way.

METRIC	IMPERIAL
4 cod steaks	4 cod steaks
grated rind and juice of 1 lemon	grated rind and juice of 1 lemon
50 g mushrooms, sliced	2 oz mushrooms, sliced
1 tomato, skinned and chopped	1 tomato, skinned and chopped
1 courgette, sliced	1 courgette, sliced
1 tablespoon chopped parsley	1 tablespoon chopped parsley
salt and pepper	salt and pepper

Place each cod steak on a square of foil large enough to enclose it. Sprinkle over the lemon juice. Mix the lemon rind with the remaining ingredients, adding salt and pepper to taste. Pile the mixture on the cod steaks.

Wrap the foil around the fish and place the parcels on a baking sheet. Bake in a preheated moderately hot oven (190°C/375°F, Gas Mark 5) for 20 minutes or until the fish flakes easily when tested with a fork. Serve in the foil parcels.

Serves 4

Haddock Charlotte

In this savoury charlotte the traditional bread lining encloses a mixture of fish, egg and milk, making a light and economical main dish.

METRIC	IMPERIAL
5 large slices of bread, crusts removed	5 large slices of bread, crusts removed
butter	butter
750 g haddock fillets, finely flaked	1½ lb haddock fillets, finely flaked
1 egg, beaten	1 egg, beaten
150 ml milk	¼ pint milk
1 teaspoon grated lemon rind	1 teaspoon grated lemon rind
1 tablespoon chopped parsley	1 tablespoon chopped parsley
salt and pepper	salt and pepper

Butter the bread, then cut the slices into fingers. Use two-thirds to line a 1.2 litre/2 pint pie dish, placing the buttered side against the dish.

Mix together the remaining ingredients, with salt and pepper to taste, and pour into the dish. Top with the remaining bread fingers, buttered sides up.

Bake in a preheated moderate oven (160°C/325°F, Gas Mark 3) for 45 to 55 minutes or until the topping is crisp and golden brown. Serve hot.

Serves 4

Summer Cod

METRIC	IMPERIAL
4 cod steaks	4 cod steaks
grated rind and juice of 1 lemon	grated rind and juice of 1 lemon
salt and pepper	salt and pepper
Sauce:	*Sauce:*
175 g cucumber, grated	6 oz cucumber, grated
150 ml plain yogurt	¼ pint plain yogurt
50 g cottage cheese, sieved	2 oz cottage cheese, sieved

Place the cod steaks in a baking dish and sprinkle with the lemon rind and juice and salt and pepper to taste. Cover and bake in a preheated moderate oven (180°C/350°F, Gas Mark 4) for 20 to 25 minutes or until the fish flakes easily when tested with a fork.

Meanwhile, make the sauce. Wring the cucumber in paper towels to extract excess moisture, then mix with the yogurt and cottage cheese. Season to taste with salt and pepper.

Transfer the cod steaks to a warmed serving dish and spoon over the sauce. Serve hot.

Serves 4

Fish

Using the oven

Timing and temperature control are the two keys to successful oven cooking. The thermometer on a modern gas or electric cooker controls the temperature, and accurate timing can be assured by using a timer.

Preheating the oven is essential for breads, cakes, biscuits and pastries. It is not so important for roast joints, casseroles, etc., but unless the cooking time is quite long you may have to add 10 minutes at the end, so nothing is saved by not preheating. However, a casserole or stew prepared ahead of time can be placed in a cold oven that is fitted with an automatic timing switch. This switch turns on the oven at a preset time, and the casserole is ready and waiting when you want it.

Most recipes give oven temperatures in Celsius, Fahrenheit, and Gas Mark, but for those that do not, here is a reference chart:

	°C	°F	Gas Mark
Very cool oven	110	225	$\frac{1}{4}$
	120	250	$\frac{1}{2}$
Cool oven	140	275	1
	150	300	2
Moderate oven	160	325	3
	180	350	4
Moderately hot oven	190	375	5
	200	400	6
Hot oven	220	425	7
	230	450	8
Very hot oven	240	475	9

Cod with Curry Topping

METRIC	IMPERIAL
4 cod steaks	4 cod steaks
50 g butter, melted	2 oz butter, melted
1–2 teaspoons curry powder	1–2 teaspoons curry powder
1 teaspoon Worcestershire sauce	1 teaspoon Worcestershire sauce
2 tablespoons sultanas	2 tablespoons sultanas
1 tablespoon sweet chutney	1 tablespoon sweet chutney
3 tablespoons fresh breadcrumbs	3 tablespoons fresh breadcrumbs
salt and pepper	salt and pepper

Arrange the cod steaks, in one layer, in a buttered baking dish. Mix together the remaining ingredients, with salt and pepper to taste, and spread over the fish.

Bake in a preheated moderately hot oven (200°C/400°F, Gas Mark 6) for about 25 minutes or until the fish flakes easily when tested with a fork.

Serves 4

Baked Cod Cutlets

METRIC	IMPERIAL
2 tablespoons oil	2 tablespoons oil
1 large onion, sliced	1 large onion, sliced
1 garlic clove, crushed	1 garlic clove, crushed
1 × 400 g can tomatoes, drained	1 × 14 oz can tomatoes, drained
1 teaspoon dried oregano	1 teaspoon dried oregano
salt and pepper	salt and pepper
4 cod cutlets	4 cod cutlets
150 ml plain yogurt	$\frac{1}{4}$ pint plain yogurt
50 g fresh breadcrumbs	2 oz fresh breadcrumbs
2 tablespoons grated Parmesan cheese	2 tablespoons grated Parmesan cheese

Heat the oil in a saucepan. Add the onion and garlic and fry until softened. Stir in the tomatoes, oregano and salt and pepper to taste. Cook gently for 5 minutes.

Spread half the tomato mixture over the bottom of a large shallow baking dish. Arrange the cutlets on top and pour over the remaining tomato mixture. Spoon over the yogurt. Mix the breadcrumbs with the cheese and sprinkle on top.

Bake in a preheated moderately hot oven (190°C/375°F, Gas Mark 5) for 20 to 30 minutes or until the top is browned and the fish flakes easily when tested with a fork. Serve hot.

Serves 4

Savoury Grilled Fish Steaks

This simple method of cooking may be used for any firm-fleshed white fish, such as cod or turbot.

METRIC	IMPERIAL
75 g butter	3 oz butter
1 tablespoon lemon juice	1 tablespoon lemon juice
1 teaspoon paprika	1 teaspoon paprika
salt and pepper	salt and pepper
4 white fish steaks	4 white fish steaks

Melt the butter in a saucepan, then heat it until it turns golden brown. Do not let it become too dark. Stir in the lemon juice, paprika and salt and pepper to taste.

Place the fish steaks in the grill pan lined with buttered foil and brush with some of the melted butter mixture. Grill for about 5 minutes on each side, brushing with the butter mixture from time to time. Serve hot, topped with any remaining butter mixture.

Serves 4

Cleaning fish

Most white fish are bought cleaned and filleted, but there may be occasions when you have to do these jobs yourself. To clean a round, scaly fish such as herring or salmon, first scrape off the scales with the back of a knife, working from the tail to head. For all large round fish, make a cut from just below the head along the belly to the vent. Open the cut and scrape out the gut. (Do this on a sheet of newspaper so that the unwanted parts may be easily disposed of.) Cut off the head, if liked, then rinse the fish inside and out under cold running water.

To fillet round fish, trim away the fins, then cut straight down the back on top of the backbone. Lift off the top fillet. Work the backbone away from the bottom fillet, from head to tail, using short sharp strokes of the knife. The skin may be removed from the fillets using a thin sharp knife. Dip the fingers of your left hand in salt (this will give you a secure grip on the skin), then take hold of the tail. Slip the knife in between flesh and skin and saw, from the tail end, keeping the knife at an angle.

Flat fish such as plaice and sole are cleaned through a semi-circular cut made just below the head on the dark side. Scrape out the gut and rinse thoroughly. Some flat fish are skinned before filleting. To do this, trim away the fins, then lossen the skin on the dark side by running your thumb under it around the fish, starting at the cut made to lean the fish. Grip the skin at the tail end firmly (salt your fingers) and peel it away. Repeat on the other side of the fish. Small flat fish are usually boned rather than filleted, in that the backbone is removed, leaving the two fillets attached to each other. For larger flat fish, the fillets may be removed in two or four pieces, as for round fish. These larger fillets are skinned after filleting.

American Fish Pie

METRIC	IMPERIAL
3 streaky bacon rashers, rinded and chopped	3 streaky bacon rashers, rinded and chopped
2 onions, chopped	2 onions, chopped
3 tomatoes, skinned and chopped	3 tomatoes, skinned and chopped
25 g flour	1 oz flour
450 ml Court Bouillon★ or chicken stock	¾ pint Court Bouillon★ or chicken stock
2 × 200 g cans tuna fish, drained and flaked	2 × 7 oz cans tuna fish, drained and flaked
salt and pepper	salt and pepper
50 g plain potato crisps, crushed	2 oz plain potato crisps, crushed
3 tablespoons grated Parmesan cheese	3 tablespoons grated Parmesan cheese
melted butter	melted butter

Fry the bacon and onions in a frying pan until the onions are softened. Stir in the tomatoes followed by the flour. Cook for 2 to 3 minutes, then stir in the stock. Bring to the boil, stirring, and simmer until thickened.

Add the tuna fish and salt and pepper to taste and mix well. Turn into a pie dish and top with the crisps mixed with the cheese. Drizzle over a little melted butter.

Bake in a preheated moderately hot oven (190°C/375°F, Gas Mark 5) for 30 minutes. Serve hot.

Serves 4 to 5

VARIATION
Make as above, using 750 g/1½ lb cooked and flaked white fish fillets instead of tuna fish, and substituting 500 g/1 lb mashed potato for the crisps and cheese.

Baked Apple Mackerel

Fresh herrings or pilchards may be used instead of mackerel.

METRIC	IMPERIAL
4 fresh mackerel fillets	4 fresh mackerel fillets
2 teaspoons made mustard	2 teaspoons made mustard
salt and pepper	salt and pepper
500 g potatoes, thinly sliced	1 lb potatoes, thinly sliced
1 onion, thinly sliced	1 onion, thinly sliced
1 teaspoon chopped fresh sage, or ½ teaspoon dried sage	1 teaspoon chopped fresh sage, or ½ teaspoon dried sage
1 large cooking apple, peeled, cored and sliced	1 large cooking apple, peeled, cored and sliced
150 ml cider or water	¼ pint cider or water

Spread the fish fillets with the mustard and season with salt and pepper. Roll up the fillets.

Cover the bottom of a lightly greased baking dish with half the potato slices. Scatter over the onion slices and season with salt, pepper and the sage. Cover with the apple slices and place the fish rolls on top. Arrange the remaining potato slices over the fissh rolls and season with salt and pepper. Pour in the cider or water, and add enough additional water to half fill the dish.

Cover and bake in a preheated moderate oven (180°C/350°F, Gas Mark 4) for 45 minutes. Uncover and bake for a further 30 minutes or until the fish flakes easily when tested with a fork and the top layer of potatoes is golden brown. Serve hot.

Serves 4

Tuna and Grapefruit Cake

This savoury 'cake' is served cold. Garnish it with lettuce and tomato, if liked.

METRIC	IMPERIAL
1 × 200 g can tuna fish, drained and flaked	1 × 7 oz can tuna fish, drained and flaked
grated rind and juice of ½ grapefruit	grated rind and juice of ½ grapefruit
25 g dried milk powder	1 oz dried milk powder
4 tablespoons cold water	4 tablespoons cold water
50 g fresh breadcrumbs	2 oz fresh breadcrumbs
1 egg, beaten	1 egg, beaten
1 small onion, grated	1 small onion, grated
½ teaspoon paprika	½ teaspoon paprika

Mix the tuna with the grapefruit rind and juice. Dissolve the milk powder in the water and add to the tuna with the remaining ingredients. Mix well.

Spoon into a lightly greased 450 ml/¾ pint shallow baking dish and smooth the top. Bake in a preheated moderate oven (180°C/350°F, Gas Mark 4) for 40 minutes or until set and golden brown. Cool slightly in the dish, then turn out on to a serving plate and leave to cool completely. Serve cold, cut into slices.

Serves 4 to 6

Herrings in Oatmeal

METRIC	IMPERIAL
4 × 350 g herrings	4 × 12 oz herrings
milk	milk
medium oatmeal	medium oatmeal
175 g butter	6 oz butter
lemon wedges to serve	lemon wedges to serve

Scrape the scales from the fish if necessary and trim the fins. Slit open the belly from the gills down to the tail and scrape out the entrails. Rinse the cavity thoroughly under cold running water. Cut off the head and tail. Open out the fish flat on a board, skin side up, and press firmly all along the backbone with the knuckles. Turn the fish over and remove the backbone in one piece using a sharp knife. Remove as many small bones as possible. Rinse the fish again and pat dry with paper towels.

Dip the fish in milk, then coat with oatmeal, shaking off any excess. Melt about one-quarter of the butter in a frying pan. Add one of the fish, skin side up, and fry until crisp and golden brown. Turn the fish over and fry the other side. Drain on paper towels and keep hot while frying the remaining three fish, using the rest of the butter.

Serve hot, with lemon wedges.

Serves 4

Smoked Haddock Bake

METRIC	IMPERIAL
4 potatoes, thinly sliced	4 potatoes, thinly sliced
225 g smoked haddock fillet, skinned and flaked	8 oz smoked haddock fillet, skinned and flaked
4 tomatoes, skinned and sliced	4 tomatoes, skinned and sliced
pepper	pepper
2 teaspoons anchovy essence	2 teaspoons anchovy essence
2 large eggs	2 large eggs
300 ml milk	½ pint milk
25 g butter	1 oz butter

Make alternate layers of potatoes, fish and tomatoes in a buttered ovenproof serving dish, seasoning each layer with pepper and ending with potatoes.

Lightly beat the anchovy essence, eggs and milk together and pour into the dish. Dot the top with the butter.

Bake in a preheated moderate oven (160°C/325°F, Gas Mark 3) for 45 minutes or until the potatoes are tender and the top is golden brown. Serve hot.

Serves 4

Coatings for frying

Food that is to be shallow or deep fried is often coated with a batter, pastry or egg and crumbs. Whichever coating is used, the food to be fried should be dry so that the coating will adhere. A batter coating should not be too thick: after dipping the fish fillet, fruit, etc. into the batter, lift it out and hold it over the bowl so that excess batter can drip off. Food to be egg-and-crumbed, such as croquettes, fish fillets, cutlets, etc., should first be coated with seasoned flour. Shake off any excess flour, then dip the food into beaten egg and finally into breadcrumbs. Press on the crumbs with a palette knife to coat evenly. If possible, chill the egg-and-crumbed food before cooking: this will help keep the coating in place.

Cubes of meat to be used in a stew or casserole are often coated with seasoned flour before browning. A quick way to do this is to place the flour in a polythene bag, add the meat, close the bag and shake lightly.

Poultry and Game

Poultry is one of the most 'affordable' of foods. And there are so many ways to prepare chicken, turkey, duck and other fowl and game birds that you need never run out of ideas. Chicken and turkey are low in fat, too, and recipes for these birds are included in almost every slimming diet. Duck works out more expensive than chicken and turkey because of the high fat content, bones and shortage of meat, but in spite of this, it is still more reasonable than many meats. You will enjoy the rich, distinctive flavour of the duck flesh and the crispy, golden skin.

Orange Chicken Casserole

Chicken is low in fat content so it is an excellent staple for a slimming diet. However, the skin of chicken is high in fat, so the skin should be removed before cooking.

METRIC	IMPERIAL
2 onions, quartered	2 onions, quartered
2 celery sticks, sliced	2 celery sticks, sliced
4 chicken portions, skinned	4 chicken portions, skinned
grated rind and juice of 2 oranges	grated rind and juice of 2 oranges
1 teaspoon dried mixed herbs	1 teaspoon dried mixed herbs
salt and pepper	salt and pepper
orange slices to garnish	orange slices to garnish

Blanch the onions and celery in boiling water for 2 minutes. Drain well. Place all the ingredients in a casserole, seasoning to taste with salt and pepper.

Cover and cook in a preheated moderate oven (180°C/350°F, Gas Mark 4) for about 1 hour or until the chicken is tender. Serve hot, garnished with orange slices.

Serves 4

Chicken Maryland

Serve this popular main dish with baked jacket potatoes, Fried Bananas (page 91) and Corn Fritters (page 91).

METRIC	IMPERIAL
25 g flour	1 oz flour
salt and pepper	salt and pepper
4 chicken portions	4 chicken portions
1 egg, beaten	1 egg, beaten
4 tablespoons fine dry breadcrumbs	4 tablespoons fine dry breadcrumbs
oil for deep frying	oil for deep frying

Season the flour with salt and pepper and use to coat the chicken portions. Dip them into beaten egg, then coat with the breadcrumbs.

Deep fry the chicken until crisp and golden brown. Drain on paper towels, then arrange on a baking sheet. Bake in a preheated moderate oven (180°C/350°F, Gas Mark 4) for 30 to 35 minutes or until the chicken is cooked through. Serve hot.

Serves 4

Choosing chicken

Chicken is so versatile. It can be grilled, fried, roasted or boiled, and the ways of using up any delicious leftovers – in casseroles, pies, salads, soups, sandwiches, pâtés – are endless. Chicken is economical too, which is what makes it such a popular choice for both large and small families.

From a slimming point of view, chicken is also a winner. Compared to other sources of protein such as beef, chicken has less fat and, as a result, it is lower in calories.

There are basically four kinds of chicken available: poussin, spring chicken, roasting chicken and boiling fowl. Poussins are baby chickens, 4–6 weeks old, and weigh 350–500 g/12 oz–1 lb. Each poussin will serve one person. There are also double poussins, which weigh about 1 kg/2 lb. These will serve two people each.

A spring chicken, about 6 weeks old, usually weighs 1.25 kg/2½ lb and will serve two or three people. Like poussins, spring chickens lend themselves to quick-cooking methods such as grilling and frying.

The most popular kind of chicken available is the roaster, which starts in weight at 1.5 kg/3 lb. Roasting chickens can be cooked in many ways other than roasting, either left whole or jointed.

Boiling fowl are older birds which take longer to cook than roasters, the length of time depending on the age of the bird (usually 8 months). They start in weight at 1.5 kg/3 lb, but can weigh much more. The average weight is 2.75 kg/6 lb. The meat on a boiling fowl is more fatty than that of other chickens, but it is also full of flavour. Use boiling fowl to make soups, stews and casseroles.

A capon is a young, sometimes castrated cock that is specially bred to be very meaty. The flavour of capon meat is excellent and the bird is usually roasted. Weight is 2.75–3.5 kg/6–8 lb.

Chickens are available fresh or frozen, either whole or jointed. If buying a frozen chicken, let it thaw completely before cooking. To hasten the thawing, put the bird under slow-running cold water. Never put a frozen chicken or any other poultry, for that matter into hot water as this will toughen the flesh.

Allow about 250 g/8 oz chicken per person, in calculating the size of chicken for a dish. And try to get the giblets, too, as these can be used to make a delicious gravy or pâté.

Chicken in Peanut Sauce

METRIC	IMPERIAL
4 tablespoons oil	4 tablespoons oil
1 onion, chopped	1 onion, chopped
2 tablespoons flour	2 tablespoons flour
salt and pepper	salt and pepper
4 chicken joints	4 chicken joints
150 ml chicken stock	¼ pint chicken stock
150 ml milk	¼ pint milk
2 tablespoons smooth peanut butter	2 tablespoons smooth peanut butter
2 tablespoons single cream	2 tablespoons single cream
50 g salted peanuts	2 oz salted peanuts

Heat the oil in a frying pan. Add the onion and fry until softened.

Season the flour with salt and pepper and use to coat the chicken joints. Add to the frying pan and brown on all sides. Transfer to a casserole.

Add the stock to the frying pan and bring to the boil, stirring to mix well with the sediment in the bottom of the pan. Stir in the milk and peanut butter and heat until smooth. Pour over the chicken.

Cover and cook in a preheated moderate oven (180°C/350°F, Gas Mark 4) for 1 hour or until the chicken is tender.

Stir in the cream, and taste and adjust the seasoning. Serve hot, sprinkled with the peanuts.

Serves 4

Old English Chicken Pie

METRIC	IMPERIAL
50 g flour	2 oz flour
salt and pepper	salt and pepper
350 g boneless chicken meat, diced	12 oz boneless chicken meat, diced
¼ quantity Sage and Onion Stuffing*	¼ quantity Sage and Onion Stuffing*
50 g butter	2 oz butter
3 skinless sausages, halved	3 skinless sausages, halved
450 ml chicken stock	¾ pint chicken stock
2 hard-boiled eggs, chopped	2 hard-boiled eggs, chopped
225 g quantity Shortcrust Pastry*	8 oz quantity Shortcrust Pastry*
beaten egg to glaze	beaten egg to glaze

Season half the flour with salt and pepper and use to coat the chicken. Form the stuffing into small balls. Melt the butter in a large frying pan. Add the chicken, sausages and stuffing balls and fry until golden brown on all sides. Remove from the pan with a slotted spoon and place in a 1.2 litre/2 pint pie dish.

Stir the remaining flour into the fat in the pan and cook for 2 minutes. Gradually stir in the stock and bring to the boil. Simmer, stirring, until thickened. Stir in the eggs and season to taste with salt and pepper. Pour this sauce over the chicken mixture in the dish.

Roll out the dough on a floured surface. Cut out a 2.5 cm/1 inch wide strip and lay over the dampened rim of the dish. Dampen the strip and lay the rest of the dough on top. Press the edges together to seal, then flute them. Make a slit in the centre of the lid and decorate with the dough trimmings. Glaze with beaten egg.

Bake in a preheated hot oven (220°C/425°F, Gas Mark 7) for 20 to 25 minutes or until the pastry is golden brown. Reduce the temperature to moderate (180°C/350°F, Gas Mark 4) and bake for a further 20 to 25 minutes. Serve hot.

Serves 6

Roast Chicken with Sweet and Sour Stuffing

Add 4 to 5 tablespoons chopped canned pineapple to the stuffing, if liked. Make gravy with the giblet stock and any drippings in the tin, and add 2 teaspoons honey or juice from the canned pineapple and a squeeze of lemon juice to give the gravy a sweet and sour flavour.

METRIC	IMPERIAL
500 g pork sausagemeat	1 lb pork sausagemeat
2 tablespoons seeded raisins	2 tablespoons seeded raisins
2 tablespoons chopped walnuts	2 tablespoons chopped walnuts
2 tablespoons chopped gherkins	2 tablespoons chopped gherkins
1 teaspoon gherkin liquid	1 teaspoon gherkin liquid
1 teaspoon dried mixed herbs	1 teaspoon dried mixed herbs
1 egg, beaten	1 egg, beaten
1 × 1.75 kg chicken	1 × 3½ lb chicken

Mix together the sausagemeat, raisins, walnuts, gherkins and liquid, herbs and egg. Stuff into the chicken and truss or secure with skewers.

Weigh the chicken and place in a roasting tin. Cover with foil and roast in a preheated moderately hot oven (200°C/400°F, Gas Mark 6) for 15 minutes per 500 g/1 lb plus 15 minutes over.

Remove the foil and roast for a further 30 minutes or until the chicken is golden brown and the juices that run out of the thigh when pierced with a skewer are clear. Serve hot.

Serves 4

Stuffed Chicken Cutlets

These chicken breasts, stuffed with sausagemeat and mushrooms, may be fried or grilled.

METRIC	IMPERIAL
225 g pork sausagemeat	8 oz pork sausagemeat
50 g mushrooms, chopped	2 oz mushrooms, chopped
1 tablespoon chopped parsley	1 tablespoon chopped parsley
salt and pepper	salt and pepper
4 chicken breasts, boned	4 chicken breasts, boned
butter	butter

Mix together the sausagemeat, mushrooms, parsley and salt and pepper to taste. Divide into four portions and press one against each chicken breast, on the underside where the bones were removed.

To fry, melt about 50 g/2 oz butter in a large frying pan. Add the chicken and fry for about 15 minutes, turning once.

To grill, baste with melted butter and cook for about 15 minutes, turning occasionally and basting with more butter from time to time. Serve hot.

Serves 4

Fried Chicken with Orange Cream

METRIC	IMPERIAL
25 g flour	1 oz flour
grated rind of 1 orange	grated rind of 1 orange
salt and pepper	salt and pepper
4 chicken breasts	4 chicken breasts
75 g butter	3 oz butter
300 ml soured cream, or double cream mixed with 2 tablespoons lemon juice	½ pint soured cream, or double cream mixed with 2 tablespoons lemon juice
2 tablespoons orange juice	2 tablespoons orange juice

Season the flour with the orange rind, salt and pepper and use to coat the chicken breasts. Melt the butter in a large frying pan. Add the chicken breasts and fry for about 15 minutes or until tender and golden brown, turning occasionally.

Transfer the chicken breasts to a warmed serving dish and keep hot. Add the cream to the pan and stir to mix with the juices. Stir in the orange juice and heat through gently. Pour over the chicken and serve hot.

Serves 4

Chicken with Spinach and Cheese

If you're slimming, replace the cheese sauce with plain yogurt mixed with 100 g/4 oz grated Edam cheese.

METRIC	IMPERIAL
500 g fresh spinach, well washed	1 lb fresh spinach, well washed
grated rind of ½ lemon	grated rind of ½ lemon
pinch of grated nutmeg	pinch of grated nutmeg
salt and pepper	salt and pepper
350 g cooked chicken meat, sliced	12 oz cooked chicken meat, sliced
300 ml hot Cheese Sauce*	½ pint hot Cheese Sauce*
3 tablespoons grated cheese	3 tablespoons grated cheese

Cook the spinach, with just the water clinging to the leaves, until tender. Drain well, pressing out all excess moisture. Chop the spinach and mix with the lemon rind, nutmeg and salt and pepper to taste. Spread over the bottom of a greased shallow baking dish.

Place the chicken on the spinach and pour over the sauce. Sprinkle the cheese on top. Bake in a preheated moderately hot oven (190°C/375°F, Gas Mark 5) for 25 to 30 minutes or until piping hot and the top is golden brown.

Serves 4

Chicken with Rice

If liked, add a few chopped nuts to the dish with the chicken, and garnish with a few more nuts or with crisp breadcrumbs.

METRIC	IMPERIAL
2 tablespoons oil	2 tablespoons oil
2 onions, chopped	2 onions, chopped
225 g long-grain rice	8 oz long-grain rice
600 ml chicken stock	1 pint chicken stock
50 g sultanas	2 oz sultanas
350 g cooked chicken meat, diced	12 oz cooked chicken meat, diced
salt and pepper	salt and pepper

Heat the oil in a saucepan. Add the onions and fry until softened. Stir in the rice and cook, stirring, for 3 to 4 minutes, then add the stock. Bring to the boil, stir once and simmer for 10 minutes.

Add the sultanas, chicken and salt and pepper to taste and simmer for a further 10 to 15 minutes or until the rice is tender and all the stock has been absorbed. Serve hot.

Serves 4 to 5

Poultry and Game

Spanish-style Chicken

METRIC	IMPERIAL
25 g flour	1 oz flour
salt and pepper	salt and pepper
8 chicken joints	8 chicken joints
50 g butter	2 oz butter
1 tablespoon olive oil	1 tablespoon olive oil
8 button onions	8 button onions
1 garlic clove, crushed	1 garlic clove, crushed
500 g tomatoes, skinned and chopped	1 lb tomatoes, skinned and chopped
300 ml chicken stock	½ pint chicken stock
100 g button mushrooms	4 oz button mushrooms

Season the flour with salt and pepper and use to coat the chicken joints. Melt the butter with the oil in a large frying pan. Add the chicken joints and fry until golden brown on all sides. Remove from the pan.

Add the onions and garlic to the pan and fry until browned all over. Stir in the tomatoes and stock and bring to the boil. Stir in the mushrooms and salt and pepper to taste.

Place the chicken joints in a casserole and pour over the tomato sauce. Cover and cook in a preheated moderate oven (160°C/325°F, Gas Mark 3) for 45 minutes to 1 hour or until the chicken is tender.

Serves 4

Apricot Chicken

METRIC	IMPERIAL
100 g fresh breadcrumbs	4 oz fresh breadcrumbs
2 tablespoons chopped parsley	2 tablespoons chopped parsley
50 g shredded suet	2 oz shredded suet
grated rind and juice of 1 lemon	grated rind and juice of 1 lemon
8–10 canned apricot halves, chopped (can syrup reserved)	8–10 canned apricot halves, chopped (can syrup reserved)
salt and pepper	salt and pepper
1 egg, beaten	1 egg, beaten
1 × 2 kg chicken	1 × 4 lb chicken

Mix together the breadcrumbs, parsley, suet, lemon rind and juice, apricots and salt and pepper to taste. Bind this stuffing with the egg.

Stuff the chicken and truss or secure with skewers. Place in a roasting tin and roast in a preheated moderate oven (180°C/350°F, Gas Mark 4) for about 2 hours or until the juices from the chicken run clear. Baste the chicken with a few tablespoons of the apricot can syrup towards the end of the cooking time.

Serves 4 to 6

Chicken in Lemon Cream Sauce

METRIC	IMPERIAL
1 × 1.5 kg young chicken, trussed	1 × 3 lb young chicken, trussed
1 bouquet garni	1 bouquet garni
2 lemons, sliced and pips removed	2 lemons, sliced and pips removed
salt and pepper	salt and pepper
50 g butter	2 oz butter
50 g flour	2 oz flour
300 ml single cream	½ pint single cream
lemon wedges to garnish	lemon wedges to garnish

Place the chicken in a large saucepan and cover with cold water. Bring to the boil, skimming off any scum that rises to the surface. Add the bouquet garni, lemons and salt and pepper to taste. Simmer for about 1¼ hours or until the chicken is tender.

Remove the chicken from the pan and keep hot. Strain the cooking liquid and reserve 300 ml/½ pint.

Melt the butter in a clean saucepan. Stir in the flour and cook for 2 minutes, then gradually stir in the reserved cooking liquid. Bring to the boil, stirring, and simmer until thickened. Stir in the cream and salt and pepper to taste. Heat through gently.

Cut the chicken into serving pieces and arrange on a warmed serving dish. Pour over the lemon cream sauce and garnish with lemon wedges. Serve hot.

Serves 4

Jointing poultry

Jointing a chicken is not difficult provided you have a sharp sturdy knife and poultry shears. Begin by removing one of the legs: slit the skin between the leg and breast, then bend the leg outwards until the bone breaks away from the carcass. Cut through this joint and the surrounding flesh and skin towards the 'parson's nose'. Remove the other leg in the same way. Cut down through the wishbone and ribs to detach each wing with a good portion of breast. Cut away the breast in one portion, leaving only the backbone and parson's nose. Discard these or use to make stock. If liked, the breast may be divided in half and each leg separated into two portions through the joint.

A small bird, such as a poussin, may be just split in half (called a spatchcock). To do this, cut through the skin and flesh on the breast with a sharp knife, then cut in half with shears on one side of the backbone. Trim away the backbone from the other side once the bird has been divided into two portions.

Devon Chicken

METRIC	IMPERIAL
25 g butter	1 oz butter
2 tablespoons oil	2 tablespoons oil
4 chicken joints	4 chicken joints
225 g small carrots, halved lengthways	8 oz small carrots, halved lengthways
225 g button onions	8 oz button onions
2 celery sticks, chopped	2 celery sticks, chopped
25 g flour	1 oz flour
450 ml dry cider	¾ pint dry cider
2 tablespoons Worcestershire sauce	2 tablespoons Worcestershire sauce
1 teaspoon dry mustard	1 teaspoon dry mustard
salt and pepper	salt and pepper
100 g frozen peas	4 oz frozen peas

Melt the butter with the oil in a large frying pan. Add the chicken joints and fry until golden brown on both sides. Transfer the joints to a casserole.

Add the carrots, onions and celery to the frying pan and fry until softened and just beginning to brown. Sprinkle over the flour and stir in well, then gradually stir in the cider. Bring to the boil, stirring, and simmer for 2 minutes. Add the Worcestershire sauce, mustard and salt and pepper to taste and mix well.

Pour the cider mixture over the chicken. Cover the casserole and cook in a preheated moderate oven (180°C/350°F, Gas Mark 4) for 1 hour.

Stir in the peas and cook for a further 10 to 15 minutes or until the chicken and vegetables are tender. Taste and adjust the seasoning before serving.

Serves 4

Chicken Drumsticks en Croûte

METRIC	IMPERIAL
8 chicken drumsticks	8 chicken drumsticks
100 g smooth chicken liver pâté	4 oz smooth chicken liver pâté
salt and pepper	salt and pepper
350 g frozen puff pastry, thawed	12 oz frozen puff pastry, thawed
1 egg, beaten	1 egg, beaten
parsley sprigs to garnish	parsley sprigs to garnish

Spread the drumsticks with the pâté, then season with salt and pepper.

Roll out the pastry dough on a floured surface to 5 mm/¼ inch thick. Cut into eight 15 cm/6 inch squares. Place a drumstick diagonally on each square. Brush the edges of the square with beaten egg, then fold over the drumstick and press together to seal.

Arrange the parcels on a baking sheet and brush with beaten egg.

Bake in a preheated moderately hot oven (200°C/400°F, Gas Mark 6) for 45 minutes or until the pastry is risen and golden brown. Serve hot or cold, garnished with parsley sprigs.

Serves 8

Spiced Tomato Chicken

METRIC	IMPERIAL
grated rind and juice of 1 lemon	grated rind and juice of 1 lemon
¼ teaspoon ground cloves	¼ teaspoon ground cloves
½ teaspoon ground cinnamon	½ teaspoon ground cinnamon
salt and pepper	salt and pepper
4 chicken joints, skinned	4 chicken joints, skinned
4 tablespoons oil	4 tablespoons oil
6 tomatoes, skinned and chopped	6 tomatoes, skinned and chopped
2 tablespoons tomato purée	2 tablespoons tomato purée
450 ml chicken stock	¾ pint chicken stock

Mix together the lemon rind and juice, spices and salt and pepper. Rub all over the chicken joints.

Heat the oil in a large frying pan. Add the chicken joints and fry until brown. Transfer to a casserole.

Add the tomatoes, tomato purée and stock to the frying pan, with any remaining spice mixture. Bring to the boil, stirring. Pour over the chicken.

Cover and cook in a preheated moderate oven (180°C/350°F, Gas Mark 4) for 45 minutes. Uncover and cook for a further 15 minutes or until the chicken is tender. Taste and adjust the seasoning.

Serves 4

Frozen stock cubes

Frozen cubes of homemade stock can transform a soup, stew or casserole. They take up very little room in the freezer.

Make stock in the usual way, then skim off all the fat and boil until reduced to one-third the original quantity. Strain the stock and cool quickly, then pour into ice cube trays. When frozen, pack the cubes into a rigid container, and return to the freezer. The stock 'cubes' may be reheated from frozen or thawed at room temperature, but the best news is that they can be added still frozen to a hot dish. They can be stored in the freezer for 3 months.

Poultry and Game

Roast Stuffed Turkey

METRIC	IMPERIAL
1 × 5 kg oven-ready turkey	1 × 10 lb oven-ready turkey
1 quantity Chestnut Stuffing*	1 quantity Chestnut Stuffing*
1 quantity Sausagemeat and Celery Stuffing*	1 quantity Sausagemeat and Celery Stuffing*
100 g butter, melted	4 oz butter, melted
salt and pepper	salt and pepper
8 streaky bacon rashers, rinded	8 streaky bacon rashers, rinded
Garnish:	*Garnish:*
225 g streaky bacon rashers, rinded and halved crossways	8 oz streaky bacon rashers, rinded and halved crossways
500 g chipolatas	1 lb chipolatas

Wipe the turkey inside and out. Stuff the neck end with chestnut stuffing and the body cavity with sausagemeat and celery stuffing. Truss the turkey, or close the openings with skewers.

Place the turkey in a roasting tin. Brush all over with melted butter and sprinkle with salt and pepper. Cover the breast with the bacon rashers.

Roast in a preheated moderate oven (160°C/325°F, Gas Mark 3) for 4 hours, basting occasionally with the drippings in the tin.

About 15 minutes before the turkey is ready, prepare the garnish. Roll up the bacon pieces and secure with wooden cocktail sticks. Grill the bacon rolls and chipolatas until golden brown and crisp. Drain on paper towels.

Untruss the turkey or remove the skewers. Place on a warmed serving platter and surround with the bacon rolls and chipolatas. Add the drippings in the tin, skimmed of fat, to the gravy and serve, with Bread Sauce* and Cranberry Sauce*.

Serves 6 to 8

Turkey Breast with Mushrooms

METRIC	IMPERIAL
25 g butter	1 oz butter
1 onion, sliced	1 onion, sliced
1 × 1 kg boned and rolled turkey breast	1 × 2 lb boned and rolled turkey breast
225 g mushrooms, sliced	8 oz mushrooms, sliced
300 ml chicken stock	½ pint chicken stock
1 bouquet garni	1 bouquet garni
¼ teaspoon grated nutmeg	¼ teaspoon grated nutmeg
salt	salt
pepper	pepper

Melt the butter in a flameproof casserole. Add the onion and fry until softened. Place the turkey breast (these joints are now available, ready boned and rolled, in many supermarkets) on top and add the remaining ingredients, with salt and pepper to taste. Bring to the boil.

Cover the casserole and transfer to a preheated moderate oven (180°C/350°F, Gas Mark 4). Cook for 1 hour or until the turkey is cooked through.

Discard the bouquet garni before serving.

Serves 4

Creamed Turkey Duchesse

Cooked chicken meat may be used instead of turkey in this recipe.

METRIC	IMPERIAL
500 g mashed potato	1 lb mashed potato
2 egg yolks	2 egg yolks
50 g butter	2 oz butter
salt and pepper	salt and pepper
100 g button mushrooms	4 oz button mushrooms
1 green pepper, cored, seeded and diced	1 green pepper, cored, seeded and diced
300 ml turkey or chicken stock	½ pint turkey or chicken stock
25 g flour	1 oz flour
150 ml milk	¼ pint milk
about 500 g cooked turkey meat, diced	about 1 lb cooked turkey meat, diced
2–3 tablespoons single cream	2–3 tablespoons single cream

Mix the potato with one of the egg yolks and half the butter. Season well with salt and pepper. Form into a border around the edge of a baking dish, making a decorative pattern on top with a fork. Lightly beat the remaining egg yolk with a few drops of water and brush over the potato border.

Bake in a preheated moderate oven (180°C/350°F, Gas Mark 4) for about 20 minutes or until piping hot and browned.

Meanwhile, place the mushrooms and green pepper in a saucepan with the stock. Bring to the boil and simmer for 10 minutes. Drain the vegetables, reserving the liquid.

Melt the remaining butter in the cleaned saucepan. Stir in the flour and cook for 2 minutes, then gradually stir in the milk and reserved vegetable cooking liquid. Bring to the boil, stirring, and simmer until thickened. Season to taste with salt and pepper.

Stir the vegetables and turkey into the sauce and heat through gently. Stir in the cream.

Pour the turkey mixture into the centre of the potato border and serve hot.

Serves 4 to 6

Checking cooking times

Cooking times given in individual recipes are intended only as a good guide, because oven temperature gauges can vary in their accuracy, and the heat under a pan on top of the stove is subject to individual judgement. So a guide to 'until done' or 'until cooked through' is useful.

For chicken, pierce the thickest part with a fine skewer: the juices that run out should be clear.

Fish, in steaks, cutlets or whole, is tested gently with the prongs of a fork: the flesh should flake easily. Fish fillets are ready when they can be easily pierced with the point of a knife.

Most vegetables are done when they can be just pierced with the point of a knife or fine skewer. At this stage they will be tender but still crisp. Potatoes need a little more cooking, until the skewer will pierce them easily.

The most accurate way to test roasted meat for doneness is to use a meat thermometer. This is inserted into the thickest part of the joint, away from bone or stuffing, before cooking begins. If you don't have a thermometer, you can test with a skewer as you would for chicken. For roast pork, the juices that run out should no longer be pink. For roast lamb, they should be pale pink or clear, depending on how well done you like lamb. The same is true for beef, with the juices red, pink or pale pink.

Casseroled Duck

METRIC	IMPERIAL
1 large duck	1 large duck
2 small apples, peeled	2 small apples, peeled
100 g prunes, soaked overnight and drained	4 oz prunes, soaked overnight and drained
12 button onions	12 button onions
1 garlic clove, crushed	1 garlic clove, crushed
4 carrots, quartered	4 carrots, quartered
450 ml duck giblet stock	¾ pint duck giblet stock
25 g flour	1 oz flour
salt and pepper	salt and pepper
4 large potatoes, sliced	4 large potatoes, sliced

Stuff the duck with the apples and prunes. Prick the skin of the duck all over, then place it in a roasting tin. Roast in a preheated hot oven (220°C/425°F, Gas Mark 7) for 30 minutes or until the skin is crisp and brown.

Meanwhile, place the onions, garlic and carrots in a saucepan. Add 300 ml/½ pint of the stock and bring to the boil. Cover and simmer for 30 minutes.

Blend the flour with the remaining cold stock and add to the saucepan of vegetables. Simmer, stirring, until thickened. Season to taste with salt and pepper, and fold in the potatoes.

Pour the vegetable mixture into a large casserole. Place the duck on top, draining off all fat. Cover and place in the oven. Reduce the temperature to moderate (160°C/325°F, Gas Mark 3) and cook for 1½ hours or until the duck is tender. Serve hot.

Serves 4

Sweet and Sour Duck with Pineapple

METRIC	IMPERIAL
3 tablespoons soy sauce	3 tablespoons soy sauce
1 tablespoon caster sugar	1 tablespoon caster sugar
½ teaspoon ground ginger	½ teaspoon ground ginger
1 garlic clove, crushed	1 garlic clove, crushed
1 × 2 kg duckling, jointed	1 × 4 lb duckling, jointed
1 × 400 g can pineapple chunks	1 × 14 oz can pineapple chunks
600 ml duck giblet or chicken stock	1 pint duck giblet or chicken stock
2 tablespoons oil	2 tablespoons oil
1 tablespoon cornflour	1 tablespoon cornflour
2 tablespoons vinegar	2 tablespoons vinegar
salt and pepper	salt and pepper

Mix together the soy sauce, sugar, ginger and garlic in a large bowl. Add the duck joints and turn to coat. Cover and leave to marinate for at least 1 hour in a cool place.

Drain the pineapple, reserving 150 ml/¼ pint of the syrup. Add the syrup to the stock.

Heat the oil in a large flameproof casserole. Drain the duck joints, reserving the marinade, and add to the pot. Fry until golden brown all over. Pour in the reserved marinade and the stock and syrup mixture and bring to the boil. Cover and transfer to a preheated moderate oven (180°C/350°F, Gas Mark 4). Cook for 1 hour.

Blend the cornflour with the vinegar. Drain the liquid from the casserole into a saucepan and stir in the cornflour mixture. Bring to the boil, stirring, and simmer until thickened. Stir in the pineapple and taste and adjust the seasoning.

Pour the pineapple sauce over the duck joints in the casserole. Return to the oven, uncovered, and cook for a further 10 minutes.

Serves 4

Poultry and Game

Country-style Rabbit

Very little liquid is used to cook the rabbit, so be sure to seal the foil tightly.

METRIC	IMPERIAL
4 rabbit joints	4 rabbit joints
1 tablespoon French mustard	1 tablespoon French mustard
225 g piece lean flank bacon, rinded and cut into 1 cm dice	8 oz piece lean flank bacon, rinded and cut into ½ inch dice
2 onions, chopped	2 onions, chopped
3 carrots, chopped	3 carrots, chopped
1 small turnip, chopped	1 small turnip, chopped
½ teaspoon dried mixed herbs	½ teaspoon dried mixed herbs
salt and pepper	salt and pepper
2 tablespoons water	2 tablespoons water

Place a piece of foil in a roasting tin, leaving enough foil hanging over the edge of the tin to enclose the contents. Place the rabbit joints on the foil and spread with the mustard. Scatter over the bacon, vegetables, herbs and salt and pepper to taste. Sprinkle over the water.

Fold over the foil to enclose and seal in the rabbit mixture. Cook in a preheated moderately hot oven (190°C/375°F, Gas Mark 5) for 1½ hours or until the rabbit is tender. Serve hot.

Serves 4

Casseroled Pigeons

METRIC	IMPERIAL
25 g butter	1 oz butter
4 streaky bacon rashers, rinded and diced	4 streaky bacon rashers, rinded and diced
2 onions, sliced	2 onions, sliced
1 carrot, sliced	1 carrot, sliced
100 g mushrooms, sliced	4 oz mushrooms, sliced
4 small oven-ready pigeons	4 small oven-ready pigeons
50 g flour	2 oz flour
600 ml chicken stock	1 pint chicken stock
salt and pepper	salt and pepper

Melt the butter in a large frying pan. Add the bacon, onions, carrot and mushrooms and fry until the onions are softened. Transfer to a casserole with a slotted spoon.

Add the pigeons to the frying pan and brown on all sides. Place in the casserole.

Stir the flour into the fat in the frying pan and cook for 3 minutes or until golden brown. Gradually stir in the stock and bring to the boil. Simmer, stirring, until thickened. Season to taste with salt and pepper, then pour into the casserole.

Cover and cook in a preheated moderate oven (180°C/350°F, Gas Mark 4) for 1¼ hours or until the pigeons are tender. Serve hot.

Serves 4

Roasting poultry and game

Roasting is an excellent method for cooking poultry and game birds because it produces succulent flesh and a golden brown skin. Some birds such as chicken, turkey and poussin and game birds should be barded before roasting, that is to say that bacon rashers or bacon fat should be laid over the breast. If barding, remove the fat for the last 10 minutes of cooking so the breast can brown. Alternatively, the bird can be basted frequently during roasting.

Birds such as goose and duck should be pricked all over before roasting so that fat can escape.

Here is a handy roasting chart for poultry and game birds.

	Oven temperature	Minutes per 500 g/1 lb
Capon	190°C/375°F, Gas 5	20 + 20 over
Chicken	190°C/375°F, Gas 5	20 + 20 over
Duck	190°C/375°F, Gas 5	20
Goose	200°C/400°F, Gas 6 OR	15 + 15 over
	180°C/350°F, Gas 4	25–30
Grouse	200°C/400°F, Gas 6	30–35
Pheasant	230°C/450°F, Gas 8 for 10 minutes, then reduce to 200°C/400°F, Gas 6	40–50 overall
Pigeon	200°C/400°F, Gas 6	40
Turkey	160°C/325°F, Gas 3	2.25–4.5 kg/5–10 lb: 3–3¾ hours overall
		4.5–5.5 kg/10–12 lb: 3¾–4 hours overall
		5.5–6.5 kg/12–14 lb: 4–4½ hours overall
		6.5–8.5 kg/14–18 lb: 4½–4¾ hours overall
	OR 230°C/450°F, Gas 8	2.25–4.5 kg/5–10 lb: 2¼–2¾ hours overall
		4.5–5.5 kg/10–12 lb: 2¾–3 hours overall
		5.5–6.5 kg/12–14 lb: 3 hours overall
		6.5–8.5 kg/14–18 lb: 3–3½ hours overall

The roast beef of England is probably
better today than ever before. The choice of
meats, and cuts, is more varied and more
generally available than even 10 years ago.
Rather than a joint of meat that was '...roast
on Sunday, cold on Monday, stewed on
Tuesday and soup on Wednesday ...', people
are buying smaller cuts and approaching
each meal individually. Thus more
interesting recipes are called for. Whether
a dish from anywhere else in the world,
or an old favourite, meat is still the heart
of a good meal.

Beef Cooked in Beer

This delicious stew is thickened with breadcrumbs, stirred in just before serving.

METRIC	IMPERIAL
3 tablespoons oil	3 tablespoons oil
1 large onion, thinly sliced	1 large onion, thinly sliced
1 kg braising steak, cut into 2.5 cm cubes	2 lb braising steak, cut into 1 inch cubes
450 ml light ale	¾ pint light ale
2 teaspoons French mustard	2 teaspoons French mustard
2 teaspoons brown sugar	2 teaspoons brown sugar
2 teaspoons malt vinegar	2 teaspoons malt vinegar
1 bay leaf	1 bay leaf
1 teaspoon dried thyme	1 teaspoon dried thyme
salt and pepper	salt and pepper
50 g fresh breadcrumbs	2 oz fresh breadcrumbs

Heat the oil in a flameproof casserole. Add the onion and fry until softened. Add the beef cubes, in batches if necessary, and fry until browned on all sides. Remove the cubes from the pot as they are browned.

Return all the beef cubes to the pan and stir in the ale, mustard, sugar, vinegar, herbs and salt and pepper to taste. Bring to the boil, then cover and transfer to a preheated moderate oven (180°C/350°F, Gas Mark 4). Cook for 2 hours or until the beef is tender.

Discard the bay leaf, Stir in the breadcrumbs. Taste and adjust the seasoning and serve hot.

Serves 6

Roasting meat

There are two basic methods of oven roasting. In one, the oven is preheated to hot (220–230°C/ 425–450°F, Gas Mark 7–8) and the meat is 'seared' for 15 to 20 minutes. This means that the surface of the meat is sealed so that the juices cannot escape. Then the oven temperature may be reduced to moderate or moderately hot (180–190°C/350–375°F, Gas Mark 4–5) and the cooking is continued according to the specified times. This method is suitable for prime quality, tender joints.

The second method uses the moderate heat right from the start of cooking. This slower roasting prevents the meat shrinking as much as with the other, 'searing' method, and retains more of the meat's vitamins.

The following chart gives roasting times for the different meats, using both methods.

| Meat | Quick roasting method | | Slow roasting method | |
	Oven temperature	Minutes per 500 g/1 lb	Oven temperature	Minutes per 500 g/1 lb
Beef				
(on the bone)	220°C/425°F, Gas 7 *then* 190°C/375°F, Gas 5	rare: 15 + 15 over medium: 20 + 20 over well done: 25 + 25 over	180°C/350°F, Gas 4	rare: 25 + 25 over medium: 30 + 30 over well done: 35 + 35 over
(boned and rolled)		rare: 20 + 20 over medium: 25 + 25 over well done: 30 + 30 over		rare: 30 + 30 over medium: 35 + 35 over well done: 40 + 40 over
(fillet)		rare: 10 well done: 15		—
Lamb				
(on the bone)	220°C/425°F, Gas 7 *then*	20 + 20 over	180°C/350°F, Gas 4	30 + 30 over
(boned and rolled)	180°C/350°F, Gas 4	25 + 25 over		35 + 35 over
Pork				
(on the bone)	220°C/425°F, Gas 7 *then*	25 + 25 over	190°C/375°F, Gas 5	35 + 35 over
(boned and rolled)	190°C/375°F, Gas 5	—		40 + 40 over
(stuffed fillet)		25 + 25 over		—
Veal				
(on the bone)	220°C/425°F, Gas 7 *then*	25 + 25 over	180°C/350°F, Gas 4	35 + 35 over
(boned and rolled)	180°C/350°F, Gas 4	30 + 30 over		40 + 40 over

Meat

Beef Pot Roast

METRIC	IMPERIAL
1 × 1.25 kg boned lean brisket of beef, rolled	1 × 2½ lb boned lean brisket of beef, rolled
150 ml red wine	¼ pint red wine
25 g dripping	1 oz dripping
8 button onions	8 button onions
4 carrots, thickly sliced	4 carrots, thickly sliced
4 celery sticks, thickly sliced	4 celery sticks, thickly sliced
10 cloves	10 cloves
2 bay leaves	2 bay leaves
salt and pepper	salt and pepper
150 ml beef stock	¼ pint beef stock
1 tablespoon cornflour	1 tablespoon cornflour
1 tablespoon water	1 tablespoon water

Place the beef in a deep dish and pour over the wine. Cover and leave to marinate for 3 to 4 hours in a cool place, turning occasionally.

Remove the meat, reserving the wine, and pat dry with paper towels. Melt the dripping in a flameproof casserole. Add the beef and brown on all sides.

Arrange the vegetables, cloves and bay leaves around the beef and season well with salt and pepper. Pour in the stock and reserved wine. Cover and transfer to a preheated moderate oven (160°C/325°F, Gas Mark 3). Cook for 3 to 3½ hours or until the beef is tender.

Place the beef on a warmed serving dish. Surround with the drained vegetables. Keep hot. Strain the cooking liquid into a saucepan and skim off any fat. Blend the cornflour with the cold water and add to the pan. Bring to the boil, stirring, and simmer until thickened. Taste and adjust the seasoning, then serve with the meat.

Serves 4 to 6

Boiled Beef with Vegetables

METRIC	IMPERIAL
2 tablespoons oil	2 tablespoons oil
2 onions, sliced	2 onions, sliced
10 small carrots, 2 sliced	10 small carrots, 2 sliced
1 turnip, sliced	1 turnip, sliced
1 leek, sliced	1 leek, sliced
1 × 1.75 kg rolled silverside of beef	1 × 3½ lb rolled silverside of beef
1 bouquet garni	1 bouquet garni
600 ml beef stock	1 pint beef stock
salt and pepper	salt and pepper
8 medium potatoes	8 medium potatoes
1 small cabbage, cut into 8 wedges	1 small cabbage, cut into 8 wedges

Heat the oil in a large flameproof casserole. Add the onions, sliced carrots, turnip and leek and fry until softened. Push to one side and place the beef in the pot. Brown on all sides.

Add the bouquet garni, stock and salt and pepper to taste. Bring to the boil, then cover and cook for 1¼ hours.

Add the potatoes and whole carrots and baste with the liquid in the casserole. Cover and cook for a further 40 minutes.

Add the cabbage and cook for 15 minutes longer or until the beef is cooked through and tender.

Place the beef on a warmed serving platter and surround with the vegetables. Serve hot.

If liked, the cooking liquid may be thickened with cornflour and served as gravy.

Serves 4 to 6

Beef Hotpot

METRIC	IMPERIAL
50 g flour	2 oz flour
salt and pepper	salt and pepper
1 kg braising steak, cut into 2.5 cm cubes	2 lb braising steak, cut into 1 inch cubes
50 g beef dripping	2 oz beef dripping
2 large onions, sliced	2 large onions, sliced
beef stock	beef stock
1 turnip, diced	1 turnip, diced
4 celery sticks, cut into 5 cm pieces	4 celery sticks, cut into 2 inch pieces
12 small carrots, quartered	12 small carrots, quartered
12 small new potatoes	12 small new potatoes
2 tablespoons chopped parsley	2 tablespoons chopped parsley

Season the flour with salt and pepper and use to coat the beef cubes. Melt the dripping in a large flameproof casserole. Add half the onions and fry until golden brown. Remove with a slotted spoon.

Add the beef cubes to the pot, in batches, and fry until browned on all sides. Remove the cubes from the pot as they are browned.

Return all the beef cubes and the browned onions to the casserole. Add enough stock to cover, then add the remaining onions, the turnip, celery and half the carrots. Bring to the boil.

Cover the casserole and transfer to a preheated moderate oven (160°C/325°F, Gas Mark 3). Cook for 1½ hours.

Stir in the remaining carrots and the potatoes. Add another 200 ml/⅓ pint beef stock and the parsley. Cover again and cook for a further 30 minutes or until the beef cubes and all the vegetables are tender.

Taste and adjust the seasoning before serving.

Serves 6

Steak and Kidney Pie

If liked, 100 g/4 oz sliced mushrooms may be spread over the cooked filling in the dish before covering with the pastry.

METRIC	IMPERIAL
1 kg chuck steak, cut into 4 cm cubes	2 lb chuck steak, cut into 1½ inch cubes
225 g ox kidney, cut into 2.5 cm cubes	8 oz ox kidney, cut into 1 inch cubes
2–3 tablespoons flour	2–3 tablespoons flour
50 g lard or beef dripping	2 oz lard or beef dripping
1 tablespoon chopped onion	1 tablespoon chopped onion
stock or water to cover	stock or water to cover
salt and pepper	salt and pepper
225 g quantity Rough Puff Pastry*	8 oz quantity Rough Puff Pastry*
beaten egg to glaze	beaten egg to glaze

Coat the steak and kidney with the flour. Melt the lard or dripping in a deep frying pan. Add the steak, kidney and onion and fry until browned on all sides. Cover with stock or water and season to taste with salt and pepper.

Bring to the boil, then cover and simmer for 1½ to 2 hours or until the meat is tender. Leave to cool, then skim off any fat from the surface.

Pack the cold filling around a pie funnel in a 1.2 litre/2 pint pie dish. Roll out the dough on a floured surface to about 5 mm/¼ inch thick. Cut out a strip of dough the same width as the rim of the dish, dampen the rim and press on the dough strip. Dampen the dough strip, then place the remaining dough on top. Press the edges together to seal.

Knock up the edges, and flute if liked. Brush the top with beaten egg and decorate with the dough trimmings.

Bake in a preheated hot oven (220°C/425°F, Gas Mark 7) for 20 minutes or until the pastry is well risen and turning brown. Reduce the temperature to moderately hot (200°C/400°F, Gas Mark 6) and bake for a further 30 minutes. If the pastry is becoming too brown, cover with foil for the remaining cooking time. Serve hot.

Serves 6

VARIATION

Steak and kidney pudding: Line a greased 1.2 litre/2 pint pudding basin with about two-thirds of a 225 g/8 oz quantity Suet Crust Pastry*. Coat the steak and kidney cubes with flour as above and put them into the pastry-lined basin. Season well with salt and pepper, then pour in enough stock or water to come one-quarter of the way up the filling. Dampen the dough edges and cover with the remaining dough rolled into a lid. Cover and steam for 3½ to 4 hours. Serve hot.

Fats for frying

When frying food such as steaks, chops, gammon steaks, or vegetables such as potatoes and onions, it is a good idea to use a mixture of butter and oil. The butter gives a good flavour and the oil can be heated to a higher temperature than butter which tends to burn.

An alternative is to use **clarified butter**, or *ghee* as it is called in India. To clarify butter, melt it until it is foaming, then skim off all the foam. Leave to cool and settle, then pour off the clear yellow liquid into a small bowl or cup. When this liquid has set, remove any liquid or sediment left. Store the clarified butter, tightly covered, in the refrigerator.

Beef Olives with Horseradish

METRIC	IMPERIAL
12 thin slices topside of beef, trimmed of fat	12 thin slices topside of beef, trimmed of fat
40 g beef dripping or lard	1½ oz beef dripping or lard
1 large onion, chopped	1 large onion, chopped
600 ml hot beef stock	1 pint hot beef stock
1½ tablespoons flour	1½ tablespoons flour
3 tablespoons water	3 tablespoons water
Stuffing:	*Stuffing:*
100 g fresh breadcrumbs	4 oz fresh breadcrumbs
50 g shredded suet	2 oz shredded suet
1½ tablespoons chopped parsley	1½ tablespoons chopped parsley
3 tablespoons creamed horseradish	3 tablespoons creamed horseradish
1 egg, beaten	1 egg, beaten
salt and pepper	salt and pepper

Mix together the stuffing ingredients, with salt and pepper to taste. Divide between the beef slices, spreading it out evenly. Roll up the slices and secure with string or wooden cocktail sticks.

Melt the dripping or lard in a frying pan. Add the beef rolls, in batches if necessary, and brown on all sides. When browned, transfer to a casserole.

Scatter the onion over the beef rolls and pour over the stock. Cover the casserole and cook in a preheated moderate oven (160°C/325°F, Gas Mark 3) for 1½ to 2 hours or until the beef is tender.

Transfer the beef rolls to a warmed serving dish. Remove the string or cocktail sticks and keep hot. Pour the cooking liquid into a saucepan. Blend the flour with the cold water and add to the pan. Bring to the boil, stirring, and simmer until thickened. Taste and adjust the seasoning, then serve this gravy with the beef olives.

Serves 6

Beef, Bean and Corn Stew

METRIC	IMPERIAL
2 tablespoons oil	2 tablespoons oil
2 onions, chopped	2 onions, chopped
1 large red pepper, cored, seeded and diced	1 large red pepper, cored, seeded and diced
750 g chuck steak, cubed	1½ lb chuck steak, cubed
1.2 litres beef stock	2 pints beef stock
2 teaspoons paprika	2 teaspoons paprika
100 g dried butter beans, soaked overnight and drained	4 oz dried butter beans, soaked overnight and drained
3 unsmoked back bacon rashers, rinded and diced	3 unsmoked back bacon rashers, rinded and diced
225 g garlic sausage, sliced (optional)	8 oz garlic sausage, sliced (optional)
salt and pepper	salt and pepper
1 × 225 g can sweetcorn kernels, drained	1 × 8 oz can sweetcorn kernels, drained

Heat the oil in a large saucepan. Add the onions, red pepper and steak cubes and fry until the onions are softened. Mix the stock with the paprika and add to the pan with the beans, bacon, sausage and salt and pepper to taste. Bring to the boil, cover and simmer for 2 hours.

Stir in the sweetcorn and simmer for a further 30 minutes or until the beef is tender. Taste and adjust the seasoning before serving.

Serves 6

Beef Risotto

METRIC	IMPERIAL
2 tablespoons oil	2 tablespoons oil
2 onions, thinly sliced	2 onions, thinly sliced
1 garlic clove, crushed	1 garlic clove, crushed
500 g minced beef	1 lb minced beef
1 × 400 g can tomatoes	1 × 14 oz can tomatoes
4 carrots, chopped	4 carrots, chopped
1 tablespoon tomato purée	1 tablespoon tomato purée
1 bay leaf	1 bay leaf
salt and pepper	salt and pepper
225 g long-grain rice	8 oz long-grain rice
600 ml water	1 pint water

Heat the oil in a large saucepan. Add the onions and garlic and fry until softened. Add the beef and fry until browned and crumbly.

Stir in the tomatoes with their liquid, the carrots, tomato purée, bay leaf and salt and pepper to taste.

Cover and cook gently for 45 minutes, stirring from time to time.

Meanwhile, cook the rice in the salted water for 15 minutes or until the rice is tender and the water has been absorbed.

Add the rice to the beef mixture and combine thoroughly. Taste and adjust the seasoning, and discard the bay leaf. Serve hot.

Serves 4

Hungarian Goulash

If freezing this stew, add the soured cream after thawing and reheating.

METRIC	IMPERIAL
4 tablespoons oil	4 tablespoons oil
1 kg lean stewing steak, cut into 2.5 cm cubes	2 lb lean stewing steak, cut into 1 inch cubes
2 onions, sliced	2 onions, sliced
1 garlic clove, crushed	1 garlic clove, crushed
1 tablespoon flour	1 tablespoon flour
2 tablespoons paprika	2 tablespoons paprika
½ teaspoon dried oregano	½ teaspoon dried oregano
½ teaspoon caraway seeds, crushed	½ teaspoon caraway seeds, crushed
2 tablespoons tomato purée	2 tablespoons tomato purée
salt and pepper	salt and pepper
600 ml beef stock	1 pint beef stock
500 g potatoes, sliced	1 lb potatoes, sliced
150 ml soured cream	¼ pint soured cream

Heat the oil in a flameproof casserole. Add the beef cubes, in batches, and brown on all sides. Remove the cubes from the pot as they are browned.

Add the onions and garlic to the casserole and fry until softened. Stir in the flour and paprika and cook, stirring, for 2 minutes. Add the oregano, caraway seeds, tomato purée and salt and pepper to taste, then gradually stir in the stock. Bring to the boil, stirring.

Return the beef cubes to the casserole. Cover and transfer to a preheated moderate oven (160°C/325°F, Gas Mark 3). Cook for 1 hour.

Stir in the potato slices. Cover again and cook for a further 1 hour or until the beef cubes and potatoes are tender.

Stir in the soured cream and cook for a final 5 minutes. Taste and adjust the seasoning.

Serves 4 to 6

Removing fat from sauces
One way of removing excess fat from a casserole, soup, etc. is to add a few ice cubes! The fat sets around the ice cubes and can then be removed with them.

Swedish Meatballs

These tangy meatballs are baked in tomato sauce and topped with yogurt.

METRIC	IMPERIAL
500 g minced beef	1 lb minced beef
1 large onion, grated	1 large onion, grated
1 garlic clove, crushed	1 garlic clove, crushed
175 g fresh breadcrumbs	6 oz fresh breadcrumbs
2 teaspoons chopped parsley	2 teaspoons chopped parsley
1 teaspoon dried thyme	1 teaspoon dried thyme
2 teaspoons soy sauce	2 teaspoons soy sauce
salt and pepper	salt and pepper
1 egg	1 egg
3 tablespoons water	3 tablespoons water
4 tablespoons oil	4 tablespoons oil
double quantity Tomato Sauce*	double quantity Tomato Sauce*
150 ml plain yogurt	¼ pint plain yogurt

Mix together the beef, onion, garlic, breadcrumbs, herbs, soy sauce and salt and pepper to taste. Beat the egg with the water and add to the mixture. Combine thoroughly using your fingers. Shape into 20 balls.

Heat the oil in a large frying pan. Add the meatballs, in batches, and fry until browned on all sides. Drain on paper towels and place in a baking dish.

Pour the tomato sauce over the meatballs. Bake in a preheated moderate oven (180°C/350°F, Gas Mark 4) for 20 minutes. Spoon over the yogurt and bake for a further 10 minutes. Serve hot, in the dish.

Serves 4

Barbecues

Having a barbecue is one of the easiest ways to entertain your friends and one of the most enjoyable.

The fuel used is charcoal, and because of the heat of the fire once started and ready for cooking, you should use long-handled tools to handle the food. Be sparing with the charcoal; you don't need more than 25 or 30 briquettes under normal circumstances. After lighting the charcoal, allow 30 to 45 minutes before cooking. By this time the charcoal should have burned down and be completely covered with grey ash. (If any briquettes are still showing black spots, they are more likely to flare and smoke when the fat from the food drips on them.)

Burning something aromatic in the coals gives more flavour to the food being cooked. Try sprigs of thyme, rosemary or bay.

Grilled Marinated Steak

Blade steaks are marinated in a tasty mixture of orange, cider and vegetables, making the steaks tender enough to grill.

METRIC	IMPERIAL
500 g beef blade steak, cut into 4 slices	1 lb beef blade steak, cut into 4 slices
225 g button mushrooms	8 oz button mushrooms
Marinade:	*Marinade:*
juice of ½ orange	juice of ½ orange
3 tablespoons lemon juice	3 tablespoons lemon juice
2 tablespoons oil	2 tablespoons oil
300 ml dry cider	½ pint dry cider
1 carrot, sliced	1 carrot, sliced
1 small onion, sliced	1 small onion, sliced
1 garlic clove, chopped	1 garlic clove, chopped
1 bay leaf	1 bay leaf
2 parsley sprigs	2 parsley sprigs
small pinch of grated nutmeg	small pinch of grated nutmeg
2 cloves	2 cloves
salt and pepper	salt and pepper

Place all the marinade ingredients, with salt and pepper to taste, in a saucepan. Bring to the boil and simmer for 5 minutes. Remove from the heat and leave to cool completely.

Put the steaks in a shallow dish and pour over the marinade. Cover and leave to marinate for 12 to 24 hours in a cool place.

Drain the meat, reserving the marinade. Grill the steaks for 1 to 2 minutes on each side or until cooked to your liking.

Meanwhile, strain the marinade into a saucepan. Add the mushrooms and poach for about 4 minutes or until just tender.

Place the steaks on a warmed serving dish. Drain the mushrooms and arrange around the steaks. Serve hot.

Serves 4

Beef and Prune Ragoût

METRIC	IMPERIAL
18 prunes	18 prunes
600 ml boiling beef stock	1 pint boiling beef stock
25 g flour	1 oz flour
salt and pepper	salt and pepper
750 g chuck steak, cut into small cubes	1½ lb chuck steak, cut into small cubes
50 g butter or dripping	2 oz butter or dripping

Meat

1 tablespoon tomato purée	1 tablespoon tomato purée
2 bay leaves	2 bay leaves
4 tomatoes, skinned	4 tomatoes, skinned

Place the prunes in a bowl and pour over the stock. Leave to soak for 12 hours (unless the prunes are tenderized in which case they need only 1 hours' soaking).

Season the flour with salt and pepper and use to coat the steak cubes. Melt the butter or dripping in a heavy-based saucepan. Add the steak cubes, in batches, and brown on all sides. Remove the cubes from the pan as they are browned. Strain the stock from the prunes and add to the pan, together with the browned beef cubes. Bring to the boil, stirring well. Stir in the tomato purée.

Finely chop six of the prunes and add to the pan, with the bay leaves. Cover and simmer for 1¾ hours.

Stir in the remaining prunes and simmer for a further 15 minutes.

Add the tomatoes and simmer for 15 minutes longer or until the steak cubes are tender. Discard the bay leaves, and taste and adjust the seasoning before serving.

Serves 4 to 5

Braised Steak

METRIC	IMPERIAL
3 tablespoons oil	3 tablespoons oil
750 g braising steak, cut into 4 pieces	1½ lb braising steak, cut into 4 pieces
1 onion, chopped	1 onion, chopped
2 carrots, sliced	2 carrots, sliced
1 swede, sliced	1 swede, sliced
450 ml beef stock	¾ pint beef stock
2 tablespoons Worcestershire sauce	2 tablespoons Worcestershire sauce
1½ teaspoons dry mustard	1½ teaspoons dry mustard
1 teaspoon dried mixed herbs	1 teaspoon dried mixed herbs
salt and pepper	salt and pepper

Heat the oil in a large frying pan. Add the steak pieces, two at a time, and brown on both sides. Remove from the pan.

Add the vegetables to the pan and fry until lightly browned. Tip the vegetables into a shallow casserole and spread out evenly. Place the steak pieces on top.

Pour the stock into the frying pan and add the remaining ingredients, with salt and pepper to taste. Bring to the boil, stirring. Pour over the steak.

Cover and cook in a preheated moderate oven (180°C/350°F, Gas Mark 4) for 1½ hours or until the beef is tender. Taste and adjust the seasoning.

Serves 4

Steak Braised with Mushrooms

METRIC	IMPERIAL
3 tablespoons oil	3 tablespoons oil
750 g braising steak, cut into 5 cm cubes	1½ lb braising steak, cut into 2 inch cubes
4 small onions, quartered	4 small onions, quartered
225 g mushrooms, sliced	8 oz mushrooms, sliced
1 teaspoon dry mustard	1 teaspoon dry mustard
1 tablespoon chopped parsley	1 tablespoon chopped parsley
2 tablespoons tomato purée	2 tablespoons tomato purée
300 ml beef stock	½ pint beef stock
salt and pepper	salt and pepper
1 tablespoon cornflour	1 tablespoon cornflour
1 tablespoon water ·	1 tablespoon water

Heat the oil in a flameproof casserole. Add the beef cubes, in batches, and brown on all sides. Remove the cubes from the pot as they are browned.

Add the onions to the casserole and fry until just softened. Stir in the mushrooms and cook for a further 2 minutes. Add the mustard, parsley, tomato purée, stock and salt and pepper to taste and mix well.

Return the beef cubes to the casserole and bring to the boil. Cover the casserole and transfer to a preheated moderate oven (180°C/350°F, Gas Mark 4). Cook for 2 hours or until the beef is tender.

Blend the cornflour with the cold water. Place the casserole over heat on top of the stove and stir in the cornflour. Simmer, stirring, until thickened. Taste and adjust the seasoning before serving.

Serves 4

Making gravy

The basis of a good **gravy** is the sediment and juices left from a roast joint. To make gravy, remove all but about 1 tablespoon of fat from the roasting tin, either by pouring off the fat, skimming with a spoon or blotting with paper towels. Add a small quantity of flour – just enough to absorb the fat that remains – and cook on top of the stove until lightly browned, stirring well to mix in all the sediment in the tin. Gradually stir in 300 to 450 ml/½ to ¾ pint stock or water used to cook vegetables and bring to the boil, stirring. Simmer until thickened. Season to taste with salt and pepper. If the colour of the gravy is rather pallid, add a little gravy browning, and be sure to stir in any juices accumulated during the carving of the meat.

Piquant Veal Stew

METRIC	IMPERIAL
1 × 225 g can tomatoes, drained	1 × 8 oz can tomatoes, drained
1 tablespoon brown sugar	1 tablespoon brown sugar
½ teaspoon dried basil	½ teaspoon dried basil
½ teaspoon dried marjoram	½ teaspoon dried marjoram
1 teaspoon grated orange rind	1 teaspoon grated orange rind
salt and pepper	salt and pepper
2 tablespoons oil	2 tablespoons oil
750 g shin of veal, cut into 7.5 cm pieces	1½ lb shin of veal, cut into 3 inch pieces
tomato purée	tomato purée
150 ml veal or chicken stock	¼ pint veal or chicken stock
25 g fresh breadcrumbs	1 oz fresh breadcrumbs
1 garlic clove, finely chopped	1 garlic clove, finely chopped
2 teaspoons grated lemon rind	2 teaspoons grated lemon rind
1 tablespoon chopped parsley	1 tablespoon chopped parsley

Place the tomatoes, sugar, herbs, orange rind and salt and pepper to taste in a saucepan. Bring to the boil, breaking up the tomatoes with a spoon, and simmer until reduced to a thick purée.

Meanwhile, heat the oil in a flameproof casserole. Add the veal pieces and brown on all sides. Pour off all oil from the pot, then add the tomato purée and stock. Bring to the boil, stirring well, and simmer for 15 minutes.

Cover the casserole and transfer to a preheated moderate oven (160°C/325°F, Gas Mark 3). Cook for 1 hour.

Mix together the breadcrumbs, garlic, lemon rind and parsley. Sprinkle over the top of the veal mixture and cook, uncovered, for a further 15 minutes. Serve hot, in the casserole.

Serves 4

Roast Veal with Cranberry Sauce

METRIC	IMPERIAL
1 × 1.5 kg boned shoulder of veal, rolled	1 × 3 lb boned shoulder of veal, rolled
salt and pepper	salt and pepper
25 g butter	1 oz butter
1 onion, chopped	1 onion, chopped
6 heaped tablespoons Cranberry Sauce*	6 heaped tablespoons Cranberry Sauce*
6 tablespoons dry cider	6 tablespoons dry cider
300 ml veal or chicken stock	½ pint veal or chicken stock
1 tablespoon cornflour	1 tablespoon cornflour
1 tablespoon water	1 tablespoon water

Season the veal with salt and pepper and place it in a deep flameproof casserole. Melt the butter in a frying pan. Add the onion and fry until softened. Stir in half the cranberry sauce and all of the cider and bring to the boil. Pour over the veal.

Roast in a preheated hot oven (220°C/425°F, Gas Mark 7) for 30 minutes per 500 g/1 lb plus 30 minutes over. Baste every 15 minutes with the juices in the casserole during the first 1½ hours, then spoon the remaining cranberry sauce over the veal, cover the casserole and complete the cooking.

Transfer the veal to a warmed serving platter and keep hot. Skim any fat from the cooking liquid in the casserole, then stir in the stock. Place the casserole on top of the stove and bring to the boil. Blend the cornflour with the cold water and add to the casserole. Simmer, stirring, until thickened. Taste and adjust the seasoning, then serve with the veal.

Serves 6 to 8

Casseroled Veal

METRIC	IMPERIAL
1 tablespoon oil	1 tablespoon oil
500 g lean pie veal, cubed	1 lb lean pie veal, cubed
1 small onion, chopped	1 small onion, chopped
100 g mushrooms, sliced	4 oz mushrooms, sliced
1 × 400 g can tomatoes	1 × 14 oz can tomatoes
300 ml chicken stock	½ pint chicken stock
good pinch of dried mixed herbs	good pinch of dried mixed herbs
2 tablespoons tomato purée	2 tablespoons tomato purée
salt and pepper	salt and pepper
50 g dried milk powder	2 oz dried milk powder
2 tablespoons cornflour	2 tablespoons cornflour
2 tablespoons water	2 tablespoons water
50 g frozen peas	2 oz frozen peas

Heat the oil in a flameproof casserole. Add the veal, onion and mushrooms and fry until the veal cubes are lightly browned on all sides. Stir in the tomatoes with their juice, stock, herbs, tomato purée and salt and pepper to taste. Bring to the boil.

Cover the casserole and transfer to a moderate oven (180°C/350°F, Gas Mark 4). Cook for 1¼ hours.

Blend the milk powder and cornflour with the cold water. Add to the casserole with the peas and stir well. Cook for a further 15 minutes or until the veal is tender and the liquid thickened. Adjust the seasoning.

Serves 4

Meat

Roasts: 'resting' and carving

Roasted joints should be allowed to 'rest' for at least 10 minutes after they come out of the oven, before carving. In this time the meat fibres relax and 'set', making it easier to carve. Cover the joint lightly so that it does not cool too quickly.

Most meat is carved across the grain so that the fibres are short and easier to digest. Lamb may be carved either across or with the grain.

Veal Parcels with Sherry Sauce

METRIC	IMPERIAL
4 streaky bacon rashers, rinded and cut into narrow strips	4 streaky bacon rashers, rinded and cut into narrow strips
100 g mushrooms, sliced	4 oz mushrooms, sliced
1 small onion, grated	1 small onion, grated
50 g butter	2 oz butter
75 g fresh breadcrumbs	3 oz fresh breadcrumbs
1 tablespoon chopped parsley	1 tablespoon chopped parsley
1 egg, beaten	1 egg, beaten
salt and pepper	salt and pepper
4 veal chops	4 veal chops
Sauce:	*Sauce:*
300 ml plain yogurt	½ pint plain yogurt
2 tablespoons sherry	2 tablespoons sherry
2 teaspoons chopped parsley	2 teaspoons chopped parsley
2 teaspoons capers	2 teaspoons capers
1 teaspoon made mustard	1 teaspoon made mustard
salt and pepper	salt and pepper

Mix together the bacon, mushrooms, onion, butter, breadcrumbs, parsley, egg and salt and pepper to taste. Cut out four squares of foil and brush with a little oil. Place a veal chop on each square of foil and top with the bacon mixture. Wrap the foil around the chops and stuffing to make neat parcels.

Place on a baking sheet and cook in a preheated hot oven (220°C/425°F, Gas Mark 7) for 40 to 45 minutes or until the chops are cooked through and tender.

About 10 minutes before the chops are ready, make the sauce. Place the yogurt, sherry and parsley in a heatproof bowl over a pan of hot water. Heat gently, then stir in the capers, mustard and salt and pepper to taste.

Serve the veal in the parcels, with the sherry sauce separately.

Serves 4

Veal Fricassée

The sauce for this dish is enriched with egg yolks and cream. Garnish with toast triangles.

METRIC	IMPERIAL
750 g stewing veal, cut into 2.5 cm cubes	1½ lb stewing veal, cut into 1 inch cubes
2 onions, chopped	2 onions, chopped
600 ml white stock	1 pint white stock
1 bouquet garni	1 bouquet garni
salt and pepper	salt and pepper
50 g butter	2 oz butter
50 g flour	2 oz flour
2 egg yolks	2 egg yolks
2 tablespoons lemon juice	2 tablespoons lemon juice
150 ml double cream	¼ pint double cream

Place the veal and onions in a saucepan and pour over almost all the stock. Bring to the boil, skimming off any scum that rises to the surface. Add the bouquet garni and salt and pepper to taste, then cover and simmer for 1½ hours or until the veal is tender.

Stir in the butter until melted. Blend the flour with the remaining cold stock and add to the pan. Simmer, stirring, until thickened. Discard the bouquet garni.

Lightly beat the egg yolks with the lemon juice and cream. Remove the pan from the heat and whisk in the egg yolk mixture. Return to the heat and cook very gently, stirring, until the sauce is thick and smooth. Do not boil. Taste and adjust the seasoning. Serve hot.

Serves 5 to 6

Barding and larding

When roasting meat that has little fat of its own – such as fillet of beef, veal, venison or the breast of poultry or a game bird – it is a good idea to provide some additional fat to prevent the meat drying out during cooking. This may be done in two ways – barding or larding. Barding means covering the meat or poultry breast with slices of fat such as streaky bacon or pork fat. This fat is usually tied on with string, and may be removed before cooking has finished to allow the meat to brown. Larding is done by inserting small strips of bacon fat or belly pork into the meat using a larding needle. The strips of fat, called lardons, are 'sewn' into the meat across the grain so that both ends of the lardon are left hanging over the surface of the meat.

Colonial Goose

Despite its name, this is really a stuffed leg of lamb!

METRIC	IMPERIAL
50 g butter	2 oz butter
1 onion, chopped	1 onion, chopped
100 g prunes, soaked overnight, drained, stoned and chopped	4 oz prunes, soaked overnight, drained, stoned and chopped
1 dessert apple, peeled, cored and chopped	1 dessert apple, peeled, cored and chopped
75 g fresh breadcrumbs	3 oz fresh breadcrumbs
½ teaspoon dried rosemary	½ teaspoon dried rosemary
1 egg, beaten	1 egg, beaten
salt and pepper	salt and pepper
1 × 2.25 kg leg of lamb, boned	1 × 4½ lb leg of lamb, boned
150 ml dry cider	½ pint dry cider
2 tablespoons flour	2 tablespoons flour
300 ml stock	½ pint stock

Melt half the butter in a frying pan. Add the onion and fry until softened. Remove from the heat and stir in the prunes, apple, breadcrumbs, rosemary, egg and salt and pepper to taste. Cool, then stuff this into the bone cavity in the lamb, and sew loosely into shape with a trussing needle and fine string.

Place the lamb in a polythene bag and add the cider. Leave to marinate for at least 4 hours, turning occasionally, in a cool place.

Drain the lamb, reserving the cider. Weigh the lamb and place in a roasting tin. Melt the remaining butter and brush over the lamb. Roast in a preheated moderate oven (180°C/350°F, Gas Mark 4) for 25 minutes per 500 g/1 lb plus 30 minutes over. Cover with foil when the lamb is browned.

Transfer the lamb to a warmed serving platter. Remove the string and keep hot.

Pour off most of the fat from the juices in the tin, then stir in the flour. Cook on top of the stove, stirring, for 2 minutes. Gradually stir in the stock and reserved cider. Bring to the boil, stirring, and simmer until thickened. Taste and adjust the seasoning.

Serve the gravy with the lamb.

Serves 4 to 6

Making good crackling
Do not rub salt into meat that is to be roasted, because salt draws juices to the surface thus delaying browning. The exception to this is, of course, roast pork where crackling is wanted. To make crisp crackling, score the skin with a sharp knife into strips about 1 cm/½ inch wide (or have the butcher do this for you). Rub it with a little oil and then with salt. After roasting, cut or break the crackling into the strips.

Thawing raw meat
For best results and to economize on fuel, completely thaw frozen meat to be roasted before cooking. This is vital with all poultry and game as they may harbour harmful salmonellae bacteria inside the body cavity which may survive freezing. Unless thawing is complete beforehand, the oven heat may not penetrate all through the bird and so kill any harmful bacteria.

Lamb and Courgette Curry

METRIC	IMPERIAL
50 g butter	2 oz butter
2 onions, chopped	2 onions, chopped
1 garlic clove, crushed	1 garlic clove, crushed
1 small dessert apple, peeled, cored and sliced	1 small dessert apple, peeled, cored and sliced
1–2 teaspoons curry paste	1–2 teaspoons curry paste
1 tablespoon curry powder	1 tablespoon curry powder
1 tablespoon flour	1 tablespoon flour
450 ml beef stock	¾ pint beef stock
1–2 tablespoons desiccated coconut	1–2 tablespoons desiccated coconut
2 tablespoons sultanas	2 tablespoons sultanas
2 tablespoons chutney	2 tablespoons chutney
500 g lean lamb from the leg or shoulder, cubed	1 lb lean lamb from the leg or shoulder, cubed
1 teaspoon sugar	1 teaspoon sugar
1 teaspoon lemon juice	1 teaspoon lemon juice
salt and pepper	salt and pepper
4 courgettes, thinly sliced	4 courgettes, thinly sliced

Melt the butter in a large saucepan. Add the onions and garlic and fry until softened. Add the apple, curry paste and powder and flour and fry, stirring, for 3 to 4 minutes. Gradually stir in the stock and bring to the boil. Simmer, stirring, until thickened.

Stir in the coconut, sultanas and chutney, then add the lamb. Cover and simmer for 1 hour.

Add the sugar, lemon juice and salt and pepper to taste. Cover again and simmer for a further 1 hour.

Stir in the courgettes. Cook, covered, for 30 minutes longer or until the lamb is tender. Taste and adjust the seasoning before serving with rice, chutney, fresh coconut, sliced bananas and other curry accompaniments.

Serves 4 to 6

Spring Lamb Casserole

METRIC	IMPERIAL
25 g butter	1 oz butter
1 tablespoon oil	1 tablespoon oil
1 kg boned shoulder of lamb, trimmed of excess fat and cut into 5 cm cubes	2 lb boned shoulder of lamb, trimmed of excess fat and cut into 2 inch cubes
6 spring onions, sliced	6 spring onions, sliced
600 ml chicken stock, or 450 ml stock and 150 ml dry white wine	1 pint chicken stock, or ¾ pint stock and ¼ pint dry white wine
750 g new potatoes	1½ lb new potatoes
1 teaspoon grated lemon rind	1 teaspoon grated lemon rind
2 tablespoons chopped parsley	2 tablespoons chopped parsley
4 tablespoons chopped fresh mint	4 tablespoons chopped fresh mint
salt and pepper	salt and pepper

Melt the butter with the oil in a flameproof casserole. Add the lamb cubes, in batches, and brown on all sides. Remove the cubes from the pot as they are browned.

Add the spring onions to the casserole and fry until softened. Stir in the stock, then add the potatoes and bring to the boil. Stir in the lemon rind, herbs and salt and pepper to taste.

Return the lamb cubes to the casserole. Cover and transfer to a preheated moderate oven (180°C/350°F, Gas Mark 4). Cook for 1 hour or until the lamb and potatoes are tender.

Taste and adjust the seasoning before serving.

Serves 6

Lamb with Dill Sauce

If fresh dill is not available, dried dill may be used. Use one-third the quantity of fresh.

METRIC	IMPERIAL
1 × 1.25 kg best end of neck of lamb	1 × 2½ lb best end of neck of lamb
1 bay leaf	1 bay leaf
few fresh dill sprigs	few fresh dill sprigs
salt and pepper	salt and pepper
50 g butter	2 oz butter
50 g flour	2 oz flour
2 tablespoons white wine vinegar	2 tablespoons white wine vinegar
1 tablespoon lemon juice	1 tablespoon lemon juice
2 teaspoons sugar	2 teaspoons sugar
1 egg yolk	1 egg yolk
2 tablespoons double cream	2 tablespoons double cream
1 tablespoon chopped fresh dill	1 tablespoon chopped fresh dill

Place the lamb in a large saucepan and add the bay leaf, dill sprigs and salt and pepper to taste. Cover with water (about 1.2 litres/2 pints) and bring to the boil. Skim off any scum that rises to the surface, then cover and simmer for 1¼ to 1½ hours or until the lamb is tender.

Transfer the lamb to a warmed serving platter and keep hot. Strain the cooking liquid and reserve 600 ml/1 pint.

Melt the butter in a saucepan. Stir in the flour and cook for 2 minutes, then gradually stir in the reserved cooking liquid. Bring to the boil, stirring, and simmer until thickened. Remove from the heat and stir in the remaining ingredients, with salt and pepper to taste. Return to the heat and cook very gently, stirring, until hot and glossy. Pour over the lamb and serve.

Serves 4 to 6

Braised Honeyed Breast of Lamb

METRIC	IMPERIAL
2 tablespoons oil	2 tablespoons oil
1 large onion, sliced	1 large onion, sliced
2 celery sticks, sliced	2 celery sticks, sliced
2 potatoes, sliced	2 potatoes, sliced
2 teaspoons flour	2 teaspoons flour
salt and pepper	salt and pepper
1 × 1 kg boned breast of lamb, rolled	1 × 2 lb boned breast of lamb, rolled
grated rind and juice of ½ orange	grated rind and juice of ½ orange
2 tablespoons clear honey	2 tablespoons clear honey
300 ml chicken stock	½ pint chicken stock

Heat the oil in a large frying pan. Add the onion, celery and potatoes, in batches if necessary, and fry until softened. Transfer to a casserole.

Season the flour with salt and pepper and rub all over the lamb. Place the lamb in the frying pan and brown on all sides. Put the lamb on top of the vegetables in the casserole.

Mix together the orange rind and juice, honey and stock and pour over the lamb. Cover and cook in a preheated moderate oven (180°C/350°F, Gas Mark 4) for about 1½ hours or until the lamb is cooked through.

Serves 4

Always under-season any dish to be frozen.

Preparing bacon and bacon rolls

Rind is easily removed from bacon rashers using scissors. If the bacon is to be fried or grilled, snip the fat to prevent it curling. To make bacon rolls, cut a rasher in half crossways, then stretch each half using the blunt side of a knife. Roll up the pieces and secure with wooden cocktail sticks, if necessary, or thread on to skewers. Grill until crisp.

Lancashire Hotpot

METRIC	IMPERIAL
3 tablespoons flour	3 tablespoons flour
salt and pepper	salt and pepper
1 kg middle neck of lamb cutlets, trimmed of excess fat	2 lb middle neck of lamb cutlets, trimmed of excess fat
4 onions, sliced	4 onions, sliced
2 lamb's kidneys, cored and sliced	2 lamb's kidneys, cored and sliced
225 g carrots, diced	8 oz carrots, diced
750 g potatoes, sliced	1½ lb potatoes, sliced
450 ml hot chicken stock	¾ pint hot chicken stock
1 bay leaf	1 bay leaf
½ teaspoon dried marjoram	½ teaspoon dried marjoram
½ teaspoon dried thyme	½ teaspoon dried thyme

Season the flour with salt and pepper and use to coat the lamb cutlets. Make alternate layers of lamb cutlets, onions, kidney slices, carrots and potatoes in a large casserole, seasoning each layer with salt and pepper. Finish with a layer of potatoes. Mix the stock with the herbs and pour into the casserole.

Cover and cook in a preheated moderate oven (180°C/350°F, Gas Mark 4) for 2 hours. Uncover and cook for a further 30 minutes or until the top layer of potatoes is golden brown. Serve hot, in the casserole.

Serves 4

VARIATION
French lamb hotpot: Very thinly slice 500 g/1 lb potatoes and 500 g/1 lb onions. Arrange half over the bottom of a long, shallow baking dish and season well with salt and pepper. Sprinkle over a good pinch of dried sage or rosemary. Place 8 small lean lamb chops on top and cover with the rest of the potatoes and onions. Season well. Add 150 ml/¼ pint stock to the dish. Cover tightly and cook in a preheated moderate oven (180°C/350°F, Gas Mark 4) for about 1¼ hours or until the lamb and vegetables are tender. Serve hot, in the dish.

Serves 4

Lamb with Vegetables

METRIC	IMPERIAL
225 g cooked lamb, cubed	8 oz cooked lamb, cubed
1 large leek, sliced	1 large leek, sliced
½ cauliflower, broken into florets	½ cauliflower, broken into florets
50 g mushrooms, sliced	2 oz mushrooms, sliced
3 carrots, sliced	3 carrots, sliced
1 onion, sliced	1 onion, sliced
salt and pepper	salt and pepper
2 tomatoes, sliced	2 tomatoes, sliced
150 ml stock	¼ pint stock

Arrange the meat and vegetables (except the tomatoes) in layers in a casserole. Season to taste with salt and pepper. Arrange the tomato slices on top and pour in the stock.

Cover and cook in a preheated moderate oven (180°C/350°F, Gas Mark 4) for 45 minutes. Serve hot.

Serves 3 to 4

French Lamb Stew

METRIC	IMPERIAL
1 aubergine, sliced	1 aubergine, sliced
salt and pepper	salt and pepper
4 tablespoons oil	4 tablespoons oil
8 lamb chops	8 lamb chops
2 onions, chopped	2 onions, chopped
1 garlic clove, crushed	1 garlic clove, crushed
1 large green pepper, cored, seeded and chopped	1 large green pepper, cored, seeded and chopped
4 courgettes, thinly sliced	4 courgettes, thinly sliced
2 tablespoons chopped parsley	2 tablespoons chopped parsley

Sprinkle the aubergine slices with salt and leave to drain for 20 minutes. Rinse and pat dry with paper towels.

Heat 2 tablespoons of the oil in a large saucepan. Add the chops, in batches, and brown on all sides. Remove from the pan.

Add the remaining oil to the pan and heat. Add the onions and garlic and fry until softened. Add the green pepper, courgettes and aubergine and season to taste with salt and pepper. Cover and cook gently for 25 minutes.

Stir in the parsley, then mix the chops into the vegetables. Cover again and cook for a further 25 to 30 minutes. Taste and adjust the seasoning.

Serves 4

Bittersweet Lamb

METRIC	IMPERIAL
1 kg lean stewing lamb, chopped	2 lb lean stewing lamb, chopped
2 tablespoons malt vinegar	2 tablespoons malt vinegar
4 tablespoons orange marmalade	4 tablespoons orange marmalade
2 tablespoons tomato ketchup	2 tablespoons tomato ketchup
2 teaspoons dry mustard	2 teaspoons dry mustard
grated rind and juice of 1 orange	grated rind and juice of 1 orange
150 ml stock	¼ pint stock
2 teaspoons cornflour	2 teaspoons cornflour
1 tablespoon water	1 tablespoon water
salt and pepper	salt and pepper

Place the lamb in a saucepan with the vinegar and add water to cover. Bring to the boil, then cover and simmer for 15 minutes. Drain the lamb.

Place the marmalade, ketchup, mustard, orange rind and juice and stock in a clean large saucepan and bring to the boil, stirring well. Add the lamb, then cover and simmer gently for 45 minutes or until the lamb is tender.

Transfer the lamb to a warmed serving dish and keep hot. Blend the cornflour with the cold water and stir into the sauce in the pan. Simmer, stirring, until thickened. Taste and adjust the seasoning, then pour the sauce over the lamb. Serve hot.

Serves 6

Stuffed Breast of Lamb

Breast of lamb can be very fatty, so trim as much fat off as possible.

METRIC	IMPERIAL
100 g dried apricots, soaked overnight, drained and chopped	4 oz dried apricots, soaked overnight, drained and chopped
1 onion, chopped	1 onion, chopped
150 g fresh breadcrumbs	5 oz fresh breadcrumbs
1 tablespoon chopped parsley	1 tablespoon chopped parsley
½ teaspoon dried thyme	½ teaspoon dried thyme
grated rind of 1 lemon	grated rind of 1 lemon
salt and pepper	salt and pepper
1 egg, beaten	1 egg, beaten
2 breasts of lamb, boned	2 breasts of lamb, boned
25 g butter, melted	1 oz butter, melted

Mix together the apricots, onion, breadcrumbs, parsley, thyme, lemon rind and salt and pepper to taste. Bind the stuffing with the egg.

Lay the lamb breasts flat, skin side down and spread over the stuffing. Roll up and secure with string.

Place the lamb in a roasting tin and brush with the melted butter. Roast in a preheated moderately hot oven (190°C/375°F, Gas Mark 5) for about 1½ hours or until the lamb is cooked through. Remove the string before serving.

Serves 6

Lamb Kebabs with Herb Sauce

Marinating the meat in this yogurt-based sauce makes the lamb very succulent. Serve the kebabs with boiled rice or crusty bread.

METRIC	IMPERIAL
500 g lean lamb from the leg, cut into 2.5 cm cubes	1 lb lean lamb from the leg, cut into 1 inch cubes
1 green pepper, cored, seeded and cut into squares	1 green pepper, cored, seeded and cut into squares
12 button mushrooms	12 button mushrooms
12 cocktail onions	12 cocktail onions
4 small tomatoes	4 small tomatoes
25 g butter, melted	1 oz butter, melted
Sauce:	*Sauce:*
300 ml tomato juice	½ pint tomato juice
150 ml plain yogurt	¼ pint plain yogurt
2 teaspoons made mustard	2 teaspoons made mustard
2 teaspoons chopped fresh mint	2 teaspoons chopped fresh mint
2 teaspoons chopped chives	2 teaspoons chopped chives
¼ teaspoon ground cinnamon	¼ teaspoon ground cinnamon
salt and pepper	salt and pepper

Mix together the ingredients for the sauce, with salt and pepper to taste, in a shallow dish. Add the lamb cubes and turn to coat. Cover and leave to marinate for 3 to 4 hours, turning occasionally, in a cool place.

Drain the lamb cubes, reserving the sauce. Thread the lamb on to four skewers, alternating with the green pepper squares, mushrooms and onions. Place a tomato on the end of each skewer.

Brush the vegetables, but not the meat, with the melted butter and grill for about 10 minutes, turning frequently, until the lamb is cooked to your liking.

Meanwhile, gently heat the sauce. Serve the kebabs with the sauce.

Serves 4

> The vegetables used in French Lamb Stew (opposite) may be cooked separately and served as Ratatouille with other meats.

Pork with Sage and Cream

METRIC	IMPERIAL
25 g flour	1 oz flour
½ teaspoon dry mustard	½ teaspoon dry mustard
salt and pepper	salt and pepper
1 kg boneless lean pork, cut into 2.5 cm cubes	2 lb boneless lean pork, cut into 1 inch cubes
4 tablespoons oil	4 tablespoons oil
1 small onion, finely chopped	1 small onion, finely chopped
450 ml chicken stock	¾ pint chicken stock
1 tablespoon grated lemon rind	1 tablespoon grated lemon rind
½ teaspoon dried savory	½ teaspoon dried savory
2 teaspoons dried sage	2 teaspoons dried sage
100 g button mushrooms, sliced	4 oz button mushrooms, sliced
150 ml single cream	¼ pint single cream

Season the flour with the mustard, salt and pepper and use to coat the pork cubes. Heat the oil in a flameproof casserole. Add the onion and fry until softened. Add the pork cubes, in batches, and fry until browned on all sides. Remove the cubes from the pot as they are browned.

Return all the pork cubes to the casserole, then add the stock and bring to the boil. Stir in the lemon rind and herbs. Cover and transfer to a preheated moderate oven (180°C/350°F, Gas Mark 4). Cook for 45 minutes.

Stir in the mushrooms and cook for a further 15 minutes.

Remove the casserole from the oven and stir in the cream. Heat through gently on top of the stove, but do not allow to boil. Taste and adjust the seasoning before serving.

Serves 4 to 6

Stuffed Pork Chops

METRIC	IMPERIAL
4 thick pork chops	4 thick pork chops
3 tablespoons oil	3 tablespoons oil
25 g fresh breadcrumbs	1 oz fresh breadcrumbs
1 small onion, grated	1 small onion, grated
1 teaspoon dried sage	1 teaspoon dried sage
grated rind of ½ lemon	grated rind of ½ lemon
salt and pepper	salt and pepper
½ egg, beaten	½ egg, beaten
300 ml dry cider	½ pint dry cider

Cut a slit in each chop to make a pocket for the stuffing. Heat the oil in a frying pan. Add the chops and brown on both sides. Drain on paper towels.

Mix together the breadcrumbs, onion, sage, lemon rind and salt and pepper to taste and bind with the egg. Divide the stuffing into four portions and place in the pockets in the chops.

Arrange the chops in a baking dish and pour over the cider. Cover and cook in a preheated moderate oven (180°C/350°F, Gas Mark 4) for 1 hour or until the chops are cooked through.

If liked, the cooking liquid may be thickened with 2 teaspoons cornflour (first blended with 2 tablespoons cold water) and served as a sauce with the chops.

Serves 4

Chinese-style Pork Balls

METRIC	IMPERIAL
500 g minced lean pork	1 lb minced lean pork
1 garlic clove, crushed	1 garlic clove, crushed
50 g fresh breadcrumbs	2 oz fresh breadcrumbs
1 egg, beaten	1 egg, beaten
salt and pepper	salt and pepper
flour for coating	flour for coating
25 g lard	1 oz lard
Sauce:	*Sauce:*
2 red or green peppers, cored, seeded and thinly sliced	2 red or green peppers, cored, seeded and thinly sliced
75 g sugar	3 oz sugar
4 tablespoons cider vinegar	4 tablespoons cider vinegar
2 tablespoons soy sauce	2 tablespoons soy sauce
300 ml stock	½ pint stock
4 canned pineapple rings, chopped	4 canned pineapple rings, chopped
4 teaspoons cornflour	4 teaspoons cornflour
2 tablespoons water	2 tablespoons water

Mix together the pork, garlic, breadcrumbs, egg and salt and pepper to taste. Divide the mixture into walnut-size balls and coat with flour.

Melt the lard in a frying pan. Add the pork balls, in batches if necessary, and fry gently for 15 to 20 minutes or until golden brown on all sides and cooked through.

Meanwhile, make the sauce. Blanch the peppers in boiling water for 5 minutes. Drain well. Place the sugar, vinegar, soy sauce and stock in the cleaned saucepan and bring to the boil, stirring to dissolve the sugar. Stir in the peppers and pineapple and simmer for 5 minutes.

Blend the cornflour with the cold water and add to the pan. Simmer, stirring, until thickened. Add salt and pepper to taste.

Drain the pork balls on paper towels and arrange on a warmed serving dish. Pour over the sauce and serve hot, with boiled rice.

Serves 4

Peasant Stew

This variation on pork and beans is an economical and very sustaining stew.

METRIC	IMPERIAL
350 g dried chick peas, soaked overnight	12 oz dried chick peas, soaked overnight
2 tablespoons oil	2 tablespoons oil
2 large onions, sliced	2 large onions, sliced
4 streaky bacon rashers, rinded and chopped	4 streaky bacon rashers, rinded and chopped
1 garlic clove, crushed	1 garlic clove, crushed
500 g belly pork, cubed	1 lb belly pork, cubed
1 × 400 g can tomatoes	1 × 14 oz can tomatoes
2 large carrots, sliced	2 large carrots, sliced
2 potatoes, diced	2 potatoes, diced
2 celery sticks, chopped	2 celery sticks, chopped
1 bay leaf	1 bay leaf
½ teaspoon dried thyme	½ teaspoon dried thyme
salt and pepper	salt and pepper

Drain the chick peas and place them in a saucepan. Cover with fresh cold water. Bring to the boil and boil for 10 minutes, then drain off the water. Cover with fresh cold water again, bring to the boil and simmer for 1½ hours or until tender. Drain, reserving the liquid.

Heat the oil in a frying pan. Add the onions, bacon and garlic and fry until the onions are softened. Add the pork cubes and brown on all sides.

Pour the pork mixture into a casserole and stir in the chick peas, the tomatoes with their juice, the vegetables, herbs and salt and pepper to taste. Add 900 ml/1½ pints of the reserved chick pea cooking liquid.

Cover the casserole and cook in a preheated moderate oven (160°C/325°F, Gas Mark 3) for 2 hours.

Remove the bay leaf, and taste and adjust the seasoning before serving.

Serves 4 to 6

Pork Braised with Cabbage

METRIC	IMPERIAL
2 tablespoons oil	2 tablespoons oil
1 × 1.5 kg shoulder of pork, boned and rolled	1 × 3 lb shoulder of pork, boned and rolled
1 large onion, sliced	1 large onion, sliced
500 g white cabbage, finely shredded	1 lb white cabbage, finely shredded
50 g seeded raisins	2 oz seeded raisins
2 tablespoons brown sugar	2 tablespoons brown sugar
½ teaspoon ground cloves	½ teaspoon ground cloves
150 ml dry cider	¼ pint dry cider
1 teaspoon celery salt	1 teaspoon celery salt
pepper	pepper
2 cooking apples, peeled, cored and sliced	2 cooking apples, peeled, cored and sliced

Heat the oil in a large frying pan. Add the pork and brown on all sides. Remove from the pan.

Add the onion and cabbage to the pan and fry until softened. Stir in the raisins, sugar and cloves.

Turn the cabbage mixture into a large casserole. Make a hollow in the centre and put in the pork. Pour in the cider and sprinkle with the celery salt and pepper to taste. Cover and cook in a preheated moderate oven (160°C/325°F, Gas Mark 3) for 2 hours.

Stir in the apples, re-cover and cook for a further 30 minutes or until the apples and vegetables are tender and the pork is cooked through.

Serves 4 to 6

Apricot-stuffed Pork

Serve with Apple Sauce*, roast potatoes and a green vegetable. Cooked fresh apricots may be used instead of canned.

METRIC	IMPERIAL
100 g fresh wholemeal breadcrumbs	4 oz fresh wholemeal breadcrumbs
50 g butter, melted	2 oz butter, melted
1 × 225 g can apricots, drained (can syrup reserved) and chopped	1 × 8 oz can apricots, drained (can syrup reserved) and chopped
75 g seeded raisins	3 oz seeded raisins
1 tablespoon chopped parsley	1 tablespoon chopped parsley
salt and pepper	salt and pepper
1 × 2.25 kg loin of pork, boned	1 × 4½ lb loin of pork, boned
oil	oil

Mix together the breadcrumbs, butter, apricots, raisins, parsley and salt and pepper to taste. Moisten with a little of the apricot can syrup.

Spread the stuffing over the pork, then roll up and tie into shape with string. Place in a roasting tin and brush with a little oil. Roast in a preheated hot oven (220°C/425°F, Gas Mark 7) for 45 minutes, then reduce the temperature to moderately hot (200°C/400°F, Gas Mark 6). Roast for a further 1¼ hours or until the pork is cooked through.

Serves 6

See page 54 for instructions on how to make and serve good pork crackling.

Herby Pork Chops

METRIC	IMPERIAL
4 pork chops	4 pork chops
salt and pepper	salt and pepper
25 g butter	1 oz butter
40 g fresh breadcrumbs	1½ oz fresh breadcrumbs
½ teaspoon ground mace	½ teaspoon ground mace
½ teaspoon dried thyme	½ teaspoon dried thyme
1 tablespoon chopped parsley	1 tablespoon chopped parsley
4 tablespoons stock	4 tablespoons stock

Season the chops with salt and pepper. Melt the butter in a large frying pan. Add the chops and fry until browned on both sides. Transfer the chops to a large shallow baking dish, arranging them in one layer.

Mix together the breadcrumbs, mace, thyme and parsley and season to taste with salt and pepper. Spread this mixture over the chops and drizzle over the fat from the frying pan and the stock.

Cover and cook in a preheated moderately hot oven (200°C/400°F, Gas Mark 6) for 20 minutes. Uncover and cook for a further 10 to 20 minutes or until the chops are cooked through and the topping is crisp and golden brown. Serve hot.

Serves 4

Barbecued Pork Chops

METRIC	IMPERIAL
2 tablespoons oil	2 tablespoons oil
2 tablespoons mild chilli sauce	2 tablespoons mild chilli sauce
2 tablespoons soy sauce	2 tablespoons soy sauce
1 tablespoon Worcestershire sauce	1 tablespoon Worcestershire sauce
1 tablespoon brown sugar	1 tablespoon brown sugar
1 tablespoon tomato purée	1 tablespoon tomato purée
1 tablespoon wine vinegar	1 tablespoon wine vinegar
1 teaspoon ground ginger	1 teaspoon ground ginger
salt and pepper	salt and pepper
4 large pork spare rib chops	4 large pork spare rib chops

Mix together the oil, chilli sauce, soy sauce, Worcestershire sauce, sugar, tomato purée, vinegar, ginger and salt and pepper to taste in a shallow dish. Add the chops and turn to coat with the mixture. Cover and leave to marinate for at least 2 hours in a cool place.

Remove the pork from the marinade, reserving the liquid, and place on the grill rack. Grill for about 10 minutes on each side or until the pork is cooked through. Brush generously with the leftover marinade from time to time.

Serves 4

Gammon with Pineapple and Sweetcorn Sauce

METRIC	IMPERIAL
4 gammon steaks	4 gammon steaks
50 g butter, melted	2 oz butter, melted
4 canned pineapple rings (can syrup reserved)	4 canned pineapple rings (can syrup reserved)
Sauce:	*Sauce:*
25 g butter	1 oz butter
1 onion, chopped	1 onion, chopped
25 g flour	1 oz flour
300 ml milk	½ pint milk
4 tablespoons canned sweetcorn kernels	4 tablespoons canned sweetcorn kernels
1 tablespoon chopped parsley	1 tablespoon chopped parsley
salt and pepper	salt and pepper

Snip the fat on the gammon steaks to prevent curling during cooking. Place the gammon on the grill rack and brush with melted butter. Grill for about 5 minutes on each side, brushing with butter from time to time.

Meanwhile, make the sauce. Melt the butter in a saucepan. Add the onion and fry until softened. Stir in the flour and cook for 2 minutes, then gradually stir in the milk. Bring to the boil, stirring, and simmer until thickened. Add the sweetcorn, parsley and salt and pepper to taste. Stir in 2 tablespoons of the syrup from the can of pineapple. Leave to heat through.

When the gammon is nearly ready, add the pineapple rings to the grill pan. Brush them with melted butter and cook until lightly browned.

Arrange the gammon and pineapple on a warmed serving dish and serve with the sauce.

Serves 4

Marinating
Meat or poultry, sometimes with vegetables, may be soaked in a flavoured liquid before cooking. This process, called marinating, tenderizes and/or flavours the meat or poultry. The liquid, called a marinade, contains vinegar, wine or lemon juice which tenderize the meat, as well as oil and seasonings.

Meat

Glazed Ham

METRIC	IMPERIAL
1 joint of bacon or ham, about 2 kg	1 joint of bacon or ham, about 4 lb
dry cider, ginger beer, ginger ale or water	dry cider, ginger beer, ginger ale or water
1 onion, halved	1 onion, halved
1 carrot, chopped	1 carrot, chopped
Glaze:	*Glaze:*
3 tablespoons brown sugar	3 tablespoons brown sugar
3 tablespoons fresh breadcrumbs	3 tablespoons fresh breadcrumbs
1 teaspoon mixed spice	1 teaspoon mixed spice
1 tablespoon golden syrup	1 tablespoon golden syrup

Soak the joint overnight in cold water to cover, unless it is sweet-cure in which case it does not require soaking.

The next day, drain the joint and place it in a large saucepan. Cover with cider, ginger beer, ginger ale or water and add the onion and carrot. Bring to the boil, them simmer very gently for two-thirds of the cooking time (see chart).

Drain the joint, reserving a few tablespoons of the cooking liquid. Remove the skin, then score the fat in a diamond pattern. Place the joint in a roasting tin.

To make the glaze, mix together all the ingredients with just enough cooking liquid from the joint to moisten to a spreading consistency. Spread the glaze over the fat on the joint.

Roast in a preheated moderately hot oven (200°C/400°F, Gas Mark 6) for the remainder of the cooking time. Serve hot or cold.

Serves 8

VARIATION
Pineapple glaze: Mix together 3 tablespoons brown sugar, 1 teaspoon made mustard and 3 tablespoons syrup from a can of pineapple rings. Spread over the fat on the joint and roast as above. Ten minutes before the end of the cooking time, arrange the pineapple rings around the joint and roast.

Ham in Redcurrant Sauce

Leftover roast pork would also be delicious served with this sweet and sour sauce.

METRIC	IMPERIAL
40 g butter	1½ oz butter
25 g brown sugar	1 oz brown sugar
3 tablespoons malt vinegar	3 tablespoons malt vinegar
3 tablespoons redcurrant jelly	3 tablespoons redcurrant jelly
1 teaspoon made mustard	1 teaspoon made mustard
pepper	pepper
4 slices of cooked ham, cut 1 cm thick	4 slices of cooked ham, cut ½ inch thick

Melt the butter in a large frying pan. Add the sugar, vinegar, jelly, mustard and pepper to taste and cook, stirring, until smooth. Add the ham slices and turn to coat with the sauce. Cook gently until the ham is piping hot.

Serves 4

Spiced Meatballs

METRIC	IMPERIAL
750 g cooked lean meat, minced	1½ lb cooked lean meat, minced
500 g cooked rice	1 lb cooked rice
2 tablespoons chopped parsley	2 tablespoons chopped parsley
1 teaspoon paprika	1 teaspoon paprika
2 teaspoons Worcestershire sauce	2 teaspoons Worcestershire sauce
2 eggs, beaten	2 eggs, beaten
salt and pepper	salt and pepper
toasted breadcrumbs to coat	toasted breadcrumbs to coat
Sauce:	*Sauce:*
50 g butter	2 oz butter
225 g potatoes, diced	8 oz potatoes, diced
500 g dessert apples, peeled, cored and diced	1 lb dessert apples, peeled, cored and diced
1 large onion, chopped	1 large onion, chopped
2 teaspoons curry powder	2 teaspoons curry powder
300 ml stock	½ pint stock
300 ml milk	½ pint milk
50 g sultanas	2 oz sultanas
50 g salted peanuts	2 oz salted peanuts

Mix together the meat, rice, parsley, paprika, Worcestershire sauce, eggs and salt and pepper to taste. Shape into 5 cm/2 inch balls and coat with toasted breadcrumbs. Arrange on a greased baking sheet.

Bake in a preheated moderate oven (180°C/350°F, Gas Mark 4) for 20 minutes or until golden brown.

Meanwhile, to make the sauce, melt the butter in a saucepan. Add the potatoes, apples and onion and fry until the onion begins to colour. Stir in the curry powder and fry for a further 2 minutes. Stir in the stock, milk, sultanas, peanuts and salt and pepper to taste and bring to the boil. Simmer gently until the vegetables and apples are tender and the sauce has reduced and thickened.

Serve the meatballs with the sauce.

Serves 6

Freezing casseroles

When making a stew or casserole, double the quantities and freeze half. Pour the stew or casserole into a rigid container, or into the foil-lined casserole if it will withstand the cold of the freezer. When frozen, the stew or casserole can easily be removed from the casserole pot and stored in a polythene bag or overwrapped in more foil. Frozen stews or casseroles may be reheated from frozen, over gentle heat, or left to thaw overnight in the refrigerator before reheating. They will keep for 1 to 3 months.

Crispy Meat Loaf

METRIC	IMPERIAL
225 g minced cooked ham	8 oz minced cooked ham
225 g minced lean beef	8 oz minced lean beef
1 onion, minced or	1 onion, minced
100 g pork sausagemeat	4 oz pork sausagemeat
1 tablespoon tomato purée	1 tablespoon tomato purée
1 egg, beaten	1 egg, beaten
1 large slice of bread, about 1 cm thick	1 large slice of bread, about ½ inch thick
5 tablespoons stock	5 tablespoons stock
salt and pepper	salt and pepper
butter	butter
crushed potato crisps	crushed potato crisps

Mix together the ham, beef, onion, sausagemeat, tomato purée and egg. Soak the bread in the stock for 15 minutes, then beat until smooth. Add to the meat mixture, season to taste and mix well.

Generously grease a 1 kg/2 lb loaf tin with butter, then coat with crisps. Pack in the meat mixture. Brush the top with melted butter and cover with a layer of crisps.

Bake in a preheated moderate oven (160°C/325°F, Gas Mark 3) for 1½ hours. Serve hot or cold.

Serves 4 to 5

Sausages and Bacon with Tomato Sauce

METRIC	IMPERIAL
350 g chipolata sausages	12 oz chipolata sausages
12 streaky bacon rashers, rinded	12 streaky bacon rashers, rinded
50 g butter	2 oz butter
1 large onion, chopped	1 large onion, chopped
1 red pepper, cored, seeded and diced	1 red pepper, cored, seeded and diced
500 g tomatoes, skinned and chopped	1 lb tomatoes, skinned and chopped
salt and pepper	salt and pepper

Prick the sausages all over. Stretch the bacon rashers with the back of a knife, then wrap a rasher around each sausage. Grill the sausages until cooked through and the bacon is browned on all sides.

Meanwhile, melt the butter in a frying pan. Add the onion and red pepper and fry until softened. Stir in the tomatoes and salt and pepper to taste. Simmer gently until the sauce is thick.

Transfer the sausages to a warmed serving dish and pour over the sauce. Serve hot.

Serves 4

Meat

Sausage and Kidney Casserole

Serve with mashed potatoes and a green vegetable.

METRIC	IMPERIAL
25 g butter	1 oz butter
225 g chipolata sausages, halved crossways	8 oz chipolata sausages, halved crossways
6 lamb's kidneys, skinned, halved and cored	6 lamb's kidneys, skinned, halved and cored
1 large onion, chopped	1 large onion, chopped
2 tablespoons flour	2 tablespoons flour
300 ml beef stock	½ pint beef stock
½ teaspoon dried thyme	½ teaspoon dried thyme
salt and pepper	salt and pepper

Melt the butter in a flameproof casserole. Add the sausage pieces and brown on all sides. Remove from the pot.

Add the kidneys to the casserole and brown lightly. Remove from the pot.

Add the onion to the casserole and fry until softened. Stir in the flour and cook for 1 minute, then gradually stir in the stock. Bring to the boil, stirring well. Add the thyme and season to taste with salt and pepper.

Return the sausages and kidneys to the casserole and mix into the sauce. Cover the casserole and transfer to a preheated moderate oven (180°C/350°F, Gas Mark 4). Cook for 30 to 40 minutes or until the kidneys are tender. Serve hot.

Serves 4

Type of offal	Basic preparation	Suggested cooking methods	Other uses
Brains	Rinse thoroughly under cold running water, then soak in water for at least 1 hour. Blanch for 5 minutes; remove membrane and skin. Simmer in water to cover (with seasonings if liked) for 15–20 minutes	Fry or braise	
Heart	Rinse thoroughly under cold running water. Cut out tubes and gristle. Rinse again and pat dry. Slice ox heart	Fry or braise, stuffed if liked	
Kidneys	Remove any fat and thin skin. Cut in half and cut out central white core and ducts. Rinse under cold running water and pat dry. Slice or chop ox kidney	Grill or fry calf's, lamb's and pig's kidneys. Braise or stew ox kidney	In steak and kidney pie and pudding
Liver	Rinse under cold running water and pat dry. Remove any membrane or gristle. Soak ox liver in milk or salted water for at least 1 hour, or blanch, before cooking to reduce strong flavour	Grill or fry calf's, lamb's and chicken liver. Braise or stew ox and pig's liver	In terrines and pâtés
Sweetbreads	Rinse thoroughly under cold running water, then soak in water for at least 2 hours. Blanch for 5 minutes; remove ducts and skin	Fry or braise	
Tail	Have butcher joint tail. Rinse under cold running water and pat dry. Remove excess fat	Braise	In soups
Tongue	Soak salted tongue in water overnight; soak fresh tongue for 2 hours. Blanch 5 minutes	Braise, allowing half the cooking time if using salted tongue, and press	
Tripe	Sold cleaned and parboiled (called 'dressed')	Stew, boil or deep fry	

Cidered Liver Ragoût

This stew uses ox liver which is very economical, although it needs long, gentle cooking to make it tender. Serve with mashed potatoes, boiled rice or noodles to take up the sauce which will be very tasty.

METRIC	IMPERIAL
25 g flour	1 oz flour
salt and pepper	salt and pepper
750 g ox liver, cut into thin strips	1½ lb ox liver, cut into thin strips
50 g butter or dripping	2 oz butter or dripping
3 onions, thinly sliced	3 onions, thinly sliced
1 garlic clove, crushed	1 garlic clove, crushed
300 ml stock	½ pint stock
300 ml dry cider	½ pint dry cider
1½ tablespoons redcurrant jelly	1½ tablespoons redcurrant jelly
½ teaspoon grated lemon rind	½ teaspoon grated lemon rind

Season the flour with salt and pepper and use to coat the liver strips. Melt the butter or dripping in a large saucepan. Add the liver strips and brown on all sides. Remove from the pan.

Add the onions and garlic to the pan and fry until softened. Stir in the stock and cider and bring to the boil. Stir in the redcurrant jelly and lemon rind. Return the liver to the pan.

Cover and simmer gently for 2 hours or until the liver is tender. Taste and adjust the seasoning before serving.

Serves 4 to 5

Oven-baked Liver Risotto

METRIC	IMPERIAL
2 tablespoons oil	2 tablespoons oil
2 onions, sliced	2 onions, sliced
1 green pepper, cored, seeded and diced	1 green pepper, cored, seeded and diced
100 g mushrooms, sliced	4 oz mushrooms, sliced
1 garlic clove, crushed (optional)	1 garlic clove, crushed (optional)
225 g long-grain rice	8 oz long-grain rice
750 ml chicken stock	1¼ pints chicken stock
50 g sultanas	2 oz sultanas
175 g chicken livers, diced	6 oz chicken livers, diced
salt and pepper	salt and pepper
50 g cheese, grated	2 oz cheese, grated
chopped parsley to garnish	chopped parsley to garnish

Heat the oil in a flameproof casserole. Add the onions, green pepper, mushrooms and garlic, if used, and fry until the onions are softened. Stir in the rice, then add the stock, sultanas, livers and salt and pepper to taste. Bring to the boil.

Cover the casserole and wrap foil around it to be sure the rice doesn't dry out. Transfer to a preheated moderate oven (180°C/350°F, Gas Mark 4) and cook for 1 hour or until the rice is tender and all the liquid has been absorbed.

Stir in the cheese with a fork. Sprinkle with parsley and serve hot.

Serves 4 to 6

Liver Kebabs with Orange Sauce

METRIC	IMPERIAL
500 g piece of calf's liver, cut about 2.5 cm thick, cubed	1 lb piece of calf's liver, cut about 1 inch thick, cubed
1 teaspoon dried mixed herbs	1 teaspoon dried mixed herbs
salt and pepper	salt and pepper
12 button mushrooms	12 button mushrooms
12 cocktail onions	12 cocktail onions
4 bacon rashers, rinded, halved crossways and rolled	4 bacon rashers, rinded, halved crossways and rolled
50 g butter, melted	2 oz butter, melted
Sauce:	*Sauce:*
thinly pared rind and juice of 2 oranges	thinly pared rind and juice of 2 oranges
300 ml beef stock	½ pint beef stock
25 g cornflour	1 oz cornflour
25 g butter	1 oz butter
1 teaspoon sugar	1 teaspoon sugar
salt and pepper	salt and pepper

First make the sauce. Place the orange rind and half the stock in a saucepan and bring to the boil. Simmer for 5 minutes, then strain the stock and return to the pan.

Blend the cornflour with the remaining cold stock and add to the pan with the remaining sauce ingredients, seasoning to taste with salt and pepper. Bring to the boil, stirring, and simmer until thickened. Leave to cook very gently while you are preparing the kebabs.

Coat the liver cubes with herbs, salt and pepper. Thread on to skewers alternately with the mushrooms, onions and bacon rolls. Brush with the melted butter and grill for about 8 minutes. Turn the kebabs and brush them with melted butter from time to time.

Serve the kebabs on a bed of rice, with the sauce separately.

Serves 4

Meat

Sausage Cakes

METRIC	IMPERIAL
500 g pork sausagemeat	1 lb pork sausagemeat
1 onion, grated	1 onion, grated
50 g fresh breadcrumbs	2 oz fresh breadcrumbs
2 tablespoons Worcestershire sauce	2 tablespoons Worcestershire sauce
1 egg, beaten	1 egg, beaten
salt and pepper	salt and pepper

Place all the ingredients, with salt and pepper to taste, in a bowl. Mix well together, using your fingers to combine the ingredients thoroughly. Divide into four or six portions and shape into flat cakes.

Grill for 5 to 8 minutes on each side or until golden brown and cooked through. Serve hot with mashed potatoes, or in soft baps like beef burgers.

Serves 4 to 6

Braised Stuffed Hearts

METRIC	IMPERIAL
4 lambs' hearts	4 lambs' hearts
25 g butter	1 oz butter
1 small onion, finely chopped	1 small onion, finely chopped
50 g fresh breadcrumbs	2 oz fresh breadcrumbs
1 teaspoon dried mixed herbs	1 teaspoon dried mixed herbs
2 tablespoons raisins	2 tablespoons raisins
1 egg, beaten	1 egg, beaten
salt and pepper	salt and pepper
450 ml beef stock	$\frac{3}{4}$ pint beef stock
150 ml dry cider	$\frac{1}{4}$ pint dry cider
4 celery stalks, chopped	4 celery stalks, chopped
3 carrots, chopped	3 carrots, chopped

Rinse the hearts and remove all tubes and gristle. Pat dry.

Melt the butter in a frying pan. Add the onion and fry until softened. Remove from the heat and stir in the breadcrumbs, herbs and raisins. Bind with the egg, then season to taste with salt and pepper. Use this mixture to stuff the hearts and sew up the openings with a needle and thread or secure with wooden cocktail sticks.

Place the hearts in a baking dish and add the stock and cider. Cover and cook in a preheated moderate oven (160°C/325°F, Gas Mark 3) for 1 hour. Add the celery and carrots, re-cover and cook for a further 1 hour or until the hearts are tender. Serve with mashed potatoes.

Serves 4

Nutritious offal

Despite its off-putting name, offal is both deliciously appetising and very nutritious. It is rich in body-building nutrients, particularly protein, iron, riboflavin, niacin and Vitamins A and B. And because much offal, such as sweetbreads and brains, is easily digestible, it is suitable for young and old.

Slimmers, too, can enjoy a lot of offal in their diets because it is low in calories. Liver or kidneys can be fried (in low-fat margarine or a non-stick pan) and finished with a delicious sauce of stock or orange juice. They can also be used to make kebabs with tomatoes and peppers, or a casserole with onion, stock and piquant seasonings such as Worcestershire sauce and mustard.

Offal is highly perishable so if possible use it the day of purchase. For storage, keep it in the refrigerator loosely wrapped; this will allow the air to circulate, thus keeping the meat dry, to inhibit bacterial growth.

Pressed Tongue

The tongue may be served hot before pressing. After removing the skin, sprinkle the tongue with browned breadcrumbs and serve with lemon wedges and parsley sauce.

METRIC	IMPERIAL
1 × 1.75–2.75 ox tongue	1 × 4–6 lb ox tongue
1 bouquet garni	1 bouquet garni
1 onion, sliced	1 onion, sliced
2 carrots, sliced	2 carrots, sliced
few black peppercorns	few black peppercorns

If the tongue has been pickled, soak it in water overnight; soak a fresh tongue for 2 hours.

Drain the tongue and place it in a saucepan with the bouquet garni, onion, carrots and peppercorns. Add fresh cold water to cover. Bring to the boil, skimming off any scum that rises, then cover and simmer for $2\frac{1}{2}$ to 3 hours for a pickled tongue, or $4\frac{1}{2}$ to 6 hours for a fresh tongue, or until tender.

Drain, reserving the cooking liquid, and plunge into cold water. Strip off the skin and remove any pieces of bone and gristle. Put into a round cake tin or bowl that will hold it comfortably (or use a tongue press). Add a little of the strained cooking liquid. Put a plate on top and weight down heavily. Leave until cold and set. Turn out to serve, with salad.

Oxtail Hotpot with Mustard Dumplings

METRIC	IMPERIAL
1 oxtail, jointed	1 oxtail, jointed
3 onions, sliced	3 onions, sliced
3 large carrots, sliced	3 large carrots, sliced
1.2 litres stock or water	2 pints stock or water
grated rind of 1 lemon	grated rind of 1 lemon
1 bouquet garni	1 bouquet garni
salt and pepper	salt and pepper
40 g cornflour	1½ oz cornflour
4 tablespoons cold water	4 tablespoons cold water
1 quantity uncooked Suet Dumplings*, made with 1 teaspoon dry mustard instead of herbs	1 quantity uncooked Suet Dumplings*, made with 1 teaspoon dry mustard instead of herbs

Place the oxtail in a large saucepan and fry until golden brown on all sides (there shouldn't be any need to add fat or oil as the oxtail is very fatty). Remove the oxtail pieces as they brown.

Add the onions and half the carrot slices and fry until softened. Return the oxtail pieces, then pour over the stock or water. Add the lemon rind, bouquet garni and salt and pepper to taste. Bring to the boil. Simmer for 1½ hours.

Add the remaining carrot slices, then simmer for a further 1 hour. Remove from the heat and leave to cool completely.

Remove the layer of fat that will have formed on the surface. Reheat the hotpot. Discard the bouquet garni. Blend the cornflour with the cold water and add to the pan. Simmer, stirring, until thickened.

Drop in the suet dumplings, cover tightly and simmer for 15 minutes. Serve hot.

Serves 4 to 6

Sweetbreads in Lemon Cream Sauce

METRIC	IMPERIAL
750 g sweetbreads	1½ lb sweetbreads
300 ml chicken stock	½ pint chicken stock
1 onion	1 onion
1 bouquet garni	1 bouquet garni
thinly pared rind and juice of 1 lemon	thinly pared rind and juice of 1 lemon
salt and pepper	salt and pepper
300 ml hot White Sauce*	½ pint hot White Sauce*
2 tablespoons cream	2 tablespoons cream
100 g button mushrooms	4 oz button mushrooms
25 g butter	1 oz butter

Place the sweetbreads in a saucepan and cover with cold water. Bring to the boil, then drain and return to the pan. Add the stock, onion, bouquet garni, lemon rind and juice and salt and pepper to taste. Bring to the boil, then simmer gently for 30 to 35 minutes or until the sweetbreads are tender.

Drain the sweetbreads, reserving 150 ml/¼ pint of the liquid. Remove any skin from the sweetbreads and keep hot.

Mix the reserved strained liquid with the white sauce. Add the sweetbreads and heat through gently. Stir in the cream, and taste and adjust the seasoning. Remove from the heat and keep hot.

Quickly fry the mushrooms in the butter, then stir into the sweetbread mixture. Serve hot.

Serves 4 to 5

Lamb's Tongues with Tomato Sauce

METRIC	IMPERIAL
25 g butter	1 oz butter
1 onion, chopped	1 onion, chopped
50 g bacon, rinded and chopped	2 oz bacon, rinded and chopped
2 celery sticks, chopped	2 celery sticks, chopped
1 × 225 g can tomatoes	1 × 8 oz can tomatoes
1 tablespoon Worcestershire sauce	1 tablespoon Worcestershire sauce
150 ml beef stock	¼ pint beef stock
salt and pepper	salt and pepper
8 lamb's tongues	8 lamb's tongues
2 tablespoons tomato purée	2 tablespoons tomato purée
2 tablespoons cornflour	2 tablespoons cornflour
3 tablespoons water	3 tablespoons water

Melt the butter in a flameproof casserole. Add the onion, bacon and celery and fry until the vegetables are softened. Stir in the tomatoes with their juice, Worcestershire sauce, stock and salt and pepper to taste. Bring to the boil.

Arrange the tongues on top. Cover and cook in a preheated moderate oven (180°C/350°F, Gas Mark 4) for about 2½ hours or until the tongues are tender.

Remove the tongues from the casserole. Trim off any bones and remove the skin. Cut each tongue into slices. Keep warm.

Skim any fat from the surface of the sauce in the casserole, then stir in the tomato purée. Blend the cornflour with the cold water and stir into the sauce. Return the casserole to the top of the stove and cook, stirring, until thickened. Taste and adjust the seasoning.

Stir in the tongue slices and reheat gently. Serve hot.

Serves 4 to 6

Meat

Brawn

METRIC
½ pig's head, gristle
  removed
2 onions, quartered
1 carrot, halved
1 turnip, quartered
4 cloves
12 peppercorns
1 mace blade
1 bouquet garni
salt and pepper

IMPERIAL
½ pig's head, gristle
  removed
2 onions, quartered
1 carrot, halved
1 turnip, quartered
4 cloves
12 peppercorns
1 mace blade
1 bouquet garni
salt and pepper

Wash the head thoroughly in tepid water, then rinse in cold water. Place in a large flameproof casserole and add water to cover. Bring slowly to the boil, skimming off the scum that rises to the surface.

Add the vegetables, cloves, peppercorns, mace blade, bouquet garni and salt and pepper to taste. Cover and transfer to a preheated moderate oven (160°C/325°F, Gas Mark 3). Cook for about 3 hours or until the flesh comes away from the bones quite easily. Skim off scum after each hour's cooking.

Remove the head from the casserole and strain the cooking liquid into a bowl. Leave to cool, then remove the meat and tongue from the head. Cut into pieces, removing all skin, gristle and fat.

Pour the cooking liquid and meat back into the casserole and bring to the boil. Boil until reduced by half. Season well with salt and pepper.

Place the meat in a mould and pour in the liquid. Chill until set to a jelly, then turn out on to a plate.

Serves 6 to 8

Tripe with Sherry Sauce

Tripe is very inexpensive, and cooked in this way with a creamy sauce it can seem very luxurious.

METRIC
750 g–1 kg tripe, cut
  into neat pieces
2 tablespoons oil
2 onions, sliced
2 carrots, sliced
100 g mushrooms,
  sliced
1 tablespoon flour
300 ml stock
salt and pepper
4 tablespoons double
  cream
1–2 tablespoons sherry

IMPERIAL
1½–2 lb tripe, cut
  into neat pieces
2 tablespoons oil
2 onions, sliced
2 carrots, sliced
4 oz mushrooms,
  sliced
1 tablespoon flour
½ pint stock
salt and pepper
4 tablespoons double
  cream
1–2 tablespoons sherry

Place the tripe in a saucepan and cover with cold water. Bring to the boil, then drain.

Heat the oil in a clean saucepan. Add the onions, carrots and mushrooms and fry until the onions are softened. Stir in the flour and cook for 2 minutes, then gradually stir in the stock. Bring to the boil, stirring.

Add the tripe and salt and pepper to taste and mix well. Cover tightly and simmer gently for 40 minutes or until the tripe is tender.

Mix the cream with the sherry and add to the pan. Cook very gently, stirring, for 5 minutes. Do not allow to boil. Taste and adjust the seasoning before serving.

Serves 4 to 6

Choosing offal

Offal, or those parts of a slaughtered animal which are left after the carcass has been cut up, is often under-rated despite being nutritious and generally inexpensive. The liver, kidneys, tongue, brains, head, heart, sweetbreads, feet, tripe, cheek and tail are economical buys as there is very little wastage, and they usually do not require lengthy preparation or cooking.

Offal from a calf is most highly prized as it is more tender and delicate in flavour than offal from other animals. Next in terms of quality comes offal from lamb. The major visible difference between the offal from different animals is size – that from beef is the largest and from lamb the smallest.

Most kinds of offal have self-explanatory names. Sweetbreads and tripe, however, may cause some confusion. Sweetbreads are the thymus glands from the throat or chest cavity (where they are called heartbreads). Tripe is the first and second stomachs from a cudchewing animal. Smooth or blanket tripe is from the first stomach, and honeycomb tripe is from the second. Other terms which may be unfamiliar are bath chap, which is the name sometimes given to the cured and boiled cheeks of a pig's head, and black pudding which is a mixture of pork fat and pig's blood packed into pig's intestines and boiled.

Sometimes classed as offal, marrow bones are from the thigh and upper front legs of beef. These bones are sawn across into manageable pieces by the butcher.

Suppers and Snacks

Preparation of food should be a challenge,
but never a burden. If you can feel it is
fun to prepare your meals, what a pleasure
it will be for everyone. Suppers and snacks
are usually quickly prepared, often using
leftovers. And quite often the dish consists
entirely of vegetables which makes the
meal economical, too. Casseroles are
versatile and interesting supper fare.
There are so many ways the cook can put
together a mouth-watering concoction. And
sandwiches can be varied by the type of
bread and filling, so that you can show your
real ingenuity.

Corned Beef Pie

METRIC	IMPERIAL
1 tablespoon oil	1 tablespoon oil
2 onions, chopped	2 onions, chopped
2 × 350 g cans corned beef, roughly chopped	2 × 12 oz cans corned beef, roughly chopped
1 egg, beaten	1 egg, beaten
2–3 carrots, cooked and diced	2–3 carrots, cooked and diced
100 g frozen peas, cooked	4 oz frozen peas, cooked
few drops of Tabasco sauce	few drops of Tabasco sauce
salt and pepper	salt and pepper
225 g quantity Short-crust Pastry*	8 oz quantity Short-crust Pastry*
beaten egg to glaze	beaten egg to glaze

Heat the oil in a frying pan. Add the onions and fry until softened. Remove from the heat and stir in the corned beef, egg, carrots, peas, Tabasco sauce and salt and pepper to taste.

Roll out half the dough on a floured surface and use to line a deep 18 to 20 cm/7 to 8 inch pie plate or tin. Spoon in the filling and spread out evenly.

Roll out the remaining dough and use to cover the filling. Press the edges together to seal and flute them. Decorate the top with dough trimmings, if liked. Glaze with beaten egg.

Bake in a preheated moderately hot oven (200°C/400°F, Gas Mark 6) for 25 to 30 minutes, then reduce the temperature to moderate (180°C/350°F, Gas Mark 4). Cook for a further 20 to 25 minutes. Serve hot or cold.

Serves 6

Decorating pies

Give your pies a decorative edge for an attractive finish. The simplest edge for a single crust pie is made by pressing the prongs of a fork into the pastry dough all around the rim of the pie dish. For a pie with two layers of pastry, first seal the edges together by 'knocking up'. To do this, place the back of a floured forefinger on top of the pie edge and, with the back of a broad-bladed knife, make indentations in the double edge. This will help the pastry to rise and will give it a flaky appearance. After knocking up, the edge may be fluted: press your thumb into the top of the edge and draw the back of a knife to one side of your thumb, making a cut about 1 cm/½ inch deep. Continue around the edge of the pie. Another finish is crimping, made by pinching the edge between the thumb and forefinger of each hand and twisting slightly in opposite directions.

Parsnip Loaf

This delicious dish is made from vegetables, cheese and eggs, so it makes a satisfying main dish. To vary, use a mixture of parsnips and swedes.

METRIC	IMPERIAL
1 kg parsnips, chopped	2 lb parsnips, chopped
2 onions, chopped	2 onions, chopped
salt and pepper	salt and pepper
75 g butter	3 oz butter
225 g Cheddar or Cheshire cheese, grated	8 oz Cheddar or Cheshire cheese, grated
2 eggs, beaten	2 eggs, beaten
50 g fresh breadcrumbs	2 oz fresh breadcrumbs
25 g flour	1 oz flour
150 ml tomato juice	¼ pint tomato juice
½ teaspoon yeast extract	½ teaspoon yeast extract

Cook the parsnips and onions in boiling salted water until tender. Drain, reserving 150 ml/¼ pint of the cooking liquid.

Mash the vegetables with 25 g/1 oz of the butter, then beat in the cheese, eggs and salt and pepper to taste. Form into a neat loaf shape on a baking sheet. Coat with the breadcrumbs and dot with 25 g/1 oz of the remaining butter.

Bake in a preheated hot oven (220°C/425°F, Gas Mark 7) for about 15 minutes or until golden brown.

Meanwhile, melt the remaining butter in a saucepan. Stir in the flour and cook for 2 minutes, then gradually stir in the tomato juice and reserved cooking liquid. Bring to the boil, stirring, and simmer until thickened. Stir in the yeast extract, and season with salt and pepper to taste.

Transfer the parsnip loaf to a warmed serving dish and serve with the sauce.

Serves 4 to 6

Toad in the Hole

METRIC	IMPERIAL
500 g large pork or beef sausages	1 lb large pork or beef sausages
1 quantity Pancake Batter*	1 quantity Pancake Batter*

Grease a shallow baking dish or roasting tin. Put the sausages in the dish and bake in a preheated hot oven (220°C/425°F, Gas Mark 7) until the sausages are browned on all sides.

Pour the batter around the sausages and return to the oven. Bake for a further 20 to 30 minutes or until the batter is risen, crisp and golden. Serve hot.

Serves 4

Pork Pie

To make the traditional Melton Mowbray pork pie, add 6 to 7 chopped anchovy fillets to the filling.

METRIC	IMPERIAL
750 g pork fillet, diced	1½ lb pork fillet, diced
100 g belly pork, diced	4 oz belly pork, diced
2 teaspoons grated lemon rind	2 teaspoons grated lemon rind
good pinch of dried sage	good pinch of dried sage
salt and pepper	salt and pepper
9 tablespoons stock	9 tablespoons stock
350 g quantity Hot Water Crusty Pastry★	12 oz quantity Hot Water Crust Pastry★
1 teaspoon powdered gelatine	1 teaspoon powdered gelatine
beaten egg to glaze	beaten egg to glaze

Mix together the pork, lemon rind, sage, salt and pepper to taste and 3 tablespoons of the stock.

To make a moulded pie, take about three-quarters of the dough (keeping the remainder warm) and flatten it slightly with your hands. Place a round or oval mould or tin on the dough and gradually pull up and mould the dough around it to give an even thickness and the right shape. Remove the mould.

Put the filling into the pastry case (it should be almost level with the top). Mould the remaining dough into a lid. Dampen the edges of the pastry case and place the lid on top. Press the edges together to seal. Make a slit in the lid and decorate with the dough trimmings.

If preferred, the dough may be rolled out and used to line a greased round deep cake tin. Cut out two rounds, one to fit the bottom of the tin and one for the lid. Roll the remaining dough into a strip as wide as the depth of the tin and as long as the circumference. Use this to line the sides of the tin.

When placing the filling in the pastry case, do not press it down too firmly as you must leave room for the jelly to be poured in after baking. Put on the lid, pinching together to seal and fluting the edges if liked. Make a slit in the centre of the pastry lid.

If the pie has been moulded, brush the top and sides with beaten egg. If baking in a tin, glaze the top only.

Bake in a preheated moderate oven (180°C/350°F, Gas Mark 4) for 1 hour, then reduce the temperature to 160°C/325°F, Gas Mark 3 and bake for a further 1 to 1¼ hours. Leave to cool.

Meanwhile, dissolve the gelatine in the remaining stock. Leave to cool until just beginning to thicken. Insert a plastic funnel or cone of foil or greaseproof paper into the slit in the lid of the pie and pour in the jelly. Leave, in a cool place, until set.

Serves 6

VARIATIONS

Veal and ham pie: Make as above, using 600 g/1¼ lb diced fillet of veal and 100 to 225 g/4 to 8 oz diced or minced cooked ham or gammon instead of the pork. Add 2 to 3 hard-boiled eggs, sliced or chopped.

Chicken and ham pie: Make as above, using 350 g/12 oz diced breast of chicken, 225 g/8 oz diced or minced chicken dark meat and 100 to 225 g/4 to 8 oz diced or minced cooked ham or gammon instead of the pork. Put half this filling in the pastry case, then press in 2 to 3 whole hard-boiled eggs. Cover with the remaining filling.

Greek Shepherds' Pie

METRIC	IMPERIAL
1 large aubergine, sliced	1 large aubergine, sliced
salt and pepper	salt and pepper
50 g butter	2 oz butter
2 onions, thinly sliced	2 onions, thinly sliced
1 large potato, thinly sliced	1 large potato, thinly sliced
500 g minced lamb	1 lb minced lamb
2 tomatoes, skinned and sliced	2 tomatoes, skinned and sliced
300 ml Béchamel Sauce★	½ pint Béchamel Sauce★
salt and pepper	salt and pepper
50 g Cheddar cheese, grated	2 oz Cheddar cheese, grated

Place the aubergine slices in a colander, sprinkle with salt and leave to drain for 30 minutes. Rinse and pat dry with paper towels.

Melt the butter in a large deep frying pan. Add the onions and fry until softened. Add the aubergine slices, in batches, and brown on both sides. Add the potato slices and fry for a few minutes on each side. Remove all the vegetables from the pan as they are fried.

Add the lamb to the pan and fry until browned and crumbly.

Arrange half the aubergines and onions on the bottom of a greased casserole and cover with half the lamb and tomatoes. Pour over one-third of the sauce and season well with salt and pepper.

Cover with the potatoes, then the remaining lamb and another third of the sauce. Finish with the remaining aubergine, tomatoes and sauce. Sprinkle the cheese on top.

Bake in a preheated moderate oven (160°C/325°F, Gas Mark 3) for 45 minutes. Serve hot, with a mixed or green salad.

Serves 4

VARIATION

Use minced beef instead of lamb, and season with ground allspice in addition to salt and pepper. Use Cheese Sauce★ instead of Béchamel, and beat 1 egg yolk into the sauce. Do not layer the sauce with the meat and vegetables, but pour it all over the top. Do not sprinkle the top with cheese. Bake as above.

Bruising seasonings
When seasonings such as garlic, root ginger and herbs such as mint are used to flavour a dish, you may want to remove them before serving. To make this easy, they should be bruised instead of chopped. Bruising is done by lightly crushing the garlic clove, piece of root ginger or herb sprig or spray without breaking it into pieces.

Jamaican Lamb Burgers

These burgers may be cooked over charcoal on a barbecue. Place the saucepan containing the sauce on the side of the barbecue grid to heat over the coals while the burgers are cooking.

METRIC	IMPERIAL
25 g butter	1 oz butter
1 onion, grated	1 onion, grated
500 g minced lamb	1 lb minced lamb
½ small green pepper, cored, seeded and diced (optional)	½ small green pepper, cored, seeded and diced (optional)
1 tablespoon tomato purée	1 tablespoon tomato purée
½ teaspoon dried thyme	½ teaspoon dried thyme
75 g fresh breadcrumbs	3 oz fresh breadcrumbs
1 teaspoon clear honey	1 teaspoon clear honey
salt and pepper	salt and pepper
Sauce:	*Sauce:*
juice of 1 lemon	juice of 1 lemon
1 tablespoon Worcestershire sauce	1 tablespoon Worcestershire sauce
1 small red pepper, cored, seeded and diced	1 small red pepper, cored, seeded and diced
2 bananas, finely chopped	2 bananas, finely chopped
1 onion, finely chopped	1 onion, finely chopped
4 mushrooms, finely chopped	4 mushrooms, finely chopped

Melt the butter in a frying pan. Add the onion and fry until softened. Tip the onion into a bowl and add the remaining burger ingredients, with salt and pepper to taste. Mix well together, using your fingers to combine the ingredients thoroughly. Divide into four or eight portions and shape each into a flat cake.

Combine the lemon juice and Worcestershire sauce in a saucepan. Brush the burgers with this mixture, then grill them for about 5 minutes on each side or until cooked through to your liking.

Meanwhile, add the remaining sauce ingredients to the saucepan and bring to the boil. Simmer for 5 minutes. Season to taste with salt and pepper.

Serve the sauce with the burgers.

Serves 4

Beef Burgers

Serve these in soft baps, with mustard, tomato ketchup, lettuce leaves and tomato slices. If liked, top each burger with a slice of cheese and grill until melted. For heartier appetites, increase the beef to 750 g/1½ lb or even 1 kg/2 lb.

METRIC	IMPERIAL
500 g minced lean beef	1 lb minced lean beef
1 small onion, grated	1 small onion, grated
1 small egg, beaten (optional)	1 small egg, beaten (optional)
1 teaspoon Worcestershire sauce	1 teaspoon Worcestershire sauce
pinch of dried mixed herbs	pinch of dried mixed herbs
salt and pepper	salt and pepper

Place all the ingredients, with salt and pepper to taste, in a bowl and mix well together, using your fingers to combine the ingredients thoroughly. Divide into four portions and shape each into a flat cake.

Grill the burgers for about 3 minutes on each side or until cooked through to your liking. Serve hot with chosen accompaniments.

Serves 4

Smoky Fish Cakes

METRIC	IMPERIAL
350 g smoked haddock fillets, cooked and flaked	12 oz smoked haddock fillets, cooked and flaked
500 g mashed potato	1 lb mashed potato
1 hard-boiled egg, chopped	1 hard-boiled egg, chopped
3 tablespoons powdered milk	3 tablespoons powdered milk
2 tablespoons chopped parsley	2 tablespoons chopped parsley
½ teaspoon dry mustard	½ teaspoon dry mustard
salt and pepper	salt and pepper
1 egg, beaten	1 egg, beaten
browned breadcrumbs	browned breadcrumbs
50 g butter	2 oz butter

Mix together the fish, potato, chopped egg, milk powder, parsley, mustard and salt and pepper to taste. Divide into eight portions and shape each into a flat cake. Brush with the beaten egg and coat with breadcrumbs.

Melt the butter in a large frying pan. Add the fish cakes and fry, in two batches if necessary, until golden brown on both sides and piping hot.

Serves 4

Deep Sea Cakes

Leftover fish and mashed potatoes make these cakes very quick to prepare.

METRIC	IMPERIAL
100 g cod fillet, cooked and flaked	4 oz cod fillet, cooked and flaked
175 g mashed potato	6 oz mashed potato
50 g flour	2 oz flour
1 teaspoon dried mixed herbs	1 teaspoon dried mixed herbs
salt and pepper	salt and pepper
50 g butter	2 oz butter

Mix together the cod, potato, flour, herbs and salt and pepper to taste. Divide into eight portions and shape each into a flat cake on a floured surface.

Melt the butter in a large frying pan. Add the fish cakes and fry, in two batches if necessary, until golden brown on both sides and piping hot.

Serves 4

Spicing up basic beefburgers

Basic beefburgers – minced beef seasoned with salt and pepper – are delicious simply served in buns or baps with tomato ketchup, mustard and pickles. But they can be made even more exciting with the addition of a few ingredients. Here are some ideas, to add to 500 g/1 lb lean minced beef:

Add 150 ml/¼ pint mild tomato chilli sauce, 25 g/1 oz fresh breadcrumbs, 1 small grated onion and 1 egg.

Add 75 g/3 oz grated mature Cheddar cheese, 1 small grated onion, 1 tablespoon Worcestershire sauce and 1 egg.

Add 75 g/3 oz chopped mushrooms, 150 ml/¼ pint soured cream or plain yogurt, 1 tablespoon tomato purée, 1 teaspoon paprika and 1 egg.

Add ½ grated dessert apple, ½ diced small green pepper, 1 teaspoon curry powder, ¼ teaspoon chilli powder (or more to taste) and 1 egg.

Add 6 tablespoons each dry white wine and chopped parsley. After shaping the burgers, wrap a streaky bacon rasher around the edge of each and secure with a cocktail stick.

Season the beef, then shape into burgers and press in 1½ tablespoons crushed black peppercorns. Fry these 'pepper burgers' in butter with a little red wine.

Barbecued Chicken Burgers

METRIC	IMPERIAL
1 kg minced chicken	2 lb minced chicken
salt and pepper	salt and pepper
2 tablespoons soy sauce	2 tablespoons soy sauce
4 tablespoons tomato ketchup	4 tablespoons tomato ketchup
½ teaspoon dry mustard	½ teaspoon dry mustard
1 tablespoon honey	1 tablespoon honey
2 teaspoons lemon juice	2 teaspoons lemon juice
2 tablespoons water	2 tablespoons water

Mix the chicken with salt and pepper to taste. Divide into six to eight portions and shape into flat cakes.

Put the remaining ingredients into a saucepan and bring to the boil. Brush the chicken burgers with this sauce and grill for 4 to 5 minutes on each side or until cooked through. Baste with the sauce from time to time. Serve with the remaining sauce.

Serves 6 to 8

Herby Chicken Cakes

METRIC	IMPERIAL
75 g butter	3 oz butter
1 onion, chopped	1 onion, chopped
500 g minced chicken	1 lb minced chicken
50 g fresh breadcrumbs	2 oz fresh breadcrumbs
1 teaspoon chopped parsley	1 teaspoon chopped parsley
pinch of dried mixed herbs	pinch of dried mixed herbs
1 egg, beaten	1 egg, beaten
salt and pepper	salt and pepper
flour for coating	flour for coating
25 g flour	1 oz flour
300 ml milk	½ pint milk

Melt 25 g/1 oz of the butter in a large frying pan. Add the onion and fry until softened. Remove from the pan with a slotted spoon.

Mix the onion with the chicken, breadcrumbs, herbs, egg and salt and pepper to taste. Divide into eight portions and shape each into a flat cake. Coat with flour.

Melt the remaining butter in the frying pan. Add the chicken cakes and fry, in two batches if necessary, until golden brown on both sides and cooked through. Remove from the pan and keep warm.

Stir the measured flour into the fat in the pan and cook, stirring, for 2 minutes. Gradually stir in the milk. Bring to the boil, stirring, and simmer until thickened. Season to taste with salt and pepper.

Pour the sauce over the chicken cakes and serve.

Serves 4

Tomato Herb Quiche

METRIC	IMPERIAL
175 g quantity Herb Shortcrust Pastry*	6 oz quantity Herb Shortcrust Pastry*
350 g tomatoes, sliced	12 oz tomatoes, sliced
1 small onion, chopped	1 small onion, chopped
1 teaspoon chopped parsley	1 teaspoon chopped parsley
½ teaspoon dried basil	½ teaspoon dried basil
½ teaspoon dried thyme	½ teaspoon dried thyme
2 tablespoons water	2 tablespoons water
salt and pepper	salt and pepper
1 egg	1 egg
250 ml milk	8 fl oz milk

Roll out the dough on a floured surface and use to line a 20 cm/8 inch flan tin.

Place the tomatoes, onion, herbs, water and salt and pepper to taste in a saucepan. Simmer for 5 minutes or until the vegetables are soft.

Lightly beat the egg with the milk. Stir into the tomato mixture, then pour into the flan case. Bake in a preheated moderate oven (180°C/350°F, Gas Mark 4) for 35 to 40 minutes or until the filling is set and the pastry is golden brown. Serve hot or cold.

Serves 4 to 6

Curried Turkey Flan

METRIC	IMPERIAL
175 g quantity Short-crust Pastry*, made with 1 teaspoon curry powder added to the dry ingredients	6 oz quantity Shortcrust Pastry*, made with 1 teaspoon curry powder added to the dry ingredients
225 g cooked turkey meat	8 oz cooked turkey meat
50 g cooked ham	2 oz cooked ham
¼ teaspoon curry powder	¼ teaspoon curry powder
¼ teaspoon ground cumin	¼ teaspoon ground cumin
1 teaspoon made mustard	1 teaspoon made mustard
salt and pepper	salt and pepper
50 g butter, melted	2 oz butter, melted
tomato slices to garnish	tomato slices to garnish

Roll out the dough on a floured surface and use to line a 20 cm/8 inch flan tin. Bake blind (see page 108), then leave to cool.

Put the turkey and ham through the mincer. Place in a bowl and add the spices, mustard and salt and pepper to taste. Mix well. Mix in the butter.

Spoon into the flan case and spread out evenly. Garnish with tomato slices and chill before serving.

Serves 4 to 6

Cheesy Vegetable Pie

METRIC	IMPERIAL
175 g quantity Cheese Shortcrust Pastry*	6 oz quantity Cheese Shortcrust Pastry*
1 egg	1 egg
150 ml milk	¼ pint milk
salt and pepper	salt and pepper
350 g mixed vegetables, chopped or sliced and cooked	12 oz mixed vegetables, chopped or sliced and cooked

Roll out the dough on a floured surface and use to line a 20 cm/8 inch flan tin.

Lightly beat the egg with the milk and salt and pepper to taste. Spread the vegetables in the flan case and pour over the egg mixture.

Bake in a preheated moderately hot oven (200°C/400°F, Gas Mark 6) for 30 to 35 minutes or until the filling is set and golden brown. Serve hot or cold.

Serves 4 to 6

Cod and Leek Quiche

METRIC	IMPERIAL
175 g quantity Cheese or Herb Shortcrust Pastry*	6 oz quantity Cheese or Herb Shortcrust Pastry*
75 g butter	3 oz butter
225 g leeks, sliced	8 oz leeks, sliced
225 g cod fillet	8 oz cod fillet
300 ml milk	½ pint milk
50 g flour	2 oz flour
salt and pepper	salt and pepper
1 tablespoon chopped parsley	1 tablespoon chopped parsley

Roll out the dough on a floured surface and use to line a 20 cm/8 inch flan tin.

Melt 25 g/1 oz of the butter in a frying pan. Add the leeks and fry gently for 5 minutes.

Meanwhile, place the cod and milk in a saucepan and poach for about 10 minutes or until the fish will flake easily when tested with a fork. Drain the cod, reserving the milk. Flake the fish, removing any skin and bone.

Melt the remaining butter in a clean saucepan. Stir in the flour and cook for 2 minutes, then gradually stir in the reserved strained milk. Bring to the boil, stirring, and simmer until thickened. Stir in the cod, leeks, parsley and salt and pepper to taste.

Pour the cod mixture into the flan case. Bake in a preheated moderately hot oven (200°C/400°F, Gas Mark 6) for 30 minutes or until the filling is golden. Serve hot.

Serves 4 to 6

Sage and Onion Quiche

METRIC	IMPERIAL
100 g self-raising flour	4 oz self-raising flour
pinch of salt	pinch of salt
50 g butter	2 oz butter
100 g mashed potato	4 oz mashed potato
Filling:	*Filling:*
50 g butter	2 oz butter
2 large onions, sliced	2 large onions, sliced
2 eggs	2 eggs
150 ml milk	$\frac{1}{4}$ pint milk
1 tablespoon chopped fresh sage	1 tablespoon chopped fresh sage
1 teaspoon chopped parsley	1 teaspoon chopped parsley
salt and pepper	salt and pepper
50 g cheese, grated	2 oz cheese, grated

Sift the flour and salt into a bowl. Rub in the butter until the mixture resembles fine crumbs. Add the potato and knead to a smooth dough.

Roll out the dough on a floured surface and use to line a 20 cm/8 inch flan tin. Bake blind (see page 108), then leave to cool slightly.

To make the filling, melt the butter in a large frying pan. Add the onions and fry until softened. Using a slotted spoon, transfer the onions to the flan case and spread out over the bottom. Lightly beat the eggs with the milk, herbs and salt and pepper to taste and pour into the flan case. Sprinkle the cheese on top.

Bake in a preheated moderately hot oven (200°C/400°F, Gas Mark 6) for 20 to 25 minutes or until the filling is set and golden brown. Serve hot or cold.

Serves 4 to 6

Quiches for picnics
Flans and quiches are delightful picnic fare. If baked in an unbreakable or foil dish, they can be easily transported in the dish, thus protecting the pastry. Or cut into wedges and carry in a sturdy rigid container.

For a change, bake the flan or quiche in a rectangular tin such as a roasting tin, and cut into squares to serve.

Because the weather is so unpredictable, picnics are often impromptu affairs. This is why a flan or quiche is an excellent standby to have in the freezer. Bake, cool and open freeze the flan or quiche, place in a rigid container, cover and overwrap. On the morning of the picnic, remove the flan or quiche from the freezer and refresh in the oven or leave to thaw at room temperature. It will be ready for lunch.

Egg and Bacon Pie

METRIC	IMPERIAL
175 g quantity Short-crust Pastry★	6 oz quantity Shortcrust Pastry★
175 g streaky bacon, rinded and chopped	6 oz streaky bacon, rinded and chopped
2 eggs	2 eggs
2 egg yolks	2 egg yolks
150 ml single cream	$\frac{1}{4}$ pint single cream
150 ml milk	$\frac{1}{4}$ pint milk
salt and pepper	salt and pepper
50 g Cheddar or Gruyère cheese, grated	2 oz Cheddar or Gruyère cheese, grated

Roll out the dough on a floured surface and use to line a 20 cm/8 inch flan tin.

Fry the bacon in a frying pan until golden brown. Drain on paper towels, then spread over the bottom of the flan case. Lightly beat the eggs and egg yolks with the cream, milk and salt and pepper to taste. Pour into the flan case. Sprinkle the cheese on top.

Bake in a preheated moderately hot oven (190°C/375°F, Gas Mark 5) for 25 to 30 minutes or until the filling is set and golden brown. Leave to cool for 10 minutes before serving, or serve cold.

Serves 4 to 6

Hot Bean and Ham Quiche

METRIC	IMPERIAL
175 g quantity Shortcrust Pastry★	6 oz quantity Shortcrust Pastry★
40 g butter	1$\frac{1}{2}$ oz butter
25 g flour	1 oz flour
300 ml milk	$\frac{1}{2}$ pint milk
1 × 275 g can broad beans, drained	1 × 10 oz can broad beans, drained
2 tablespoons chopped parsley	2 tablespoons chopped parsley
225 g cooked ham, diced	8 oz cooked ham, diced
salt and pepper	salt and pepper

Roll out the dough on a floured surface and use to line a 20 cm/8 inch flan tin. Bake blind (see page 108), then allow to cool slightly.

Meanwhile, melt the butter in a saucepan. Stir in the flour and cook for 1 minute, then gradually stir in the milk. Bring to the boil, stirring, and simmer until thickened. Add the beans, parsley, ham and salt and pepper to taste and mix well. Heat through gently.

Pour the bean mixture into the flan case and serve hot.

Serves 4 to 6

Pizza Bolognese

If mozzarella or fontina cheese is not available, Cheddar may be used instead.

METRIC	IMPERIAL
4 tablespoons olive oil	4 tablespoons olive oil
100 g back bacon, rinded and chopped	4 oz back bacon, rinded and chopped
1 onion, chopped	1 onion, chopped
1 garlic clove, crushed	1 garlic clove, crushed
1 carrot, diced	1 carrot, diced
1 celery stick, diced	1 celery stick, diced
225 g minced beef	8 oz minced beef
300 ml beef stock, or half stock and half dry white wine	½ pint beef stock, or half stock and half dry white wine
4 tablespoons tomato purée	4 tablespoons tomato purée
salt and pepper	salt and pepper
1 quantity Yeast Pizza Dough*	1 quantity Yeast Pizza Dough*
75 g mozzarella or fontina cheese, cut into strips	3 oz mozzarella or fontina cheese, cut into strips

Heat the oil in a large saucepan. Add the bacon, onion, garlic, carrot and celery and fry until the vegetables are beginning to soften. Add the beef and fry until browned and crumbly.

Pour off the excess fat from the pan, then add the stock, tomato purée and salt and pepper to taste. Stir well, then bring to the boil and simmer for about 25 minutes or until the sauce is thick.

Meanwhile, roll out the risen dough on a floured surface to one large or two smaller rounds about 1 cm/½ inch thick. Transfer to a greased baking sheet and push up the edge of the round(s) to make a rim. Leave in a warm place to rise for 10 to 15 minutes.

Bake the dough base in a preheated moderately hot oven (200°C/400°F, Gas Mark 6) for 15 minutes.

Spread the bolognese sauce over the dough base and arrange the cheese strips on top. Return to the oven and bake for a further 15 to 20 minutes or until the base is cooked through and the top is golden brown.

Serves 2 to 4

Tuna and Cheese Pizza

If liked, a 300 g/10 oz packet of white bread mix may be used instead of the yeast pizza dough. Follow the packet directions.

METRIC	IMPERIAL
1 quantity Tomato Yeast Pizza Dough*	1 quantity Tomato Yeast Pizza Dough*
25 g butter	1 oz butter
1 large onion, sliced	1 large onion, sliced
1 × 200 g can tuna fish, drained and flaked	1 × 7 oz can tuna fish, drained and flaked
175 g Cheddar cheese, grated	6 oz Cheddar cheese, grated
salt and pepper	salt and pepper

Roll out the risen dough on a floured surface to one large or two smaller rounds about 1 cm/½ inch thick. Transfer to a greased baking sheet and push up the edge of the round(s) to make a rim. Leave to rise in a warm place for 30 minutes.

Meanwhile, melt the butter in a frying pan. Add the onion and fry until softened. Drain the onion on paper towels, then spread over the dough base. Scatter over the tuna and sprinkle the cheese on top. Season to taste with salt and pepper.

Bake in a preheated moderately hot oven (200°C/400°F, Gas Mark 6) for 30 to 35 minutes or until the base is risen and golden brown and the topping is golden.

Serves 2 to 4

Sardine Pancake Pizzas

METRIC	IMPERIAL
oil for frying	oil for frying
½ quantity Pancake Batter*	½ quantity Pancake Batter*
1 × 225 g can tomatoes	1 × 8 oz can tomatoes
good pinch of dried mixed herbs	good pinch of dried mixed herbs
300 ml hot Cheese Sauce*	½ pint hot Cheese Sauce*
1 × 100 g can sardines, drained	1 × 4 oz can sardines, drained
50 g cheese, grated	2 oz cheese, grated
black olives to garnish	black olives to garnish

Lightly oil a 25 cm/10 inch pancake or frying pan and heat it. Pour about one-quarter of the batter into the pan and tilt so that the bottom is covered evenly in a thickish layer. Cook until the underside is golden brown, then flip or turn over the pancake and cook the other side. Slide the pancake out of the pan and keep warm while you make three more pancakes.

Tip the tomatoes into a saucepan and add the herbs. Heat through, breaking up the tomatoes with a spoon.

Place a pancake on each of two flameproof serving plates. Spread over half the tomatoes. Cover with the remaining pancakes and spread the cheese sauce on top. Add the rest of the tomatoes and arrange the sardines on top. Sprinkle over the cheese and garnish with olives.

Grill until the sardines are heated through and the cheese has melted. Serve hot.

Serves 2

Quick Potato Pizza

This is an excellent way of using up leftover cooked chicken.

METRIC	IMPERIAL
1 large packet instant mashed potato granules	1 large packet instant mashed potato granules
1 teaspoon dried mixed herbs	1 teaspoon dried mixed herbs
4 tomatoes, sliced	4 tomatoes, sliced
225 g cooked chicken meat, chopped	8 oz cooked chicken meat, chopped
salt and pepper	salt and pepper
100 g cheese, grated	4 oz cheese, grated
4 tablespoons Cranberry Sauce★	4 tablespoons Cranberry Sauce★

Mix the potato granules with the herbs, then make up the potato mixture according to the directions on the packet.

Spread the potato in an even layer on a greased ovenproof plate. Cover with the tomatoes and chicken and season with salt and pepper. Sprinkle over the grated cheese and then top with spoonfuls of cranberry sauce.

Bake in a preheated moderately hot oven (200°C/400°F, Gas Mark 6) for 15 minutes. Serve hot.

Serves 2 to 4

Bacon and Olive Scone Pizza

METRIC	IMPERIAL
1 quantity Scone Dough (see page 146)	1 quantity Scone Dough (see page 146)
1 quantity Tomato Sauce★	1 quantity Tomato Sauce★
6 streaky bacon rashers, rinded	6 streaky bacon rashers, rinded
100 g Cheddar cheese, grated	4 oz Cheddar cheese, grated
6 stuffed olives, halved	6 stuffed olives, halved

Roll out the dough on a floured surface to one large or two smaller rounds about 1 cm/½ inch thick. Transfer to a greased baking sheet and push up the edge of the round(s) to make a rim.

Spread the tomato sauce over the dough, then arrange the bacon rashers on top like the spokes of a wheel. Sprinkle over the cheese and garnish with the olives.

Bake in a preheated moderately hot oven (200°C/400°F, Gas Mark 6) for 20 to 25 minutes or until the base is risen and cooked and the topping is golden. Serve hot.

Serves 2 to 4

Lamb and Kidney Pancakes

METRIC	IMPERIAL
25 g butter	1 oz butter
350 g lambs' kidneys, cored and chopped	12 oz lambs' kidneys, cored and chopped
2 tablespoons flour	2 tablespoons flour
300 ml Beef Stock★	½ pint Beef Stock★
100 g cooked lamb, chopped	4 oz cooked lamb, chopped
salt and pepper	salt and pepper
8 hot Pancakes★	8 hot Pancakes★

Melt the butter in a saucepan. Add the kidneys and fry until lightly browned all over. Sprinkle over the flour and stir in well, then gradually stir in the stock. Simmer, stirring, until thickened. Add the lamb and salt and pepper to taste and heat through gently.

Using a slotted spoon, divide the lamb and kidney mixture between the pancakes and roll them up. Arrange in a warmed serving dish and pour over the liquid. Serve hot.

Serves 4

Pizzas for all

In Italy, the word pizza means a pie, and it can be savoury or sweet, open or covered. When we say pizza, we mean a flat, round, open pie, with a savoury topping. The base can be pastry or bread dough, a large scone, or a pancake. We even make quick snacks with slices of bread and call them 'instant pizzas'.

Freezing pancakes

Pancakes keep very well in the freezer. Stack them, interleaved with greaseproof paper, and wrap the stack in foil or a polythene bag. Seal and freeze. Store for up to 4 months. To use the pancakes, unwrap them and spread out to thaw at room temperature for 30 minutes. Reheat, covered, in a preheated moderately hot oven (200°C/400°F, Gas Mark 6) for 10 to 15 minutes.

Pancakes may also be frozen filled. Pack them in a foil container, separating the layers with foil. Cover and seal. Store for up to 2 months. To serve, unwrap the pancakes and place on a greased baking sheet. Brush with melted butter if not coated with a sauce. Reheat from frozen in a preheated moderate oven (180°C/350°F, Gas Mark 4) for 35 minutes.

Cornish Pasties

Do not make the filling too moist or it will seep out of the pastry. Add only half the stock at first, then gradually add the remainder. For more economical pasties, use lean minced beef instead of rump steak.

METRIC	IMPERIAL
500 g rump steak, diced	1 lb rump steak, diced
2 medium potatoes, diced	2 medium potatoes, diced
2 medium onions, chopped	2 medium onions, chopped
1 small swede, diced (optional)	1 small swede, diced (optional)
2 tablespoons stock	2 tablespoons stock
salt and pepper	salt and pepper
450 g quantity Shortcrust Pastry*	1 lb quantity Shortcrust Pastry*
beaten egg to glaze	beaten egg to glaze

Mix together the steak and vegetables and moisten with the stock. Season to taste with salt and pepper.

Roll out the dough on a floured surface and cut out four rounds about the size of tea plates. Put the meat mixture in the centre of each round. Dampen the edges and bring them up to meet over the filling. Press together to seal and flute.

Place the pasties on a baking sheet and glaze with beaten egg. Bake in a preheated hot oven (220°C/425°F, Gas Mark 7) for 15 to 20 minutes or until the pastry is golden brown, then reduce the temperature to moderate (180°C/350°F, Gas Mark 4). Bake for a further 25 to 30 minutes. Serve hot or cold.

Makes 4

VARIATION

Gammon pasties: Make the filling as above, using 600 g/1¼ lb diced lean cooked gammon instead of steak, and 1 dessert apple, peeled, cored and chopped, instead of swede. Add a pinch of dried sage and use only 1 tablespoon stock.

Cheddar Scotch Eggs

METRIC	IMPERIAL
4 hard-boiled eggs, halved crossways	4 hard-boiled eggs, halved crossways
75 g Cheddar cheese, grated	3 oz Cheddar cheese, grated
25 g butter	1 oz butter
salt and pepper	salt and pepper
350 g pork sausagemeat	12 oz pork sausagemeat
flour for coating	flour for coating
1 egg, beaten	1 egg, beaten
dry breadcrumbs	dry breadcrumbs
oil for deep frying	oil for deep frying

Carefully remove the yolks from the egg white halves. Mash the yolks with the cheese, butter and salt and pepper to taste. Press the mixture into the egg white halves and reshape the four eggs. Divide the sausage-meat into four portions and wrap around the eggs.

Season the flour with salt and pepper and use to coat the eggs. Dip in beaten egg, then roll in breadcrumbs.

Deep fry until crisp and brown. Drain on paper towels and leave to cool before serving.

Makes 4

Stuffed Sausage Loaves

These loaves may also be served cold which makes them ideal picnic fare.

METRIC	IMPERIAL
2 Vienna loaves	2 Vienna loaves
175 g unsalted butter	6 oz unsalted butter
1 kg pork sausages	2 lb pork sausages
2 green peppers, cored, seeded and diced	2 green peppers, cored, seeded and diced
4 sticks celery, chopped	4 sticks celery, chopped
100 g button mushrooms, sliced	4 oz button mushrooms, sliced
350 g cheese, grated	12 oz cheese, grated
2 eggs, beaten	2 eggs, beaten
salt and pepper	salt and pepper

Split open the loaves lengthways, leaving them attached on one side. Scoop out the soft bread centres and spread out on a baking sheet. Dry out in a preheated moderately hot oven (190°C/375°F, Gas Mark 5) until crisp.

Melt half the butter and brush over the insides of the bread shells.

Melt the remaining butter in a frying pan. Add the sausages and fry until browned on all sides. Remove from the pan and cut into 1 cm/½ inch thick slices.

Add the green peppers, celery and mushrooms to the pan and fry, stirring frequently, until softened. Remove from the heat and drain off any excess fat.

Place the crisped bread centres in a polythene bag and crush with a rolling pin to make fine crumbs. Add to the vegetables with the sausage slices, cheese, eggs and salt and pepper to taste and mix well. Fill the bread shells with the mixture. Wrap in foil.

Bake in the moderately hot oven for 25 to 30 minutes or until the bread shells are crisp. Serve hot or cold with salad.

Serves 6 to 8

When planning food for picnics, always remember to include things that will be moist to eat.

Suppers and snacks

Vegetable Tortilla

This is really a flat omelette. Cut it into wedges to serve. It is also very delicious cold and could be taken on picnics.

METRIC	IMPERIAL
25 g butter	1 oz butter
1 large onion, sliced	1 large onion, sliced
1 teaspoon yeast extract	1 teaspoon yeast extract
4 eggs	4 eggs
3 tablespoons water	3 tablespoons water
salt and pepper	salt and pepper
225 g potatoes, cooked and diced	8 oz potatoes, cooked and diced
100 g green beans, cooked	4 oz green beans, cooked

Melt the butter in a 20 cm/8 inch diameter frying pan. Add the onion and fry until softened. Stir in the yeast extract.

Whisk the eggs with the water and salt and pepper to taste and pour into the pan. Stir to mix with the onions. Add the potatoes and beans. Cook gently, stirring occasionally and shaking the pan gently, until the tortilla is set.

Place under the grill and cook for 2 to 3 minutes to brown the top. Serve hot.

Serves 3 to 4

Ham and Noodle Omelette

METRIC	IMPERIAL
8 eggs	8 eggs
salt and pepper	salt and pepper
175 g egg noodles, cooked and chopped	6 oz egg noodles, cooked and chopped
225 g cooked ham, diced	8 oz cooked ham, diced
25 g cheese, grated	1 oz cheese, grated
2 tablespoons chopped parsley	2 tablespoons chopped parsley
50 g butter	2 oz butter

Lightly beat the eggs with salt and pepper to taste. Stir in the noodles, ham, cheese and parsley.

Melt one-quarter of the butter in a frying pan. Pour in one-quarter of the egg mixture and cook over moderate heat, lifting the set edges of the omelette to allow the liquid egg to run on to the pan. When the omelette is lightly set and the underside is golden brown, slide out of the pan on to a plate. Turn back into the pan to cook the other side. Remove the omelette from the pan and keep hot while you cook three more omelettes in the same way.

Serve hot, with a green salad.

Serves 4

Smoked Mackerel Omelettes

METRIC	IMPERIAL
6 eggs	6 eggs
4 tablespoons milk	4 tablespoons milk
salt and pepper	salt and pepper
50 g butter	2 oz butter
225 g smoked mackerel fillets, skinned and flaked	8 oz smoked mackerel fillets, skinned and flaked
tomato slices to garnish	tomato slices to garnish

Whisk the eggs with the milk and salt and pepper to taste. Melt one-quarter of the butter in a frying pan. Pour in one-quarter of the egg mixture and cook over moderate heat, lifting the set edges of the omelette to allow the liquid egg to run on to the pan.

When the omelette is just set, pile one-quarter of the mackerel into the centre. Fold over the omelette and slide on to a warmed serving plate. Keep hot while you make three more omelettes in the same way. Serve hot or cold garnished with tomato slices.

Serves 4

Vegetable garnishes
Vegetable flowers are very pretty garnishes. Radish roses are among the most popular and are very easy to make, especially if you have a special implement that cuts out the central rose shape with one push. If using a knife, make thin cuts aound the radish, almost to the base, to resemble open petals. Cut a second row of petals inside the first, then place the radishes in iced water. They will open out into lovely 'roses'.

Onion chrysanthemums are made in a similar way to radish roses, using pickling onions or the fat white bulbs of spring onions. Do not trim the root off as this will hold the flower together. Make cuts downwards almost to the base, first dividing the onion into quarters, then into eighths, then into sixteenths, etc. Chill in iced water for 1 hour, until the flower has opened up. To lessen the strong onion smell, freeze the onion chrysanthemums, in a polythene bag, for 30 minutes before using.

For tomato roses, only the skin is used. Cut a slice from the stalk end of a tomato, keeping it attached to the skin on one side. Then peel away the remaining skin in a spiral fashion, taking some of the flesh with the skin. Place the slice on a flat surface and wind the skin round to form the rose. Secure with a cocktail stick.

Spaghetti with Simple Sauce

METRIC	IMPERIAL
225 g minced beef	8 oz minced beef
1 large onion, chopped	1 large onion, chopped
1 × 400 g can tomatoes, drained	1 × 14 oz can tomatoes, drained
600 ml Beef Stock*	1 pint Beef Stock*
salt and pepper	salt and pepper
350 g spaghetti	12 oz spaghetti
grated cheese to serve	grated cheese to serve

Fry the beef, in its own fat, in a frying pan until browned and crumbly. Stir in the onion and tomatoes and cook for a further 5 minutes. Add the stock and bring to the boil. Season to taste with salt and pepper, then cover and simmer for 15 to 20 minutes.

Meanwhile, cook the spaghetti in boiling salted water until tender. Drain well.

Place the spaghetti in a warmed serving dish and pour over the sauce. Serve with grated cheese.

Serves 4

VARIATION
Fry 1 crushed garlic clove with the beef. Substitute red wine for half the beef stock, and add ½ teaspoon each dried basil and oregano with the seasoning.

Noodles with Mushroom and Bacon Sauce

METRIC	IMPERIAL
3 tablespoons oil	3 tablespoons oil
100 g bacon, rinded and diced	4 oz bacon, rinded and diced
225 g mushrooms, sliced	8 oz mushrooms, sliced
1 garlic clove, crushed	1 garlic clove, crushed
4 tomatoes, skinned and chopped	4 tomatoes, skinned and chopped
1 tablespoon chopped parsley	1 tablespoon chopped parsley
½ teaspoon dried oregano	½ teaspoon dried oregano
salt and pepper	salt and pepper
350 g egg noodles	12 oz egg noodles
25 g Parmesan cheese, grated	1 oz Parmesan cheese, grated

Heat the oil in a large saucepan. Add the bacon and fry until crisp. Add the mushrooms and fry for a further 3 minutes. Stir in the garlic, tomatoes, herbs and salt and pepper to taste. Cover and cook gently for 5 minutes.

Meanwhile, cook the noodles in boiling salted water until just tender. Drain well and add to the sauce. Fold together gently, then fold in the cheese. Serve hot.

Serves 4

Pasta – shapes and cooking

Pasta has become a basic and popular part of the English diet. Macaroni cheese and spaghetti bolognese are almost thought of as national dishes! But don't limit yourself to macaroni and spaghetti – there are so many different shapes of pasta and they can be used almost interchangeably. Here are some of the shapes available:

canneloni – large tubes that may be ridged; stuffed and served in a sauce
conchiglie – shells; large ones are stuffed
ditali – thimbles
farfalle – bow ties
fettucine – thin, flat noodles
fusilli – twisted spaghetti
lasagne – broad flat noodles; may be green or have ruffled edges
ravioli – little pillows that are stuffed with cheese or meat filling
rigatoni – macaroni that has fine lengthways ridges
stellette – little stars
vermicelli – very fine spaghetti

Pasta can be served in many different ways – as an accompaniment in the same way as potatoes and rice are served (tossed with butter or olive oil, seasonings, herbs, grated cheese, cream etc.), as a starter or main dish topped with a sauce, added to soups and casseroles, or even to make a hot or cold pudding.

To cook pasta, bring a large pan of salted water to the boil (use about 1.5 litres/2½ pints of water to 225 g/8 oz of pasta). Add the pasta gradually so the water does not come off the boil, then simmer, stirring occasionally, until the pasta is *al dente*, or firm to the tooth. Test by removing a piece of pasta, cool it slightly and pinch it between two fingernails or bite it. It should be tender but still firm. According to the freshness and type of pasta, this can take between 3 and 12 minutes.

Spaghetti should be cooked whole in the long strands: do not break them to fit them in the pan. Instead, put in one end of the bunch of spaghetti strands and gradually push in the rest as that in the pan softens.

If you are cooking pasta for a casserole, undercook it a little so it won't be mushy. When cooking lasagne, it helps to add a little oil to the water. This will prevent the sheets of pasta from sticking together.

Drain the pasta and serve immediately, if it is to be served hot. Lasagne or pasta to be stuffed should be dried on a clean tea towel first.

Suppers and snacks

Beef and Spinach Cannelloni

If you cannot find cannelloni tubes, sheets of lasagne may be used instead. Spread them with the filling and roll up like Swiss rolls.

METRIC	IMPERIAL
500 g cannelloni tubes	1 lb cannelloni tubes
salt and pepper	salt and pepper
2 tablespoons oil	2 tablespoons oil
1 onion, chopped	1 onion, chopped
1 garlic clove, crushed	1 garlic clove, crushed
500 g minced beef	1 lb minced beef
500 g fresh spinach, well washed	1 lb fresh spinach, well washed
1 egg	1 egg
75 g Parmesan cheese, grated	3 oz Parmesan cheese, grated
½ teaspoon dried oregano	½ teaspoon dried oregano
25 g butter	1 oz butter
150 ml chicken stock	¼ pint chicken stock

Cook the cannelloni tubes in boiling salted water until just tender. Drain and leave to dry on a tea towel.

Heat the oil in a frying pan. Add the onion and garlic and fry until softened. Add the beef and fry until browned and crumbly.

Meanwhile, cook the spinach, with just the water clinging to the leaves after washing, until tender. Drain well, pressing out all excess moisture, and chop.

Add the spinach to the beef mixture, with the egg, 25 g/1 oz of the cheese, the oregano and salt and pepper to taste and mix well. Divide the filling between the cannelloni tubes and place them, in one layer, in a large buttered baking dish.

Sprinkle over the remaining cheese and dot with the butter. Pour in the stock. Bake in a preheated moderate oven (180°C/350°F, Gas Mark 4) for 30 minutes or until the top is golden brown. Serve hot.

Serves 4 to 6

VARIATION

Golden ham cannelloni: Cook the cannelloni tubes as above. To make the filling, add 175 g/6 oz chopped cooked ham, 4 chopped hard-boiled eggs and 100 g/4 oz fresh breadcrumbs to double quantity coating consistency White Sauce*. Stuff into the cannelloni tubes and chill for 1 hour. Dust with flour, dip into beaten egg and coat with fresh breadcrumbs. Deep fry until crisp and golden and serve hot, with Tomato Sauce*.

> Remember when cooking a stew or casserole to under season, and to cool quickly. If the stew or casserole is to be thickened, use cornflour or thicken when reheating.

Macaroni with Frankfurters

This is macaroni cheese with a difference. If you have any leftover cooked ham or gammon, or cooked sausages, use them instead of frankfurters.

METRIC	IMPERIAL
100 g macaroni	4 oz macaroni
salt and pepper	salt and pepper
300 ml hot Cheese Sauce*	½ pint hot Cheese Sauce*
pinch of cayenne pepper	pinch of cayenne pepper
8 frankfurter sausages, chopped	8 frankfurter sausages, chopped
100 g frozen peas, cooked	4 oz frozen peas, cooked

Cook the macaroni in boiling salted water until tender. Drain well and return to the pan. Add the cayenne to the sauce, then pour into the pan with the macaroni. Stir to coat well.

Add the frankfurters and peas and heat through gently, stirring frequently. Serve piping hot.

Serves 4

Kedgeree

This dish has Anglo-Indian origins, but the popular concoction of rice, fish, eggs and sometimes cream is much more extravagant than its parent, *kitchri* or *khichri*, which combined rice with lentils.

METRIC	IMPERIAL
175 g smoked haddock	6 oz smoked haddock
50 g butter	2 oz butter
175 g cooked long-grain rice	6 oz cooked long-grain rice
3 hard-boiled eggs, chopped	3 hard-boiled eggs, chopped
salt and pepper	salt and pepper
1 egg, beaten	1 egg, beaten

Cook the fish in simmering water for about 10 minutes. Drain and flake, removing any bones.

Melt the butter in a large deep frying pan. Stir in the rice and fish, then add the chopped eggs and salt and pepper to taste. Heat through gently.

Add the beaten egg and cook gently, stirring, until the mixture is creamy. Serve hot.

Serves 4

VARIATION

Use 1 × 200 g/7 oz can red salmon, drained and flaked, instead of the smoked haddock, and 3 tablespoons double cream instead of the beaten egg. Season with a pinch of cayenne pepper.

Chilli Con Carne

For a quicker chilli, use a 425 g/15 oz can red kidney beans, well drained, instead of dried beans. Add the canned beans 5 minutes before the cooking time is finished.

METRIC	IMPERIAL
350 g dried red kidney beans, soaked overnight	12 oz dried red kidney beans, soaked overnight
25 g butter	1 oz butter
1 large onion, chopped	1 large onion, chopped
500 g minced beef	1 lb minced beef
1 × 400 g can tomatoes	1 × 14 oz can tomatoes
2 tablespoons tomato purée	2 tablespoons tomato purée
1–2 teaspoons chilli powder	1–2 teaspoons chilli powder
150 ml Beef Stock★	¼ pint Beef Stock★
salt and pepper	salt and pepper.

Drain the beans and place in a saucepan. Cover with fresh cold water. Bring to the boil and simmer for 1 hour or until tender. Drain well.

Melt the butter in a large saucepan. Add the onion and beef and fry until the beef is browned and crumbly. Stir in the tomatoes with their juice, tomato purée, chilli powder, stock and salt and pepper to taste. Bring to the boil, stirring well. Stir in the beans.

Cover and simmer for 30 minutes. Taste and adjust the seasoning before serving.

Serves 4

Dried vegetables

Dried vegetables should be soaked before cooking. To do this, place them in a bowl, cover with lukewarm water and leave to soak for 8 hours or overnight. If they are left any longer, change the water or the beans may ferment.

When you are short of time, use the quick-soak method. Place the beans in a saucepan, cover with water and bring to the boil. Boil for 2 minutes, then remove from the heat. Leave to soak for 1 hour.

To cook, drain the beans and place them in a saucepan. Cover with fresh water and bring to the boil. Simmer for 1½ to 2 hours or until tender. If the cooking liquid is to be used to make a sauce, alter the method as follows: place the drained beans in a saucepan, cover with water and bring to the boil. Boil rapidly for 10 minutes, then drain the beans and discard the water. Return the beans to the pan and cover with fresh water. Bring to the boil and simmer for 1½ hours or until tender.

Salt should not be added to the beans while they are cooking as it would harden them.

Stuffed Cabbage Leaves

METRIC	IMPERIAL
8 large cabbage leaves	8 large cabbage leaves
salt and pepper	salt and pepper
1 tablespoon oil	1 tablespoon oil
1 onion, chopped	1 onion, chopped
350 g minced beef	12 oz minced beef
500 g frozen mixed vegetables, thawed	1 lb frozen mixed vegetables, thawed
1 tablespoon Worcestershire sauce	1 tablespoon Worcestershire sauce
½ teaspoon dried mixed herbs	½ teaspoon dried mixed herbs
1 × 225 g can tomatoes	1 × 8 oz can tomatoes
2 teaspoons made mustard	2 teaspoons made mustard

Blanch the cabbage leaves in boiling salted water for 2 minutes, then drain well. Remove any coarse stalks.

Heat the oil in a frying pan. Add the onion and fry until softened. Add the beef and fry until browned and crumbly. Stir in the mixed vegetables, Worcestershire sauce, herbs, salt and pepper to taste.

Divide the beef mixture between the cabbage leaves and roll them up, tucking in the sides to make neat parcels. Place in a shallow baking dish.

Chop the tomatoes with their juice and mix with the mustard. Pour over the cabbage rolls. Cover and cook in a preheated moderate oven (180°C/350°F, Gas Mark 4) for 45 minutes. Serve hot.

Serves 4

VARIATION

Chicken stuffed cabbage leaves: Substitute 500 g/1 lb minced cooked chicken meat for the beef. Omit the mixed vegetables and Worcestershire sauce, and add 50 g/2 oz fresh breadcrumbs and a pinch of ground ginger. Omit the mustard and add 150 ml/¼ pint chicken stock with the tomatoes. Increase the cooking time to 1 hour.

Leek and Bacon Casserole

Serve this with baked jacket potatoes to make an unusual and economical mid-week supper.

METRIC	IMPERIAL
75 g butter	3 oz butter
4 leeks, cut into 1 cm pieces	4 leeks, cut into ½ inch pieces
300 ml dry cider	½ pint dry cider
pinch of dried sage	pinch of dried sage
salt and pepper	salt and pepper
2 dessert apples, peeled, cored and sliced	2 dessert apples, peeled, cored and sliced
4 thick streaky bacon rashers, rinded	4 thick streaky bacon rashers, rinded

Melt 50 g/2 oz of the butter in a frying pan. Add the leeks and toss to coat. Fry until golden brown. Stir in the cider, sage and salt and pepper to taste and pour into a casserole.

Cover and cook in a preheated moderate oven (160°C/325°F, Gas Mark 3) for 40 minutes.

Meanwhile, melt the remaining butter in the frying pan. Add the apples and toss to coat. Arrange the apples on top of the leek mixture and cover with the bacon rashers.

Return to the oven, uncovered, and bake for a further 25 to 30 minutes. Serve hot.

Serves 4

Vegetable Hotpot

Take a break from meat and serve this casserole for a mid-week supper. It needs no accompaniment.

METRIC	IMPERIAL
2 tablespoons oil	2 tablespoons oil
2 onions, sliced	2 onions, sliced
3 carrots, sliced	3 carrots, sliced
2 celery sticks, sliced	2 celery sticks, sliced
1 large leek, sliced	1 large leek, sliced
1 × 425 g can red kidney beans, drained	1 × 15 oz can red kidney beans, drained
1 × 400 g can tomatoes	1 × 14 oz can tomatoes
300 ml Beef Stock★	½ pint Beef Stock★
1 tablespoon yeast extract	1 tablespoon yeast extract
salt and pepper	salt and pepper
750 g potatoes, thinly sliced	1½ lb potatoes, thinly sliced
15 g butter	½ oz butter

Heat the oil in a flameproof casserole. Add the onions, carrots, celery and leek and fry until softened. Stir in the kidney beans, tomatoes with their juice, stock, yeast extract and salt and pepper to taste. Arrange the potato slices on top, seasoning each layer with salt and pepper. Dot the top with the butter.

Cover and transfer to a preheated moderate oven (180°C/350°F, Gas Mark 4). Cook for 1½ hours.

Remove the lid and cook for a further 30 minutes or until the potatoes are tender and the top is golden brown. Serve hot, in the casserole.

Serves 4

Beef and Cabbage Bake

METRIC	IMPERIAL
500 g cooked beef, minced	1 lb cooked beef, minced
300 ml milk	½ pint milk
50 g fresh breadcrumbs	2 oz fresh breadcrumbs
1 tablespoon tomato purée	1 tablespoon tomato purée
pinched of dried mixed herbs	pinch of dried mixed herbs
salt and pepper	salt and pepper
1 small cabbage, shredded	1 small cabbage, shredded
25 g butter	1 oz butter

Mix together the beef, milk, breadcrumbs, tomato purée, herbs and salt and pepper to taste. Place in a large baking dish. Cover and bake in a preheated moderate oven (180°C/350°F, Gas Mark 4) for 25 minutes.

Meanwhile, cook the cabbage in boiling salted water until just tender. Drain well, then return to the pan. Add the butter and toss until the butter has melted and coated the cabbage.

Spread the cabbage over the beef mixture. Return to the oven, uncovered, and bake for a further 10 minutes. Serve hot.

Serves 4 to 6

Cauliflower Basket

METRIC	IMPERIAL
1 large cauliflower	1 large cauliflower
salt and pepper	salt and pepper
300 ml hot Cheese Sauce★ (made with half cooking liquid from the cauliflower, if liked)	½ pint hot Cheese Sauce★ (made with half cooking liquid from the cauliflower, if liked)
2 hard-boiled eggs, chopped	2 hard-boiled eggs, chopped
1 tablespoon chopped gherkins	1 tablespoon chopped gherkins
1 tablespoon chopped parsley	1 tablespoon chopped parsley
1 tablespoon chopped chives	1 tablespoon chopped chives
25 g Cheddar cheese, grated	1 oz Cheddar cheese, grated

Cook the cauliflower in boiling salted water until tender. Drain well. Scoop out the centre of the cauliflower and chop it coarsely. Place the outside of the cauliflower (the 'basket') in a flameproof serving dish and keep hot.

Add the chopped cauliflower to the sauce, with the eggs, gherkins, parsley and chives. Mix well, then spoon into the cauliflower basket. Sprinkle over the cheese.

Grill until the cheese has melted and the top is lightly browned. Serve hot.

Serves 4

Welsh Rarebit

Use a strongly flavoured cheese to make this popular savoury.

METRIC	IMPERIAL
25 g butter	1 oz butter
1 egg, beaten	1 egg, beaten
1 teaspoon made mustard	1 teaspoon made mustard
175–225 g cheese, grated	6–8 oz cheese, grated
few drops of Worcestershire sauce	few drops of Worcestershire sauce
salt and pepper	salt and pepper
3 tablespoons ale	3 tablespoons ale
3 tablespoons single cream	3 tablespoons of single cream
4 slices of toast	4 slices of toast

Melt the butter in a heavy-based saucepan. Add the egg, mustard, cheese, Worcestershire sauce and salt and pepper to taste. Cook very gently, gradually stirring in the ale and cream, until the mixture is thick and smooth.

Spread on the toast, leaving a border clear all around as the cheese mixture will run. Grill until golden brown. Serve hot.

Serves 4

VARIATIONS

Buck rarebit: Make as above, then top each serving with a hot poached egg.

York rarebit: Butter the toast and spread with a little made mustard, then top each slice with a thin slice of cooked ham. Warm under the grill for a few minutes. Add the cheese mixture and complete as above.

Cheese Double Deckers

Children will enjoy these attractive sandwiches. With a bowl of soup they make a sustaining lunch.

METRIC	IMPERIAL
225 g Edam cheese	8 oz Edam cheese
4 crisp bread rolls	4 crisp bread rolls
butter	butter
8 lettuce leaves	8 lettuce leaves
2 tomatoes, sliced	2 tomatoes, sliced
4 tablespoons tomato pickle	4 tablespoons tomato pickle
cucumber slices	cucumber slices

Cut half the cheese into four slices and grate the remainder. Make two diagonal cuts almost through each roll. Butter the cut surfaces.

Place half the lettuce, the tomatoes, pickle and cheese slices in one cut, and put the remaining lettuce, cucumber and grated cheese in the other cut.

Serves 4

Toasted Egg, Bacon and Mushroom Sandwiches

METRIC	IMPERIAL
25 g butter	1 oz butter
8 streaky bacon rashers, rinded and chopped	8 streaky bacon rashers, rinded and chopped
225 g mushrooms, sliced	8 oz mushrooms, sliced
2 eggs	2 eggs
1 teaspoon dried mixed herbs	1 teaspoon dried mixed herbs
salt and pepper	salt and pepper
8 slices of buttered bread	8 slices of buttered bread

Melt the butter in a large frying pan. Add the bacon and fry until golden brown. Stir in the mushrooms and fry for a further 4 minutes.

Lightly beat the eggs with the herbs and salt and pepper to taste. Pour into the pan and cook, stirring occasionally, until lightly set and scrambled.

Spread four of the bread slices with the egg mixture and place the remaining bread slices on top, buttered sides down. Toast the sandwiches under the grill until both sides are golden brown. Serve hot.

Serves 4

Hot Ham and Peach Sandwiches

METRIC	IMPERIAL
500 g cooked ham, finely chopped or minced	1 lb cooked ham, finely chopped or minced
50 g fresh breadcrumbs	2 oz fresh breadcrumbs
1 egg, beaten	1 egg, beaten
4 slices of bread, toasted	4 slices of bread, toasted
4 canned peach halves	4 canned peach halves
150 ml hot Cheese Sauce★	¼ pint hot Cheese Sauce★

Mix together the ham, breadcrumbs and egg. Divide into four portions and shape each into a flat cake. Grill for 4 minutes on each side.

Arrange the toast, in one layer, in a shallow flame-proof serving dish, or on a baking sheet. Top each slice of toast with a ham cake. Place a peach half on top and pour over the sauce.

Grill until the sauce is bubbly and golden brown. Serve hot.

Serves 4

Suppers and snacks

Bacon, Potato and Cheese Fry-up

Use leftover cooked potatoes or drained canned potatoes to make this quick, substantial snack. A frying pan with a flameproof handle is needed.

METRIC	IMPERIAL
50 g butter	2 oz butter
1 large onion, chopped	1 large onion, chopped
225 g back bacon, rinded and chopped	8 oz back bacon, rinded and chopped
1 red pepper, cored, seeded and diced	1 red pepper, cored, seeded and diced
750 g potatoes, cooked and sliced	1½ lb potatoes, cooked and sliced
salt and pepper	salt and pepper
175 g cheese, grated	6 oz cheese, grated

Melt the butter in a large frying pan. Add the onion and bacon and fry, stirring occasionally, until the onion is softened. Add the red pepper and potatoes and cook, stirring frequently, for a further 5 minutes.

Season to taste with salt and pepper and scatter the cheese over the top. Place the pan under a preheated grill and cook until the cheese has melted and is golden brown. Cut into wedges to serve.

Serves 4

Curried Ham and Cheese Toasty

METRIC	IMPERIAL
8 slices of bread	8 slices of bread
butter	butter
4 slices of cheese	4 slices of cheese
4 slices of cooked ham	4 slices of cooked ham
1 large banana, sliced	1 large banana, sliced
pinch of curry powder	pinch of curry powder

Spread the bread slices with butter. Cover four slices with cheese and then with ham. Top with the banana slices and sprinkle over the curry powder. Place the remaining bread slices on top, buttered side down.

Toast the sandwiches under the grill until they are golden brown on both sides. Serve hot.

Serves 4

VARIATION
Ham and tomato toasty: Cover four slices of buttered bread, wholemeal if liked, with four slices of cooked ham. Top with tomato slices and chutney. Finish as above.

Speedy sandwiches
More quick sandwich ideas:

Top slices of toast with sliced mushrooms and tomatoes. Grill to heat through. Meanwhile, mix together chopped spring onions and cottage cheese with pineapple. Moisten with a little mayonnaise and spoon on top of the tomatoes. Return to the grill and cook until golden brown.

Mash a can of anchovy fillets, in their oil, with 1 tablespoon grated onion, 2 tablespoons chopped parsley and 1 tablespoon lemon juice. Spread over slices of buttered toast and grill for 2 minutes. Cut into fingers to serve.

Mash a can of sardines, in their oil, with 2 tablespoons mayonnaise, 1 egg yolk and 1 teaspoon dried mixed herbs. Spread over slices of toast and top with slices of Cheddar cheese. Grill until the cheese is melted and bubbling.

Mix a can of flaked crabmeat (after removing all trace of shell and cartilage) with the juice of ½ lemon, 2 tablespoons tomato purée, 25 g/1 oz softened butter and salt and pepper to taste. Pile on buttered slices of toast and top with a slice of tomato. Grill gently for 3 to 4 minutes to heat through.

Fry 1 finely chopped small onion in butter with ½ teaspoon dried sage until softened. Add 225 g/8 oz finely chopped chicken livers and fry, stirring occasionally, until the livers are no longer pink inside. Season to taste and add a squeeze of lemon juice. Pile onto buttered slices of toast or fried bread.

Fry 1 sliced small onion in butter with 225 g/8 oz sliced mushrooms until softened. Stir in 2 tablespoons fresh breadcrumbs, ¼ teaspoon dried mixed herbs and salt and pepper to taste, then bind with 1 beaten egg. Arrange sliced cooked chicken meat on buttered slices of bread and top with the mushroom mixture. Bake in a preheated moderately hot oven (200°C/400°F, Gas Mark 6) for about 20 minutes.

Fry chopped onion and sliced courgettes in olive oil until softened, then stir in a little dried Italian seasoning. Cover buttered slices of bread with sliced hard-boiled eggs and tomatoes, then top with the courgette mixture. Sprinkle over grated cheese and grill gently until the cheese has melted.

Spread garlic- and herb-flavoured cream cheese over slices of wholemeal toast and top with slices of avocado (sprinkled with lemon juice to prevent discoloration) and sprigs of watercress.

Vegetables and Salads

Visiting the greengrocer or fruit and
vegetable section at the supermarket is a
shopping experience that has changed
perhaps more than any other in the last
20 years. New vegetables and salad items
have been introduced so regularly that no
sooner have we become accustomed to a new
item when yet another appears in the shops.
Although this sometimes seems confusing,
it is surprising how we adopt new items as
firm favourites. Avocados, courgettes,
artichokes and corn on the cob would have
been specialty items a few years ago, but
now it would be hard to imagine a good
greengrocer without them. The way we
prepare and present vegetables has changed,
too. Scalloped Potatoes, Cabbage Pancakes
and Stuffed Courgettes, for example, are
a long way from the over-boiled methods
of the past.

Cheese and Potato Ring

The centre of this ring could be filled with other vegetables to make a meatless main dish.

METRIC	IMPERIAL
50 g butter	2 oz butter
750 g old potatoes, coarsely grated	1½ lb old potatoes, coarsely grated
500 g onions, coarsely grated	1 lb onions, coarsely grated
175 g cheese, coarsely grated	6 oz cheese, coarsely grated
salt and pepper	salt and pepper
paprika	paprika

Melt the butter in a frying pan. Add the potatoes and onions and toss to coat. Remove from the heat and mix in half the cheese. Season well with salt, pepper and paprika.

Pack the mixture into a well-greased 20 cm/8 inch ring tin and press down well. Cover and bake in a preheated moderate oven (180°C/350°F, Gas Mark 4) for 45 minutes.

Turn out the ring on to an ovenproof serving plate. Sprinkle over the remaining cheese and return to the oven. Bake for a further 5 to 10 minutes or until the cheese has melted. Serve hot.

Serves 4 to 6

Red Cabbage with Apple

METRIC	IMPERIAL
500 g red cabbage, shredded	1 lb red cabbage, shredded
25 g butter	1 oz butter
1 large onion, sliced	1 large onion, sliced
1 cooking apple, peeled, cored and sliced	1 cooking apple, peeled, cored and sliced
1 tablespoon soft brown sugar	1 tablespoon soft brown sugar
2 tablespoons red wine vinegar	2 tablespoons red wine vinegar
4 tablespoons water	4 tablespoons water
salt and pepper	salt and pepper

Blanch the cabbage in boiling water to cover for 4 minutes. Drain well.

Melt the butter in a large saucepan. Add the onion and apple and cook for 3 minutes. Stir in the cabbage, sugar, vinegar, water and salt and pepper to taste. Bring to the boil, then cover and simmer for 15 minutes or until the cabbage and apple are tender. Stir occasionally and add a little more water if necessary. Serve hot.

Serves 4

Scalloped Potatoes

METRIC	IMPERIAL
750 g potatoes, very thinly sliced	1½ lb potatoes, very thinly sliced
2 onions, thinly sliced	2 onions, thinly sliced
300 ml hot milk	½ pint hot milk
50 g butter	2 oz butter
salt and pepper	salt and pepper

Make alternate layers of the potatoes and onions in a buttered ovenproof serving dish, ending with potatoes. Stir the milk and butter together until the butter has melted, then season to taste with salt and pepper. Pour over the potatoes.

Bake in a preheated moderate oven (180°C/350°F, Gas Mark 4) for about 1¼ hours or until the potatoes are tender and the top is crisp and golden brown.

Serves 6

Boston Baked Beans

METRIC	IMPERIAL
500 g dried haricot beans, soaked overnight	1 lb dried haricot beans, soaked overnight
2 large tomatoes, chopped	2 large tomatoes, chopped
1–2 tablespoons black treacle	1–2 tablespoons black treacle
2 teaspoons made mustard	2 teaspoons made mustard
salt and pepper	salt and pepper
350 g fat salt pork, diced	12 oz fat salt pork, diced
2 onions, thinly sliced	2 onions, thinly sliced

Drain the beans and place them in a large saucepan. Cover with fresh cold water, bring to the boil and boil for 5 minutes. Drain the beans and throw away the water. Return the beans to the saucepan, cover with fresh cold water again and bring to the boil. Simmer for 10 minutes.

Drain the beans, reserving 300 ml/½ pint of the liquid. Pour the liquid back into the pan and add the tomatoes. Bring to the boil and simmer until the tomatoes have pulped. Sieve the mixture and stir in the treacle, mustard and salt and pepper to taste.

Put the beans, pork and onions in a deep casserole and pour over the tomato mixture. Combine thoroughly.

Cover tightly and cook in a preheated very cool oven (120°C/250°F, Gas Mark ½) for about 5 hours or until the beans are very tender. Check halfway through the cooking; if the beans seem dry, add a little boiling water. Serve hot.

Serves 8

Vegetables and Salads

Cabbage Pancakes

METRIC	IMPERIAL
1 small green cabbage, shredded	1 small green cabbage, shredded
salt	salt
1 quantity Pancake Batter*	1 quantity Pancake Batter*
oil for frying	oil for frying

Cook the cabbage in boiling salted water until just tender. Drain well, then mix with the pancake batter.

Lightly oil a 25 cm/10 inch pancake or frying pan and heat it. Pour a little batter into the pan and tilt so that the bottom is covered with a thin layer. Cook over high heat until the underside of the pancake is golden brown, then flip or turn over the pancake and cook the other side. Slide the pancake out of the pan and keep warm while you cook the remaining pancakes in the same way. Serve hot.

Serves 4 to 6

Cottage Potatoes

METRIC	IMPERIAL
4 large potatoes	4 large potatoes
225 g cottage cheese	8 oz cottage cheese
2 tomatoes, skinned and chopped	2 tomatoes, skinned and chopped
1 tablespoon chopped chives	1 tablespoon chopped chives
2 tablespoons single cream	2 tablespoons single cream
salt and pepper	salt and pepper

Prick the potatoes with a fork, then bake in a pre-heated moderately hot oven (190°C/375°F, Gas Mark 5) for 1¼ hours or until tender.

Cool slightly, then cut a slice from the side of each potato. Scoop most of the potato flesh from the skins into a bowl. Reserve the skins. Add the remaining ingredients, with salt and pepper to taste, to the potato flesh and mix together thoroughly. Spoon back into the potato skins and replace the 'lids'. Return to the oven to reheat for about 5 minutes. Serve hot.

Serves 4

VARIATION

Bacon-stuffed potatoes: While the potatoes are baking, fry 75 g/3 oz rinded and chopped bacon until crisp. Drain on paper towels. Scoop the potato flesh from the skins as above and mix with the bacon, 50 g/2 oz butter, 25 g/1 oz chopped walnuts, 50 g/2 oz grated cheese, 1 tablespoon chopped parsley and salt and pepper to taste. Spoon back into the potato skins, replace the 'lids' and reheat for 15 minutes.

Baked Jerusalem Artichokes

METRIC	IMPERIAL
500 g Jerusalem artichokes, peeled	1 lb Jerusalem artichokes, peeled
300 ml milk	½ pint milk
300 ml water	½ pint water
salt and pepper	salt and pepper
100 g mushrooms, chopped	4 oz mushrooms, chopped
1 onion, chopped	1 onion, chopped
25 g butter	1 oz butter
25 g flour	1 oz flour
25 g fresh breadcrumbs	1 oz fresh breadcrumbs
25 g cheese, grated	1 oz cheese, grated

Place the artichokes in a large saucepan with the milk and water and add about ½ teaspoon salt. Bring to the boil, then simmer for about 10 minutes or until tender.

Drain the artichokes, reserving 450 ml/¾ pint of the liquid. Place the artichokes in a casserole and cover with the mushrooms and onion.

Melt the butter in the saucepan. Stir in the flour and cook for 2 minutes, then gradually stir in the reserved cooking liquid. Bring to the boil, stirring, and simmer until thickened. Season to taste with salt and pepper and pour over the vegetables in the casserole.

Cover and bake in a preheated moderate oven (180°C/350°F, Gas Mark 4) for 15 minutes.

Mix together the breadcrumbs and cheese and sprinkle over the top. Bake, uncovered, for a further 15 minutes.

Serves 4 to 6

Roasting potatoes

Roast potatoes are a popular accompaniment to a roasted joint, and are cooked with it in the following way: Peel medium size potatoes that are of an even size, then place them in a saucepan. Cover with water and bring to the boil. Drain well. Lightly score the surface of each potato with a fork. Arrange the potatoes in the roasting tin around the meat (or in a separate tin in which some dripping has been melted) and turn to coat with the fat. Cook for about 45 minutes, turning and basting halfway through the cooking. To test if the potatoes are ready, pierce them with a fine skewer. Drain the potatoes on paper towels, sprinkle with salt and serve hot.

Braised Celery

METRIC	IMPERIAL
3 heads of celery, cut into 12.5 cm pieces	3 heads of celery, cut into 5 inch pieces
15 g dripping or lard	½ oz dripping or lard
2 bacon rashers, rinded and chopped	2 bacon rashers, rinded and chopped
2 carrots, diced	2 carrots, diced
2 onions, chopped	2 onions, chopped
50 g mushrooms, chopped	2 oz mushrooms, chopped
2 tomatoes, skinned and chopped	2 tomatoes, skinned and chopped
1 bouquet garni	1 bouquet garni
300 ml chicken or herb stock	½ pint chicken or herb stock
salt and pepper	salt and pepper

Arrange the celery pieces in a shallow casserole.

Melt the dripping or lard in a frying pan. Add the bacon and fry for 2 minutes. Stir in the carrots, onions, mushrooms and tomatoes and fry until lightly browned. Add the bouquet garni, stock and salt and pepper to taste and bring to the boil.

Pour the vegetable mixture over the celery. Cover and cook in a preheated moderate oven (180°C/350°F, Gas Mark 4) for 1½ to 1¾ hours or until the celery is tender.

Transfer the celery to a warmed serving dish and keep hot. Strain the cooking liquor into a saucepan and bring to the boil. Boil until reduced to a glaze. Pour over the celery and serve hot.

Serves 6

Country-style Beans

METRIC	IMPERIAL
50 g butter	2 oz butter
2 onions, grated	2 onions, grated
2 carrots, grated	2 carrots, grated
450 ml water	¾ pint water
salt and pepper	salt and pepper
750 g French beans	1½ lb French beans

Melt the butter in a saucepan. Add the onions and carrots and fry until softened. Stir in the water and salt and pepper to taste and bring to the boil.

Add the beans and simmer until just tender. Drain off any remaining water and serve hot.

Serves 4 to 6

VARIATIONS
Use cooked or canned butter or haricot beans instead of French beans, and reduce the water to 300 ml/½ pint. Add the beans to the liquid and heat gently.

Glazed Carrots

METRIC	IMPERIAL
75 g butter	3 oz butter
750 g young carrots	1½ lb young carrots
4 sugar lumps	4 sugar lumps
½ teaspoon salt	½ teaspoon salt
chicken stock	chicken stock

Melt the butter in a saucepan. Add the carrots, sugar, salt and enough stock to half cover the carrots. Cook gently, shaking the pan occasionally, until the carrots are tender.

Transfer the carrots to a warmed serving dish and keep hot. Boil the liquid in the pan until reduced to a rich glaze. Pour over the carrots, toss to coat and serve hot.

Serves 6

Moulded Sprouts

METRIC	IMPERIAL
750 g Brussels sprouts	1½ lb Brussels sprouts
salt and pepper	salt and pepper
225 g mashed potato	8 oz mashed potato
25 g butter	1 oz butter
1 egg, beaten	1 egg, beaten
2 tablespoons single cream or top of milk	2 tablespoons single cream or top of milk
¼ teaspoon grated nutmeg	¼ teaspoon grated nutmeg

Cook the sprouts in boiling salted water until tender. Drain well, then purée in a blender or food processor, or sieve them.

Mix the puréed sprouts with the mashed potato, butter, egg, cream or milk, nutmeg and salt and pepper to taste.

Pack into a well-greased 18 cm/7 inch round deep cake tin. Place in a roasting tin and add enough hot water to the roasting tin to come halfway up the sides of the cake tin.

Bake in a preheated moderately hot oven (190°C/375°F, Gas Mark 5) for 45 minutes or until a knife inserted into the sprout mould comes out clean. Leave to cool in the tin for 5 minutes, then turn out on to a warmed serving plate. Serve hot.

Serves 4 to 6

Chips
Potatoes cut into chips are soaked in water before cooking to remove excess starch (which would make them stick together when frying). They must be drained and thoroughly dried before frying because water left on them could make the hot fat spit.

Vegetables and Salads

Baked Stuffed Tomatoes

METRIC	IMPERIAL
8 large tomatoes	8 large tomatoes
1 tablespoon oil	1 tablespoon oil
1 garlic clove, crushed	1 garlic clove, crushed
1 large onion, chopped	1 large onion, chopped
2 celery sticks, diced	2 celery sticks, diced
100 g back bacon, rinded and diced	4 oz back bacon, rinded and diced
50 g fresh breadcrumbs	2 oz fresh breadcrumbs
1 teaspoon dried oregano	1 teaspoon dried oregano
4 tablespoons chopped parsley	4 tablespoons chopped parsley
salt and pepper	salt and pepper
25 g Parmesan cheese, grated	1 oz Parmesan cheese, grated

Cut the tops off the tomatoes and scoop out the insides. Discard the seeds and chop the pulp.

Heat the oil in a frying pan. Add the garlic, onion, celery and bacon and fry until the vegetables are softened. Remove from the heat and stir in the breadcrumbs, herbs, tomato pulp and salt and pepper to taste. Stuff the tomatoes with this mixture. Sprinkle the cheese on top, then replace the tomato 'lids' on a slant.

Arrange in a greased baking dish. Cover and bake in a preheated moderate oven (180°C/350°F, Gas Mark 4) for about 20 minutes or until piping hot and the tomatoes are tender. Serve hot.

Serves 4

Corn Fritters

Serve with sausages, bacon or Chicken Maryland.

METRIC	IMPERIAL
100 g plain flour	4 oz plain flour
2 teaspoons baking powder	2 teaspoons baking powder
¼ teaspoon salt	¼ teaspoon salt
1 egg, beaten	1 egg, beaten
150 ml milk	¼ pint milk
1 × 300 g can sweetcorn kernels	1 × 11 oz can sweetcorn kernels
oil for shallow frying	oil for shallow frying

Sift the flour, baking powder and salt into a bowl. Add the egg and milk and beat to a smooth batter. Drain the sweetcorn, reserving 2 tablespoons of the liquid. Add the reserved liquid and the sweetcorn to the batter and mix well.

Heat the oil in a frying pan. Put spoonsful of the batter into the oil and fry until golden brown on both sides. Drain on paper towels and serve hot.

Serves 4 to 6

Preparing vegetables

Some vegetables, such as aubergine, are salted before cooking to remove any bitterness. Other vegetables, like courgettes, may be salted if they are to be stuffed; the salting removes excess moisture which would make the stuffing too soggy. To salt vegetables, slice them (or prepare as specified in the recipe), then layer on a plate or in a colander, sprinkling each layer with salt. Leave for about 15 minutes. Rinse the vegetables and pat dry with paper towels. The French name for this salting process is *dégorger*.

Sugared Turnips

METRIC	IMPERIAL
750 g turnips, thickly sliced	1½ lb turnips, thickly sliced
salt and pepper	salt and pepper
25 g butter	1 oz butter
1 tablespoon brown sugar	1 tablespoon brown sugar
120 ml chicken stock	4 fl oz chicken stock

Cook the turnips in boiling salted water for 20 to 30 minutes or until almost tender. Drain well.

Melt the butter in the cleaned saucepan. Stir in the sugar until dissolved, then add the stock. Bring to the boil. Return the turnips to the pan and turn to coat with the sauce. Cook gently for 8 to 10 minutes or until the turnips are glazed and tender.

Season to taste with salt and pepper and serve hot.

Serves 4 to 6

Fried Bananas

These are usually served with Chicken Maryland, but are equally good with bacon or ham.

METRIC	IMPERIAL
4 small bananas, or 2 large bananas	4 small bananas, or 2 large bananas
3 tablespoons flour	3 tablespoons flour
salt and pepper	salt and pepper
oil for deep frying	oil for deep frying

If using large bananas, cut them in half. Season the flour with salt and pepper and use to coat the bananas.

Deep fry until crisp and golden brown. Drain on paper towels and serve hot.

Serves 4

Mild Vegetable Curry

METRIC	IMPERIAL
4 tablespoons oil	4 tablespoons oil
2 onions, sliced	2 onions, sliced
1 garlic clove, crushed	1 garlic clove, crushed
1 tablespoon curry powder	1 tablespoon curry powder
1 teaspoon turmeric	1 teaspoon turmeric
1 small cauliflower, broken into florets	1 small cauliflower, broken into florets
4 carrots, sliced	4 carrots, sliced
2 medium turnips, diced	2 medium turnips, diced
1 tablespoon tomato purée	1 tablespoon tomato purée
300 ml chicken stock	½ pint chicken stock
salt	salt
150 ml plain yogurt	¼ pint plain yogurt

Heat the oil in a saucepan. Add the onions and garlic and fry until softened. Stir in the curry powder and turmeric and fry for a further 2 minutes.

Add the cauliflower, carrots, turnips, tomato purée, stock and salt to taste and mix well. Bring to the boil, then cover and simmer for 40 to 45 minutes or until the vegetables are very tender.

Stir in the yogurt and heat through gently without boiling. Serve with boiled rice.

Serves 4

Garlic
Garlic is a much misunderstood seasoning. This member of the onion family is available fresh and should be used sparingly unless the dish it seasons is to be cooked for a long time.

When using garlic uncooked in a salad, try rubbing the salad bowl with the cut side of a garlic clove. Or add a whole or halved garlic clove to the oil or vinegar to be used to make the dressing, and leave to infuse for 24 hours. Never add the crushed garlic clove, raw, to a salad or dressing unless it is intended to have a very strong garlic flavour.

To crush a garlic clove you can use a special implement called a garlic crusher. Or sprinkle the clove with salt (this softens the garlic, making it easy to crush) and crush with the flat side of a knife or the back of a spoon. After preparing garlic for cooking, rinse your hands in cold water, rub with a piece of lemon and then with salt, then rinse in cold water again. Wash with warm water and soap, and the smell should be gone. Garlic on the breath can be covered up by chewing a sprig of parsley!

Steamed Suet Dumplings

These light dumplings will make any dish with which they are served, or in which they are cooked, more satisfying. And they will make it more economical by stretching it further.

METRIC	IMPERIAL
100 g plain flour	4 oz plain flour
1½ teaspoons baking powder	1½ teaspoons baking powder
½ teaspoon salt	½ teaspoon salt
1 tablespoon chopped fresh herbs (see below), or 1 teaspoon dried mixed herbs	1 tablespoon chopped fresh herbs (see below), or 1 teaspoon dried mixed herbs
50 g shredded suet	2 oz shredded suet

Sift the flour, baking powder and salt into a bowl. Stir in the herbs and suet. Add just enough cold water to bind to a soft but not sticky dough.

With floured hands, shape the dough into eight balls. Drop into boiling salted water or stock, or place on a stew or casserole. Cover and simmer gently for 15 minutes or until well risen and fluffy. Drain if necessary and serve hot.

Note: Vary the herbs according to the main ingredient of the soup, stew or casserole. With lamb, use parsley or mint, lemon thyme with veal or chicken, and sage or savory with pork or duck.

Serves 4

VARIATION
Roasted dumplings: If serving the dumplings with a roast, cook them with the meat in the oven. Place them in the hot fat around the joint 20 or 30 minutes before the end of the roasting time. Baste with a little of the fat and roast until risen and golden brown. Drain on paper towels before serving. If liked, finely chopped onion or grated lemon rind may be added instead of the herbs, or in addition to them.

Stuffed Courgettes

Choose medium to large courgettes to make this dish.

METRIC	IMPERIAL
1 large slice of bread, crusts removed	1 large slice of bread, crusts removed
milk	milk
500 g courgettes	1 lb courgettes
4 mushrooms, chopped	4 mushrooms, chopped
2 anchovy fillets, chopped	2 anchovy fillets, chopped
2 bacon rashers, rinded and chopped	2 bacon rashers, rinded and chopped
3 tablespoons grated Parmesan cheese	3 tablespoons grated Parmesan cheese

Vegetables and Salads

½ teaspoon dried basil
salt and pepper
1 egg yolk
1 tablespoon fresh
 breadcrumbs
oil

½ teaspoon dried basil
salt and pepper
1 egg yolk
1 tablespoon fresh
 breadcrumbs
oil

Soak the bread in the milk for 10 minutes, then squeeze dry.

Blanch the courgettes in boiling water for 3 minutes. Drain well. Cut in half lengthways and scoop out the seeds. Discard the seeds. Hollow out the courgette shells and chop the scooped-out flesh. Mix together the chopped flesh, mushrooms, anchovies, bacon, 2 tablespoons of the cheese, the basil and salt and pepper to taste. Bind with the egg yolk.

Fill the courgette shells with the mixture and arrange, in one layer, in a baking dish. Mix the remaining cheese with the breadcrumbs and sprinkle over the tops. Drizzle over a little oil.

Bake in a preheated moderate oven (180°C/350°F, Gas Mark 4) for 40 minutes. Serve hot.

Serves 4

Tomato Stuffed Marrow

If more convenient, canned tomatoes may be used instead of fresh. Use 2 × 400 g/14 oz cans, and drain and mash the tomatoes before adding.

METRIC	IMPERIAL
1 medium marrow, peeled and halved lengthways	1 medium marrow, peeled and halved lengthways
salt and pepper	salt and pepper
75 g butter	3 oz butter
2 onions, chopped	2 onions, chopped
500 g tomatoes, skinned and chopped	1 lb tomatoes, skinned and chopped
75 g fresh breadcrumbs	3 oz fresh breadcrumbs
2 tablespoons chopped parsley	2 tablespoons chopped parsley

Scoop out the seeds from the marrow halves with a spoon. Sprinkle the marrow with salt, then leave to drain for 30 minutes.

Meanwhile, melt 50 g/2 oz of the butter in a frying pan. Add the onions and fry until softened. Stir in the tomatoes, breadcrumbs, parsley and salt and pepper to taste.

Rinse the marrow and dry with paper towels. Put the tomato mixture into the marrow halves, then press them back together. Tie or skewer the marrow to keep the shape and place in a roasting tin.

Melt the remaining butter and pour over the marrow. Bake in a preheated moderate oven (180°C/350°F, Gas Mark 4) for 1 hour, basting once or twice with the butter in the tin. Serve hot, cut into slices.

Serves 4 to 6

Stuffed Mushrooms

These mushrooms may be served as a starter.

METRIC	IMPERIAL
4 large flat open mushrooms	4 large flat open mushrooms
15 g butter	½ oz butter
1 streaky bacon rasher, rinded and diced	1 streaky bacon rasher, rinded and diced
25 g fresh breadcrumbs	1 oz fresh breadcrumbs
50 g Cheddar cheese, grated	2 oz Cheddar cheese, grated
1 tablespoon chopped parsley	1 tablespoon chopped parsley
grated rind of ¼ lemon	grated rind of ¼ lemon
salt and pepper	salt and pepper

Trim the stalks from the mushrooms level with the caps, then chop the stalks finely. Melt the butter in a frying pan. Add the bacon and chopped mushroom stalks and fry until the bacon is crisp. Remove the pan from the heat and stir in the breadcrumbs, cheese, parsley, lemon rind and salt and pepper to taste.

Arrange the mushroom caps, rounded sides down, on a greased baking sheet. Divide the stuffing between them. Bake in a preheated moderate oven (160°C/325°F, Gas Mark 3) for 15 to 20 minutes or until the mushrooms are tender and the stuffing golden brown. Serve hot.

Serves 2 to 4

Creamed Spinach

Many vegetables are delicious creamed in this way.

METRIC	IMPERIAL
1.5 kg spinach	3 lb spinach
50 g butter	2 oz butter
4 tablespoons single cream	4 tablespoons single cream
pinch of grated nutmeg	pinch of grated nutmeg
salt and pepper	salt and pepper

Place the spinach in a saucepan and cover. Do not add any water: there should be enough left clinging to the leaves after washing. Cook until the spinach is wilted and tender, stirring occasionally.

Tip the spinach onto a plate and place another plate on top. Press together to squeeze out all excess water from the spinach. Purée in a blender or food mill, or press through a sieve.

Melt the butter in the saucepan. Add the puréed spinach, cream, nutmeg and salt and pepper to taste and reheat gently. Serve hot.

Serves 4

Minted Orange Salad

Serve this refreshing salad as an unusual accompaniment to roast pork or lamb. For a more sophisticated taste, add 1½ tablespoons brandy to the dressing.

METRIC	IMPERIAL
4 oranges, peeled and thinly sliced	4 oranges, peeled and thinly sliced
1 tablespoon chopped fresh mint	1 tablespoon chopped fresh mint
5 tablespoons olive oil	5 tablespoons olive oil
1½ tablespoons lemon juice	1½ tablespoons lemon juice

Arrange the orange slices, slightly overlapping, on a serving dish. Sprinkle over the mint. Mix the oil with the lemon juice and pour over the oranges.

Serves 4

Baked Bean Salad

METRIC	IMPERIAL
1 × 425 g can baked beans	1 × 15 oz can baked beans
4 spring onions, chopped	4 spring onions, chopped
100 g French beans, cooked and chopped	4 oz French beans, cooked and chopped
1 small green pepper, cored, seeded and diced	1 small green pepper, cored, seeded and diced
3 tablespoons French Dressing*	3 tablespoons French Dressing*

Place all the ingredients in a bowl and fold together gently. Chill lightly before serving.

Serves 4

Orange Pork Salad

METRIC	IMPERIAL
1 large orange	1 large orange
3 tablespoons mayonnaise	3 tablespoons mayonnaise
1 × 350 g can chopped ham and pork, diced	1 × 12 oz can chopped ham and pork, diced
2 heads of chicory, chopped	2 heads of chicory, chopped
4 celery sticks, chopped	4 celery sticks, chopped
4 spring onions, chopped	4 spring onions, chopped

Grate the rind from the orange and mix with the mayonnaise. Fold in the meat.

Remove all the pith from the orange and slice.

Mix together the chicory, celery and spring onions and spread out on a serving plate. Spoon the meat mixture into the centre and surround with the orange slices. Chill lightly before serving.

Serves 4

Sweetcorn Salad

This salad is delicious with hot or cold meats.

METRIC	IMPERIAL
1 × 300 g can sweetcorn kernels, drained	1 × 11 oz can sweetcorn kernels, drained
1 celery stick, chopped	1 celery stick, chopped
1 large tomato, chopped	1 large tomato, chopped
2 tablespoons French Dressing*	2 tablespoons French Dressing*

Mix together all the ingredients. Chill lightly before serving.

Serves 4

Choosing pulses
Pulses, or dried peas and beans, are a rich source of protein, minerals and vitamins, and can be stored in an airtight container for up to 9 months without losing any of their goodness. Buy pulses from a store with a good turnover of stock to be sure they are fresh and haven't been on the shelf for several months before you buy them.

The many types of dried beans include broad or Windsor (large, round, flattish and brown), butter (large, white, kidney-shaped), lima (large, green, oval), flageolet (pale green, oval), haricot (usually white, oval), kidney (large, dark red, kidney-shaped), black-eye (small, white with black spot), pinto or borlotti (brown- or pink-speckled), black, brown and soya (beige, round). Other pulses are whole green peas, split green and yellow peas, chick peas and lentils.

To prepare pulses for cooking, pick them over to remove any grit or stones, then soak overnight in water to cover. (Alternatively, if time is short, cover with water, bring to the boil, then soak for 2 hours.) Discard the soaking water and simmer in fresh water until tender. If the cooking water is wanted for a sauce, etc., bring to the boil and boil for 10 minutes, then discard the water and replace with fresh to complete the cooking. This will reduce flatulence caused by beans.

Vegetables and Salads

Chicken and Avocado Salad

Try some unusual pasta shapes for this salad – small conchiglie, farfalle and stellette, for example. See the information on pasta on page 80.

METRIC	IMPERIAL
175 g pasta shapes	6 oz pasta shapes
salt	salt
1 tablespoon oil	1 tablespoon oil
1 large ripe avocado, peeled, stoned and cubed	1 large ripe avocado, peeled, stoned and cubed
1 quantity French Dressing★	1 quantity French Dressing★
225 g cooked chicken meat, cut into strips	8 oz cooked chicken meat, cut into strips
2 celery sticks, sliced	2 celery sticks, sliced
10 black olives, stoned	10 black olives, stoned

Cook the pasta in boiling salted water until just tender. Drain well. Mix with the oil and allow to cool.

Fold the avocado into the dressing. Add the chicken, celery, olives and pasta and toss together gently. Chill lightly before serving.

Serves 4 to 6

Preparing peppers and tomatoes

If a recipe calls for a green or red pepper to be peeled, this is how to do it. Bake the pepper in a preheated moderately hot oven (200°C/400°F, Gas Mark 6) for 3 to 4 minutes or until the skin chars, then rub off the skin using a rough tea towel. If you have a gas cooker, you can char the pepper by holding it with a long fork in the gas flame.

Tomatoes are skinned in the same way as many fruits; place them in a bowl, cover with boiling water and leave for 30 seconds. Drain the tomatoes and slip off the skins. Some recipes require that the tomato seeds be removed, and this can easily be done with a teaspoon. The seeds are not harmful, but they may spoil the appearance of the finished dish. Also, if making a soup or sauce that is puréed, the seeds may impart a bitter flavour after blending. (If you make the purée with a sieve, there is no need to remove the seeds first.)

Smoked Mackerel Salad

Other smoked fish may be used instead of mackerel. Serve as a main dish salad, with brown bread and butter.

METRIC	IMPERIAL
225 g white cabbage, shredded	8 oz white cabbage, shredded
1 large carrot, grated	1 large carrot, grated
3 tablespoons mayonnaise	3 tablespoons mayonnaise
salt and pepper	salt and pepper
lettuce leaves	lettuce leaves
4 smoked mackerel fillets	4 smoked mackerel fillets
2 hard-boiled eggs, sliced	2 hard-boiled eggs, sliced
watercress or slices of lemon to garnish	watercress or slices of lemon to garnish

Mix together the cabbage, carrot, mayonnaise and salt and pepper to taste. Line a large serving platter with lettuce leaves and spread the cabbage mixture on top.

Arrange the mackerel fillets on the cabbage mixture and top with the egg slices. Garnish with watercress or lemon and serve.

Serves 4

Mixed Bean Salad

METRIC	IMPERIAL
100 g dried haricot beans, soaked overnight	4 oz dried haricot beans, soaked overnight
100 g dried red kidney beans, soaked overnight	4 oz dried red kidney beans, soaked overnight
100 g dried butter beans, soaked overnight	4 oz dried butter beans, soaked overnight
4 spring onions, chopped	4 spring onions, chopped
1 red pepper, cored, seeded and diced	1 red pepper, cored, seeded and diced
1 quantity French Dressing★	1 quantity French Dressing★

Drain all the beans and put them in separate saucepans. Cover with fresh cold water. Bring to the boil and boil for 10 minutes, then drain off the water. Cover with fresh cold water again, bring to the boil and simmer for 1 to 1½ hours or until tender. Drain the beans and cool.

Mix all the beans with the spring onions and red pepper. Fold through the dressing. Chill for 1 hour before serving.

Serves 6

Mixed Vegetable Salad

This is a clever way to use up leftover cooked vegetables.

METRIC	IMPERIAL
2 carrots, cooked and diced	2 carrots, cooked and diced
225 g potatoes, cooked and diced	8 oz potatoes, cooked and diced
100 g peas, cooked	4 oz peas, cooked
100 g French beans, cooked and chopped	4 oz French beans, cooked and chopped
1 × 300 g can sweetcorn kernels, drained	1 × 11 oz can sweetcorn kernels, drained
4 tablespoons mayonnaise	4 tablespoons mayonnaise
salt and pepper	salt and pepper

Place the vegetables in a bowl. Add the mayonnaise and fold together gently. Season to taste with salt and pepper. Chill lightly before serving.

Serves 4

Egg and Potato Salad

Serve this unusual moulded salad with cooked ham or other meats.

METRIC	IMPERIAL
750 g potatoes, diced	1½ lb potatoes, diced
3 hard-boiled eggs, sliced	3 hard-boiled eggs, sliced
1 tablespoon gelatine	1 tablespoon gelatine
2 tablespoons water	2 tablespoons water
3 tablespoons mayonnaise	3 tablespoons mayonnaise
2 teaspoons chopped chives	2 teaspoons chopped chives
1 small onion, grated	1 small onion, grated
salt and pepper	salt and pepper
shredded lettuce to serve	shredded lettuce to serve

Cook the potatoes in boiling water for about 10 minutes or until just tender. Drain well.

Line a 1 kg/2 lb loaf tin with greaseproof paper. Arrange the egg slices to cover the bottom of the tin.

Dissolve the gelatine in the water. Add the mayonnaise, chives, onion, potatoes and salt and pepper to taste and mix well. Spoon into the tin on top of the egg slices. Cover and chill until set.

Line a serving plate with shredded lettuce. Turn the moulded salad out of the tin, using the paper to pull it out gently, and place on the lettuce.

Serves 6

Waldorf Salad

This delicious, crunchy salad is an American favourite. Serve it with cold meats.

METRIC	IMPERIAL
4 celery sticks, diced	4 celery sticks, diced
1 red dessert apple, cored and chopped	1 red dessert apple, cored and chopped
1 green dessert apple, cored and chopped	1 green dessert apple, cored and chopped
50 g walnuts, chopped	2 oz walnuts, chopped
150 ml Mayonnaise*	¼ pint Mayonnaise*

Place all the ingredients in a bowl and fold together gently. Cover and chill before serving.

Serves 4

VARIATION

Curried apple and potato salad: Drain a 750 g/1½ lb can new potatoes. If the potatoes are very small, leave them whole. Otherwise, thickly slice the potatoes. Mix with 1 chopped dessert apple, 2 tablespoons chopped walnuts, 2 tablespoons sultanas, 150 ml/¼ pint Mayonnaise*, 1 tablespoon sweet mango chutney, 1 teaspoon curry paste and salt and pepper to taste.

Winter Macaroni Salad

If preferred, French Dressing* may be used instead of the yogurt dressing suggested here.

METRIC	IMPERIAL
50 g short-cut plain or wholemeal macaroni	2 oz short-cut plain or wholemeal macaroni
salt	salt
2 carrots, chopped	2 carrots, chopped
2 celery sticks, chopped	2 celery sticks, chopped
¼ small white cabbage, finely shredded	¼ small white cabbage, finely shredded
2 dessert apples, cored and chopped	2 dessert apples, cored and chopped
2 tablespoons seeded raisins	2 tablespoons seeded raisins
2 tablespoons chopped walnuts	2 tablespoons chopped walnuts
1 quantity Honey Yogurt Dressing*	1 quantity Honey Yogurt Dressing*

Cook the macaroni in boiling salted water until just tender. Drain and rinse with cold water. Cool.

Mix the macaroni with the vegetables, apples, raisins and walnuts. Fold through the dressing. Chill lightly before serving.

Serves 4 to 6

Vegetables and Salads

Red Cabbage Salad

METRIC	IMPERIAL
2 dessert apples, peeled, cored and thinly sliced	2 dessert apples, peeled, cored and thinly sliced
1 quantity French Dressing* (made with French mustard)	1 quantity French Dressing* (made with French mustard)
500 g red cabbage, finely shredded	1 lb red cabbage, finely shredded
2 tablespoons sultanas	2 tablespoons sultanas
1 bunch of watercress, stalks removed	1 bunch of watercress, stalks removed

Toss the apples in the dressing to coat well. Add the cabbage, sultanas and watercress and mix well.

Serves 4

Simple Rice Salad

METRIC	IMPERIAL
100 g long-grain rice	4 oz long-grain rice
1 × 300 g can sweetcorn kernels, drained	1 × 11 oz can sweetcorn kernels, drained
1 large pickled cucumber, chopped	1 large pickled cucumber, chopped
4 tablespoons French Dressing*	4 tablespoons French Dressing*

Cook the rice in boiling salted water until it is tender.
Mix the cooled rice with the remaining ingredients and chill lightly before serving.

Serves 4 to 6

Nutty Apple Coleslaw

METRIC	IMPERIAL
500 g white cabbage, finely shredded	1 lb white cabbage, finely shredded
1 carrot, grated	1 carrot, grated
1 celery stick, chopped	1 celery stick, chopped
1 onion, finely chopped	1 onion, finely chopped
1 red dessert apple, cored and sliced	1 red dessert apple, cored and sliced
2 tablespoons seeded raisins	2 tablespoons seeded raisins
25 g walnuts, chopped	1 oz walnuts, chopped
150 ml Mayonnaise*	¼ pint Mayonnaise*

Place all the ingredients in a bowl and mix together thoroughly. Chill before serving.

Serves 4 to 6

Mandarin Rice Salad

METRIC	IMPERIAL
225 g long-grain rice	8 oz long-grain rice
salt and pepper	salt and pepper
1 × 300 g can mandarin oranges	1 × 11 oz can mandarin oranges
1 onion, thinly sliced	1 onion, thinly sliced
½ cucumber, diced	½ cucumber, diced
120 ml vegetable oil	4 fl oz vegetable oil
2 tablespoons lemon juice	2 tablespoons lemon juice

Cook the rice in boiling salted water until tender. Drain if necessary and allow to cool.

Drain the mandarin oranges, reserving 3 tablespoons of the syrup. Add the oranges, onion and cucumber to the rice.

Mix the reserved orange syrup with the oil, lemon juice and salt and pepper to taste. Pour this dressing over the rice mixture and fold together gently. Chill lightly before serving.

Serves 4

Some simple garnishes

Many cooks go no further than a little parsley, watercress or mint, or lemon wedges or slices, in garnishing a dish. For some even that is adventurous. But garnishes make a dish more pleasing to the eye, and thus more tempting.

A garnish must be edible, and should never overpower the flavour of the dish, nor the presentation.

Here are some ideas for simple garnishes: gherkins sliced into a fan shape, overlapping slices of stuffed green olives, an anchovy fillet rolled around a caper, twisted slices of cucumber (mark the sides of the cucumber with the prongs of a fork before slicing), sieved hard-boiled egg, croûtons, fried apple or pineapple rings, small raw or cooked vegetable shapes, or chopped chives or spring onions sprinkled over a dollop of whipped cream or soured cream.

To make celery curls, use thick stalks from the celery heart. Cut the stalks into 5 cm/2 inch pieces, then make very fine cuts into the two ends of each piece, cutting about one-third of the way in from each side. If the stalks are very thick, make cuts downwards across the width as well as downwards across the length. Place the pieces of celery in iced water and leave until the ends have curled up.

Puddings

Always leave room at the end of the meal for dessert. Even the most satisfied will find a little space for any one of the delicious recipes in this chapter. Those with a sweet tooth will need no encouragement for recipes like Butterscotch Meringue Pie or Hot Chocolate Soufflé. And there are sturdy steamed puddings for winter days, and even recipes for those with their slim figure in mind. Why not spoil yourself and your family with one of these delicious desserts?

Butterscotch Meringue Pie

METRIC	IMPERIAL
175 g quantity Short-crust Pastry*	6 oz quantity Shortcrust Pastry*
50 g plain flour	2 oz plain flour
100 g soft brown sugar	4 oz soft brown sugar
200 ml milk	⅓ pint milk
50 g butter	2 oz butter
2 eggs, separated	2 eggs, separated
1 teaspoon vanilla essence	1 teaspoon vanilla essence
100 g caster sugar	4 oz caster sugar

Roll out the dough on a floured surface and use to line a 20 cm/8 inch flan tin. Bake blind (see page 108) and allow to cool slightly.

Mix the flour with the brown sugar in a saucepan. Gradually stir in the milk. Bring to the boil, stirring, then remove from the heat. Stir in the butter until melted, then beat in the egg yolks and vanilla essence. Pour into the flan case.

Whisk the egg whites until stiff. Add 2 tablespoons of the caster sugar and continue whisking for about 1 minute or until glossy. Fold in the remaining caster sugar.

Pile the meringue on top of the butterscotch filling, pulling it into peaks. Bake in a preheated cool oven (140°C/275°F, Gas Mark 1) for 30 to 40 minutes or until the meringue is golden brown. Serve hot.

Serves 6

VARIATION

Lemon meringue pie: To make the filling, mix together 4 tablespoons cornflour, 300 ml/½ pint water, the grated rind and juice of 1 lemon and 100 g/4 oz caster sugar in a saucepan. Bring to the boil, stirring, and simmer until thickened. Cool slightly, then beat in 2 egg yolks. Pour into the flan case and cover with meringue as above. Bake in a preheated cool oven (150°C/300°F, Gas Mark 2) for 20 to 30 minutes.

Guards' Pudding

METRIC	IMPERIAL
175 g fresh breadcrumbs	6 oz fresh breadcrumbs
75 g caster sugar	3 oz caster sugar
2 eggs, beaten	2 eggs, beaten
75 g butter, melted	3 oz butter, melted
4 tablespoons raspberry jam	4 tablespoons raspberry jam
¼ teaspoon bicarbonate of soda	¼ teaspoon bicarbonate of soda
1 teaspoon water	1 teaspoon water

Mix together the breadcrumbs, sugar, eggs, butter and jam. Dissolve the soda in the water and stir thoroughly into the mixture. Turn into a well-greased 900 ml/1½ pint pudding basin.

Cover and steam for 2 hours. Serve hot with cream or Custard*.

Serves 4

Steamed Chocolate Chip Pudding

METRIC	IMPERIAL
175 g self-raising flour	6 oz self-raising flour
½ teaspoon baking powder	½ teaspoon baking powder
75 g fresh breadcrumbs	3 oz fresh breadcrumbs
100 g shredded suet	4 oz shredded suet
100 g caster sugar	4 oz caster sugar
100 g plain chocolate, chopped	4 oz plain chocolate, chopped
2 eggs, beaten	2 eggs, beaten
150 ml milk	¼ pint milk

Sift the flour and baking powder into a bowl. Stir in the breadcrumbs, suet, sugar and chocolate. Add the eggs and milk and mix to a soft consistency.

Turn into a greased 1.2 litre/2 pint pudding basin. Cover and steam for 1¼ to 1½ hours.

Turn out and serve hot, with Chocolate Sauce*.

Serves 4 to 6

Steaming puddings

A steamed pudding must be covered before cooking to prevent the steam which condenses on the saucepan lid from dripping on to the pudding and making it soggy.

To cover a rich fruit or suet pudding, place a piece of buttered side down, on top and cover with a piece of foil or a cotton square that is three times wider than the top of the basin. Make a pleat in the centre of the paper and foil or cotton lid to allow for the pudding to expand, then tie on below the rim with string. If not using a cotton lid, make a looped knot in the string so that the pudding basin can be removed from the saucepan. If using cotton, knot the opposite corners of the square together over the basin, thus making a handle.

Cover steamed sponge puddings with buttered foil, tied on securely.

Steamed Sponge Pudding

METRIC	IMPERIAL
100 g butter	4 oz butter
100 g caster sugar	4 oz caster sugar
2 eggs, beaten	2 eggs, beaten
175 g self-raising flour	6 oz self-raising flour
few drops of vanilla essence	few drops of vanilla essence
3 tablespoons milk	3 tablespoons milk

Cream the butter with the sugar until light and fluffy. Beat in the eggs. Sift the flour into the bowl. Add the vanilla essence and milk and mix together thoroughly.

Turn into a greased 1.2 litre/2 pint pudding basin. Cover and steam for 1¼ to 1½ hours. Serve hot, with warmed jam or Fruit Sauce★.

Serves 4 to 6

VARIATIONS

Lemon pudding: Make as above, creaming the finely grated rind of 1 lemon with the butter and sugar. Substitute lemon juice for half the milk.

Fudge pudding: Make as above, increasing the butter to 150 g/5 oz, and using soft brown sugar instead of caster. Replace 1 tablespoon of the milk with golden syrup. Coat the inside of the basin with a generous layer of butter and brown sugar. Serve with Chocolate Sauce★.

Bread and Butter Pudding

METRIC	IMPERIAL
butter	butter
4 large slices of bread	4 large slices of bread
100 g mixed dried fruit	4 oz mixed dried fruit
600 ml milk	1 pint milk
2 eggs	2 eggs
3 tablespoons sugar	3 tablespoons sugar
pinch of grated mutmeg	pinch of grated nutmeg

Butter the bread, then cut each slice into four triangles. Arrange in a pie dish in layers with the fruit.

Heat the milk in a saucepan until it is almost boiling. Lightly beat the eggs with 2 tablespoons of the sugar, then gradually whisk in the hot milk. Strain over the bread and fruit in the dish. Sprinkle the nutmeg and the remaining sugar on top.

Place the dish in a roasting tin and pour in enough hot water to come halfway up the sides of the dish. Bake in a preheated cool oven (150°C/300°F, Gas Mark 2) for about 45 minutes or until the pudding is set and golden brown. Serve hot.

Serves 4 to 5

Hot Chocolate Soufflé

This soufflé is light and very moist.

METRIC	IMPERIAL
75 g plain chocolate	3 oz plain chocolate
300 ml milk	½ pint milk
75 g butter	3 oz butter
50 g flour	2 oz flour
50 g caster sugar	2 oz caster sugar
4 eggs, separated	4 eggs, separated
icing sugar to dredge	icing sugar to dredge

Place the chocolate and milk in a saucepan and heat gently until the chocolate has melted. Remove from the heat.

Melt the butter in another saucepan. Stir in the flour and cook for 2 minutes, then gradually stir in the chocolate milk. Bring to the boil, stirring, and simmer until thickened. Remove from the heat and stir in the sugar until dissolved. Cool slightly, then beat in the egg yolks.

Whisk the egg whites until stiff and fold into the chocolate mixture. Spoon into a greased 15 cm/6 inch soufflé dish and smooth the surface. Bake in a preheated moderately hot oven (190°C/375°F, Gas Mark 5) for 40 minutes or until puffed up. Dredge with sifted icing sugar and serve immediately.

Serves 4 to 5

Almond Noodle Pudding

METRIC	IMPERIAL
225 g vermicelli	8 oz vermicelli
salt	salt
50 g butter	2 oz butter
50 g sultanas	2 oz sultanas
25 g chopped mixed candied peel	1 oz chopped mixed candied peel
75 g flaked almonds	3 oz flaked almonds
¼ teaspoon ground cinnamon	¼ teaspoon ground cinnamon
50 g caster sugar	2 oz caster sugar
2 eggs, beaten	2 eggs, beaten

Cook the vermicelli in boiling salted water until just tender. Drain well, then return to the saucepan. Add the butter, sultanas, peel, 50 g/2 oz of the almonds, the cinnamon and sugar and mix together well. Add the eggs and combine thoroughly.

Pour into a buttered baking dish and sprinkle over the remaining almonds. Bake in a preheated moderate oven (180°C/350°F, Gas Mark 4) for 30 minutes or until golden brown and set. Serve hot, with whipped cream.

Serves 4

Rice Pudding

METRIC	IMPERIAL
3 tablespoons pudding rice	3 tablespoons pudding rice
50 g sugar	2 oz sugar
600 ml milk	1 pint milk
½ teaspoon grated nutmeg	½ teaspoon grated nutmeg
15 g butter	½ oz butter

Mix together the rice, sugar, milk and nutmeg in a shallow baking dish. Add the butter.

Bake in a preheated hot oven (230°C/450°F, Gas Mark 8) for 10 to 15 minutes or until the pudding is bubbling and a skin has formed. Reduce the temperature to very cool (140°C/275°F, Gas Mark 1) and bake for a further 1 hour or until the pudding is soft and creamy and the skin is golden. Serve hot.

Serves 4

VARIATION
Orange meringue rice pudding: Bake as above, reducing the sugar to 25 g/1 oz and the nutmeg to a pinch. Add the grated rind of 1 orange. Whisk 2 egg whites until stiff and fold in 50 g/2 oz caster sugar. Spread or pipe this meringue over the rice pudding. Increase the oven temperature to hot again and bake for a further 10 minutes or until the meringue is set and lightly golden. Serve hot.

Nut Soufflé Omelette

METRIC	IMPERIAL
6 eggs, separated	6 eggs, separated
2 teaspoons caster sugar	2 teaspoons caster sugar
2 tablespoons water	2 tablespoons water
25 g blanched almonds, finely chopped	1 oz blanched almonds, finely chopped
50 g butter	2 oz butter
hot apricot or other jam	hot apricot or other jam

Lightly beat the egg yolks with the sugar and water. Stir in the nuts. Whisk the egg whites until stiff and fold into the mixture.

Melt half the butter in a 15 cm/6 inch omelette pan. Pour in half the egg mixture and cook gently. When the omelette is half cooked, place the pan under the grill and cook until lightly browned.

Make a shallow cut across the centre of the omelette. Spread jam on one half and fold over the other half. Slide on to a warmed serving plate and keep hot while you cook the second omelette.

Serve hot, cut in half.

Serves 4

Orange Baked Apples

METRIC	IMPERIAL
4 large cooking apples	4 large cooking apples
3 tablespoons orange marmalade	3 tablespoons orange marmalade
grated rind of 1 orange	grated rind of 1 orange
2 tablespoons orange juice	2 tablespoons orange juice

Core the apples, then make a cut in the skin around the circumference of each apple to prevent the skin bursting during baking.

Mix together the marmalade, and orange rind and juice. Stuff into the apples and arrange in a baking dish.

Bake in a preheated moderate oven (180°C/350°F, Gas Mark 4) for about 1 hour or until the apples are tender. Serve hot, with cream, ice cream or Custard★.

Serves 4

Puddings on a diet
If you have a tendency to gain weight easily or if you are trying to slim, you will be wise to avoid rich or over-sweetened desserts. Overweight is simply the result of consuming too much food, the excess being stored as body fat, and the only way to lose weight is to cut down on energy-rich foods which contain sugar and starch so that the body will draw on fat reserves for energy.

This doesn't mean you have to cut out desserts from your diet altogether: fruit desserts can be delicious without being too sweet or rich. Plain yogurt makes an excellent substitute for cream in fruit mousses and cold soufflés; fruit such as damsons, cooking apples and pears can be baked with citrus juices (oranges and lemons) and spices; fresh summer berry fruits can be puréed to make a sauce for other fruits such as peaches and apricots; dried fruit can be cooked in spiced water to make a compôte, or further to a purée to be served as a sauce or used as a base for a mousse – just fold in stiffly whisked egg whites. Where fresh or dried fruits are a little tart, use honey for sweetening as it has fewer calories than sugar.

Queen of Puddings

METRIC	IMPERIAL
75 g fresh breadcrumbs	3 oz fresh breadcrumbs
25 g granulated sugar	1 oz granulated sugar
2 teaspoons grated lemon rind	2 teaspoons grated lemon rind
25 g butter	1 oz butter
450 ml milk	¾ pint milk
2 eggs, separated	2 eggs, separated
50 g caster sugar	2 oz caster sugar
2 tablespoons raspberry jam	2 tablespoons raspberry jam
sugar to dredge	sugar to dredge

Mix together the breadcrumbs and granulated sugar. Place the lemon rind, butter and milk in a saucepan and heat until the butter has melted. Pour over the crumb mixture and leave to soak for 30 minutes.

Beat the egg yolks into the crumb mixture, then pour into a well-greased 900 ml/1½ pint baking dish. Bake in a preheated moderate oven (160°C/325°F, Gas Mark 3) for 30 minutes or until firm and set.

Whisk the egg whites until stiff. Fold in the caster sugar. Spread the jam over the top of the baked pudding base, then cover with the meringue. Dredge with sugar.

Return to the oven and bake for a further 30 minutes or until crisp and golden. Serve hot or cold.

Serves 4

Toffee Sultana Pudding

METRIC	IMPERIAL
100 g self-raising flour	4 oz self-raising flour
100 g fresh bread-crumbs	4 oz fresh bread-crumbs
100 g shredded suet	4 oz shredded suet
100 g sugar	4 oz sugar
100 g sultanas	4 oz sultanas
2 eggs, beaten	2 eggs, beaten
milk	milk
brown sugar	brown sugar
2 tablespoons golden syrup	2 tablespoons golden syrup

Sift the flour into a bowl and stir in the breadcrumbs, suet, sugar and sultanas. Add the eggs and enough milk to bind to a sticky mixture.

Grease a 1.2 litre/2 pint pudding basin and coat with brown sugar. Put the golden syrup at the bottom of the basin, then spoon in the pudding mixture.

Cover and steam for about 2 hours. Serve hot, with warmed jam or golden syrup.

Serves 4 to 6

VARIATION

Traditional Christmas pudding: Sift the flour with 1 teaspoon mixed spice, ½ teaspoon ground cinnamon and ½ teaspoon grated nutmeg. Use soft brown sugar instead of granulated. Add 350 g/12 oz seeded raisins, 100 g/4 oz currants, 100 g/4 oz chopped mixed candied peel and 50 g/2 oz chopped blanched almonds with the sultanas. Omit the milk and add 150 ml/¼ pint ale or beer. Add 1 cooking apple, peeled, cored and grated, the grated rind and juice of 1 lemon and 2 tablespoons brandy or sherry. Divide the mixture between two or three greased pudding basins. Cover and steam for 5 hours. Cool, then replace the covers. Store in a cool, dry place, and steam for a further 2 to 3 hours on Christmas Day. Serve with Brandy Butter★.

Orange Chocolate Tart

METRIC	IMPERIAL
225 g quantity Short-crust Pastry★	8 oz quantity Shortcrust Pastry★
2 tablespoons orange marmalade	2 tablespoons orange marmalade
1 large egg	1 large egg
50 g butter, softened	2 oz butter, softened
50 g caster sugar	2 oz caster sugar
40 g self-raising flour	1½ oz self-raising flour
1½ tablespoons cocoa powder	1½ tablespoons cocoa powder
2 tablespoons thawed frozen concentrated orange juice	2 tablespoons thawed frozen concentrated orange juice
milk to glaze	milk to glaze

Roll out the dough on a floured surface and use to line an 18 cm/7 inch flan tin. Reserve the dough trimmings. Spread the marmalade over the bottom of the flan case.

Place the egg, butter and sugar in a bowl and beat until well mixed. Sift the flour and cocoa powder into the bowl and beat in thoroughly. Beat in the orange juice. Pour into the flan case.

Roll out the dough trimmings and cut into strips. Lay over the filling in a lattice pattern. Glaze with milk.

Bake in a preheated moderately hot oven (190°C/375°F, Gas Mark 5) for 30 to 35 minutes or until the filling has risen and set and the pastry is golden brown. Serve warm.

Serve 6

Vanilla essence

To make your own vanilla essence, add 2 split vanilla pods to 250 ml/8 fl oz vodka, cover and leave for 1 month.

Spiced Apple Raisin Crumble

METRIC	IMPERIAL
500 g cooking apples, peeled, cored and sliced	1 lb cooking apples, peeled, cored and sliced
100 g seeded raisins	4 oz seeded raisins
1 tablespoon lemon juice	1 tablespoon lemon juice
2 tablespoons chopped blanched almonds	2 tablespoons chopped blanched almonds
sugar to taste	sugar to taste
Topping:	*Topping:*
100 g plain flour	4 oz plain flour
½ teaspoon ground cinnamon	½ teaspoon ground cinnamon
50 g butter	2 oz butter
50 g sugar	2 oz sugar

Place the apples, raisins, lemon juice and almonds in a baking dish and add sugar to taste. Cook in a preheated moderate oven (180°C/350°F, Gas Mark 4) for 10 to 15 minutes.

Meanwhile, make the topping. Sift the flour and cinnamon into a bowl. Rub in the butter until the mixture resembles fine crumbs. Stir in the sugar.

Sprinkle the topping over the fruit mixture and return to the oven. Bake for a further 25 to 30 minutes or until the topping is golden brown.

Serve hot, with cream or Custard*.

Serves 4 to 5

Nutty Apple Pie

METRIC	IMPERIAL
225 g quantity Short-crust Pastry*	8 oz quantity Shortcrust Pastry*
500 g cooking apples, peeled, cored and thinly sliced	1 lb cooking apples, peeled, cored and thinly sliced
50 g walnuts, chopped	2 oz walnuts, chopped
50 g seeded raisins	2 oz seeded raisins
100 g soft brown sugar	4 oz soft brown sugar
grated rind of 1 lemon	grated rind of 1 lemon
½ teaspoon ground cinnamon	½ teaspoon ground cinnamon
milk to glaze	milk to glaze

Divide the dough into two portions, one slightly larger than the other. Roll out the larger portion on a floured surface and use to line a 23 cm/9 inch pie plate. Mix together the apples, walnuts, raisins, sugar, lemon rind and cinnamon and spoon into the pastry case.

Roll out the remaining dough to make a lid for the pie. Press the edges together to seal. Make a slit in the lid and brush with milk.

Bake in a preheated hot oven (220°C/425°F, Gas Mark 7) for 20 minutes, then reduce the temperature to moderate (180°C/350°F, Gas Mark 4). Bake for a further 35 minutes or until the apples are tender (test with a skewer) and the pastry golden brown.

Serves 4

Pastry – rubbing in

Recipes for pastry instruct you to rub the fat into the flour. To do this, use fat that is firm but not hard. Place the fat in the bowl containing the flour and cut it into small pieces with a table knife through the flour so that the pieces of fat don't stick together. Now switch to your fingertips to rub the pieces of fat and flour together, until the mixture resembles fine crumbs. Don't rub in beyond this point until the crumbs become large and oily because that will result in tough pastry.

Another way to rub in is to use a pastry blender or two table knives. Because you don't touch the fat directly, the heat of your fingertips cannot make it oily, and the resulting pastry is sure to be light.

Pastry: tips for rolling out

All pastry shrinks when it is baked, as water is driven off. However, this shrinkage should not be noticeable, unless the pastry dough was stretched when rolling out and lining the tin. Avoid stretching the dough when rolling out by rolling on a well-floured surface, in the same direction, using a steady even pressure. Leave the rolled-out dough to relax for about 10 minutes before lifting it on the rolling pin and placing it over the tin. Do not stretch it tautly over the bottom of the tin and push it up the sides, but allow plenty of slack. Then chill for 30 minutes before baking.

Freezing pastry

Pastry is another freezer standby. The uncooked dough, divided into usable quantities, can be wrapped in polythene bags and frozen for 3 to 6 months. Thaw completely before using. Unbaked pastry cases can be open frozen and then transferred to a polythene bag. If more than one pastry case is made, interleave the stack with foil, greaseproof paper or freezer tissue. The pastry cases may be baked from frozen, or thawed at room temperature and used as fresh. They will keep for 3 to 6 months.

Puddings

Rhubarb and Ginger Soufflé

This hot soufflé is made with a bread sauce base, rather than the more traditional butter and flour based white sauce.

METRIC	IMPERIAL
500 g rhubarb, chopped	1 lb rhubarb, chopped
50 g sugar	2 oz sugar
50 g butter	2 oz butter
50 g fresh breadcrumbs	2 oz fresh breadcrumbs
200 ml milk	⅓ pint milk
4 eggs, separated	4 eggs, separated
½ teaspoon ground ginger	½ teaspoon ground ginger

Place the rhubarb in a saucepan with half the sugar and a very little water. Poach the fruit until very soft. Drain off most of the liquid.

Place the butter, breadcrumbs and milk in another saucepan and heat, stirring, until smooth and thickened. Cool slightly, then beat in the egg yolks, ginger, remaining sugar and rhubarb. Whisk the egg whites until stiff and fold into the mixture.

Spoon into a greased 15 cm/6 inch soufflé dish. Bake in a preheated moderately hot oven (200°C/400°F, Gas Mark 6) for 35 to 40 minutes or until well risen. Serve immediately.

Serves 4

Sugar Plum Tart

METRIC	IMPERIAL
100 g quantity French Flan Pastry★	4 oz quantity French Flan Pastry★
3 egg yolks	3 egg yolks
1 tablespoon sugar	1 tablespoon sugar
300 ml plain yogurt	½ pint plain yogurt
½ teaspoon ground cinnamon	½ teaspoon ground cinnamon
500 g dessert plums, halved and stoned	1 lb dessert plums, halved and stoned
25 g blanched almonds	1 oz blanched almonds
40 g demerara sugar	1½ oz demerara sugar

Roll out the dough on a floured surface and use to line a 20 cm/8 inch flan tin. Bake blind (see page 108), then allow to cool slightly.

Lightly beat together the egg yolks, sugar, yogurt and cinnamon. Pour into the flan case. Arrange the plums on top, cut sides up.

Bake in a preheated moderately hot oven (200°C/400°F, Gas Mark 6) for 35 to 40 minutes or until the filling is set.

Place an almond in the hollow of each plum half. Sprinkle over the demerara sugar. Grill until the top is golden brown. Serve warm.

Serves 6

Pineapple and Vanilla Pancakes

METRIC	IMPERIAL
300 ml hot Custard★	½ pint hot Custard★
25 g icing sugar, sifted	1 oz icing sugar, sifted
½ teaspoon vanilla essence	½ teaspoon vanilla essence
1 × 425 g can pineapple chunks, drained	1 × 15 oz can pineapple chunks, drained
8 hot Pancakes★	8 hot Pancakes★
icing sugar to dredge	icing sugar to dredge

Mix together the custard, sugar and vanilla essence. Fold in the pineapple.

Divide the mixture between the pancakes and roll them up. Arrange in a warmed serving dish and dredge with icing sugar. Serve hot.

Serves 4

VARIATIONS

Apple cream pancakes: Peel, core and slice 500 g/1 lb cooking apples and cook with ½ teaspoon ground cinnamon and 4 tablespoons rose hip syrup until very soft. Beat to a smooth purée. Divide the apple purée between the pancakes and roll them up. Sprinkle with sugar and top with whipped cream. Serve hot.

Cherry pancakes: Drain a 425 g/15 oz can black cherries and divide between the pancakes. Roll them up and arrange in a baking dish. Sprinkle liberally with flaked almonds and sifted icing sugar. Heat through in a preheated moderately hot oven (200°C/400°F, Gas Mark 6) for 10 mintues. Serve hot with cream.

Baked Bananas

This is a quick and simple pudding.

METRIC	IMPERIAL
25 g butter	1 oz butter
50 g brown sugar	2 oz brown sugar
juice of 2 oranges	juice of 2 oranges
8 small bananas	8 small bananas
desiccated coconut	desiccated coconut

Place the butter, sugar and orange juice in a saucepan and heat until the butter has melted and the sugar dissolved.

Arrange the bananas in a buttered baking dish and pour over the melted mixture. Press a layer of coconut over the bananas.

Bake in a preheated moderate oven (180°C/350°F, Gas Mark 4) for about 25 minutes or until the bananas are tender and the top is golden brown. Serve hot, with cream.

Serves 4

Hawaiian Pudding

METRIC	IMPERIAL
6 canned pineapple rings (can syrup reserved)	6 canned pineapple rings (can syrup reserved)
6 oranges, peeled	6 oranges, peeled
50 g butter	2 oz butter
50 g caster sugar	2 oz caster sugar
4 tablespoons orange juice	4 tablespoons orange juice
75 g nuts, chopped	3 oz nuts, chopped

Place the pineapple rings, in one layer, on the bottom of a buttered baking dish. Put an orange on each pineapple ring.

Melt the butter in a saucepan. Stir in the sugar until dissolved. Remove from the heat and stir in 150 ml/¼ pint of the pineapple can syrup and the orange juice. Pour over the fruit in the baking dish.

Cover and cook in a preheated moderately hot oven (190°C/375°F, Gas Mark 5) for 45 minutes.

Sprinkle the nuts over the oranges, and serve hot with cream.

Serves 6

Apricot and Almond Tart

METRIC	IMPERIAL
175 g quantity Short-crust Pastry*	6 oz quantity Shortcrust Pastry*
1 × 425 g can apricot halves, drained	1 × 15 oz can apricot halves, drained
50 g butter	2 oz butter
2 tablespoons caster sugar	2 tablespoons caster sugar
1 egg	1 egg
1½ tablespoons golden syrup	1½ tablespoons golden syrup
25 g self-raising flour, sifted	1 oz self-raising flour, sifted
50 g ground almonds	2 oz ground almonds

Roll out the dough on a floured surface and use to line an 18 cm/7 inch flan tin. Bake blind (see page 108) and cool slightly.

Arrange the apricot halves, rounded sides up, in the flan case. Cream the butter and sugar together until light and fluffy. Beat in the egg and syrup, then fold in the flour and almonds. Pour over the apricots and spread out evenly.

Bake in a preheated moderately hot oven (200°C/400°F, Gas Mark 6) for about 35 minutes or until the top is firm and golden. Serve hot.

Serves 6

Malvern Puddings

METRIC	IMPERIAL
500 g cooking apples, peeled, cored and sliced	1 lb cooking apples, peeled, cored and sliced
4 tablespoons water	4 tablespoons water
1 teaspoon ground cinnamon	1 teaspoon ground cinnamon
1 teaspoon mixed spice	1 teaspoon mixed spice
sugar to taste	sugar to taste
300 ml hot Custard*	½ pint hot Custard*
25 g cornflakes, crushed	1 oz cornflakes, crushed
25 g nuts, chopped	1 oz nuts, chopped

Place the apples in a saucepan with the water and half the spices. Poach gently until very soft. Add sugar to taste and stir until dissolved.

Divide the apples between six individual flame-proof serving dishes and pour over the custard. Mix together the cornflakes, nuts and remaining spice and sprinkle over the top.

Grill until the tops are golden brown. Serve hot.

Serves 6

Mandarin Custard Crunch

METRIC	IMPERIAL
1 × 300 g can mandarin oranges	1 × 11 oz can mandarin oranges
milk	milk
3 tablespoons custard powder	3 tablespoons custard powder
1 tablespoon caster sugar	1 tablespoon caster sugar
Topping:	*Topping:*
2 tablespoons cocoa powder	2 tablespoons cocoa powder
50 g butter	2 oz butter
50 g soft brown sugar	2 oz soft brown sugar
4 slices white bread, crusts removed and cut into 1 cm cubes	4 slices white bread, crusts removed and cut into ½ inch cubes

Drain the oranges, reserving the syrup. Add enough milk to the syrup to make up to 450 ml/¾ pint. Dissolve the custard powder and sugar in a little of the orange milk. Pour the remaining milk into a saucepan and bring to just below boiling point. Stir into the custard mixture, then pour back into the pan. Simmer until thickened. Fold in the mandarin oranges. Pour into a flameproof dish and keep hot.

For the topping, place the cocoa, butter and sugar in a saucepan and heat, stirring, until melted and smooth. Fold in the bread cubes to coat on all sides.

Pile the topping on the custard. Grill until the topping is crisp. Serve hot.

Serves 4

Puddings

Rich Cherry Batter Pudding

Other fruit in season, such as plums, apples and pears, may be used instead of cherries.

METRIC	IMPERIAL
3 eggs	3 eggs
75 g caster sugar	3 oz caster sugar
75 g plain flour	3 oz plain flour
¼ teaspoon salt	¼ teaspoon salt
250 ml milk	8 fl oz milk
75 g butter	3 oz butter
350 g ripe cherries, stoned	12 oz ripe cherries, stoned
2 tablespoons icing sugar	2 tablespoons icing sugar

Whisk the eggs with the caster sugar until thick and foamy. Sift the flour and salt into the bowl. Add the milk and beat until smooth. Melt 50 g/2 oz of the butter and stir into the batter.

Pour enough batter into a large baking tin to make a 5 mm/¼ inch thick layer on the bottom. Bake in a preheated hot oven (220°C/425°F, Gas Mark 7) for 5 minutes or until just beginning to set.

Spread the cherries over the baked batter base, then pour the remaining batter over the top. Dot with the rest of the butter. Return to the oven and bake for a further 30 minutes or until set. If the top is browning too quickly, cover with foil.

Sprinkle with the icing sugar and serve hot or cold.

Serves 4

Dried Fruit Salad

METRIC	IMPERIAL
600 ml water	1 pint water
2 tablespoons clear honey	2 tablespoons clear honey
1 teaspoon ground cinnamon	1 teaspoon ground cinnamon
2 cloves	2 cloves
2 tablespoons lemon juice	2 tablespoons lemon juice
100 g dried apricots	4 oz dried apricots
100 g prunes	4 oz prunes
100 g dried apples	4 oz dried apples
100 g dried figs	4 oz dried figs
50 g sultanas	2 oz sultanas
25 g walnut halves	1 oz walnut halves
25 g flaked almonds	1 oz flaked almonds

Place the water, honey, cinnamon, cloves and lemon juice in a saucepan and bring to the boil. Stir in the apricots, prunes, apples and figs. Cover and simmer for 15 minutes or until the fruits are softened.

Stir in the sultanas and nuts. Serve hot.

Serves 4 to 6

Apple Pan Dowdy

This apple batter pudding is turned out upside-down to serve.

METRIC	IMPERIAL
3 large cooking apples, peeled, cored and sliced	3 large cooking apples, peeled, cored and sliced
2 tablespoons brown sugar	2 tablespoons brown sugar
2 tablespoons golden syrup	2 tablespoons golden syrup
good pinch of grated nutmeg	good pinch of grated nutmeg
good pinch of ground cinnamon	good pinch of ground cinnamon
100 g self-raising flour	4 oz self-raising flour
pinch of salt	pinch of salt
50 g caster sugar	2 oz caster sugar
1 egg, beaten	1 egg, beaten
4 tablespoons milk	4 tablespoons milk
50 g butter, melted	2 oz butter, melted
sugar to dredge	sugar to dredge

Place the apples in a greased 900 ml/1½ pint pie dish and sprinkle over the brown sugar, syrup and spices. Cover and bake in a preheated moderate oven (180°C/350°F, Gas Mark 4) for 15 to 20 minutes or until the apples are nearly tender.

Meanwhile, sift the flour and salt into a bowl and stir in the caster sugar. Add the egg, milk and butter and whisk until smooth.

Pour the batter over the apples and dredge with sugar. Return to the oven, uncovered. Bake for a further 30 to 35 minutes or until the batter has set and is golden brown. Invert on to a warmed serving dish and serve hot, with cream.

Serves 4

Preventing discoloration of fruit and vegetables

Some fruits such as apples, bananas and avocados (yes, they are a fruit) will discolour if their peeled or cut surfaces are left exposed to the air for very long before serving. For this reason they should be sprinkled with lemon juice immediately after peeling or cutting. Apples can be dropped into cold acidulated water (to which lemon juice or vinegar have been added) as they are chopped or sliced.

Potatoes should be kept covered with water once they have been peeled or they will turn brown. But as with any vegetable, do not prepare them too long before cooking, leaving them soaking in water, as the vitamins they contain will be drawn out into the water.

HOT AND COLD PUDDINGS FOR SPECIAL OCCASIONS

Treacle Tart

METRIC	IMPERIAL
175 g quantity Short-crust Pastry★	6 oz quantity Shortcrust Pastry★
225 g golden syrup	8 oz golden syrup
50 g fresh white breadcrumbs	2 oz fresh white breadcrumbs
grated rind of 1 lemon	grated rind of 1 lemon
juice of ½ lemon	juice of ½ lemon

Roll out the dough on a floured surface and use to line a 20 cm/8 inch pie plate. Reserve the dough trimmings.

Place the remaining ingredients in a saucepan and heat gently until just melted. Pour into the pastry case. Cut the dough trimmings into strips and lay in a lattice pattern over the filling.

Bake in a preheated moderate oven (180°C/350°F, Gas Mark 4) for 30 minutes or until the pastry is lightly browned. Serve warm or cold.

Serves 4 to 6

VARIATION

Dorset treacle tart: For the filling, mix together 5 tablespoons golden syrup, 1 tablespoon black treacle, 50 g/2 oz fresh white breadcrumbs, 1 medium cooking apple, peeled, cored and chopped, and 50 g/ 2 oz mixed dried fruit. Decorate with a lattice of the dough trimmings as above. Bake in a preheated moderately hot oven (200°C/400°F, Gas Mark 6) for 35 to 40 minutes. Serve hot.

Profiteroles

Be sure to slit the side of each bun after baking, to allow the steam to escape. If this is not done, the buns may become soggy and flat.

METRIC	IMPERIAL
1 quantity Choux Pastry★	1 quantity Choux Pastry★
300 ml double cream	½ pint double cream
Sauce:	*Sauce:*
225 g plain chocolate	8 oz plain chocolate
50 g unsalted butter	2 oz unsalted butter
4 tablespoons milk	4 tablespoons milk
2 tablespoons rum (optional)	2 tablespoons rum (optional)

Pipe or spoon the choux pastry in small buns on greased baking sheets, leaving room for spreading. Bake in a preheated moderately hot oven (200°C/ 400°F, Gas Mark 6) for 25 to 30 minutes or until the buns are puffed up and golden brown. Slit each bun and cool on a wire rack.

To make the sauce, place the chocolate, butter and milk in a heatproof bowl over a pan of simmering water and stir until melted and smooth. Remove from the heat and stir in the rum, if using. Keep the sauce warm over the water.

Whip the cream until thick and use to fill the buns. Pile them up in a pyramid on a serving dish and pour over the sauce. Serve immediately.

Serves 4 to 6

French Apple Flan

METRIC	IMPERIAL
175 g quantity French Flan Pastry★	6 oz quantity French Flan Pastry★
500 g cooking apples, peeled and cored	1 lb cooking apples, peeled and cored
100 g golden syrup	4 oz golden syrup
2 teaspoons lemon juice	2 teaspoons lemon juice
100 g apricot jam	4 oz apricot jam

Roll out the dough on a floured surface and use to line a 20 cm/8 inch flan tin. Bake blind (see page 108) and allow to cool slightly.

Grate half the apples and mix with the syrup and lemon juice. Spread evenly in the pastry case. Thinly slice the remaining apples and arrange over the top, in concentric circles, slightly overlapping.

Warm the jam, then sieve it. Brush over the apple slices. Bake in a preheated moderate oven (180°C/ 350°F, Gas Mark 4) for 30 to 35 minutes. Serve hot or cold.

Serves 4 to 6

Baking blind
Flan cases are often baked blind, that is to say empty, if they are to be filled with an uncooked or cold mixture. To bake a flan case blind, prick the pastry all over with a fork, then line it with a piece of greaseproof paper or foil. Cover with a layer of dried beans or rice to keep the pastry from rising during baking. Bake in a preheated moderately hot oven (200°C/400°F, Gas Mark 6) for 15 to 20 minutes or until the sides of the flan are crisp and set. Lift out the paper or foil and beans or rice. Remove the metal ring too if the case is being baked in a loose-bottomed tin. Return the pastry case to the oven and bake for a further 5 minutes to crisp the bottom.

Puddings

Mincemeat and Pineapple Tart

METRIC	IMPERIAL
175 g quantity Rich or Sweet Shortcrust Pastry*	6 oz quantity Rich or Sweet Shortcrust Pastry*
500 g Mincemeat*	1 lb Mincemeat*
1 × 375 g can crushed pineapple, drained	1 × 13 oz can crushed pineapple, drained
1 teaspoon mixed spice	1 teaspoon mixed spice
150 ml double cream	¼ pint double cream

Roll out the dough on a floured surface and use to line a 20 cm/8 inch flan tin.

Mix together the mincemeat, pineapple and spice. Spread over the bottom of the flan case.

Bake in a preheated moderately hot oven (190°C/ 375°F, Gas Mark 5) for 20 to 25 minutes or until set and the pastry is golden brown. Allow to cool.

Whip the cream until thick and use to decorate the tart just before serving.

Serves 6

Chocolate Cream Swiss Roll

METRIC	IMPERIAL
6 eggs, separated	6 eggs, separated
¼ teaspoon vanilla essence	¼ teaspoon vanilla essence
225 g caster sugar	8 oz caster sugar
50 g cocoa powder	2 oz cocoa powder
100 g plain chocolate	4 oz plain chocolate
2 tablespoons water	2 tablespoons water
300 ml Chantilly Cream*	½ pint Chantilly Cream*
whipped cream or more Chantilly Cream to decorate	whipped cream or more Chantilly Cream to decorate

Place the egg yolks, vanilla essence and sugar in a heatproof bowl placed over a pan of simmering water and whisk until very thick and pale. (If using an electric beater, no heat is needed.) Remove from the heat.

Sift the cocoa into the bowl and fold in. Whisk the egg whites until stiff and fold in. Pour into a greased and lined 33 × 21 cm/13 × 8½ inch Swiss roll tin and spread evenly into the corners.

Bake in a preheated moderate oven (180°C/350°F, Gas Mark 4) for 20 minutes or until the cake is springy to the touch. Turn out the cake on to a sheet of greaseproof paper sprinkled with caster sugar.

Melt the chocolate with the water in a heavy-based saucepan and spread over the cake. Cover with the Chantilly Cream, then roll up the cake.

Place the cake on a serving platter and decorate with whipped cream or more Chantilly Cream. Serve soon after filling.

Serves 6 to 8

Rum Babas

If liked, the babas may be filled with fruit instead of, or in addition to, whipped cream.

METRIC	IMPERIAL
40 g caster sugar	1½ oz caster sugar
6 tablespoons lukewarm milk	6 tablespoons lukewarm milk
15 g dried yeast	½ oz dried yeast
225 g strong plain flour	8 oz strong plain flour
½ teaspoon salt	½ teaspoon salt
4 eggs, beaten	4 eggs, beaten
100 g butter, softened	4 oz butter, softened
5 tablespoons clear honey, warmed	5 tablespoons clear honey, warmed
whipped cream	whipped cream
Syrup:	*Syrup:*
225 g sugar	8 oz sugar
300 ml water	½ pint water
grated rind and juice of 1 large orange	grated rind and juice of 1 large orange
4 tablespoons clear honey	4 tablespoons clear honey
5 tablespoons rum (optional)	5 tablespoons rum (optional)

Dissolve 1 teaspoon of the sugar in the milk. Sprinkle the yeast over the top and leave in a warm place until frothy.

Sift the flour and salt into a bowl. Stir in the remaining sugar. Make a well in the centre and put in the yeast liquid, eggs and butter. Beat to make a smooth, soft dough.

Divide the dough between 12 to 16 greased individual baba (ring) moulds, filling them only half full. Cover and leave to rise in a warm place for 30 to 40 minutes or until risen to the tops of the moulds.

Bake in a preheated moderately hot oven (200°C/ 400°F, Gas Mark 6) for 10 to 15 minutes or until golden brown.

Meanwhile, make the syrup. Dissolve the sugar in the water in a saucepan, then bring to the boil. Boil for 1 minute. Remove from the heat and stir in the orange rind and juice, honey and rum, if used.

Place the cooked babas on a wire rack over a tray or baking sheet. Spoon over the syrup to soak the babas. Leave to cool.

Just before serving, brush the babas with the warmed honey and fill the centres with whipped cream.

Makes 12 to 16

VARIATION
Currant babas: Beat in 100 g/4 oz currants with the eggs and butter. Make the syrup with 4 tablespoons golden syrup, 4 tablespoons water and 2 tablespoons rum. After soaking the babas with the syrup, glaze with 3 tablespoons apricot jam heated with 2 tablespoons water.

110

COLD FRUIT PUDDINGS

Apricot Chocolate Rice Cake

This 'cake' is really a cold rice pudding, set with gelatine. Canned apricots can be substituted.

METRIC	IMPERIAL
450 ml milk	¾ pint milk
75 g sugar	3 oz sugar
175 g plain chocolate, grated	6 oz plain chocolate, grated
100 g pudding rice	4 oz pudding rice
few drops of vanilla essence	few drops of vanilla essence
15 g powdered gelatine	½ oz powdered gelatine
2 tablespoons water	2 tablespoons water
50 g butter	2 oz butter
12 apricots, halved and stoned	12 apricots, halved and stoned
300 ml double cream	½ pint double cream

Place the milk, sugar and chocolate in a heavy-based saucepan and bring to the boil, stirring to melt the chocolate and dissolve the sugar.

Blanch the rice in boiling water for 2 minutes. Drain well and add to the chocolate milk. Stir well, then simmer gently for 25 minutes or until the rice is very tender and the milk has been absorbed. Stir in the vanilla essence.

Dissolve the gelatine in the water. Add to the rice mixture with the butter and stir well until the butter has melted. Allow to cool.

Reserve four of the apricots and chop the rest. Fold into the rice mixture. Whip the cream until thick and fold in.

Arrange the reserved apricot halves over the bottom of a greased 20 cm/ 8 inch round loose-bottomed cake tin. Spread the rice mixture on top and chill until set.

Turn out to serve, with cream.

Serves 6

Banana Cream Syllabub

METRIC	IMPERIAL
3 ripe bananas	3 ripe bananas
2 tablespoons lemon juice	2 tablespoons lemon juice
2 tablespoons white wine	2 tablespoons white wine
2 tablespoons caster sugar	2 tablespoons caster sugar
300 ml double cream	½ pint double cream

Mash the bananas with the lemon juice, wine and sugar. Whip the cream until thick and fold into the banana mixture. Spoon into dessert glasses and chill for about 30 minutes before serving.

Serves 4 to 6

Using gelatine
To dissolve gelatine, first sprinkle it over a small quantity of the measured cold liquid to be set. Leave to soak and swell, then add to the remaining liquid. It is a good idea to strain the soaked gelatine into the remaining liquid to be sure that no undissolved particles are there to mar the finished smooth texture of the dish.

The setting strength of gelatine (in other words how much liquid the gelatine will set) varies from brand to brand, so be sure to read the instructions on the packet to be sure you are using the correct amount.

Fresh Orange Jelly

METRIC	IMPERIAL
2–3 large oranges	2–3 large oranges
1 small lemon	1 small lemon
300 ml water	½ pint water
50–75 g sugar	2–3 oz sugar
1 tablespoon powdered gelatine	1 tablespoon powdered gelatine

Pare the rind thinly from the oranges and lemon. Place in a saucepan with the water and bring to the boil. Simmer for 10 minutes.

Strain the liquid into a bowl and stir in the sugar until dissolved. Squeeze the juice from the fruit and add to the liquid. Measure it; it should be 600 ml/1 pint. If not, add more water or orange juice.

Dissolve the gelatine in a little of the liquid, then stir into the remaining liquid. Pour into a dampened mould or basin and chill until set. Turn out to serve.

Serves 4

Gingered Pineapple Dessert

METRIC	IMPERIAL
50 g butter, melted	2 oz butter, melted
75 g ginger nuts, crushed	3 oz ginger nuts, crushed
50 g cornflakes, crushed	2 oz cornflakes, crushed
25 g walnuts, chopped	1 oz walnuts, chopped
1 × 350 g can pineapple chunks, drained and chopped	1 × 12 oz can pineapple chunks, drained and chopped
1 tablespoon ginger marmalade	1 tablespoon ginger marmalade
300 ml thick Custard*	½ pint thick Custard*

Mix together the butter, ginger nuts, cornflakes and walnuts. Combine the pineapple, marmalade and custard. Make alternate layers of the two mixtures in four dessert glasses. Cover and chill before serving.

Serves 4

Puddings

Lemon Refrigerator Cheesecake

Make the crumb crust in a loose-bottomed flan tin.

METRIC	IMPERIAL
350 g cream cheese	12 oz cream cheese
75 g caster sugar	3 oz caster sugar
grated rind of 1 lemon	grated rind of 1 lemon
juice of 2 lemons	juice of 2 lemons
15 g powdered gelatine	½ oz powdered gelatine
2 tablespoons cold water	2 tablespoons cold water
150 ml double cream	¼ pint double cream
1 × 20 cm chocolate Crumb Crust*	1 × 8 inch chocolate Crumb Crust*
grated chocolate to decorate	grated chocolate to decorate

Beat the cream cheese until softened, then beat in the sugar and lemon rind and juice until smooth. Dissolve the gelatine in the water and stir thoroughly into the cheese mixture. Whip the cream until stiff and fold into the mixture.

Pour the cheese filling into the crumb crust. Chill until set.

Remove the metal ring and place the cheesecake on a serving plate. Decorate with grated chocolate.

Serves 6

Biscuit crumb crusts

A biscuit crumb crust is a delicious alternative to pastry for a sweet pie or flan. Many kinds of biscuits can be used – plain digestives, chocolate digestives, ginger nuts, shortbread, bourbon biscuits – even those broken ones sold cheaply at the grocers. To crush the biscuits, place them in a polythene bag and roll over with a rolling pin.

Slightly stale, soft biscuits can be used too. Refresh them in a preheated moderate oven (180°C/350°F, Gas Mark 4) for 15 minutes before crushing.

To make a basic crumb crust, mix 225 g/8 oz crushed biscuits with 100 g/4 oz melted butter. Press over the bottom and up the sides of a 20 cm/8 inch flan dish, then press an 18 cm/7 in flan dish into the crumb mixture to make it an even depth all over. Bake in a preheated moderately hot oven (190°C/375°F, Gas Mark 5) for about 5 minutes or until the edges are browned, then cool. Alternatively, the crumb crust may just be chilled until firm.

Try adding one of the following to the basic crumb mixture: 4–6 tablespoons chopped nuts, a good pinch of ground cinnamon or ginger or grated nutmeg, 1 teaspoon of grated orange or lemon rind, or 25 g/1 oz desicated coconut.

Summer Pudding

If you prefer, use a stale close-textured plain cake, such as Madeira cake, instead of white bread. Cake will make a sweeter pudding.

METRIC	IMPERIAL
500 g raspberries	1 lb raspberries
500 g mixed redcurrants, blackcurrants and strawberries	1 lb mixed redcurrants, blackcurrants and strawberries
75 g sugar	3 oz sugar
3 tablespoons water	3 tablespoons water
1 small loaf of white bread, 1 day old, crusts removed	1 small loaf of white bread, 1 day old, crusts removed

Place the fruit in a saucepan with the sugar and water. Bring to the boil, stirring to dissolve the sugar. Simmer for 1 minute, then remove from the heat and cool.

Cut all but five slices of bread in half diagonally. Place one whole slice on the bottom of a greased 1.2 litre/2 pint pudding basin. Line the sides of the basin with the bread triangles, closely overlapping them. Spoon the fruit into the basin, reserving the juice. Place the remaining whole bread slices on top, cutting them to fit.

Cover with a plate that will just fit inside the basin and place a heavy weight on top. Leave overnight.

The next day, turn out the pudding on to a serving plate. Use the reserved juice to cover any white patches. Serve with whipped cream.

Serves 6

Strawberries Cordon Bleu

METRIC	IMPERIAL
500 g strawberries, hulled	1 lb strawberries, hulled
100 g ratafias or macaroons, crushed	4 oz ratafias or macaroons, crushed
grated rind and juice of 1 orange	grated rind and juice of 1 orange
2 tablespoons caster sugar	2 tablespoons caster sugar
150 ml double cream	¼ pint double cream

Gently mix the strawberries with the ratafia or macaroon crumbs and the orange rind. Divide between four dessert glasses.

Stir together the orange juice and sugar until the sugar has dissolved. Whip the cream until thick, then whisk in the orange mixture. Pile on top of the strawberries. Cover and chill lightly before serving.

Serves 4

Oranges in Caramel Sauce

If you want to serve this dessert for a special occasion you could add 2 tablespoons orange liqueur to the syrup just before serving.

METRIC	IMPERIAL
4 large oranges	4 large oranges
100 g caster sugar	4 oz caster sugar
4 tablespoons water	4 tablespoons water

Thinly pare the rind from the oranges, being careful not to take any of the white pith. Cut the rind into fine shreds and place in a saucepan. Cover with water, bring to the boil and simmer for 10 minutes. Drain well.

Remove all the white pith from the oranges, then slice them thinly. Re-assemble the oranges and secure with cocktail sticks. Place in a small bowl.

Put the sugar and water in a saucepan and bring to the boil, stirring to dissolve the sugar. Boil until the syrup turns a rich caramel colour. Stir in the orange rind shreds. Pour over the oranges. Cover and chill overnight.

The next day, allow the oranges to return to room temperature before serving.

Serves 4

Fresh Fruit Salad

The fruits in this refreshing salad may be varied according to what is in season. If liked, add 1–2 tablespoons orange liqueur for a special occasion.

METRIC	IMPERIAL
100 g sugar	4 oz sugar
300 ml water	½ pint water
juice of ½ lemon	juice of ½ lemon
2 oranges, peeled and segmented	2 oranges, peeled and segmented
2 bananas, thickly sliced	2 bananas, thickly sliced
2 dessert apples, peeled, cored and sliced	2 dessert apples, peeled, cored and sliced
50 g black grapes, halved and pipped	2 oz black grapes, halved and pipped
50 g green grapes, halved and pipped	2 oz green grapes, halved and pipped
1 pear, peeled, cored and sliced	1 pear, peeled, cored and sliced

Dissolve the sugar in the water in a saucepan, then bring to the boil. Boil for 5 minutes. Remove from the heat, stir in the lemon juice and allow to cool.

Place the fruit in a bowl and pour over the syrup. Fold together gently. Cover and leave in a cool place for 2 to 3 hours before serving.

Serves 4

Strawberry Almond Shortcake

METRIC	IMPERIAL
225 g plain flour	8 oz plain flour
¼ teaspoon salt	¼ teaspoon salt
75 g caster sugar	3 oz caster sugar
100 g butter	4 oz butter
50 g almonds, toasted and finely chopped	2 oz almonds, toasted and finely chopped
1 egg	1 egg
3 tablespoons single cream	3 tablespoons single cream
150 ml double cream	¼ pint double cream
25 g icing sugar, sifted	1 oz icing sugar, sifted
225 g strawberries, hulled and sliced	8 oz strawberries, hulled and sliced
toasted almonds to decorate	toasted almonds to decorate

Sift the flour, salt and caster sugar into a bowl. Rub in the butter until the mixture resembles fine crumbs. Stir in the almonds. Mix the egg with the single cream and use to bind the rubbed-in mixture to a soft dough.

Divide the dough in half and press over the bottoms of two greased 20 cm/8 inch sandwich tins. Bake in a preheated hot oven (220°C/425°F, Gas Mark 7) for 15 to 20 minutes or until lightly browned. Cool on a wire rack.

Whip the double cream with the icing sugar until thick. Fold two-thirds of the cream into the strawberries.

Place one of the shortcake rounds on a serving plate. Pile the strawberry and cream mixture on top. Place the second shortcake round on the filling and press down lightly. Decorate the top with the remaining whipped cream and toasted almonds.

Serves 4 to 6

Orange and Banana Dessert

METRIC	IMPERIAL
2 oranges, peeled and sliced	2 oranges, peeled and sliced
4 bananas, sliced	4 bananas, sliced
2 tablespoons lemon juice	2 tablespoons lemon juice
1 egg white	1 egg white
150 ml orange or mandarin flavoured yogurt	¼ pint orange or mandarin flavoured yogurt

Mix together the oranges, bananas and lemon juice. Whisk the egg white and fold into the yogurt. Fold through the fruit mixture.

Divide between dessert glasses and serve.

Serves 4

Strawberry Cheesecake

This baked cheesecake is made with curd or cottage cheese instead of the richer cream cheese. It is no less delicious, though, and is a luscious dessert to serve when strawberries are in season.

METRIC	IMPERIAL
1 × 20 cm Crumb Crust★	1 × 8 inch Crumb Crust★
150 ml double cream	¼ pint double cream
175–225 g strawberries	6–8 oz strawberries
Filling:	*Filling:*
500 g curd or cottage cheese, sieved	1 lb curd or cottage cheese, sieved
100 g caster sugar	4 oz caster sugar
grated rind of 1 lemon	grated rind of 1 lemon
1 large egg, beaten	1 large egg, beaten
25 g sultanas	1 oz sultanas
milk to glaze	milk to glaze

Beat together the cheese, sugar, lemon rind and egg until smooth. Fold in the sultanas. Spoon into the crumb crust and spread out evenly. Brush the top of the filling with milk.

Bake in a preheated moderately hot oven (190°C/375°F, Gas Mark 5) for 40 to 45 minutes or until the filling is firm. Leave to cool.

Whip the cream until thick. Spread or pipe over the top of the cheesecake and decorate with the strawberries, whole or sliced.

Serves 8

Nuts

To toast almonds, first blanch them by placing them in a bowl and covering with boiling water. Leave until cool, then drain and push off the skins with your fingers. Rinse the nuts and dry thoroughly. Spread out on a baking sheet and toast in a preheated moderate oven (180°C/350°F, Gas Mark 4) for 7 to 8 minutes. The almonds may be chopped, shredded or flaked before toasting.

Shelled hazelnuts are skinned after toasting. Bake as above, then rub briskly in a rough cloth to remove the skins.

To skin chestnuts, place them in a saucepan, cover with water and bring to the boil. Remove the pan from the heat. Take the chestnuts from the pan one at a time, using a slotted spoon, and remove the peel and inner skin, using a small sharp knife. Hold the nuts in a tea towel as you do this because they will be hot. If the skins don't come away easily, return the nuts to the hot water for a few more minutes.

Strawberry Meringue Gâteau

METRIC	IMPERIAL
50 g butter	2 oz butter
350 g caster sugar	12 oz caster sugar
4 eggs, separated	4 eggs, separated
100 g self-raising flour, sifted	4 oz self-raising flour, sifted
5 tablespoons milk	5 tablespoons milk
1 tablespoon chopped almonds	1 tablespoon chopped almonds
150 ml double cream	¼ pint double cream
175 g strawberries, halved	6 oz strawberries, halved

Cream the butter with 100 g/4 oz of the sugar until light and fluffy. Beat in the egg yolks one at a time, adding a tablespoon of flour with each. Fold in the remaining flour alternately with the milk. Divide the mixture between two greased and lined 23 cm/9 inch sandwich tins.

Whisk the egg whites until stiff, then gradually whisk in the remaining sugar. Spread evenly over the cake mixture and sprinkle with the almonds.

Bake in a preheated moderate oven (180°C/350°F, Gas Mark 4) for 35 to 40 minutes or until the meringue is crisp. Cool on a wire rack.

Whip the cream until thick. Sandwich the cake layers together with the cream and strawberries.

Cream Horns

METRIC	IMPERIAL
350 g frozen puff pastry, thawed	12 oz frozen puff pastry, thawed
1 egg, beaten	1 egg, beaten
3 tablespoons sugar	3 tablespoons sugar
100 g jam	4 oz jam
300 ml Chantilly Cream★	½ pint Chantilly Cream★
12 strawberries	12 strawberries

Roll out the dough on a floured surface to about 5 mm/¼ inch thick. Cut into 12 long strips about 2.5 cm/1 inch wide. Brush one side of each strip with water, then wind around the outside of 12 greased cream horn tins, slightly overlapping the dough so there are no gaps. Brush with beaten egg and sprinkle with the sugar.

Place on a baking sheet and bake in a preheated hot oven (230°C/450°F, Gas Mark 8) for 20 to 25 minutes or until puffed and golden brown. Cool.

When cold, remove the tins carefully from the pastry. Put a spoonful of jam into the bottom of the pastry horns, then fill with the cream. Top each horn with a strawberry.

Makes 12

Preparing a soufflé dish

To prepare a soufflé dish for a cold soufflé, fold a piece of greaseproof paper or foil in half and tie it around the dish so that the paper or foil extends 5 cm/2 inches above the rim. Alternatively, the paper collar may be secured with clear sticky tape. Brush the inside of the dish and the paper collar with melted butter.

To remove the paper collar from the set soufflé, carefully run a warmed knife around the soufflé, between it and the paper collar. Then peel off the collar.

Orange and Lemon Soufflé

This cold soufflé, set with gelatine, is not as rich as soufflés made with double cream. Plain yogurt is used here and the result is tart-sweet and refreshing.

METRIC	IMPERIAL
4 eggs, separated	4 eggs, separated
100 g light brown sugar	4 oz light brown sugar
grated rind and juice of 2 lemons	grated rind and juice of 2 lemons
grated rind and juice of 2 oranges	grated rind and juice of 2 oranges
15 g powdered gelatine	½ oz powdered gelatine
150 ml plain yogurt	¼ pint plain yogurt

Prepare an 18 cm/7 inch soufflé dish (see above).

Place the egg yolks, sugar, lemon rind and juice, orange rind and half the orange juice in a heatproof bowl placed over a pan of hot water. Whisk until very thick and the mixture will make a ribbon trail on itself when the whisk is lifted. Remove from the heat and continue whisking until cool. (If using an electric beater, no heat is needed.)

Dissolve the gelatine in the remaining orange juice. Add to the whisked mixture with the yogurt and mix together thoroughly.

Whisk the egg whites until stiff and fold into the mixture. Spoon into the soufflé dish and chill until set. Carefully peel off the paper collar before serving.

Serves 4 to 6

VARIATION

Orange and almond soufflé: Use the grated rind and juice of 3 oranges and 1 lemon. Replace the brown sugar with caster sugar, and add a few drops of almond essence with the yogurt. After peeling off the paper collar from the set soufflé, press crushed macaroons on to the side. Decorate the top of the soufflé with piped whipped cream and toasted flaked almonds.

Blackberry and Apple Mousse

METRIC	IMPERIAL
500 g cooking apples, peeled, cored and sliced	1 lb cooking apples, peeled, cored and sliced
100 g blackberries	4 oz blackberries
100 g sugar	4 oz sugar
150 ml water	¼ pint water
15 g powdered gelatine	½ oz powdered gelatine
juice of 1 lemon	juice of 1 lemon
2 egg whites	2 egg whites

Place the apples, blackberries, half the sugar and the water in a saucepan. Poach gently, covered, until very tender.

Sieve the fruit mixture into a bowl. Dissolve the gelatine in the lemon juice and stir into the fruit purée. Cool until beginning to thicken.

Whisk the egg whites until stiff. Gradually whisk in the remaining sugar. Fold into the fruit mixture.

Divide between dessert glasses and chill until set.

Serves 4

Caramel Delight

This quickly-made dessert will have everyone guessing how you made it.

METRIC	IMPERIAL
3 Mars bars	3 Mars bars
1 tablespoon instant coffee powder	1 tablespoon instant coffee powder
2 tablespoons hot water	2 tablespoons hot water
6 egg whites	6 egg whites
grated chocolate to decorate	grated chocolate to decorate

Melt the Mars bars in a heatproof bowl over a pan of hot water. Remove from the heat. Dissolve the coffee in the water and add to the Mars bars. Whisk well until smooth, then leave to cool.

Whisk the egg whites until stiff. Fold into the coffee caramel mixture. Spoon into individual dessert glasses and chill for about 30 minutes before serving.

Sprinkle with grated chocolate to decorate.

Serves 4 to 6

Macerating fruits

Fruits may be soaked in a liquid before serving or cooking. This process, called maceration, is just to flavour, and the liquid usually includes brandy, wine or a liqueur.

Puddings

Baked Custards

METRIC	IMPERIAL
4 eggs	4 eggs
25 g caster sugar	1 oz caster sugar
600 ml milk	1 pint milk
To decorate:	*To decorate:*
whipped cream	whipped cream
25 g toasted flaked	1 oz toasted flaked
almonds	almonds

Lightly beat the eggs with the sugar until the sugar has dissolved. Heat the milk until almost boiling, then whisk into the egg mixture. Strain into four individual baking dishes.

Place the dishes in a roasting tin and pour enough boiling water around them to come halfway up the sides of the dishes. Bake in a preheated moderate oven (160°C/325°F, Gas Mark 3) for 25 to 30 minutes or until set. Leave to cool completely.

Decorate each custard with a whirl of cream and a few almonds. Chill before serving.

Serves 4

VARIATIONS

Crème caramel: Dissolve 100 g/4 oz caster sugar in 4 tablespoons water, then bring to the boil and boil until the syrup turns a golden caramel colour. Divide the caramel syrup between four 150 ml/¼ pint dariole moulds and tilt the moulds so the caramel coats the insides evenly. Make the custard as above, using 2 eggs, 25 g/1 oz caster sugar and 450 ml/¾ pint milk. Flavour with a few drops of vanilla essence, if liked. Strain the custard into the moulds. Bake in a water bath as above in a preheated moderately hot oven (190°C/375°F, Gas Mark 5) for 45 minutes or until set. Cool, then chill well. Unmould to serve. Alternatively, crème caramel may be made in a 600 ml/1 pint mould. Bake for about 1 hour.

Caramelized rich custard: Make the custard as above, using 4 egg yolks, 50 g/2 oz caster sugar, 600 ml/1 pint double cream and 1 teaspoon vanilla essence. Strain into a shallow baking dish and bake in a water bath as above in a preheated cool oven (150°C/300°F, Gas Mark 2) for 1 hour or until set. Cool and chill overnight. Sprinkle 25 g/1 oz caster sugar over the top of the custard and grill until the sugar melts and caramelizes. Cool before serving.

Custard tart: Line an 18 cm/7 inch flan tin with 175 g/6 oz quantity Shortcrust Pastry*. Make the custard as above, using 2 eggs, 25 g/1 oz caster sugar and 300 ml/½ pint milk. Strain into the flan case and sprinkle over ½ teaspoon grated nutmeg. Bake in a preheated moderately hot oven (200°C/400°F, Gas Mark 6) for 10 minutes, then reduce the temperature to moderate (180°C/350°F, Gas Mark 4). Bake for a further 20 to 25 minutes or until the custard filling is set and the pastry is golden brown. Serve warm or cold.

Using a bain marie
A water bath, or *bain marie*, is used for cooking delicate mixtures such as custards in the oven. The bain marie prevents the oven heat reaching the food directly, which might cause it to curdle. To make a *bain marie*, use a large tin such as a roasting tin. Place the dish containing the custard, etc. in the tin and pour around enough hot water to come halfway up the sides of the dish. Bake according to the instructions in the recipe.

A double boiler, and a heatproof bowl placed over a saucepan of hot water, are top-of-the-stove versions of the *bain marie*. They are used to cook delicate mixtures and to keep them warm.

Chocolate Apples and Pears

Granny Smith apples and Conference pears would be best for this dessert. If preferred, the fruit may be poached in non-alcoholic apple juice.

METRIC	IMPERIAL
4 firm apples or pears	4 firm apples or pears
300 ml cider	½ pint cider
25 g sugar	1 oz sugar
175 g plain chocolate	6 oz plain chocolate

Leaving the stalk intact, peel the fruit thinly. Carefully remove the core from the bottom, leaving the fruit whole.

Place the cider and sugar in a saucepan and bring to the boil, stirring to dissolve the sugar. Add the fruit and poach gently for about 3 minutes. Do not allow the fruit to become too soft. Remove with a slotted spoon, and cool on paper towels.

Melt the chocolate in a heatproof bowl over a pan of hot water. Thin slightly with the cider syrup, then use to coat the fruit. Serve with the remaining cider syrup.

Serves 4

VARIATION

Cranberry apples and pears: Peel the fruit as above, then halve lengthways and remove the cores. Mix together 150 g/5 oz cranberry sauce, 4 tablespoons red wine or water and ¼ teaspoon ground cinnamon in a saucepan and heat until melted and smooth. Add the fruit, cover and cook gently until tender. Lift the fruit on to a serving dish. Allow the sauce to cool until it becomes syrupy, then spoon over the fruit to coat. Serve chilled.

Honey Lemon Whip

This frothy dessert has only 190 calories per serving. If you find it too tart, increase the amount of honey.

METRIC	IMPERIAL
150 ml plain yogurt	¼ pint plain yogurt
1½ tablespoons clear honey, warmed	1½ tablespoons clear honey, warmed
grated rind and juice of ½ lemon	grated rind and juice of ½ lemon
1 egg white	1 egg white

Mix together the yogurt, honey and lemon rind and juice. Whisk the egg white until stiff and fold into the yogurt mixture.

Divide between three dessert glasses and chill lightly before serving.

Serves 3

Rich Raspberry Soufflé

Other fruits may be used instead of raspberries. Firm fruits should be cooked before sieving.

METRIC	IMPERIAL
500 g raspberries	1 lb raspberries
3 eggs, separated	3 eggs, separated
100 g caster sugar	4 oz caster sugar
100 g caster sugar	4 oz caster sugar
1½ teaspoons powdered gelatine	1½ teaspoons powdered gelatine
2 tablespoons water	2 tablespoons water
300 ml double cream	½ pint double cream
whipped cream to decorate	whipped cream to decorate

Prepare a 15 cm/6 inch soufflé dish (see page 114).

Sieve the raspberries, then measure the purée: there should be 150 ml/¼ pint. Place the purée in a heatproof bowl with the egg yolks and sugar and lightly beat together. Place the bowl over a pan of simmering water and whisk until the mixture is very thick and creamy and will make a ribbon trail on itself when the whisk is lifted. (If using an electric beater, no heat is needed.) Remove from the heat and continue beating until cool.

Dissolve the gelatine in the water and stir into the whisked mixture. Cool until the mixture is beginning to thicken.

Whip the cream until thick and fold into the mixture. Whisk the egg whites until stiff and fold in. Spoon into the soufflé dish and chill until set.

Carefully remove the paper collar and decorate the top of the soufflé with whipped cream.

Serves 5 to 6

Apricot Custard Mousse

If liked, this delectable dessert may be decorated with piped whipped cream, glacé cherries and angelica.

METRIC	IMPERIAL
150 g dried apricots, soaked overnight	5 oz dried apricots, soaked overnight
3 eggs, separated	3 eggs, separated
75 g caster sugar	3 oz caster sugar
600 ml milk	1 pint milk
15 g powdered gelatine	½ oz powdered gelatine
grated rind and juice of 1 lemon	grated rind and juice of 1 lemon
150 ml double cream	¼ pint double cream

Place the apricots in a saucepan and add enough cold water just to cover. Cook gently until the apricots are very tender and almost all the water has been absorbed. Cool slightly, then purée in a blender or food processor, or sieve the apricots.

Lightly beat the egg yolks with the sugar. Stir in all but 3 tablespoons of the milk. Pour into a heatproof bowl placed over a pan of simmering water and cook, stirring, until the custard thickens. Do not allow to boil. Remove from the heat.

Dissolve the gelatine in the remaining milk. Add to the custard and mix well. Cool until just beginning to set, then mix in the apricot purée and lemon rind and juice.

Whip the cream until thick and fold into the apricot mixture. Whisk the egg whites until stiff and fold in. Spoon into a 1.2 litre/2 pint decorative mould. Cover and chill until set.

Dip the mould quickly into hot water, then turn out the mousse on to a serving dish.

Serve 4 to 6

Cream – whipping and freezing

Whipped double cream may be stretched by folding in a stiffly beaten egg white (add the white of 1 large egg to 300 ml/½ pint cream). This stretched cream may be served in the same way as you would any whipped cream, but it is not suitable for piping.

Whipped evaporated milk may be served in the same way as whipped cream. It is more economical and also lower in calories!

Unwhipped cream does not freeze successfully as it separates on thawing; however, whipped cream can be frozen. Pipe it in small rosettes on to a sheet of foil placed on a rigid surface, like a baking sheet, and open freeze. When frozen, pack the rosettes into a rigid container and return to the freezer.

Freezing puddings

Puddings freeze successfully. Make them in the special freezer foil containers, then cool quickly and wrap in foil or a polythene bag. Storage time is 3 months. To use, reheat the pudding from frozen, allowing extra time.

Puddings suitable for freezing include steamed sponge and suet puddings, fruit crumbles, charlottes and baked sponge puddings. Cold puddings such as blancmange and baked custard do not freeze successfully as they separate when thawed. Clear jellies should not be frozen because they go cloudy and 'weep' on thawing.

Blackcurrant Shortbread Tart

METRIC	IMPERIAL
1 quantity Shortbread dough (see page 144)	1 quantity Shortbread dough (see page 144)
40 g cornflour	1½ oz cornflour
50 g caster sugar	2 oz caster sugar
1 egg, beaten	1 egg, beaten
450 ml milk	¾ pint milk
150 ml double cream	¼ pint double cream
Topping:	*Topping:*
225 g blackcurrants	8 oz blackcurrants
2 tablespoons sugar	2 tablespoons sugar
2 teaspoons arrowroot	2 teaspoons arrowroot
2 tablespoons water	2 tablespoons water

Press the chilled dough over the bottom and up the sides of a 20 cm/8 inch flan tin. Prick all over, then bake in a preheated moderate oven (160°C/325°F, Gas Mark 3) for 30 to 40 minutes or until pale golden. Allow to cool before removing from the tin.

Mix together the cornflour, sugar, egg and 3 tablespoons of the milk. Heat the remaining milk until almost boiling, then stir into the cornflour mixture. Pour back into the saucepan and cook, stirring, until the custard thickens. Remove from the heat and allow to cool.

Whip the cream until thick. Whisk the cooled custard until smooth, then fold in the cream. Spread out in the flan case. Chill.

For the topping, place the blackcurrants in a saucepan with the sugar and cook gently for about 10 minutes or until the fruit is soft. Drain off the juice into another saucepan. Blend the arrowroot with the water and add to the juice. Bring to the boil, stirring, and simmer until clear and thickened. Stir in the blackcurrants and cool. Spread over the custard filling in the flan case. Serve chilled.

Serves 6 to 8

Hazelnut Muesli Yogurt

If you find this too tart, add a little clear honey to sweeten to taste. Serve for breakfast or as a nourishing, filling snack anytime.

METRIC	IMPERIAL
50 g hazelnuts	2 oz hazelnuts
100 g muesli	4 oz muesli
600 ml plain yogurt	1 pint plain yogurt

Spread out the hazelnuts on a baking sheet. Toast in a preheated moderate oven (160°C/325°F, Gas Mark 3) for about 15 minutes or until a pale biscuit colour. Cool, then rub off the skins in a tea towel. Grind or pound the nuts to the texture of coarse breadcrumbs.

Mix together the nuts, muesli and yogurt. Chill for at least 1 hour before serving.

Serves 4 to 6

Apricot Creams

Here a familiar pudding is given a new twist – pasta is used instead of rice.

METRIC	IMPERIAL
75 g miniature pasta shapes	3 oz miniature pasta shapes
600 ml milk	1 pint milk
2 tablespoons sugar	2 tablespoons sugar
few drops of vanilla essence	few drops of vanilla essence
1 × 225 g can apricots, drained and chopped	1 × 8 oz can apricots, drained and chopped
150 ml double cream	¼ pint double cream

Place the pasta and milk in a saucepan and bring to the boil, stirring. Simmer gently for 30 minutes or until the pasta is very soft, adding more milk if necessary. Stir in the sugar and vanilla essence and allow to cool.

Fold the apricots into the pasta mixture. Whip the cream until thick and fold in. Spoon into dessert glasses and chill lightly before serving.

Serves 4

VARIATION

Caramelized peach creams: Make the pasta mixture as above, adding 1 egg with the sugar and vanilla essence. Return to the heat and cook gently for 1 minute, stirring. Pour into a flameproof serving dish and arrange 1 × 425 g/15 oz can peach halves, drained, on top. Sprinkle over 3 tablespoons soft brown sugar. Grill until the sugar has melted and caramelized. Serve hot.

Gooseberry Fool

Other fruits may be used instead of gooseberries, and just sieved to a purée if a soft fruit such as raspberries or strawberries is chosen.

METRIC	IMPERIAL
500 g gooseberries	1 lb gooseberries
100 g caster sugar	4 oz caster sugar
2 teaspoons custard powder	2 teaspoons custard powder
150 ml milk	¼ pint milk
150 ml double cream	¼ pint double cream

Place the gooseberries and sugar in a saucepan. Add a little water, then simmer gently until the gooseberries are tender. Purée the gooseberries in a blender or food processor then sieve them, or sieve them.

Make a thick custard with the custard powder and milk, according to the instructions on the custard packet. Stir into the gooseberry purée and cool.

Whip the cream until thick and fold into the gooseberry mixture. Taste and add more sugar if too tart. Spoon into dessert glasses and chill for at least 3 hours before serving.

Serves 4

Chocolate Macaroon Trifle

METRIC	IMPERIAL
8 macaroons	8 macaroons
3 tablespoons orange juice	3 tablespoons orange juice
2 tablespoons rum	2 tablespoons rum
25 g cornflour	1 oz cornflour
450 ml milk	¾ pint milk
50 g sugar	2 oz sugar
175 g plain chocolate, broken into pieces	6 oz plain chocolate, broken into pieces
150 ml double cream	¼ pint double cream
To decorate:	*To decorate:*
whipped cream	whipped cream
blanched almonds	blanched almonds

Place the macaroons over the bottom of a serving dish. Mix the orange juice with the rum and pour over the biscuits.

Dissolve the cornflour in the milk in a saucepan. Add the sugar and bring to the boil, stirring until thickened. Remove from the heat and add the chocolate. Stir until melted and smooth. Leave to cool, stirring occasionally. Stir in the cream.

Pour the chocolate mixture over the biscuits and chill until fairly firm. Decorate with whipped cream and almonds before serving.

Serves 4 to 6

Preparing grapes

The instruction to peel grapes may seem unnecessary, and even impossible, but as some grapes have rather tough skins – particularly the large purple ones – they can be indigestible. To peel grapes easily, dip the whole bunch into boiling water for a few seconds. Then make a shallow slit in the skin of each grape and slip off the skins.

Seeding, or pipping, is also easily accomplished using the point of a knife or potato peeler.

This peeling method may also be used for peaches, apricots, nectarines and some plums.

Mandarin Pavlovas

This impressive dessert is not difficult to make. Just remember to fold the sugar and cornflour very gently into the beaten egg whites, using a metal spoon. Other fruits, canned or fresh, may be used instead of mandarin oranges.

METRIC	IMPERIAL
3 egg whites	3 egg whites
175 g caster sugar	6 oz caster sugar
2 teaspoons cornflour	2 teaspoons cornflour
1 teaspoon lemon juice	1 teaspoon lemon juice
½ teaspoon vanilla essence	½ teaspoon vanilla essence
150 ml double cream	¼ pint double cream
1 × 450 g can mandarin oranges, drained	1 × 1lb can mandarin oranges, drained

Whisk the egg whites until stiff. Gradually whisk in half the sugar. Fold in the remaining sugar, the cornflour, lemon juice and vanilla essence.

Draw four 7.5 cm/3 inch circles on each of three sheets of non-stick silicone paper. Place the paper on three baking sheets.

Put the meringue mixture into a piping bag fitted with a large plain or star nozzle. Pipe into the circles, starting in the centres, to make flat rounds. Bake in a preheated cool oven (140°C/275°F, Gas Mark 1) for 30 minutes, then reduce the temperature to 120°C/250°F, Gas Mark ½. Bake for a further 30 to 40 minutes or until the meringue rounds are crisp and dry.

Cool slightly, then carefully peel the rounds off the paper. Cool on wire racks.

Whip the cream until thick. Spread or pipe the cream over the tops of half the meringue rounds and cover with the mandarin oranges. Place the remaining rounds on top. Serve soon after assembling so that the meringue doesn't become soggy.

Serves 6

Puddings

Chantilly Meringues

METRIC	IMPERIAL
2 egg whites	2 egg whites
100 g caster sugar	4 oz caster sugar
caster sugar to dredge	caster sugar to dredge
300 ml Chantilly Cream★	½ pint Chantilly Cream★

Whisk the egg whites until stiff. Add 1 tablespoon of the sugar and continue whisking for 1 minute or until the mixture is very stiff and glossy, then carefully fold in the remaining sugar with a metal spoon.

Put the meringue into a piping bag fitted with a 1 cm/½ inch plain tube. Pipe in small rounds on a baking sheet lined with non-stick silicone paper. Alternatively, the meringues may be shaped with two spoons. Make an even number of meringues. Dredge with a little sugar.

Bake in a preheated very cool oven (120°C/225°F, Gas Mark ¼) for 3 to 4 hours or until the meringues are crisp and firm to the touch. Cool on a wire rack.

Carefully peel the meringues off the paper. Sandwich them together in pairs with a dollop of the Chantilly cream.

Serves 4

Butterscotch Flan

A Crumb Crust★ may be used instead of the cornflake flan case, if preferred.

METRIC	IMPERIAL
1 × 20 cm Cornflake Flan Case★	1 × 8 inch Cornflake Flan Case★
Filling:	*Filling:*
100 g soft brown sugar	4 oz soft brown sugar
50 g plain flour	2 oz plain flour
450 ml milk	¾ pint milk
2 egg yolks	2 egg yolks
25 g butter	1 oz butter
½ teaspoon vanilla essence	½ teaspoon vanilla essence
150 ml double cream	¼ pint double cream
grated chocolate to decorate	grated chocolate to decorate

Place the brown sugar, flour and milk in a saucepan and heat, stirring, until thickened. Simmer, stirring, for 2 to 3 minutes. Remove from the heat and stir in the egg yolks. Return to the heat and cook for a further 1 minute. Stir in the butter and vanilla essence until smooth.

Pour the filling into the flan case. Chill until set.

Whip the cream until thick and pipe or spread over the top of the filling. Decorate with grated chocolate.

Serves 6 to 8

Chocolate Mousse

This smooth, creamy dessert has a hint of ginger to enliven the flavour.

METRIC	IMPERIAL
100 g plain chocolate	4 oz plain chocolate
300 ml milk	½ pint milk
3 eggs, separated	3 eggs, separated
50 g caster sugar	2 oz caster sugar
¼ teaspoon ground ginger	¼ teaspoon ground ginger
15 g powdered gelatine	½ oz powdered gelatine
2 tablespoons water	2 tablespoons water
250 ml double cream	8 fl oz double cream
To decorate:	*To decorate:*
whipped cream	whipped cream
chopped nuts	chopped nuts

Place the chocolate and milk in a heavy-based saucepan and melt over gentle heat. Remove from the heat and cool slightly.

Cream the egg yolks, sugar and ginger together. Stir in the chocolate milk, then pour back into the saucepan. Cook gently, stirring, until the custard thickens. Do not allow to boil. Strain into a bowl and leave to cool.

Dissolve the gelatine in the water. Stir into the cooled custard. Chill until beginning to set.

Whip the cream until thick and fold into the chocolate mixture. Whisk the egg whites until stiff and fold in. Spoon into individual dessert glasses and chill until set. Serve decorated with whipped cream and chopped nuts.

Serves 4

Serving fresh pineapple

A sweet, ripe, fresh pineapple, served in slices plain or sprinkled with a little sweet liqueur such as kirsch, makes a delightful dessert. Here is a method of peeling and coring a pineapple that avoids wasting any of the sweet flesh. Cut off the bottom with a serrated-edge knife. Then, holding the pineapple firmly at the top or crown end, make cuts downwards between the 'eyes' at a 45° angle using a sharp stainless steel knife. Peel away the strips of 'eyes' with your fingers. Cut off the top or crown and slice the pineapple thickly crossways. Remove the core from each slice with a special coring implement or with a grapefruit knife.

Chopped fresh pineapple mixed with another fruit such as melon cubes or balls, fresh strawberries, or sliced bananas, makes a simple and superb fruit salad. Serve it with cream or vanilla ice cream, if you want to gild the lily.

Vanilla Ice Cream

Store-bought vanilla ice cream is very good, but it just can't compete with the homemade variety, with its rich, creamy texture and golden colour. Serve it plain, or with sweet or fruity sauces, or spoon it over fresh or baked fruit, steamed and baked puddings or warm fruit pies and gâteaux.

METRIC	IMPERIAL
300 ml milk	½ pint milk
1 vanilla pod, halved lengthways	1 vanilla pod, halved lengthways
4 egg yolks	4 egg yolks
100 g caster sugar	4 oz caster sugar
pinch of salt	pinch of salt
300 ml double cream	½ pint double cream
2 tablespoons iced water	2 tablespoons iced water

Place the milk and vanilla pod in a saucepan and heat until the milk is almost boiling. Remove from the heat and leave to infuse for about 20 minutes.

Beat the egg yolks, sugar and salt together until very pale and thick. Gradually strain in the milk, whisking constantly. Pour the mixture into the saucepan and cook very gently, stirring, until the custard is thick enough to coat the back of a wooden spoon. Remove from the heat and allow to cool, stirring occasionally. Chill.

Whip the cream with the iced water until thick. Lightly whisk the cream into the custard. Pour into freezer trays and freeze until half-frozen. Beat thoroughly to break down the ice crystals, then return to the freezer trays and freeze until firm. (If liked, beat again when half frozen.)

Remove from the freezer 30 minutes before serving.

Note: 2 teaspoons vanilla essence may be used instead of the vanilla pod. Add the essence to the cooled custard.

VARIATIONS

Vanilla ice milk: Make as above, using 750 ml/1¼ pints milk, 1 vanilla pod, 6 egg yolks, 275 g/10 oz caster sugar and a pinch of salt. Omit the double cream and iced water.

Rich coffee ice cream: Make as above, using 150 ml/¼ pint each single cream and strong black coffee instead of the milk. Omit the vanilla pod.

Tea ice cream: Make as above, using 150 ml/¼ pint milk and 150 ml/¼ pint strong tea. Omit the vanilla pod.

Almond macaroon ice cream: Make as above, substituting ½ teaspoon almond essence for the vanilla (add to the cooled custard). Fold in 50 g/2 oz crushed ratafias or macaroons with the cream.

Chocolate chip ice cream: After beating the half-frozen ice cream, fold in 100 g/4 oz finely grated plain chocolate. Continue freezing as above.

Gooseberry Ice Cream

METRIC	IMPERIAL
500 g gooseberries	1 lb gooseberries
100 g granulated sugar	4 oz granulated sugar
300 ml water	½ pint water
4 egg yolks	4 egg yolks
100 g icing sugar, sifted	4 oz icing sugar, sifted
300 ml double cream	½ pint double cream
2 tablespoons iced water	2 tablespoons iced water
green food colouring	green food colouring

Place the gooseberries in a saucepan with the granulated sugar and water and bring to the boil, stirring to dissolve the sugar. Cover and simmer for about 5 minutes or until tender. Cool slightly, then purée the fruit in a blender or food processor and strain out the seeds. Alternatively, sieve the fruit. Chill.

Beat the egg yolks with the icing sugar in a heat-proof bowl over a saucepan of simmering water. When the mixture is lukewarm, remove the bowl from the heat and continue beating until the mixture has tripled its original volume. Chill.

Whip the cream with the iced water until thick. Lightly whisk together the cream, gooseberry purée and egg mixture, then tint a pale green with food colouring.

Pour into freezer trays and freeze until half-frozen. Beat thoroughly to break down the ice crystals, then return to the freezer trays and freeze until firm. Remove from the freezer 30 minutes before serving.

Makes 1 litre/1¾ pints

VARIATION

Strawberry ice cream: Purée 350 g/12 oz strawberries in a blender or food processor or by sieving. Stir in 75 g/3 oz sugar and the juices of 1 orange and 1 lemon. Chill the fruit purée. Make the ice cream as above, substituting the strawberry purée for the gooseberry purée.

Vanilla

Vanilla comes from an orchid plant. It grows as a long pod filled with small beans, and we use both the whole pod and the extracted essence.

Vanilla sugar, which is available in small sachets, is easy to make at home. Bury a vanilla pod in a container of caster suger, cover tightly and leave for at least 1 week before using. (The sugar will keep just as ordinary sugar does.)

Vanilla sugar may be used in any recipe where both vanilla and sugar are called for — in fruit desserts, whipped cream, custards, cakes and other puddings.

Puddings

Chocolate Ice Cream

METRIC	IMPERIAL
6 egg yolks	6 egg yolks
100 g caster sugar	4 oz caster sugar
600 ml milk	1 pint milk
225 g plain chocolate, grated	8 oz plain chocolate, grated
1 teaspoon vanilla essence	1 teaspoon vanilla essence

Beat the egg yolks and sugar together until very pale and thick. Gradually whisk in the milk. Pour the mixture into a saucepan and cook very gently, stirring, until the custard thickens enough to coat the back of a wooden spoon. Remove from the heat and leave to cool for 5 minutes.

Stir in the chocolate until it has melted, then stir in the vanilla essence. Pour into freezer trays and freeze until half-frozen. Beat thoroughly to break down the ice crystals, then return to the freezer trays and freeze until firm. Remove from the freezer 30 minutes before serving.

Makes 1 litre/1¾ pints

Blackcurrant Sorbet

METRIC	IMPERIAL
500 g blackcurrants	1 lb blackcurrants
juice of 2 oranges	juice of 2 oranges
175 g caster sugar	6 oz caster sugar
2 egg whites	2 egg whites
2 tablespoons icing sugar	2 tablespoons icing sugar

Purée the blackcurrants in a blender or sieve them. Mix the purée with the orange juice and caster sugar and stir until the sugar has dissolved. Pour into freezer trays and freeze until slushy.

Whisk the egg whites until foamy. Add the icing sugar and continue whisking until stiff. Whisk the half-frozen fruit mixture to break down all the ice crystals, then lightly whisk in the egg whites.

Return to the freezer trays and freeze until firm. If liked, whisk the sorbet again when it is half frozen, then freeze until firm.

Makes 1 litre/ 1¾ pints

VARIATION
Citrus sorbet: Thinly pare the rind from 4 lemons and 1 orange. Place the rind in a saucepan with 450 ml/¾ pint water and 225 g/8 oz sugar. Bring to the boil, stirring to dissolve the sugar. Boil for 5 minutes, then cool. Squeeze the juice from the lemons and orange and mix with the sugar syrup. Strain into freezer trays and freeze until slushy. Continue with the egg whites as above.

Making ice cream

You don't need a freezer to make ice cream: the frozen food compartment of your refrigerator will do very well. Just turn the temperature control in the refrigerator to its lowest setting one hour before putting the ice cream mixture into the frozen food compartment.

Most ice creams need to be whisked several times during the freezing process, to prevent ice crystals forming (these would ruin the texture of the finished ice cream). But an electric ice cream-maker, or *sorbetière*, will do the whisking for you. This machine, three-quarters full of ice cream mixture, is placed in the freezer compartment, with the flex hanging out to be plugged in. The paddle in the machine moves constantly, stirring the ice cream as it freezes. There is also an electric ice cream machine that is operated independently of the refrigerator. It requires a quantity of ice to do the freezing.

Old-fashioned, hand-operated ice cream buckets, sometimes called churn freezers, are also effective. Ice and coarse rock salt, called freezing salt, are placed in a container around that holding the ice cream mixture. The paddle, or dasher, is moved by cranking the handle. This requires a lot of stamina and patience, so a team of willing 'crankers' would be a great help.

*

A water ice or sorbet, which is basically a frozen fruit-flavoured syrup, is best frozen in a churn. But if a small quantity of gelatine is added (to help prevent ice crystals), it can be still-frozen in the freezer compartment of the refrigerator, and whisked, at intervals, two or three times.

Strawberry Yogurt Lollies

Other fruit yogurts may be used instead of strawberry. Black cherry and apricot are particularly good.

METRIC	IMPERIAL
1 teaspoon powdered gelatine	1 teaspoon powdered gelatine
150 ml milk	¼ pint milk
250 ml strawberry yogurt	8 fl oz strawberry yogurt

Place the gelatine and milk in a saucepan and stir over low heat until the gelatine has dissolved. Remove from the heat and stir in the yogurt.

Pour into ice lolly moulds and freeze until firm. For longer storage in the freezer, unmould the lollies and stack between sheets of greaseproof paper or foil. Overwrap in paper or foil.

Makes 6

Sugar syrup

In making confectionery, the boiling of sugar syrup is a major factor, and the instructions in a recipe for the stage to which the syrup is boiled must be followed carefully. Stir until the sugar has dissolved, then stop stirring. Brush down the sides of the pan using a wet bristle brush, to wash all crystals back into the liquid, then add a sugar thermometer. (Be sure that the thermometer has been heated in hot water first so that it won't break, and clip it on to the side of the pan so that the bulb is not touching the bottom.) Boil until the correct stage has been reached.

If you want to double check your thermometer, or if you are making sweets without a thermometer, here are the temperatures, stages and tests you can do by pouring the syrup into a bowl of cold water:

Temperature	Stage	Cold-water test
110°C/230°F	thread	syrup poured slowly from spoon forms a 5 cm/2 inch thread
116°C/240°F	soft ball	syrup can be shaped into a ball, but flattens when removed from the water
121°C/250°F	hard ball	syrup can be shaped into a hard, pliable ball that does not flatten when removed from the water
125°C/260°F	soft crack	syrup separates into threads that bend but do not break
150°C/300°F	hard crack	syrup separates into hard, brittle threads that crack

Marzipan Fruits

METRIC
100 g caster sugar
100 g icing sugar, sifted
225 g ground almonds
1 teaspoon lemon juice
few drops of almond essence
1 egg or 2 egg yolks
food colourings
cloves

IMPERIAL
4 oz caster sugar
4 oz icing sugar, sifted
8 oz ground almonds
1 teaspoon lemon juice
few drops of almond essence
1 egg or 2 egg yolks
food colourings
cloves

Mix together the sugars and ground almonds. Add the lemon juice, almond essence and egg or egg yolks and mix to a firm but manageable paste. Turn onto a lightly sugared surface and knead until smooth.

Divide the marzipan into four or more portions. Tint one portion yellow for bananas, one orange for oranges, one deep pink for strawberries and one green for apples, pears and grapes.

To shape bananas, break off a small piece of yellow marzipan and shape into a half-moon with one end blunt and the other tapering off. Paint on brown markings with food colouring.

For oranges, roll the marzipan into small balls and roll gently on a grater to give the textured skin. Press in a clove at one end for the calyx.

Shape the pink marzipan into strawberries, then roll in granulated sugar to give the effect of seeds. Shape the hull from a little green marzipan.

Roll green marzipan into balls for apples or more elongated shapes for pears. Paint one side of each apple with red food colouring and stick in a clove to represent the calyx. Paint marks on pears with brown food colouring. For grapes, roll green marzipan into very small balls and press lightly together to make a bunch. If preferred, the marzipan for grapes may be tinted purple with the appropriate food colouring or a mixture of red and blue.

Crunchy Chocolate Fudge

You don't need a sugar thermometer to make this mouth-watering fudge.

METRIC
175 g digestive biscuits, finely crushed, or cake crumbs
2 tablespoons golden syrup
100 g unsalted butter
50 g sugar
50 g cocoa powder
few drops of vanilla essence

IMPERIAL
6 oz digestive biscuits, finely crushed, or cake crumbs
2 tablespoons golden syrup
4 oz unsalted butter
2 oz sugar
2 oz cocoa powder
few drops of vanilla essence

Spread out the crumbs on a baking sheet and bake in a preheated moderate oven (160°C/325°F, Gas Mark 3) for 3 to 5 minutes or until crisp. Allow to cool.

Place the syrup, butter and sugar in a saucepan and heat until melted and smooth. Stir in the cocoa powder until dissolved and evenly mixed. Remove from the heat and stir in the crumbs and vanilla essence.

Pour into a greased 18 cm/7 inch square tin and spread evenly into the corners. Chill until set.

Cut into 2.5 cm/1 inch squares to serve.

Makes about 49

Puddings

Nut Brittle

METRIC	IMPERIAL
150 ml water	¼ pint water
15 g butter	½ oz butter
450 g sugar	1 lb sugar
6 tablespoons golden syrup	6 tablespoons golden syrup
225 g nuts, chopped	8 oz nuts, chopped
pinch of cream of tartar	pinch of cream of tartar

Place the water and butter in a heavy-based saucepan and heat until the butter has melted. Add the sugar and golden syrup and stir until the sugar has dissolved. Bring to the boil and boil to the hard crack stage (see box, opposite, on Sugar Syrup).

Add the nuts and cream of tartar and cook for a further 2 to 3 minutes, stirring well.

Pour into a flat buttered tin and leave to set. Break into pieces to serve, and store, wrapped in greaseproof paper, in an airtight tin.

Simple Truffles

METRIC	IMPERIAL
225 g stale chocolate or coffee cake, finely crumbled	8 oz stale chocolate or coffee cake, finely crumbled
50 g ground almonds	2 oz ground almonds
25 g soft brown sugar	1 oz soft brown sugar
1 tablespoon apricot jam	1 tablespoon apricot jam
1 tablespoon rum, or	1 tablespoon rum, or
½ teaspoon rum essence	½ teaspoon rum essence
75 g plain chocolate	3 oz plain chocolate
50 g chocolate vermicelli	2 oz chocolate vermicelli

Mix together the cake crumbs, almonds, sugar, jam and rum or rum essence. Shape the mixture into walnut-size balls.

Melt the chocolate in a heatproof bowl over a pan of hot water. Dip the balls into the chocolate to coat on all sides, then roll in the vermicelli.

Leave to set on greaseproof paper.

Makes about 20

Peppermint Fondant Creams

METRIC	IMPERIAL
2 egg whites	2 egg whites
450 g icing sugar, sifted	1 lb icing sugar, sifted
few drops of oil of peppermint or peppermint essence	few drops of oil of peppermint or peppermint essence

Whisk the egg whites until frothy, then gradually whisk in the sugar. Halfway through adding the sugar, you will have to knead it in. Knead in the flavouring.

Roll out the fondant on a surface sprinkled with icing sugar and cut into small shapes. Leave to dry and harden before serving.

Caramels

METRIC	IMPERIAL
100 g soft brown sugar	4 oz soft brown sugar
150 ml milk	¼ pint milk
350 g golden syrup	12 oz golden syrup
40 g butter	1½ oz butter
¼ teaspoon vanilla essence	¼ teaspoon vanilla essence

Place all the ingredients, except the vanilla essence, in a saucepan and bring to the boil, stirring. Boil until the hard ball stage is reached (see box, opposite, on Sugar Syrup).

Remove from the heat and stir in the vanilla essence. Pour into a well oiled 18 cm/7 inch square tin. Mark into 2.5 cm/1 inch squares and leave to set.

Makes about 49

Making sweets

At Christmastime, birthdays, Mother's Day, or anytime you want to give a gift, make that gift more special by giving something you have made yourself. Homemade sweets and chocolates, in particular, are very welcome.

At Easter, you could give a gaily painted egg box filled with your own chocolate eggs. These are simply made using a real egg: prick both ends, blow out the insides, rinse and leave to dry. Then seal up one hole and funnel melted chocolate into the other. When the chocolate has set, carefully crack the egg shell and peel it away. Decorate the chocolate eggs with piped icing and crystallized flowers or nuts.

A sweet bag can be made to present any firm, non-sticky sweets. Cut out a 20 cm/8 inch square of a pretty fabric and hem the edges with lace. Place the sweets in the centre, gather up the fabric and tie into a bag with a ribbon.

Other containers for sweets can be made from small, rigid cardboard boxes (covered and lined with attractive paper or fabric), pretty tins or glass jars (decorated with ribbon), small straw baskets lined with tissue paper or doilies, and paper cones made from doilies (thread ribbon around the top edge).

Any sweets that might stick together, such as marzipan fruits or chocolates, should be placed in individual paper or foil cases. These can be bought from good stationers.

Baking

Countless books about baking have been
written, and thousands of recipes for breads,
cakes and biscuits have been handed down
from generation to generation. This is
because it is such a pleasure to share baking
skills and ideas with someone else. Many a
friendship has been cemented over a cup
of tea or coffee and a delicious baked treat.
Cakes and biscuits are such sociable foods.
The lovely fragrance of homemade breads,
cakes and biscuits cannot be matched. Just
step into any kitchen when these treats are
fresh from the oven and you'll find your
mouth watering.

Basic White Bread

This basic bread can be baked in plain loaf shapes, or as a cob, cottage or farmhouse loaf. See below for shaping instructions. If preferred, the loaves may be glazed with egg beaten with a little milk before baking.

METRIC	IMPERIAL
1 teaspoon caster sugar	1 teaspoon caster sugar
900 ml lukewarm water	1½ pints lukewarm water
15 g dried yeast	½ oz dried yeast
1.5 kg strong plain flour	3 lb strong plain flour
1 tablespoon salt	1 tablespoon salt
25 g lard or margarine	1 oz lard or margarine
salted water to glaze	salted water to glaze

Stir the sugar into the water until dissolved. Sprinkle the yeast on top and leave in a warm place until frothy.

Sift the flour and salt into a bowl. Rub in the lard or margarine. Make a well in the centre and put in the yeast liquid. Mix to a firm dough.

Turn out on to a floured surface and knead for 10 minutes or until the dough is smooth and elastic. Cover and leave to rise in a warm place for 1½ hours or until doubled in size.

Knock back the dough, then knead again for 5 minutes. Divide the dough into four portions and shape each into a loaf. Place in four greased 500 g/1 lb loaf tins. (Or use two 1 kg/2 lb loaf tins.) Cover and leave to prove in a warm place for about 1 hour or until the dough has risen to the tops of the tins.

Brush the tops of the loaves with salted water, then bake in a preheated hot oven (230°C/450°F, Gas Mark 8) for 30 to 40 minutes or until the bread sounds hollow when tapped on the bottom. (Larger loaves will take 45 to 55 minutes baking.) Cool on a wire rack.

Makes four 500 g/1 lb loaves (or two 1 kg/2 lb loaves)

SHAPING VARIATIONS
Cob loaf: Divide the dough in half and shape each portion into a smooth round. Place on a floured baking sheet and dust with flour. Prove and bake as above.
Cottage loaf: Break off one-quarter of the dough and shape into a ball. Form the remaining dough into a large ball and place on a floured baking sheet. Put the small ball on top of the large ball and push the handle of a wooden spoon through the centre of the loaf, almost to the bottom. Prove and bake as above.
Farmhouse loaf: Shape the dough to fit the loaf tins as above. Make a lengthways cut through the top of each loaf with a sharp knife. Prove and bake as above.

Proving bread dough
The second rising, called proving, may be done overnight in the refrigerator.

Rosemary Bread

Fresh rosemary is essential for this bread.

METRIC	IMPERIAL
½ teaspoon caster sugar	½ teaspoon caster sugar
300 ml lukewarm water	½ pint lukewarm water
7 g dried yeast	¼ oz dried yeast
350 g strong plain flour	12 oz strong plain flour
1 teaspoon salt	1 teaspoon salt
100 g wholemeal flour	4 oz wholemeal flour
2 tablespoons chopped fresh rosemary	2 tablespoons chopped fresh rosemary

Dissolve the sugar in the water. Sprinkle the yeast on top and leave in a warm place until frothy.

Sift the plain flour and salt into a bowl and stir in the wholemeal flour and three-quarters of the rosemary. Make a well in the centre and put in the yeast liquid. Mix to a dough.

Turn out on to a floured surface and knead for 5 minutes or until smooth and elastic. Cover and leave to rise in a warm place for 1½ hours or until doubled in size.

Knock back the dough and knead for 3 minutes. Shape into a loaf and place in a greased 500 g/1 lb loaf tin. Cover and leave to prove in a warm place for 45 minutes or until doubled in size.

Sprinkle the remaining rosemary on top. Bake in a preheated very hot oven (240°C/475°F, Gas Mark 9) for 15 minutes, then reduce the temperature to moderately hot (190°C/375°F, Gas Mark 5). Bake for a further 25 minutes or until the bread sounds hollow when tapped on the bottom. Cool on a wire rack.

Makes a 500 g/1 lb loaf

Ploughman's Loaf

METRIC	IMPERIAL
½ teaspoon caster sugar	½ teaspoon caster sugar
300 ml lukewarm milk	½ pint lukewarm milk
7 g dried yeast	¼ oz dried yeast
450 g strong plain flour	1 lb strong plain flour
salt and pepper	salt and pepper
65 g butter, melted	2½ oz butter, melted
1 onion, thinly sliced	1 onion, thinly sliced
1 garlic clove, crushed (optional)	1 garlic clove, crushed (optional)
1 egg yolk	1 egg yolk
1½ tablespoons soured cream	1½ tablespoons soured cream

Dissolve the sugar in the milk. Sprinkle the yeast on top and leave in a warm place until frothy.

Sift the flour and 1 teaspoon salt into a bowl. Make a well in the centre and put in the yeast liquid and

Baking

40 g/1½ oz of the butter. Mix to a dough.

Turn out on to a floured surface and knead for 10 minutes or until smooth and elastic. Cover and leave to rise in a warm place for 1½ hours or until doubled in size.

Heat the remaining butter in a frying pan. Add the onion and garlic, if used, and fry until softened. Season to taste with salt and pepper. Remove from the pan with a slotted spoon and spread over the bottom of a greased 20 cm/8 inch round cake tin. Reserve the butter in the frying pan.

Knock back the dough and knead for 4 minutes. Shape into a 20 cm/8 inch round and place on the onion in the tin. Brush with the reserved butter. Cover and leave to prove in a warm place for 30 minutes or until doubled in size.

Beat the egg yolk with the soured cream and salt and pepper to taste. Spread over the top of the dough. Bake in a preheated hot oven (220°C/425°F, Gas Mark 7) for 10 minutes, then reduce the temperature to moderately hot (190°C/375°F, Gas Mark 5). Bake for a further 20 minutes. Cool on a wire rack.

Makes a 20 cm/8 inch round bread

Milk Twist

METRIC	IMPERIAL
½ teaspoon caster sugar	½ teaspoon caster sugar
300 ml lukewarm milk	½ pint lukewarm milk
7 g dried yeast	¼ oz dried yeast
450 g strong plain flour	1 lb strong plain flour
2 teaspoons salt	2 teaspoons salt
15 g lard	½ oz lard
1 egg, beaten	1 egg, beaten
1 tablespoon sea salt	1 tablespoon sea salt

Stir the sugar into the milk until dissolved. Sprinkle the yeast on top and leave in a warm place until frothy.

Sift the flour and salt into a bowl. Rub in the lard. Make a well in the centre and put in the yeast liquid. Mix to a dough.

Turn out on to a floured surface and knead for 10 minutes or until the dough is smooth and elastic. Cover and leave to rise in a warm place for 1½ hours or until doubled in size.

Knock back the dough, then knead again for 5 minutes. Divide the dough in half and shape each piece into a roll about 35 cm/14 inches long. Press one end of each roll together and twist together to form a loaf. Seal the other ends with a little beaten egg. Place on a greased baking sheet. Cover and leave to prove in a warm place for 30 minutes or until doubled in size.

Brush all over with beaten egg and sprinkle with the sea salt. Bake in a preheated moderately hot oven (200°C/400°F, Gas Mark 6) for 30 to 35 minutes or until golden brown. Cool on a wire rack.

Makes a 500 g/1 lb loaf

Freezing bread and bread dough

Bread can be frozen as unrisen dough, risen dough, part-baked and completely baked.

To freeze unrisen dough, increase the amount of yeast by 50% and freeze in a greased polythene bag, leaving a little space for expansion. Storage time is 1 month. To use the dough, reseal the bag so that there is plenty of room for rising, then leave to rise at room temperature for 6 hours. Use as for fresh dough.

Risen dough should also have the yeast increased by 50% if you intend to freeze it. After the first rising, knock back the dough, shape into a loaf (or another shape) and place in a greased tin or wrap in foil. Risen dough will also keep for 1 month in the freezer. To use, thaw at room temperature, then prove.

Part-baked breads and rolls should be cooled quickly and then wrapped in foil or a polythene bag. Freeze for 4 months. Bake from frozen.

Cool baked bread quickly and wrap as for part-baked bread. To use, thaw at room temperature for 3 hours, or refresh, wrapped in foil, in a preheated hot oven (220°C/425°F, Gas Mark 7) for 45 minutes. Storage time in the freezer is 6 months.

Crumpets

If you don't have crumpet rings, use 7.5 cm/3 inch plain metal pastry cutters.

METRIC	IMPERIAL
½ teaspoon caster sugar	½ teaspoon caster sugar
600 ml lukewarm milk	1 pint lukewarm milk
7 g dried yeast	¼ oz dried yeast
450 g strong plain flour	1 lb strong plain flour
1 teaspoon salt	1 teaspoon salt
½ teaspoon bicarbonate of soda	½ teaspoon bicarbonate of soda
2 teaspoons warm water	2 teaspoons warm water

Dissolve the sugar in a little of the milk. Sprinkle the yeast on top and leave in a warm place until frothy.

Sift the flour and salt into a bowl. Make a well in the centre and put in the yeast liquid and remaining milk. Beat well for 5 minutes, then cover and leave to rise in a warm place for 1 hour.

Dissolve the soda in the water. Add to the batter and beat for 3 to 4 minutes. Cover and leave in a warm place for 45 minutes.

Grease a griddle or heavy-based frying pan and six crumpet rings. Heat the griddle or pan and place the rings on top. Pour about 2 tablespoons of batter into each ring and cook until the tops of the crumpets have set and the bottoms are golden brown. Remove the rings and turn the crumpets over. Cook for a further 3 minutes. Serve toasted and buttered.

Makes about 20

Muffins

Muffins are traditionally cooked on a griddle, but a heavy-based frying pan will do just as well. Serve toasted on both sides, split open and buttered.

METRIC	IMPERIAL
½ teaspoon caster sugar	½ teaspoon caster sugar
4 tablespoons lukewarm water	4 tablespoons lukewarm water
7 g dried yeast	¼ oz dried yeast
25 g butter	1 oz butter
300 ml lukewarm milk	½ pint lukewarm milk
450 g strong plain flour	1 lb strong plain flour
½ teaspoon salt	½ teaspoon salt
1 egg, beaten	1 egg, beaten

Dissolve the sugar in the water. Sprinkle the yeast on top and leave in a warm place until frothy.

Stir the butter into the milk until melted.

Sift the flour and salt into a bowl. Make a well in the centre and put in the yeast liquid, milk mixture and egg. Mix to a dough.

Turn out on to a floured surface and knead until smooth and elastic. Cover and leave to rise in a warm place for 1½ hours or until doubled in size.

Knock back the dough, then roll out to 1 cm/½ inch thick. Cut out 6 cm/2½ inch rounds. Cook on a greased griddle until lightly browned on both sides.

Wholemeal Bread

METRIC	IMPERIAL
50 g soft brown sugar	2 oz soft brown sugar
450 ml lukewarm water	¾ pint lukewarm water
15 g dried yeast	½ oz dried yeast
900 g wholemeal flour	2 lb wholemeal flour
1 teaspoon salt	1 teaspoon salt

Dissolve 1 teaspoon of the sugar in the water. Sprinkle the yeast on top and leave in a warm place until frothy.

Place the flour, salt and remaining sugar in a bowl. Make a well in the centre and put in the yeast liquid. Mix to a dough.

Turn out on to a floured surface and knead for 10 minutes or until the dough is smooth and elastic. Cover and leave to rise in a warm place for 1½ hours or until doubled in size.

Knock back the dough, then knead again for 5 minutes. Shape into a loaf and place in a greased 1 kg/2 lb loaf tin. Cover and leave to prove in a warm place for 30 to 45 minutes or until risen to the top of the tin.

Bake in a preheated hot oven (230°C/450°F, Gas Mark 8) for 15 minutes, then reduce the temperature to moderately hot (200°C/400°F, Gas Mark 6). Bake for a further 30 to 35 minutes or until the bread sounds hollow when tapped on the bottom. Cool on a wire rack.

Makes a 1 kg/2 lb loaf

VARIATION
Wheatmeal bread: Reduce the quantity of yeast to 7 g/¼ oz and use 350 g/12 oz each wholemeal flour and strong plain flour. Rub 15 g/½ oz lard into the flours before adding the yeast liquid. After kneading the dough, shape it into a slightly flattened round about 23 cm/9 inches across and sprinkle with cracked wheat. Place on a baking sheet and leave it to rise for 1½ hours or until doubled in size. Bake in a preheated hot oven (230°C/450°F, Gas Mark 8) for 40 to 45 minutes. Alternatively, bake in two well-greased clay flower pots for 30 to 40 minutes.

Selkirk Bannock

METRIC	IMPERIAL
100 g soft brown sugar	4 oz soft brown sugar
450 ml lukewarm milk	¾ pint lukewarm milk
7 g dried yeast	¼ oz dried yeast
450 g strong plain flour	1 lb strong plain flour
225 g wholemeal flour	8 oz wholemeal flour
1½ teaspoons salt	1½ teaspoons salt
1 egg, beaten	1 egg, beaten
100 g butter, softened	4 oz butter, softened
100 g lard, softened	4 oz lard, softened
225 g sultanas	8 oz sultanas
100 g currants	4 oz currants
100 g chopped mixed candied peel	4 oz chopped mixed candied peel

Dissolve ½ teaspoon of the sugar in the milk. Sprinkle over the yeast and leave in a warm place until frothy.

Place the flours and salt in a bowl. Make a well in the centre and put in the yeast liquid and the egg. Mix to a dough and knead well for 5 minutes. Cover and leave to rise in a warm place for 1½ hours or until doubled in size.

Knock back the dough, then beat in the butter and lard with a wooden spoon. Turn out on to a floured surface and roll or push out into a large square. Sprinkle over the dried fruit, peel and remaining sugar. Fold the dough over the fruit mixture, then knead well to distribute it evenly.

Divide the dough in half and shape each portion into a loaf. Place in two greased 500 g/1 lb loaf tins. Cover and leave to prove in a warm place for 30 minutes or until risen to the tops of the tins.

Bake in a preheated moderately hot oven (200°C/400°F, Gas Mark 6) for 50 to 60 minutes or until a skewer inserted into the centre of the loaves comes out clean. Cool in the tins for 10 minutes, then turn out on to a wire rack to cool completely.

Makes two 500 g/1 lb loaves

Kneading

The kneading of dough is important to develop the gluten, and make the bread rise. Place the dough on a floured surface and push it with the heels of your hands. Fold it back towards you and push out again. Be aggressive and work the dough hard. Kneading by hand takes about 10 minutes to make the dough smooth and elastic; using a dough hook on an electric mixer is much faster (and less tiring).

The kneaded dough is left to rise in a warm, draught-free place until doubled in size. It is then 'knocked back', or punched with the fists to remove all the air bubbles and return the dough to its original size. The dough is shaped and then left to rise again.

Baking bread

To give home-baked bread a crusty finish, brush it with beaten egg yolk before baking. Another method is to place a pan of water in the bottom of the oven when preheating it. Leave the water in the oven for two-thirds of the baking time: the steam from it will give the bread a nice golden crust.

To test if a loaf of bread is done, tip it out of the tin and rap the bottom with your knuckles. It should sound hollow. If it doesn't, bake for a few more minutes.

Devonshire Splits

Split open these sweet buns and fill with whipped or clotted cream and jam.

METRIC	IMPERIAL
75 g caster sugar	3 oz caster sugar
300 ml lukewarm milk	$\frac{1}{2}$ pint lukewarm milk
7 g dried yeast	$\frac{1}{4}$ oz dried yeast
450 g strong plain flour	1 lb strong plain flour
$\frac{1}{2}$ teaspoon salt	$\frac{1}{2}$ teaspoon salt
$\frac{1}{2}$ teaspoon ground cinnamon	$\frac{1}{2}$ teaspoon ground cinnamon
50 g butter	2 oz butter

Dissolve $\frac{1}{2}$ teaspoon of the sugar in the milk. Sprinkle the yeast over the top and leave in a warm place until frothy.

Sift the flour, salt and cinnamon into a bowl and stir in the remaining sugar. Rub in the butter. Make a well in the centre and pour in the yeast liquid. Mix to a dough.

Turn out on to a floured surface and knead for 5 minutes or until smooth and elastic. Cover and leave to rise in a warm place for 1$\frac{1}{2}$ hours or until doubled in size.

Knock back the dough and knead lightly. Divide into 14 to 16 pieces and shape each into a ball. Place, well spaced apart, on a greased baking sheet and flatten the balls slightly. Cover and leave to prove in a warm place for 30 minutes or until doubled in size.

Bake in a preheated hot oven (220°C/425°F, Gas Mark 7) for 15 minutes. Cool on a wire rack.

Makes 14 to 16

Barm Brack

This yeasted fruit loaf from Ireland is traditionally baked at Halloween.

METRIC	IMPERIAL
100 g caster sugar	4 oz caster sugar
300 ml lukewarm milk	$\frac{1}{2}$ pint lukewarm milk
7 g dried yeast	$\frac{1}{4}$ oz dried yeast
450 g strong plain flour	1 lb strong plain flour
$\frac{1}{2}$ teaspoon salt	$\frac{1}{2}$ teaspoon salt
$\frac{1}{2}$ teaspoon ground cinnamon	$\frac{1}{2}$ teaspoon ground cinnamon
1 teaspoon grated nutmeg	1 teaspoon grated nutmeg
50 g butter	2 oz butter
2 eggs, beaten	2 eggs, beaten
175 g sultanas	6 oz sultanas
175 g currants	6 oz currants
100 g chopped mixed candied peel	4 oz chopped mixed candied peel
Glaze:	*Glaze:*
2 tablespoons caster sugar	2 tablespoons caster sugar
3 tablespoons boiling water	3 tablespoons boiling water

Dissolve 1 teaspoon of the sugar in the milk. Sprinkle the yeast on top and leave in a warm place until frothy.

Sift the flour, salt and spices into a bowl. Stir in the remaining sugar, then rub in the butter. Make a well in the centre and put in the yeast liquid and eggs. Mix to a dough.

Turn out on to a floured surface and knead for about 10 minutes or until smooth and elastic. Knead in the dried fruit and peel. Cover and leave to rise in a warm place for 1$\frac{1}{2}$ hours or until doubled in size.

Knock back the dough, then knead again for 3 minutes. Divide the dough in half and shape each portion into a loaf. Place in two greased 500 g/1 lb loaf tins. Cover and leave to prove in a warm place for 30 minutes or until risen almost to the tops of the tins.

Bake in a preheated moderately hot oven (200°C/400°F, Gas Mark 6) for 50 to 60 minutes or until the loaves sound hollow when tapped on the bottom.

To make the glaze, dissolve the sugar in the water. Brush over the tops of the loaves 2 to 3 minutes before the end of the baking time. Cool on a wire rack.

Makes two 500 g/1 lb loaves

> **Yeast**
> Fresh bakers' yeast is active and alive, which is why it is highly perishable, whereas dried yeast, in granular form, is in an inert state and will not become active until it is mixed with a warm liquid. To substitute fresh for dried yeast, just double the quantity.

Lardy Cake

METRIC	IMPERIAL
50 g caster sugar	2 oz caster sugar
300 ml lukewarm milk	½ pint lukewarm milk
7 g dried yeast	¼ oz dried yeast
450 g strong plain flour	1 lb strong plain flour
1 teaspoon salt	1 teaspoon salt
100 g lard, cut into pieces	4 oz lard, cut into pieces
40 g currants	1½ oz currants
40 g sultanas	1½ oz sultanas
1 teaspoon mixed spice	1 teaspoon mixed spice
Glaze:	*Glaze:*
3 tablespoons caster sugar	3 tablespoons caster sugar
3 tablespoons boiling water	3 tablespoons boiling water

Dissolve ½ teaspoon of the sugar in the milk. Sprinkle the yeast over the top and leave in a warm place until frothy.

Sift the flour and salt into a bowl. Make a well in the centre and pour in the yeast liquid. Mix to a dough.

Turn out on to a floured surface and knead for 5 minutes or until smooth and elastic. Cover and leave to rise in a warm place for 1½ hours or until doubled in size.

Knock back the dough and knead for 3 minutes. Roll out to an oblong about 5 mm/¼ inch thick. Dot one-third of the lard over the dough, leaving a margin of 1 cm/½ inch clear around the edges. Mix together the dried fruit, spice and remaining sugar and sprinkle one-third over the dough. Fold into three, seal the edges by pressing with the rolling pin and give the dough a half turn.

Roll out into an oblong again and repeat the process twice, using up the lard and fruit mixture. Shape into a round about 20 cm/8 inches in diameter and place on a greased baking sheet. Score a pattern on top with a sharp knife. Cover and leave to prove in a warm place for 30 minutes or until doubled in size.

Bake in a preheated moderately hot oven (200°C/400°F, Gas Mark 6) for 30 minutes.

Make the glaze by dissolving the sugar in the water. Brush over the cake and bake for a further 10 minutes. Cool on a wire rack for 5 minutes before serving.

Makes a 20 cm/8 inch round cake

Raisin Bread

METRIC	IMPERIAL
350 g seeded raisins	12 oz seeded raisins
5 tablespoons sweet white wine or sherry	5 tablespoons sweet white wine or sherry
175 g soft brown sugar	6 oz soft brown sugar
450 ml lukewarm milk	¾ pint lukewarm milk
15 g dried yeast	½ oz dried yeast
450 g wholemeal flour	1 lb wholemeal flour
450 g rye flour	1 lb rye flour
1½ teaspoons salt	1½ teaspoons salt
175 g butter, melted	6 oz butter, melted
75 g black treacle	3 oz black treacle

Place the raisins and wine or sherry in a saucepan and simmer gently for 20 minutes.

Meanwhile, dissolve 1 teaspoon of the sugar in the milk. Sprinkle the yeast on top and leave in a warm place until frothy.

Place the flours and salt in a bowl. Stir in the remaining sugar. Make a well in the centre and put in the yeast liquid, butter and treacle. Mix to a dough.

Turn out on to a floured surface and knead for 10 minutes or until smooth and elastic. Cover and leave to rise in a warm place for 1½ hours or until doubled in size.

Drain the raisins, if necessary, and allow to cool.

Knock back the dough, then knead again for 5 minutes, working in the raisins. Divide the dough in half and shape each portion into a loaf. Place in two greased 500 g/1 lb loaf tins. Cover and leave to prove in a warm place for 30 to 40 minutes or until doubled in size.

Bake in a preheated very hot oven (240°C/475°F, Gas Mark 9) for 15 minutes, then reduce the temperature to hot (220°C/425°F, Gas Mark 7). Bake for a further 25 to 30 minutes or until the loaves sound hollow when tapped on the bottom. Cool slightly on a wire rack.

Makes two 500 g/1 lb loaves

> **Star rating for freezing**
> The star markings on the freezing compartment of a refrigerator indicate the length of time frozen foods may be stored, and these markings correspond to symbols on the packets of food. One large white star is followed by one, two or three dark stars, and indicate the following: one dark star – a temperature of −6°C/21°F and storage time of 1 week; two dark stars – a temperature of −12°C/10°F and storage time of 1 month; three dark stars – a temperature of −18°C/0°F and storage time of 3 months.

Baking

Bath Buns

Home-made Bath buns are a delicious, and very filling treat at tea-time.

METRIC	IMPERIAL
75 g caster sugar	3 oz caster sugar
4 tablespoons lukewarm water	4 tablespoons lukewarm water
7 g dried yeast	¼ oz dried yeast
450 g strong plain flour	1 lb strong plain flour
½ teaspoon salt	½ teaspoon salt
50 g butter	2 oz butter
150 ml lukewarm milk	¼ pint lukewarm milk
2 eggs, beaten	2 eggs, beaten
100 g currants	4 oz currants
50 g chopped mixed candied peel	2 oz chopped mixed candied peel
Glaze:	*Glaze:*
½ egg, beaten	½ egg, beaten
1 tablespoon milk	1 tablespoon milk
2 tablespoons crushed lump sugar	2 tablespoons crushed lump sugar

Dissolve ½ teaspoon of the sugar in the water. Sprinkle the yeast over the top and leave in a warm place until frothy.

Sift the flour and salt into a bowl and stir in the remaining sugar. Rub in the butter. Make a well in the centre and put in the yeast liquid, milk and eggs. Mix to a dough.

Turn out on to a floured surface and knead for 5 minutes or until smooth and elastic. Cover and leave to rise in a warm place for 1½ hours or until doubled in size.

Knock back the dough, then knead in the currants and peel. Divide the dough into 12 portions and place, well spaced apart, on a greased baking sheet. Cover and leave to prove in a warm place for 30 minutes or until doubled in size.

To make the glaze, beat the egg with the milk. Brush over the buns and sprinkle with the sugar. Bake in a preheated moderately hot oven (200°C/400°F, Gas Mark 6) for 20 to 25 minutes. Cool on a wire rack.

Makes 12

VARIATION

Hot cross buns: Use only 50 g/2 oz sugar, and add 2 teaspoons mixed spice with the flour and salt. Use only 1 egg. Reduce the amount of currants and peel to 25 g/1 oz each and add 50 g/2 oz sultanas. Before baking the buns, score a cross on each with a sharp knife. Glaze the warm baked buns with a mixture of 1 tablespoon each caster sugar, milk and water. Alternatively, the crosses may be made with strips of Shortcrust Pastry★ before baking. For a sweeter bun, they can be added after baking using thick Glacé Icing★.
Makes 12

Lemon Doughnuts

METRIC	IMPERIAL
25 g caster sugar	1 oz caster sugar
5 tablespoons lukewarm milk	5 tablespoons lukewarm milk
7 g dried yeast	¼ oz dried yeast
225 g strong plain flour	8 oz strong plain flour
½ teaspoon salt	½ teaspoon salt
¼ teaspoon grated nutmeg	¼ teaspoon grated nutmeg
grated rind and juice of 1 lemon	grated rind and juice of 1 lemon
50 g butter, melted	2 oz butter, melted
1 egg, beaten	1 egg, beaten
oil for deep frying	oil for deep frying
caster sugar to dredge	caster sugar to dredge

Dissolve ½ teaspoon of the sugar in the milk. Sprinkle the yeast over the top and leave in a warm place until frothy.

Sift the flour, salt and nutmeg into a bowl. Stir in the remaining sugar and the lemon rind. Make a well in the centre and put in the yeast liquid, lemon juice, butter and egg. Mix to a dough.

Turn out on to a floured surface and knead for 5 minutes or until smooth and elastic. Cover and leave to rise in a warm place for about 1 hour or until doubled in size.

Knock back the dough and knead for 4 minutes. Roll out to 5 mm/¼ inch thick and cut out 7.5 cm/3 inch rounds. With a 2.5 cm/1 inch cutter, remove the centres of the rounds to make rings. Cover and leave to prove in a warm place for 20 minutes or until puffy.

Deep fry in oil heated to 190°C/375°F for about 4 minutes or until golden brown. Drain on paper towels and dredge with caster sugar. Serve warm or cold.

Makes about 12

Refreshing stale bread
Stale bread and rolls can be refreshed so that they are moist and soft again. To do this, sprinkle a loaf of bread, or part of a loaf, lightly with water and place it in a heavy brown paper bag (such as you get in many supermarkets). Twist the end of the bag closed and place in a preheated cool oven (150°C/300°F, Gas Mark 2). Heat for 15 minutes. For rolls, dampen the brown paper bag well, place the rolls inside and heat in the oven for 5 to 7 minutes.

Date and Orange Rolls

These delicious rolls are made by enclosing a sweet spicy filling in a rich buttery dough, rolling it up like a Swiss roll and slicing it. After baking, the rolls are coated with orange Glacé Icing.*

METRIC	IMPERIAL
100 g caster sugar	4 oz caster sugar
3 tablespoons lukewarm milk	3 tablespoons lukewarm milk
7 g dried yeast	¼ oz dried yeast
450 g strong plain flour	1 lb strong plain flour
1 teaspoon salt	1 teaspoon salt
3 tablespoons soured cream	3 tablespoons soured cream
2 tablespoons orange juice	2 tablespoons orange juice
175 g butter, melted	6 oz butter, melted
2 eggs, beaten	2 eggs, beaten
75 g dates, stoned and chopped	3 oz dates, stoned and chopped
grated rind of 2 large oranges	grated rind of 2 large oranges
25 g chopped mixed candied peel	1 oz chopped mixed candied peel
¼ teaspoon ground cinnamon	¼ teaspoon ground cinnamon
¼ teaspoon mixed spice	¼ teaspoon mixed spice
double quantity Orange Glacé Icing*	double quantity Orange Glacé Icing*

Dissolve ½ teaspoon of the sugar in the milk. Sprinkle over the yeast and leave in a warm place until it is frothy.

Sift the flour and salt into a bowl. Stir in 50 g/2 oz of the remaining sugar. Make a well in the centre and put in the yeast liquid, soured cream, orange juice, 150 g/5 oz of the butter and the eggs. Mix to a dough.

Turn out on to a floured surface and knead for 10 minutes or until smooth and elastic. Cover and leave to rise in a warm place for 1½ hours or until doubled in size.

Knock back the dough, then roll out to a 30 cm/12 inch square. Brush with the remaining butter. Mix together the dates, orange rind, peel, spices and remaining sugar and sprinkle over the dough, leaving a 1 cm/½ inch border clear all around. Roll up like a Swiss roll, pressing the edges well together to seal completely.

Cut into 4 cm/1½ inch thick slices and place, cut sides up and not quite touching, on a baking sheet. Cover and leave to prove in a warm place for 30 minutes or until risen and touching.

Bake in a preheated moderately hot oven (190°C/375°F, Gas Mark 5) for 30 to 35 minutes or until golden brown. Coat the buns with the glacé icing, then cool on a wire rack.

Makes 12 to 15

Mincemeat Pinwheel Buns

METRIC	IMPERIAL
40 g caster sugar	1½ oz caster sugar
4 tablespoons lukewarm water	4 tablespoons lukewarm water
7 g dried yeast	¼ oz dried yeast
225 g strong plain flour	8 oz strong plain flour
1 teaspoon salt	1 teaspoon salt
grated rind and juice of ½ orange	grated rind and juice of ½ orange
1 egg, beaten	1 egg, beaten
4 heaped tablespoons Mincemeat*	4 heaped tablespoons Mincemeat*
1 large cooking apple, peeled, cored and grated	1 large cooking apple, peeled, cored and grated
2 tablespoons clear honey, warmed	2 tablespoons clear honey, warmed

Dissolve ½ teaspoon of the sugar in the water. Sprinkle the yeast over the top and leave in a warm place until frothy.

Sift the flour and salt into a bowl. Stir in the orange rind and the remaining sugar. Make a well in the centre and put in the yeast liquid, orange juice and egg. Mix to a dough.

Turn out on to a floured surface and knead for 5 minutes or until smooth and elastic. Cover and leave to rise in a warm place for 1 hour or until doubled in size.

Knock back the dough and knead for 2 minutes. Roll out to a 15 × 30 cm/6 × 12 inch rectangle. Mix the mincemeat with the apple and spread over the dough, leaving a 1 cm/½ inch border clear all around. Roll up like a Swiss roll, pressing the edges together to seal, and cut into 1 cm/½ inch thick slices. Place the slices, cut sides up, in greased bun tins. Cover and leave to prove in a warm place for 30 minutes or till doubled in size.

Bake in a preheated moderately hot oven (200°C/400°F, Gas Mark 6) for 20 to 30 minutes or until golden brown. Brush with the honey, then cool on a wire rack.

Makes about 12

Golden Ring Yeast Cake

METRIC	IMPERIAL
4 teaspoons caster sugar	4 teaspoons caster sugar
150 ml lukewarm milk	¼ pint lukewarm milk
2 teaspoons dried yeast	2 teaspoons dried yeast
100 g strong plain flour	4 oz strong plain flour
pinch of salt	pinch of salt
50 g ground almonds	2 oz ground almonds
50 g butter	2 oz butter

50 g seeded raisins	2 oz seeded raisins
1 egg, beaten	1 egg, beaten
4 oranges, peeled and segmented	4 oranges, peeled and segmented
Syrup:	*Syrup:*
225 g caster sugar	8 oz caster sugar
300 ml water	½ pint water

Dissolve 1 teaspoon of the sugar in the milk. Sprinkle the yeast over the top and leave in a warm place until frothy.

Sift the flour and salt into a bowl. Stir in the remaining sugar and almonds, then rub in the butter. Stir in the raisins. Make a well in the centre and put in the yeast liquid and egg. Beat to make a smooth, soft batter.

Pour into a greased 18 to 20 cm/7 to 8 inch ring tin. Cover and leave to rise in a warm place until the batter has risen to the top of the tin.

Bake in a preheated moderately hot oven (200°C/400°F, Gas Mark 6) for 20 to 25 minutes or until golden brown and springy to the touch. Cool on a wire rack.

To make the syrup, dissolve the sugar in the water, then bring to the boil and boil until the syrup reaches 112°C/230°F on a sugar thermometer. Remove from the heat.

Place a plate under the rack on which the cake has cooled. Spoon the syrup over the cake until it has all been absorbed. Leave to cool.

Place the cake on a serving plate and fill the centre of the ring with orange segments. Serve with whipped cream.

Serves 4 to 6

Granny's Tea Bread

METRIC	IMPERIAL
225 g self-raising flour	8 oz self-raising flour
½ teaspoon salt	½ teaspoon salt
25 g soft brown sugar	1 oz soft brown sugar
50 g walnuts, chopped	2 oz walnuts, chopped
75 g seeded raisins	3 oz seeded raisins
1 tablespoon golden syrup	1 tablespoon golden syrup
150 ml milk	¼ pint milk

Sift the flour and salt into a bowl. Stir in the sugar, walnuts and raisins. Add the syrup and milk and beat until well combined.

Turn into a greased and bottom-lined 15 cm/6 inch round cake tin. Bake in a preheated moderate oven (180°C/350°F, Gas Mark 4) for about 45 minutes or until the cake has risen and a skewer inserted into the centre comes out clean. Turn out and cool on a wire rack.

Makes a 15 cm/6 inch round cake

Nutty Orange Tea Bread

The surprise in this moist tea cake is the addition of grated plain chocolate, to give a layered effect.

METRIC	IMPERIAL
350 g self-raising flour	12 oz self-raising flour
pinch of salt	pinch of salt
75 g caster sugar	3 oz caster sugar
50 g nuts, chopped	2 oz nuts, chopped
50 g chopped mixed candied peel	2 oz chopped mixed candied peel
grated rind of 2 oranges	grated rind of 2 oranges
2 eggs	2 eggs
150 ml orange juice	¼ pint orange juice
2 tablespoons milk	2 tablespoons milk
50 g butter, melted	2 oz butter, melted
50 g plain chocolate, grated	2 oz plain chocolate, grated

Sift the flour and salt into a bowl. Stir in the sugar, nuts, peel and orange rind. Lightly beat the eggs with the orange juice, milk and butter and add to the dry ingredients. Mix together well.

Spoon one-third of the mixture into a greased and floured 1 kg/2 lb loaf tin. Sprinkle over one-third of the chocolate. Repeat the layers twice.

Bake in a preheated moderate oven (160°C/325°F, Gas Mark 3) for about 1 hour or until a skewer inserted into the centre of the cake comes out clean. Cool on a wire rack.

Makes a 1 kg/2 lb cake

Cake faults

If a cake sinks in the centre as it cools, this may be because too much liquid was used to make it or because the oven was not hot enough. If a cake rises in the centre as it bakes, the oven may have been too hot.

Both these faults can be easily disguised. The cake that has sunk in the centre can be turned upside-down before icing, or be topped with whipped cream and fruit so the hollow is filled up. The cake that has peaked in the centre can be sliced level with a knife before icing.

It is preferable always to use the size of tin stated in a recipe. If the tin is too large, the finished cake may be pale and flat-looking. If the tin is too small or too shallow, the mixture will rise up over the edges, producing a very uneven and unattractive cake.

Fig Loaf

This tea bread is made without fat. If liked, use skimmed milk instead of whole milk.

METRIC	IMPERIAL
100 g All-Bran	4 oz All-Bran
100 g dark soft brown sugar	4 oz dark brown sugar
100 g dried figs, chopped	4 oz dried figs, chopped
2 teaspoons black treacle	2 teaspoons black treacle
300 ml milk	½ pint milk
100 g self-raising flour	4 oz self-raising flour

Place the All-Bran, sugar, figs, treacle and milk in a bowl and mix well. Leave to soak for 30 minutes.

Sift the flour into the bowl and combine thoroughly. Turn into a greased 500 g/1 lb loaf tin. Bake in a preheated moderate oven (180°C/350°F, Gas Mark 4) for 45 to 60 minutes or until a skewer inserted into the centre comes out clean. Cool on a wire rack.

Makes a 500 g/1 lb loaf

VARIATION
Bran fruit loaf: Use 150 g/5 oz caster sugar instead of brown sugar, and 275 g/10 oz mixed dried fruit instead of the figs. Omit the treacle.

Banana Cake

This cake may be iced with plain or Walnut Butter-cream*.

METRIC	IMPERIAL
100 g butter	4 oz butter
100 g soft brown sugar	4 oz soft brown sugar
2 eggs	2 eggs
150 g plain flour	5 oz plain flour
2 teaspoons baking powder	2 teaspoons baking powder
2 ripe bananas, mashed	2 ripe bananas, mashed
25 g walnuts, chopped	1 oz walnuts, chopped

Cream the butter with the sugar until light and fluffy. Beat in the eggs one at a time, adding a spoonful of flour with each. Sift the remaining flour and the powder into the bowl and beat into the creamed mixture with the bananas. Fold in the walnuts.

Turn into a greased and lined 18 cm/7 inch round deep cake tin. Bake in a preheated moderate oven (180°C/350°F, Gas Mark 4) for 1 hour or until a skewer inserted into the centre of the cake comes out clean. Cool on a wire rack.

Makes an 18 cm/7 inch round cake

Cherry and Almond Cake

METRIC	IMPERIAL
100 g butter	4 oz butter
100 g caster sugar	4 oz caster sugar
2 eggs, beaten	2 eggs, beaten
50 g glacé cherries, chopped	2 oz glacé cherries, chopped
100 g plain flour, sifted	4 oz plain flour, sifted
50 g ground almonds	2 oz ground almonds
few drops of almond essence	few drops of almond essence

Cream the butter with the sugar until light and fluffy. Beat in the eggs. Mix the cherries with the flour, then fold into the creamed mixture with the ground almonds and almond essence.

Turn into a greased and lined 15 cm/6 inch round deep cake tin. Bake in a preheated moderate oven (160°C/325°F, Gas Mark 3) for 1½ to 1¾ hours or until a skewer inserted into the centre of the cake comes out clean. Cool in the tin for 5 minutes, then turn out on to a wire rack to cool completely.

Makes a 15 cm/6 inch cake

Spiced Currant Scones

METRIC	IMPERIAL
225 g self-raising flour	8 oz self-raising flour
1 teaspoon salt	1 teaspoon salt
½ teaspoon ground cinnamon	½ teaspoon ground cinnamon
50 g butter	2 oz butter
50 g caster sugar	2 oz caster sugar
1 egg, beaten	1 egg, beaten
4 tablespoons milk	4 tablespoons milk
50 g currants	2 oz currants
milk to glaze	milk to glaze

Sift the flour, salt and cinnamon into a bowl. Rub in the butter until the mixture resembles fine crumbs. Stir in the sugar. Add the egg and milk and mix to a soft dough. Work in the currants.

Roll out the dough on a floured surface to about 1 cm/½ inch thick and cut into 5 cm/2 inch rounds. Place on a greased baking sheet and brush with milk.

Bake in a preheated hot oven (220°C/425°F, Gas Mark 7) for 10 minutes. Cool on a wire rack. Serve split and buttered.

Makes 12

VARIATION
Cheese scones: Omit the sugar, cinnamon and currants. Add 50 g/2 oz grated Cheddar cheese, ½ teaspoon dry mustard and ¼ teaspoon pepper with the egg and milk. Brush with beaten egg before baking.

Baking

Rich Date Cake

This cake will keep well, wrapped in foil or stored in an airtight tin. Try serving it cut in thin slices spread with cream cheese.

METRIC	IMPERIAL
150 g butter	5 oz butter
150 g soft brown sugar	5 oz soft brown sugar
2 tablespoons black treacle	2 tablespoons black treacle
2 eggs	2 eggs
225 g wholemeal flour	8 oz wholemeal flour
2 teaspoons baking powder	2 teaspoons baking powder
1 teaspoon ground cinnamon	1 teaspoon ground cinnamon
6 tablespoons milk	6 tablespoons milk
225 g stoned dates, chopped	8 oz stoned dates, chopped

Cream the butter with the sugar and treacle until light and fluffy. Beat in the eggs one at a time, adding a spoonful of flour with each. Add the remaining flour, the baking powder and cinnamon and mix into the creamed mixture alternately with the milk. Fold in the dates.

Turn into a greased and lined 18 cm/7 inch round deep cake tin. Bake in a preheated moderate oven (160°C/325°F, Gas Mark 3) for $1\frac{3}{4}$ to 2 hours or until a skewer inserted into the centre of the cake comes out clean. Cool on a wire rack.

Makes an 18 cm/7 inch round cake

Dutch Apple Walnut Cake

METRIC	IMPERIAL
175 g unsalted butter	6 oz unsalted butter
175 g caster sugar	6 oz caster sugar
3 eggs, beaten	3 eggs, beaten
grated rind and juice of 1 lemon	grated rind and juice of 1 lemon
2 dessert apples, peeled, quartered and cored	2 dessert apples, peeled, quartered and cored
75 g walnut halves	3 oz walnut halves
175 g self-raising flour, sifted	6 oz self-raising flour, sifted
3 tablespoons apricot jam, warmed and sieved	3 tablespoons apricot jam, warmed and sieved

Cream the butter with the sugar until light and fluffy. Gradually beat in the eggs, then beat in the lemon rind and juice. Chop one of the apple quarters and stir into the creamed mixture. Reserve eight walnut halves and chop the remainder. Fold the chopped walnuts into the cake mixture with the flour.

Turn into a greased and lined 18 cm/7 inch round cake tin. Level the surface. Arrange the remaining apple quarters and reserved walnut halves around the top edge.

Bake in a preheated moderate oven (160°C/325°F, Gas Mark 3) for 1 to $1\frac{1}{2}$ hours or until the cake will spring back when lightly pressed in the centre. Cool in the tin for a few minutes, then turn out on to a wire rack to cool completely. Glaze the top of the cake with the jam.

Makes an 18 cm/7 inch round cake

Honey Spice Cake

METRIC	IMPERIAL
50 g butter	2 oz butter
150 g honey	5 oz honey
150 g demerara sugar	5 oz demerara sugar
275 g plain flour	10 oz plain flour
1 teaspoon bicarbonate of soda	1 teaspoon bicarbonate of soda
1 teaspoon baking powder	1 teaspoon baking powder
1 teaspoon mixed spice	1 teaspoon mixed spice
1 teaspoon ground cinnamon	1 teaspoon ground cinnamon
1 teaspoon ground ginger	1 teaspoon ground ginger
100 g chopped mixed candied peel	4 oz chopped mixed candied peel
1 egg, beaten	1 egg, beaten
150 ml milk	$\frac{1}{4}$ pint milk
50 g nuts, chopped	2 oz nuts, chopped

Place the butter, honey and sugar in a saucepan and heat until melted and smooth. Cool.

Sift the flour, soda, baking powder and spices into a bowl. Stir in the peel. Add the egg, milk and honey mixture and beat until well combined.

Turn into a greased and lined 1 kg/2 lb loaf tin and sprinkle the nuts on top. Bake in a preheated moderate oven (180°C/350°F, Gas Mark 4) for $1\frac{1}{4}$ to $1\frac{1}{2}$ hours or until a skewer inserted into the centre comes out clean. Cool in the tin for 5 minutes, then turn out on to a wire rack to cool completely.

Makes a 1 kg/2 lb loaf

Testing cakes

There are two methods used to test whether a cake is cooked. Sponge cakes are tested by lightly pressing the centre with a fingertip: the cake should spring back. Creamed or fruit cakes are tested by inserting a fine skewer into the centre: it should come out clean.

Cake decorations
Decorate iced rich fruit cakes with seasonal shapes: Father Christmas, Easter chicks, Halloween pumpkin jack-o-lanterns and black cats, Harvest Festival fruits and vegetables, and flowers for Mother's Day. These shapes can be moulded from Almond Paste* or fondant icing, or piped in Royal Icing.* Other shapes can be made by rolling out Almond Paste* and cutting out shapes using special cutters or templates you have made yourself and a sharp knife.

Simnel Cake

METRIC	IMPERIAL
175 g butter	6 oz butter
175 g soft brown sugar	6 oz soft brown sugar
3 eggs, beaten	3 eggs, beaten
225 g plain flour	8 oz plain flour
pinch of salt	pinch of salt
1½ teaspoons mixed spice	1½ teaspoons mixed spice
175 g seeded raisins	6 oz seeded raisins
175 g sultanas	6 oz sultanas
100 g currants	4 oz currants
75 g chopped mixed candied peel	3 oz chopped mixed candied peel
2 tablespoons milk	2 tablespoons milk
750 g Almond Paste★	1½ lb Almond Paste★
warmed honey to glaze	warmed honey to glaze
angelica to decorate	angelica to decorate

Cream the butter with the sugar until light and fluffy. Beat in the eggs. Sift the flour, salt and spice into the bowl and mix well. Fold in the dried fruit, peel and milk.

Roll out one-third of the almond paste to an 18 cm/7 inch round. Spoon half the cake mixture into a greased and lined 18 cm/7 inch round deep cake tin and smooth the surface. Place the almond paste round on top and cover with the remaining cake mixture.

Bake in a preheated cool oven (150°C/300°F, Gas Mark 2) for 2¾ to 3 hours or until a skewer inserted into the centre of the cake comes out clean. Cool in the tin.

Roll out half the remaining almond paste to an 18 cm/7 inch round. Brush the top of the cake with honey and lightly press on the almond paste round. Flute the edges of the paste round.

Roll the remaining almond paste into 12 small balls and arrange in a ring on the top of the cake. Decorate with angelica leaves. If liked, tie a yellow ribbon around the side of the cake.

Makes an 18 cm/7 inch round cake

Dundee Cake

METRIC	IMPERIAL
225 g plain flour	8 oz plain flour
½ teaspoon baking powder	½ teaspoon baking powder
1½ teaspoons mixed spice	1½ teaspoons mixed spice
225 g butter, softened	8 oz butter, softened
225 g caster sugar	8 oz caster sugar
grated rind of 1 orange	grated rind of 1 orange
4 eggs, beaten	4 eggs, beaten
100 g seeded raisins	4 oz seeded raisins
100 g sultanas	4 oz sultanas
100 g currants	4 oz currants
50 g chopped mixed candied peel	2 oz chopped mixed candied peel
75 g glacé cherries, chopped	3 oz glacé cherries, chopped
50 g blanched almonds, split	2 oz blanched almonds, split

Sift the flour, baking powder and spice into a bowl. Add the butter, sugar, orange rind and eggs and beat with a wooden spoon until smooth and well mixed. Stir in the dried fruit, peel and cherries.

Turn into a greased and lined 20 cm/8 inch round deep cake tin and smooth the top. Arrange the almonds in concentric circles on top.

Bake in a preheated moderate oven (160°C/325°F, Gas Mark 3) for 2¼ to 2½ hours or until a skewer inserted into the cake comes out clean. Cool in the tin for 10 minutes, then turn out on to a wire rack.

Makes a 20 cm/8 inch round cake

Bran and Nut Muffins

METRIC	IMPERIAL
75 g bran	3 oz bran
1 large egg	1 large egg
250 ml milk	8 fl oz milk
100 g plain flour	4 oz plain flour
2 teaspoons baking powder	2 teaspoons baking powder
pinch of salt	pinch of salt
50 g sugar	2 oz sugar
25 g butter, melted	1 oz butter, melted
25 g walnuts, chopped	1 oz walnuts, chopped

Mix together the bran, egg and milk and leave to soak for 15 minutes. Sift the flour, baking powder and salt into the bowl. Add the sugar, butter and walnuts and mix together thoroughly.

Divide between greased deep patty or muffin tins. Bake in a preheated moderately hot oven (190°C/375°F, Gas Mark 5) for 20 minutes or until firm.

Makes 12 to 16

Baking

Scotch Pancakes

METRIC	IMPERIAL
100 g self-raising flour	4 oz self-raising flour
pinch of salt	pinch of salt
1 egg, beaten	1 egg, beaten
150 ml milk	$\frac{1}{4}$ pint milk
fat for frying	fat for frying

Sift the flour and salt into a bowl. Add the egg, then gradually whisk in the milk to make a smooth batter.

Lightly grease a griddle or heavy-based frying pan and heat it. Drop the batter in tablespoonsful on to the pan and cook for 1 to 2 minutes or until the surface is covered with bubbles. Turn over the scones with a palette knife and cook the other sides.

Lift the scones on to a tea towel on a wire rack, wrap in the towel and keep warm until all the scones are cooked.

Makes 10 to 12

Rich Fruit Cake

This cake is suitable for all special occasions – Christmas, birthdays, anniversaries and even a tiered wedding cake. For two tiers, double the quantities and bake in two round tins, 20 cm/8 inches and 25 cm/10 inches in diameter respectively, or two square tins, 18 cm/7 inches and 23 cm/9 inches across respectively. Test the smaller cake after $2\frac{1}{2}$ hours baking.

METRIC	IMPERIAL
350 g plain flour	12 oz plain flour
$\frac{1}{2}$ teaspoon ground cinnamon	$\frac{1}{2}$ teaspoon ground cinnamon
$\frac{1}{2}$ teaspoon grated nutmeg	$\frac{1}{2}$ teaspoon grated nutmeg
$\frac{1}{2}$ teaspoon mixed spice	$\frac{1}{2}$ teaspoon mixed spice
500 g currants	1 lb currants
225 g sultanas	8 oz sultanas
100 g seeded raisins	4 oz seeded raisins
100 g prunes, stoned and chopped	4 oz prunes, stoned and chopped
50 g glacé cherries, chopped	2 oz glacé cherries, chopped
50 g chopped mixed candied peel	2 oz chopped mixed candied peel
2 tablespoons milk	2 tablespoons milk
5 tablespoons brandy or sherry	5 tablespoons brandy or sherry
225 g butter	8 oz butter
225 g soft brown sugar	8 oz soft brown sugar
1 tablespoon black treacle	1 tablespoon black treacle
5 large eggs, beaten	5 large eggs, beaten

Sift the flour with the spices. Place the dried fruit, cherries and peel in a bowl and sprinkle with the milk and 2 tablespoons of the brandy or sherry.

Cream the butter with the sugar until light and fluffy. Beat in the treacle, then gradually beat in the eggs. Fold in the flour and fruit mixtures.

Turn into a greased and double-lined 20 cm/8 inch square or 23 cm/9 inch round deep cake tin. Make a slight hollow in the centre.

Bake in a preheated moderate oven (160°C/325°F, Gas Mark 3) for 1 hour, then reduce the temperature to very cool (140°C/275°F, Gas Mark 1). Bake for a further 2 to 3 hours or until a skewer inserted into the centre of the cake comes out clean. Cool in the tin for a few minutes, then turn out on to a wire rack to cool completely. Wrap the cold cake in foil and store for a few weeks.

Make holes in the base of the cake and spoon in the remaining brandy. Rewrap in foil and store. One week before the cake is required, cover with Almond Paste*. Leave to harden, then cover with Royal Icing* and decorate to suit the occasion.

Makes a 20 cm/8 inch square or 23 cm/9 inch round cake

Decorating a fruit cake

To decorate a rich fruit cake, first cover it with Almond Paste* before adding the icing. The paste prevents the white icing being stained by the fruit cake. Roll out one-third of the almond paste on a surface dusted with icing sugar to a round or square the same size as the top of the cake. Brush the top of the cake with warmed, sieved apricot jam and place the almond paste on top. Press on lightly. Roll out the remaining almond paste to a strip long enough to go around the side of the cake. If the cake is square, cut the strip into four equal portions. Brush the side of the cake with jam, then lightly press on the almond paste. Make the joins as neat as possible, then leave to dry for 2 to 3 days. If the icing is added too soon, the oils from the almond paste may seep through it.

To ice the cake, put the prepared Royal icing* on top of the cake and, working with a palette knife, gradually spread the icing over the top and down the sides until it is completely covered. For a flat surface, draw the palette knife or a steel ruler across the top of the cake in a single movement to make the surface absolutely smooth. Smooth the sides in the same way, keeping the joins neat. For a rough surface, draw up the icing into peaks using the tip of the palette knife. Leave the icing to dry for 24 hours before adding any decorations.

Gingerbread

If liked, cover the gingerbread with Lemon Glacé Icing* and decorate with chopped preserved ginger.

METRIC	IMPERIAL
50 g butter	2 oz butter
50 g soft brown sugar	2 oz soft brown sugar
50 g black treacle	2 oz black treacle
50 g golden syrup	2 oz golden syrup
175 g wholemeal flour	6 oz wholemeal flour
2 teaspoons ground ginger	2 teaspoons ground ginger
1 teaspoon bicarbonate of soda	1 teaspoon bicarbonate of soda
5 tablespoons warm milk	5 tablespoons warm milk
1 egg, beaten	1 egg, beaten

Place the butter, sugar, treacle and syrup in a saucepan and heat until melted and smooth. Cool.

Place the flour and ginger in a bowl. Make a well in the centre and put in the syrup mixture. Dissolve the soda in the milk and add to the bowl with the egg. Beat well until thoroughly combined.

Pour into a greased and lined 28 × 18 cm/11 × 7 inch baking tin. Bake in a preheated moderate oven (180°C/350°F, Gas Mark 4) for about 40 minutes or until well risen and springy to the touch. Cool in the tin for 15 minutes, then turn out on to a wire rack to cool completely. Cut into slices to serve.

Makes about 15 slices

VARIATIONS
Fruity gingerbread: Increase the butter, brown sugar and treacle to 100 g/4 oz each. Omit the golden syrup. Use 100 g/4 oz each plain and wholemeal flour, and add 2 teaspoons ground cinnamon. Increase the milk to 150 ml/¼ pint, and add 50 g/2 oz mixed dried fruit to the mixture. Spoon into a greased 1 kg/2 lb loaf tin and bake in a preheated cool oven (150°C/300°F, Gas Mark 2) for about 1 hour.
Parkin: Increase the butter, brown sugar and golden syrup to 100 g/4 oz each. Omit the treacle. Use 100 g/4 oz each plain flour and medium or fine oatmeal instead of the wholemeal flour. Reduce the bicarbonate of soda to ½ teaspoon. Turn into a greased and lined 20 cm/8 inch square tin and bake in a preheated moderate oven (160°C/325°F, Gas Mark 3) for 1 to 1¼ hours. When cold, wrap in foil and store for 3 to 4 days before serving.

Cooling cakes
When a cake is cooked, leave it to cool for a few seconds before turning it out on to a wire rack to cool completely. Fruit cakes should be left longer in the tin before turning out, or cooled completely in the tin.

Chocolate cake decorations
Iced cakes can be given a finishing decorative touch by adding jellies and other small sweets, chocolate shavings, walnut halves, chopped nuts, or crystallized flowers.

Chocolate, in particular, lends itself to many cake and dessert decorations. Use the dark, glossy, plain chocolate as this is easiest to cut after melting and keeps its sheen. Melt the chocolate in a heatproof bowl placed over a pan of simmering water.

To make chocolate squares and triangles, pour the melted chocolate on to waxed paper or foil in a thin layer and leave to set. Cut into shapes with aspic or petits fours cutters or a sharp knife and carefully peel away the paper or foil.

Chocolate curls are made by pouring the melted chocolate on to a cold, smooth surface such as marble and spreading it out into a 3 mm/⅛ inch layer. When the chocolate has set, use a long-bladed knife held at a 45° angle to shave off the chocolate into curls.

Chocolate leaves are not as difficult as you might think. Spread melted chocolate over the backs of washed and dried rose leaves and leave to set, chocolate side up. Carefully peel off the leaf, trying not to touch the chocolate.

Easy Marmalade Cake

METRIC	IMPERIAL
100 g self-raising flour	4 oz self-raising flour
100 g butter, softened	4 oz butter, softened
100 g caster sugar	4 oz caster sugar
2 large eggs	2 large eggs
5 tablespoons chunky marmalade	5 tablespoons chunky marmalade
1 quantity Vanilla or Orange Glacé Icing*	1 quantity Vanilla or Orange Glacé Icing*

Sift the flour into a bowl. Add the butter, sugar and eggs and beat well with a wooden spoon until pale and smooth. Stir in 3 tablespoons of the marmalade.

Turn into a greased and lined 20 cm/8 inch round cake tin and smooth the top. Bake in a preheated moderate oven (180°C/350°F, Gas Mark 4) for 35 to 40 minutes or until the cake will spring back when lightly pressed in the centre. Cool in the tin for 5 minutes, then turn out on to a wire rack to cool completely.

Spread the remaining marmalade over the cake, then pour over the glacé icing and spread evenly. Leave to set before serving.

Makes a 20 cm/8 inch round cake

Baking

Quick Orange Cake

METRIC	IMPERIAL
250 g plain flour	9 oz plain flour
1 teaspoon baking powder	1 teaspoon baking powder
pinch of salt	pinch of salt
175 g butter, softened	6 oz butter, softened
225 g caster sugar	8 oz caster sugar
grated rind of 1 orange	grated rind of 1 orange
3 eggs	3 eggs
icing sugar to dredge	icing sugar to dredge

Sift the flour, baking powder and salt into a bowl. Add the butter, sugar, orange rind and eggs and beat together with a wooden spoon until pale and smooth. Turn into a greased and lined 18 or 20 cm/7 or 8 inch square cake tin.

Bake in a preheated cool oven (150°C/300°F, Gas Mark 2) for 1¼ to 1½ hours or until the cake springs back when lightly pressed in the centre. Cool on a wire rack.

Dredge the top with icing sugar before serving.

Makes an 18 or 20 cm/7 or 8 inch square cake

Devil's Food Cake

METRIC	IMPERIAL
175 g plain flour	6 oz plain flour
¼ teaspoon baking powder	¼ teaspoon baking powder
1 teaspoon bicarbonate of soda	1 teaspoon bicarbonate of soda
50 g cocoa powder	2 oz cocoa powder
100 g butter, softened	4 oz butter, softened
275 g caster sugar	10 oz caster sugar
2 eggs, beaten	2 eggs, beaten
250 ml water	8 fl oz water
½ quantity Chocolate Buttercream★	½ quantity Chocolate Buttercream★
1 quantity American Frosting★	1 quantity American Frosting★

Sift the flour with the baking powder, soda and cocoa powder. Cream the butter and sugar together until light and fluffy. Beat in the eggs. Fold in the flour mixture and water alternately.

Divide the mixture between two greased and lined 20 cm/8 inch sandwich tins. Bake in a preheated moderate oven (180°C/350°F, Gas Mark 4) for 50 to 60 minutes or until the cakes spring back when lightly pressed in the centres. Cool on a wire rack.

Sandwich the cake layers together with the buttercream. Cover the top and sides of the cake with American frosting, swirling it on to make a decorative pattern.

Makes a 20 cm/8 inch sandwich cake

Candied fruit and peel

Making candied fruit and peel at home does take time, but it is a very easy process, and it is so much more economical than buying expensive candied fruits.

Fruits used for candying should be perfect and firm, not over-ripe. Prepare the fruits as you would for cooking, by peeling and stoning where necessary. Weigh the fruit, place it in a saucepan and cover with water. Bring to the boil and simmer until the fruit is just soft but not overcooked. Drain, reserving the cooking water.

For every 500 g/1 lb of fruit, make a syrup from 300 ml/½ pint of the cooking water and 175 g/6 oz sugar. Pour the hot syrup over the fruit and leave 24 hours. Then every day for 3 days: drain off the syrup into a saucepan and add 50 g/2 oz sugar. Bring to the boil and pour back over the fruit.

The 4th day, drain off the syrup and add 75 g/3 oz sugar. Bring to the boil and pour over the fruit. Leave for 2 days, then repeat this step. Let the fruit soak for 4 days. Finally, drain the fruit and dry in a warm place such as an airing cupboard.

Decorative cake icing

To make a feathered pattern on the top of an iced cake, pipe parallel lines, equally spaced apart, on the top of the still-wet icing, using a contrasting coloured icing. Draw a cocktail stick or a fine skewer across the lines in one direction, at equal intervals. Turn the cake around and draw the cocktail stick or skewer between the first set of marks, in the opposite direction.

A cobweb pattern is made by piping a contrasting coloured icing on to the top of the cake in a spiral, starting in the centre. Draw a skewer from the centre to the edge at regular intervals, then draw the skewer from the edge to the centre between the first marks.

*

Icing run-outs, which are raised designs made with royal icing, can be piped straight onto a cake or onto non-stick parchment or waxed paper and attached to the cake when dry. Draw the outline of the shape on paper, then trace onto the cake by pricking with a pin. Pipe the outline using a fine writing tube, then fill in with flowing royal icing.

Victoria Sandwich

This rich sponge cake is used as the basis for many cakes and puddings, and is very useful to have on hand in the freezer. To freeze, place the cooled cakes one on top of the other with greaseproof paper or foil between them and place in a polythene bag or wrap in foil. Seal, label and freeze. Thaw in the wrappings at room temperature for 3 hours, and fill and ice just before serving.

METRIC	IMPERIAL
175 g butter	6 oz butter
175 g caster sugar	6 oz caster sugar
3 eggs, beaten	3 eggs, beaten
175 g self-raising flour	6 oz self-raising flour
pinch of salt	pinch of salt
about 2 tablespoons warm water	about 2 tablespoons warm water
jam	jam
sifted icing sugar	sifted icing sugar

Beat the butter with the sugar until light and fluffy. Beat in the eggs. Sift the flour and salt into the bowl and fold in until well combined. Add enough water to make a soft dropping consistency.

Divide between two greased and bottom-lined 18 cm/7 inch sandwich tins. Bake in a preheated moderately hot oven (190°C/375°F, Gas Mark 5) for about 20 minutes or until well risen and golden and the cakes have shrunk away from the sides of the tins. Cool on a wire rack.

Sandwich the cakes together with jam, then dredge the top of the cake with icing sugar.

Makes an 18 cm/7 inch sandwich cake

VARIATIONS
The cake may be filled with Buttercream* or whipped cream and iced with Buttercream* or Glacé Icing*. Caster sugar may be used to dredge the top instead of icing sugar. Lemon curd may be used instead of jam for the filling.

Butterfly cakes: Divide the mixture between greased and floured patty tins, or use paper cake cases. Bake in a preheated moderately hot oven (200°C/400°F, Gas Mark 6) for 10 to 12 minutes. When cold, cut a slice from the top of each cake and cut the slices in half. Pipe or spread a little Buttercream* or whipped cream on each cake and press in the two halves of the top slice to form 'wings'. Dust with sifted icing sugar if liked.

Iced fancies: Make up the basic mixture for Victoria Sandwich and pour it into a lined Swiss roll tin 30 × 20 cm/12 × 8 inches, spreading it evenly into the corners. Bake as above at 190°C/375°F, Gas Mark 5 for about 20 minutes. Allow to cool slightly, then turn out onto a wire rack and carefully peel off the lining paper. When cold, cut the cake into four strips with a sharp knife. From the strips, cut squares, rectangles, triangles and, using a 4 cm/1½ inch pastry cutter, rounds. Ice the little sponge shapes with glacé icing and decorate with silver balls, glacé cherries, chocolate vermicelli etc.

Coffee and walnut sandwich: Flavour the basic mixture with 2 teaspoons coffee essence or 2 teaspoons instant coffee dissolved in 1 tablespoon water. Fill and top the cake with Coffee or Mocha Buttercream* and decorate with halved walnuts.

Chocolate Sandwich Cake

If preferred, the cake layers may be sandwiched together with whipped cream instead of buttercream. Or use Mocha or Walnut Buttercream* instead of chocolate.

METRIC	IMPERIAL
100 g butter	4 oz butter
100 g caster sugar	4 oz caster sugar
2 eggs	2 eggs
100 g self-raising flour, sifted	4 oz self-raising flour, sifted
25 g cocoa powder	1 oz cocoa powder
1 tablespoon hot water	1 tablespoon hot water
2/3 quantity Chocolate Buttercream*	2/3 quantity Chocolate Buttercream*
sifted icing sugar to dredge	sifted icing sugar to dredge

Cream the butter with the sugar until light and fluffy. Beat in the eggs one at a time, adding a spoonful of the flour with each. Dissolve the cocoa powder in the water, then add to the bowl with the remaining flour. Mix together well until smooth.

Divide the mixture between two greased and lined 18 cm/7 inch sandwich tins. Bake in a preheated moderately hot oven (190°C/375°F, Gas Mark 5) for about 20 minutes or until well risen and firm to the touch. Cool on a wire rack.

Place one cake layer on a serving plate and spread over the buttercream. Place the other cake layer on top and press down gently. Dredge the top of the cake with icing sugar.

Makes an 18 cm/7 inch sandwich cake

Chocolate Banana Sandwich Cake

This moist cake is irresistible, and is very attractively decorated.

METRIC	IMPERIAL
175 g unsalted butter	6 oz unsalted butter
175 g caster sugar	6 oz caster sugar
3 eggs	3 eggs
225 g self-raising flour	8 oz self-raising flour
2 ripe bananas, mashed	2 ripe bananas, mashed

1 quantity Chocolate Buttercream*
chocolate vermicelli
double quantity Glacé Icing*
2 teaspoons cocoa powder
1 teaspoon hot water

1 quantity Chocolate Buttercream*
chocolate vermicelli
double quantity Glacé Icing*
2 teaspoons cocoa powder
1 teaspoon hot water

Cream the butter with the sugar until light and fluffy. Beat in the eggs one at a time, adding a spoonful of flour with each. Sift the remaining flour into the bowl. Add the bananas and fold together thoroughly.

Divide the mixture between two greased 20 cm/8 inch sandwich tins. Bake in a preheated moderately hot oven (190°C/375°F, Gas Mark 5) for 25 to 30 minutes or until the cakes spring back when lightly pressed. Cool on a wire rack.

Sandwich the cake layers together with half the buttercream. Spread the remaining buttercream over the side of the cake, then roll in vermicelli.

Spread three-quarters of the glacé icing over the top of the cake. Dissolve the cocoa in the hot water and add to the remaining icing. Mix until evenly coloured. Place the chocolate icing in a piping bag fitted with a small plain nozzle and pipe straight lines across the top of the cake. Pipe another series of straight lines at right angles to the first lines to form squares. Leave it to set before serving.

Makes a 20 cm/8 inch sandwich cake

Sponge Sandwich

Whereas the Victoria Sandwich is made by the creaming method, this is a whisked sponge. It is feather-light in texture but, being fatless, must be eaten as fresh as possible. If very well sealed, it can be frozen successfully.

METRIC	IMPERIAL
3 large eggs	3 large eggs
100 g caster sugar	4 oz caster sugar
75 g plain flour, sifted	3 oz plain flour, sifted

Place the eggs and sugar in a heatproof bowl placed over a pan of simmering water. Whisk until the mixture is very thick and pale and will make a ribbon trail on itself when the whisk is lifted. (If using an electric beater, no heat is needed.) Remove from the heat.

Gently but thoroughly fold in the flour. Divide the mixture between two greased and floured 18 cm/7 inch sandwich tins.

Bake in a preheated moderately hot oven (200°C/400°F, Gas Mark 6) for about 15 minutes or until the cakes will spring back when lightly pressed in the centres. Cool slightly in the tins, then turn out on to a wire rack. Sandwich together with jam.

Makes an 18 cm/7 inch sandwich cake

VARIATIONS

Orange or lemon sponge: Make as above, adding the finely grated rind of 1 orange or lemon and 1 tablespoon hot orange or lemon juice with the flour. Sandwich the cake layers together with orange or lemon curd or marmalade and whipped cream. Decorate the top with crystallized orange or lemon slices.

Coffee sponge: Add 1 tablespoon very strong hot coffee with the flour.

Sponge flan case: Make as above, using only 2 eggs and 75 g/3 oz sugar. Bake in a 20 to 23 cm/8 to 9 inch flan tin for 10 to 12 minutes. Cool before filling with fruit.

Cake tins

To prepare a shallow cake tin for baking, first brush the sides and bottom with melted fat. Place a round of buttered greaseproof paper in the bottom of the tin and dust it lightly with flour. The paper lining will prevent the bottom of the cake sticking to the tin and make it easier to turn out. For richer cake mixtures, and tins that are over 5 cm/2 inches deep, the sides of the tin should be lined with paper as well. To do this, measure the circumference of the tin with a piece of string. Cut out a strip of greaseproof paper 2.5 cm/1 inch longer than the circumference, and 2.5 cm/1 inch wider than the depth of the tin. Fold down 1 cm/½ inch of the long edge and make cuts in the fold, about 2.5 cm/1 inch apart. Butter the paper strip and place it in the tin against the sides, with the folded edge on the bottom. Place the bottom round in the tin so that it is over the fold.

If a recipe calls for a tin size you do not have, do not despair. In a smaller tin, the mixture will be deeper, so increase the baking time by about 5 minutes. For a larger tin, where the mixture will be more shallow, decrease the baking time by 5 minutes.

You should not, however, necessarily expect perfect results if you have to substitute a different size of tin. See page 133, Cake faults, for some of the imperfections that could occur.

If you want to substitute a round tin for a square one, here is a guide: 18 cm/7 inch round use 12.5 cm/5 inch square, 20 cm/8 inch round use 18 cm/7 inch square, 23 cm/9 inch round use 20 cm/8 inch square, 25 cm/10 inch round use 23 cm/9 inch square, 28 cm/11 inch round use 25 cm/10 inch square, 30 cm/12 inch round use 28 cm/11 inch square, and 35 cm/14 inch round use 30 cm/12 inch square.

Baking

Lemon Mimosa Cake

METRIC	IMPERIAL
100 g butter	4 oz butter
100 g caster sugar	4 oz caster sugar
7 tablespoons lemon curd	7 tablespoons lemon curd
grated rind of ½ lemon	grated rind of ½ lemon
2 large eggs	2 large eggs
225 g self-raising flour	8 oz self-raising flour
1 quantity Lemon Glacé Icing*	1 quantity Lemon Glacé Icing*
10 mimosa balls	10 mimosa balls
19 angelica leaves	19 angelica leaves

Cream the butter with the sugar until light and fluffy. Beat in 3 tablespoons of the lemon curd, the lemon rind and eggs. Sift the flour into the bowl and mix in well.

Turn into a greased and bottom-lined 18 cm/7 inch round cake tin. Bake in a preheated moderate oven (160°C/325°F, Gas Mark 3) for 55 minutes or until a skewer inserted into the centre of the cake comes out clean. Cool in the tin for 5 minutes, then turn out on to a wire rack to cool completely.

Cut the cake into two layers and sandwich back together with the remaining lemon curd. Spread the icing over the top of the cake. Arrange two mimosa balls and three angelica leaves in the centre of the cake and decorate the edge with the remaining mimosa balls and angelica leaves. Leave to set.

Makes an 18 cm/7 inch sandwich cake

Chocolate Walnut Cookies

METRIC	IMPERIAL
100 g butter	4 oz butter
50 g caster sugar	2 oz caster sugar
175 g self-raising flour	6 oz self-raising flour
2 tablespoons condensed milk	2 tablespoons condensed milk
25 g walnuts, finely chopped	1 oz walnuts, finely chopped
100 g plain chocolate, grated	4 oz plain chocolate, grated

Cream the butter with the sugar until light and fluffy. Sift the flour into the bowl and work into the creamed mixture alternately with the milk. Add the walnuts and chocolate and mix well.

Roll the dough into small balls and place on greased baking sheets, well spaced apart. Flatten the balls slightly with a fork.

Bake in a preheated moderate oven (180°C/350°F, Gas Mark 4) for about 15 minutes or until golden brown. Cool on a wire rack.

Makes about 24

Whisked Butter Sponge

METRIC	IMPERIAL
3 large eggs, separated	3 large eggs, separated
75 g caster sugar	3 oz caster sugar
75 g plain flour	3 oz plain flour
50 g unsalted butter, melted	2 oz unsalted butter, melted
Chocolate Fudge Icing* grated chocolate to decorate	Chocolate Fudge Icing* grated chocolate to decorate

Place the egg yolks and sugar in a heatproof bowl placed over a pan of simmering water and whisk until very pale and thick and the mixture will leave a ribbon trail on itself when the whisk is lifted. Remove from the heat and whisk until cool. (If using an electric beater, no heat is needed.)

Fold in half the flour. Whisk the egg whites until stiff and fold in. Pour the melted butter around the edge of the bowl and fold in. Fold in the remaining flour.

Spoon into a greased and lined 18 cm/7 inch round cake tin. Bake in a preheated moderate oven (180°C/350°F, Gas Mark 4) for 30 to 35 minutes or until the cake springs back when lightly pressed in the centre. Cool in the tin for 5 minutes, then turn out on to a wire rack to cool completely.

Spread the icing over the top and sides of the cake and sprinkle grated chocolate on top.

Makes an 18 cm/7 inch round cake

Date Crunchies

METRIC	IMPERIAL
175 g dates, stoned and chopped	6 oz dates, stoned and chopped
2 tablespoons water	2 tablespoons water
1 tablespoon clear honey	1 tablespoon clear honey
225 g wholemeal flour	8 oz wholemeal flour
75 g soft brown sugar	3 oz soft brown sugar
100 g rolled oats	4 oz rolled oats
150 g butter, melted	5 oz butter, melted

Place the dates, water and honey in a saucepan and simmer until the dates are soft.

Mix together the flour, sugar and oats. Add the butter to bind the dry ingredients. Press half the mixture evenly over the bottom of a greased 18 cm/7 inch square cake tin. Cover with the date mixture, then sprinkle over the remaining oat mixture and press it down well.

Bake in a preheated moderate oven (180°C/350°F, Gas Mark 4) for 55 to 60 minutes. Cut into bars, then leave to cool in the tin.

Makes 18

Baking

Florentines

METRIC	IMPERIAL
50 g butter	2 oz butter
50 g sugar	2 oz sugar
50 g walnuts, finely chopped	2 oz walnuts, finely chopped
2 tablespoons diced mixed candied peel	2 tablespoons diced mixed candied peel
2 tablespoons finely chopped glacé cherries	2 tablespoons finely chopped glacé cherries
1½ tablespoons chopped sultanas	1½ tablespoons chopped sultanas
1 tablespoon single cream	1 tablespoon single cream
75 g plain chocolate, melted	3 oz plain chocolate, melted

Place the butter and sugar in a saucepan and heat gently until the butter has melted and the sugar dissolved. Remove from the heat and stir in the remaining ingredients, except the chocolate.

Drop teaspoonsful of the mixture on to greased baking sheets, well spaced apart. Bake in a preheated moderate oven (180°C/350°F, Gas Mark 4) for 10 minutes or until golden brown. Quickly press into neat rounds with a palette knife, then cool slightly on the baking sheets. Transfer to a wire rack to cool.

Spread the chocolate over the backs of the biscuits and mark in a wavy pattern with a fork. Leave to set.

Makes about 20

Easter Biscuits

METRIC	IMPERIAL
100 g butter	4 oz butter
100 g caster sugar	4 oz caster sugar
1 egg yolk	1 egg yolk
225 g plain flour	8 oz plain flour
½ teaspoon ground cinnamon	½ teaspoon ground cinnamon
50 g currants	2 oz currants
caster sugar to dredge	caster sugar to dredge

Cream the butter with the sugar until light and fluffy. Beat in the egg yolk. Sift the flour and cinnamon into the bowl and mix well. Work in the currants.

Roll out the dough on a floured surface to about 5 mm/¼ inch thick and cut out 7.5 cm/3 inch rounds with a fluted cutter. Place on a greased baking sheet and prick with a fork.

Bake in a preheated moderate oven (180°C/350°F, Gas Mark 4) for 10 to 12 minutes or until pale golden. Cool on a wire rack.

Dredge with caster sugar before serving.

Makes about 12

Maids of Honour

METRIC	IMPERIAL
175 g quantity Flaky, Puff or Rough Puff Pastry*	6 oz quantity Flaky, Puff or Rough Puff Pastry*
100 g ground almonds	4 oz ground almonds
50 g caster sugar	2 oz caster sugar
1 egg	1 egg
1 egg yolk	1 egg yolk
25 g flour	1 oz flour
1 teaspoon orange flower water	1 teaspoon orange flower water
pinch of grated lemon rind	pinch of grated lemon rind

Roll out the dough until wafer thin and cut into rounds to line 12 to 15 deep patty tins.

Mix together the remaining ingredients and divide between the pastry cases. Bake in a preheated hot oven (220°C/425°F, Gas Mark 7) for 10 minutes, then reduce the temperature to moderate (180°C/350°F, Gas Mark 4). Bake for a further 15 minutes or until the pastry is golden brown and the filling is set. Cool in the tins.

Makes 12 to 15

VARIATION
Line the tins with pastry as above, then put 1 teaspoon of jam in cach. Mix together 175 g/6 oz sieved cottage cheese, 50 g/2 oz sultanas, ½ teaspoon almond essence, 2 tablespoons ground almonds and 2 eggs. Divide between the pastry cases and bake as above. When the cakes are cooked, ice with Glacé Icing* flavoured with a few drop of almond essence.

Batch cooking

Batch cooking can make life easier for the busy cook with a freezer. To batch cook is to cook a large quantity of the same food especially for the freezer. So when you feel like baking, don't make just one or two loaves of bread or one cake for teatime, make five or more. Keep one for immediate use and freeze the rest, or freeze them all.

Cakes are ideal foods for batch cooking, whether they be plain or fruity, large or small, or fancy gâteaux. They can be frozen whole or in slices. Fancy gâteaux decorated with buttercream should be packed in a rigid container so the decoration is not damaged in the freezer. To use the cakes, leave them to thaw at room temperature for 1 to 4 hours.

Plain and fruit cakes will keep for 4 to 6 months in the freezer; gâteaux with buttercream will keep for 3 months. If you want to freeze a fresh cream cake, it will keep for 2 months.

Brownies

These moist squares of chocolate and nut cake will be immensely popular with all the family.

METRIC	IMPERIAL
100 g butter	4 oz butter
100 g plain chocolate	4 oz plain chocolate
100 g soft brown sugar	4 oz soft brown sugar
100 g self-raising flour	4 oz self-raising flour
pinch of salt	pinch of salt
2 eggs, beaten	2 eggs, beaten
50 g walnuts, chopped	2 oz walnuts, chopped
1–2 tablespoons milk	1–2 tablespoons milk

Place the butter and chocolate in a heavy-based saucepan and heat gently until melted. Remove from the heat and stir in the sugar until dissolved. Leave to cool.

Sift the flour and salt into a bowl. Add the chocolate mixture and eggs and mix well. Stir in the walnuts, then add enough milk to make a soft dropping consistency.

Pour into a greased 20 cm/8 inch square cake tin. Bake in a preheated moderate oven (180°C/350°F, Gas Mark 4) for about 30 minutes or until a skewer inserted into the centre of the cake comes out clean.

Cool in the tin, then cut into squares to serve.

Makes about 16

Shortbread

METRIC	IMPERIAL
150 g plain flour	5 oz plain flour
pinch of salt	pinch of salt
25 g ground rice	1 oz ground rice
50 g caster sugar	2 oz caster sugar
100 g butter	4 oz butter
caster sugar to dredge	caster sugar to dredge

Sift the flour, salt and ground rice into a bowl and stir in the sugar. Add the butter and rub in, then knead to make a smooth dough. Do not allow the dough to become sticky. Cover and chill for 30 minutes.

Press the dough into an 18 cm/7 inch round or fluted flan ring placed on a greased baking sheet, or into a shortbread mould. If using a mould, turn out on to the baking sheet. Prick all over with a fork, then mark the plain round into wedges. Chill for 15 minutes.

Bake in a preheated moderate oven (160°C/325°F, Gas Mark 3) for 40 to 45 minutes or until pale golden. Allow to cool slightly on the baking sheet, then transfer to a wire rack to cool completely. Dredge with sugar before serving.

Makes about 8 wedges

Honey Chocolate Biscuits

METRIC	IMPERIAL
50 g plain flour	2 oz plain flour
50 g custard powder	2 oz custard powder
50 g butter	2 oz butter
50 g plain chocolate, finely chopped	2 oz plain chocolate, finely chopped
1 tablespoon clear honey	1 tablespoon clear honey
1 egg yolk	1 egg yolk

Sift the flour and custard powder into a bowl. Rub in the butter until the mixture resembles fine crumbs. Stir in the chocolate. Add the honey and egg yolk and mix to a dough.

Roll out the dough on a floured surface to 1 cm/½ inch thick. Cut out 5 cm/2 inch rounds and place on greased baking sheets.

Bake in a preheated cool oven (150°C/300°F, Gas Mark 2) for 25 to 30 minutes or until golden brown. Cool on a wire rack.

Makes 15

Caramel Fingers

METRIC	IMPERIAL
100 g unsalted butter	4 oz unsalted butter
50 g caster sugar	2 oz caster sugar
175 g plain flour	6 oz plain flour
Topping:	*Topping:*
1 small can condensed milk	1 small can condensed milk
100 g caster sugar	4 oz caster sugar
100 g unsalted butter	4 oz unsalted butter
2 tablespoons golden syrup	2 tablespoons golden syrup
175 g plain chocolate, melted	6 oz plain chocolate, melted

Cream the butter with the sugar until light and fluffy. Sift the flour into the bowl and work into the creamed mixture to make a smooth dough.

Press the dough evenly over the bottom of a greased 20 cm/8 inch square tin. Prick all over. Bake in a preheated moderate oven (180°C/350°F, Gas Mark 4) for 20 to 30 minutes or until golden brown. Cool in the tin for 5 minutes, then cool on a wire rack.

To make the topping, place the milk, sugar, butter and syrup in a saucepan and heat, stirring to dissolve the sugar. Bring to the boil and boil for 6 to 8 minutes, stirring constantly. Allow to cool slightly.

Replace the biscuit base in the tin and pour over the caramel topping. Leave to cool.

Spread the melted chocolate over the caramel. Mark into fingers. Allow to set before cutting.

Makes 24

Chocolate Coconut Slices

METRIC	IMPERIAL
100 g unsalted butter	4 oz unsalted butter
175 g caster sugar	6 oz caster sugar
2 eggs	2 eggs
100 g ground rice	4 oz ground rice
100 g desiccated coconut	4 oz desiccated coconut
100 g sultanas	4 oz sultanas
100 g glacé cherries, chopped	4 oz glacé cherries, chopped
175 g plain chocolate, melted	6 oz plain chocolate, melted

Cream the butter with the sugar until light and fluffy. Beat in the eggs, then fold in the rice, coconut, sultanas and cherries. Spread evenly in a greased and lined 28 × 18 cm/11 × 7 inch baking tin.

Bake in a preheated moderate oven (160°C/325°F, Gas Mark 3) for 30 minutes. Leave to cool in the tin.

Pour the melted chocolate over the biscuit base. Leave until set, then cut into bars to serve.

Makes 12

Christmas Plait

METRIC	IMPERIAL
225 g Mincemeat*	8 oz Mincemeat*
50 g glacé cherries, chopped	2 oz glacé cherries, chopped
50 g blanched almonds, chopped	2 oz blanched almonds, chopped
350 g frozen puff pastry, thawed	12 oz frozen puff pastry, thawed
1 egg, beaten	1 egg, beaten
1 quantity Lemon Glacé Icing*	1 quantity Lemon Glacé Icing*
To decorate:	*To decorate:*
glacé cherries, halved	glacé cherries, halved
flaked almonds	flaked almonds

Mix together the mincemeat, cherries and almonds. Roll out the dough on a floured surface to a 30 × 35 cm/12 × 14 inch rectangle. Lightly score the rectangle into three equal portions lengthways. Make 7.5 cm/3 inch long cuts, 2.5 cm/1 inch apart, at an angle of 45°, down the two outside thirds. Spread the mincemeat mixture down the centre third.

Dampen the outside edges, then fold over the strips alternately to give a plaited effect. Seal the ends. Place on a baking sheet and brush with beaten egg.

Bake in a preheated hot oven (220°C/425°F, Gas Mark 7) for 20 minutes. Allow to cool, then spoon over the glacé icing. Decorate with cherries and almonds and leave to set before serving.

Serves 6

Freezing biscuit dough

Unbaked biscuit dough freezes well and makes a useful standby in the freezer as the biscuits can be baked from frozen. Cut them into shapes or pipe on to trays and open freeze, then pack in rigid freezer containers. Alternatively, form the dough into long rolls and wrap in freezer foil. Thaw the dough in the refrigerator for 1 to 2 hours, then slice and bake. The biscuits can be stored in the freezer for up to 6 months.

Baked biscuits can be frozen successfully, too, although they will keep well in an air-tight tin. Pack in rigid containers, separating each biscuit with freezer tissue to prevent breakages. Thaw at room temperature, then refresh in a moderately hot oven for 5 minutes.

Crunchy Apple Cake

METRIC	IMPERIAL
100 g self-raising flour	4 oz self-raising flour
50 g ground almonds	2 oz ground almonds
75 g butter	3 oz butter
50 g soft brown sugar	2 oz soft brown sugar
1 teaspoon lemon juice	1 teaspoon lemon juice
1 small egg, beaten	1 small egg, beaten
Filling:	*Filling:*
500 g cooking apples, peeled, cored and chopped	1 lb cooking apples, peeled, cored and chopped
75 g soft brown sugar	3 oz soft brown sugar
1 teaspoon lemon juice	1 teaspoon lemon juice
Topping:	*Topping:*
75 g self-raising flour	3 oz self-raising flour
1 teaspoon ground cinnamon	1 teaspoon ground cinnamon
50 g butter	2 oz butter
50 g soft brown sugar	2 oz soft brown sugar

Sift the flour into a bowl and stir in 25 g/1 oz of the almonds. Rub in the butter until the mixture resembles fine crumbs. Stir in the sugar. Add the lemon juice and egg and mix to a stiff dough.

Press the dough over the bottom of a greased 20 cm/8 inch loose-bottomed cake tin. Sprinkle over the remaining almonds and chill for 20 minutes.

Mix together the ingredients for the filling and spread over the cake base.

For the topping, sift the flour and cinnamon into a bowl. Rub in the butter until the mixture resembles fine crumbs. Stir in the sugar. Sprinkle the topping over the filling.

Bake in a preheated moderate oven (180°C/350°F, Gas Mark 4) for 1 to 1¼ hours or until the topping is golden brown. Cool in the tin for 10 minutes, then turn out on to a wire rack to cool completely.

Makes a 20 cm/8 inch round cake

Rich Vanilla Buns

METRIC	IMPERIAL
225 g self-raising flour	8 oz self-raising flour
175 g butter	6 oz butter
150 g caster sugar	5 oz caster sugar
$\frac{1}{4}$ teaspoon vanilla essence	$\frac{1}{4}$ teaspoon vanilla essence
2 eggs, beaten	2 eggs, beaten
few crushed sugar lumps	few crushed sugar lumps

Sift the flour into a bowl. Rub the butter in until the mixture resembles fine crumbs. Stir in the sugar. Add the vanilla essence and eggs and bind to a sticky dough.

Drop teaspoonful of the mixture on to greased and floured baking sheets, leaving room for spreading. Shape into rounds with the help of a second teaspoon. Sprinkle over the crushed sugar.

Bake in a preheated moderately hot oven (200°C/400°F, Gas Mark 6) for 12 to 15 minutes or until risen and golden brown. Leave to cool on the baking sheets for a few minutes, then transfer to a wire rack to cool completely.

Makes 12 to 14

VARIATIONS

Jam buns: Make as above, using only 100 g/4 oz butter and adding a little milk with the eggs. After shaping into rounds on the baking sheets, make an indentation in each with a floured finger. Put a little jam in the hollow, then bring up the bun around the jam almost to enclose it. Sprinkle the buns with caster sugar instead of crushed sugar lumps. Bake as above.

Orange buns: Make as above, omitting the vanilla essence and adding the grated rind of 2 oranges and a little chopped candied orange peel with the sugar. Omit the crushed sugar topping and bake as above. When cool, dredge with sifted icing sugar.

Chocolate Crackles

METRIC	IMPERIAL
100 g plain chocolate	4 oz plain chocolate
100 g butter	4 oz butter
4 tablespoons golden syrup	4 tablespoons golden syrup
100 g cornflakes	4 oz cornflakes
50 g walnuts, chopped	2 oz walnuts, chopped

Place the chocolate, butter and syrup in a heavy-based saucepan and heat gently. Remove from the heat and fold in the cornflakes and walnuts.

Cool slightly, then drop by heaped spoonfuls into paper cases. Cool until firm.

Makes 12 to 16

Scones

Use this simple dough as the base for quick pizzas and other savoury snacks.

METRIC	IMPERIAL
225 g self-raising flour	8 oz self-raising flour
$\frac{1}{2}$ teaspoon salt	$\frac{1}{2}$ teaspoon salt
50 g butter	2 oz butter
150 ml milk	$\frac{1}{4}$ pint milk

Sift the flour and salt into a bowl. Rub in the butter until the mixture resembles fine crumbs. Stir in the milk and mix to a smooth, soft dough.

Roll out the dough on a floured surface to 2 cm/$\frac{3}{4}$ inch thick and cut out 6 cm/2$\frac{1}{2}$ inch rounds. Place on a floured baking sheet.

Dust the rounds with more flour, then bake in a preheated hot oven (230°C/450°F, Gas Mark 8) for 7 to 10 minutes or until risen and golden brown. Serve hot, or cool on a wire rack.

Makes about 12

VARIATIONS

Buttermilk soda scones: Use plain flour and sift with 1 teaspoon bicarbonate of soda and 1 teaspoon cream of tartar. Reduce the butter to 25 g/1 oz and use buttermilk instead of milk. Roll out and cut into rounds as above, then bake in a preheated hot oven (220°C/425°F, Gas Mark 7) for about 10 minutes.

Girdle scones: Use plain flour and sift it with 1 tablespoon baking powder and 1 teaspoon caster sugar. Divide the dough in half and roll out each portion to a round about 1 cm/$\frac{1}{2}$ inch thick on a floured surface. Cut each round into four wedges and dredge them with flour. Cook the scones on a lightly greased girdle or heavy-based frying pan for about 5 minutes on each side or until risen and golden brown. Serve hot, split and spread thickly with butter. Makes 8

Raising agents for cakes

To give cakes and biscuits a light, open texture, several methods may be employed. Air may be beaten into whole eggs or egg whites, or raising agents may be used. Just as yeast is used for bread, so baking powder, bicarbonate of soda and self-raising flour are used as raising agents for cakes.

When mixed with liquid and heated, bicarbonate of soda produces carbon dioxide gas which causes a cake mixture to puff up. Cream of tartar, sour milk, yogurt, vinegar and other acid substances may be added to speed up this chemical reaction.

Baking powder is a mixture of bicarbonate of soda and one of these acid powders (usually cream of tartar). Self-raising flour has baking powder added.

DOUGHNUTS AND BISCUITS

Baking

Baking Powder Doughnuts

METRIC	IMPERIAL
225 g self-raising flour	8 oz self-raising flour
pinch of salt	pinch of salt
25 g butter, melted	1 oz butter, melted
1 egg, beaten	1 egg, beaten
25–50 g sugar	1–2 oz sugar
6–7 tablespoons milk	6–7 tablespoons milk
oil for deep frying	oil for deep frying
caster sugar to dredge	caster sugar to dredge

Sift the flour and salt into a bowl. Add the butter, egg, sugar and milk and mix to a soft dough. If sticky, cover and let stand for about 10 minutes.

Roll the dough into balls, or roll out and cut into rings. Deep fry in oil heated to 190°C/375°F until golden brown, turning with a slotted spoon. Do not crowd the pan.

Drain on paper towels, then coat with sugar.

Makes about 8

VARIATION

To make jam doughnuts: Press your finger or the handle of a wooden spoon into the balls of dough, then fill with jam. Bring the dough up to enclose the jam completely and roll into neat balls again.

Brandy Snaps

Despite their fragile appearance, these biscuits can be frozen very successfully. Pack them carefully in rigid containers with greaseproof paper or foil between the layers. Fill with cream after thawing.

METRIC	IMPERIAL
50 g butter	2 oz butter
50 g demerara sugar	2 oz demerara sugar
3 tablespoons golden syrup	3 tablespoons golden syrup
50 g plain flour	2 oz plain flour
1 teaspoon ground ginger	1 teaspoon ground ginger
½ teaspoon lemon juice	½ teaspoon lemon juice
150 ml double cream, whipped, or Chantilly Cream★	¼ pint double cream, whipped, or Chantilly Cream★

Place the butter, sugar and syrup in a saucepan and heat gently until melted and smooth. Remove from the heat. Sift the flour and ginger into the pan. Add the lemon juice and mix together well.

Place heaped teaspoonsful of the mixture on greased baking sheets, well spaced apart, and bake in a preheated moderate oven (180°C/350°F, Gas Mark 4) for 15 to 20 minutes.

Leave to cool on the baking sheet for 1 minute, then remove the biscuits one at a time and roll around the greased handle of a wooden spoon. Slide off on to a wire rack to cool completely.

It is best to bake these biscuits in batches as they cannot be shaped easily once cooled and hardened. If the last one or two on the baking sheet is too hard to roll, return it to the oven for 1 to 2 minutes to soften.

Fill with whipped cream just before serving.

Makes 12

VARIATION

Brown walnut snaps: Make as above, using 50 g/2 oz each butter and dark brown sugar, 75 g/3 oz golden syrup and 65 g/2½ oz self-raising flour. Add 40 g/1½ oz finely chopped walnuts to the mixture. Bake in a preheated moderately hot oven (190°C/375°F, Gas Mark 5) for 6 minutes, then roll and cool as above. Fill with 150 ml/¼ pint double cream whipped with ½ teaspoon instant coffee powder and 25 g/1 oz sifted icing sugar.

Flapjacks

METRIC	IMPERIAL
100 g demerara sugar	4 oz demerara sugar
100 g butter	4 oz butter
3 tablespoons golden syrup	3 tablespoons golden syrup
175 g porridge oats	6 oz porridge oats
50 g desiccated coconut	2 oz desiccated coconut
1 teaspoon baking powder	1 teaspoon baking powder
½ teaspoon salt	½ teaspoon salt
1 egg, beaten	1 egg, beaten

Place the sugar, butter and syrup in a saucepan and heat gently until melted and smooth. Remove from the heat and stir in the remaining ingredients.

Press into a greased 20 cm/8 inch shallow square cake tin. Bake in a preheated moderate oven (180°C/350°F, Gas Mark 4) for 20 to 30 minutes or until firm to the touch.

Cool for 5 minutes, then cut into squares. Leave to cool in the tin.

Makes about 16

VARIATION

Spiced flapjacks: Make as above, using 50 g/2 oz each demerara sugar and butter, 3 tablespoons golden syrup and 100 g/4 oz rolled oats. Add ½ teaspoon mixed spice, ground cinnamon or ground ginger to the mixture. Press into a greased 18 cm/7 inch round cake tin and bake in a preheated moderate oven (180°C/350°F, Gas Mark 4) for 20 to 25 minutes. Cut into squares and leave to cool in the tin.

Apple and Banana Triangles

METRIC	IMPERIAL
100 g self-raising flour	4 oz self-raising flour
1 teaspoon ground cinnamon	1 teaspoon ground cinnamon
50 g butter, softened	2 oz butter, softened
100 g soft brown sugar	4 oz soft brown sugar
1 egg, beaten	1 egg, beaten
1 ripe banana, mashed	1 ripe banana, mashed
5 tablespoons apple purée	5 tablespoons apple purée
25 g walnuts, chopped	1 oz walnuts, chopped
1 quantity Spice Buttercream* (made with cinnamon)	1 quantity Spice Buttercream* (made with cinnamon)
8 walnut halves	8 walnut halves

Sift the flour and cinnamon into a bowl. Add the butter, sugar, egg, banana and apple and beat with a wooden spoon until smooth. Stir in the walnuts. nuts.

Turn into a greased and lined 20 cm/8 inch round cake tin. Bake in a preheated moderate oven (180°C/350°F, Gas Mark 4) for 35 to 45 minutes or until firm and golden brown. Cool on a wire rack.

Cut the cake into eight wedges. Put the buttercream into a piping bag fitted with a star nozzle and pipe a border around each cake triangle. Pipe a star in the centre of each and press in a walnut half.

Makes 8

Oatmeal Biscuits

Serve with butter and cheese, or with jam.

METRIC	IMPERIAL
225 g self-raising flour	8 oz self-raising flour
½ teaspoon salt	½ teaspoon salt
225 g medium oatmeal	8 oz medium oatmeal
150 g butter	5 oz butter
50 g golden syrup	2 oz golden syrup
about 4 tablespoons hot water	about 4 tablespoons hot water

Sift the flour and salt into a bowl and stir in the oatmeal. Rub in the butter until the mixture resembles fine crumbs. Dissolve the syrup in half the hot water and add to the bowl. Knead well, adding as much of the remaining water as necessary to make a firm dough.

Roll out the dough on a floured surface to about 5 mm/¼ inch thick. Cut into rounds or squares and arrange on greased baking sheets.

Bake in a preheated moderate oven (160°C/325°F, Gas Mark 3) for about 15 minutes. Cool on the baking sheet.

Makes 20 to 24

Coconut Macaroons

METRIC	IMPERIAL
2 egg whites	2 egg whites
150–175 g caster sugar	5–6 oz caster sugar
about 175 g desiccated coconut	about 6 oz desiccated coconut
glacé cherries to decorate	glacé cherries to decorate

Whisk the egg whites until frothy. Whisk in the sugar, then gradually stir in the coconut. The mixture should be just firm enough to roll into balls.

Roll into balls and place on baking sheets lined with rice paper, leaving room for spreading. Press a cherry half into each ball.

Bake in a preheated moderate oven (180°C/350°F, Gas Mark 4) for 18 to 20 minutes. For sticky macaroons, put a dish of water in the oven while baking.

Leave to cool on the baking sheets, then cut out the macaroons (the rice paper is edible).

Makes 10 to 12

VARIATION
Almond macaroons: Use ground almonds instead of coconut and flavour the mixture with a few drops of almond essence. Top with blanched almonds instead of cherries.

Lemon Chocolate Fingers

METRIC	IMPERIAL
100 g butter	4 oz butter
50 g icing sugar, sifted	2 oz icing sugar, sifted
2 teaspoons lemon juice	2 teaspoons lemon juice
75 g plain flour	3 oz plain flour
75 g self-raising flour	3 oz self-raising flour
½ quantity Lemon Buttercream*	½ quantity Lemon Buttercream*
50 g plain chocolate	2 oz plain chocolate

Cream the butter with the sugar until light and fluffy. Beat in the lemon juice. Sift the flours into the bowl and mix to a stiff dough.

Place the dough in a piping bag fitted with a 1 cm/½ inch fluted nozzle and pipe in 6 cm/2½ inch lengths on greased baking sheets, spacing well apart. Bake in a preheated moderately hot oven (190°C/375°F, Gas Mark 5) for 10 to 15 minutes or until golden brown. Cool on a wire rack.

Sandwich together in pairs with the buttercream.

Melt the chocolate in a heatproof bowl placed over a pan of simmering water. Remove from the heat. Dip both ends of the biscuits into the chocolate, then leave to cool on a wire rack until the chocolate has set.

Makes 12

Chocolate Chip Refrigerator Cookies

If chocolate drops are not available, use finely chopped plain chocolate. The roll of dough can be kept in the refrigerator for up to 4 days, and sliced and baked when wanted.

METRIC	IMPERIAL
225 g plain flour	8 oz plain flour
1 teaspoon baking powder	1 teaspoon baking powder
100 g unsalted butter	4 oz unsalted butter
75 g chocolate drops	3 oz chocolate drops
175 g caster sugar	6 oz caster sugar
1 egg, beaten	1 egg, beaten
1 teaspoon vanilla essence	1 teaspoon vanilla essence

Sift the flour and baking powder into a bowl. Rub in the butter until the mixture resembles fine crumbs. Stir in the chocolate drops and sugar, then add the egg and vanilla essence and mix to a stiff dough.

Shape the dough into a roll about 45 cm/18 inches long (or into two rolls if more convenient). Wrap in foil and chill for 1 hour.

Unwrap the dough roll and cut into thin slices. Place the slices, well spaced apart, on greased baking sheets. Bake in a preheated moderately hot oven (190°C/375°F, Gas Mark 5) for 10 to 12 minutes or until golden brown. Cool on a wire rack.

Makes about 40

Madeleines

METRIC	IMPERIAL
3 eggs, separated	3 eggs, separated
75 g caster sugar	3 oz caster sugar
75 g plain flour, sifted	3 oz plain flour, sifted
5 tablespoons jam, warmed and sieved	5 tablespoons jam, warmed and sieved
desiccated coconut	desiccated coconut
8 glacé cherries, halved	8 glacé cherries, halved

Whisk the egg whites until stiff. Gradually whisk in the sugar alternately with the egg yolks. Fold in the flour.

Divide the mixture between 15 to 16 greased dariole moulds, filling them three-quarters full. Bake in a preheated moderately hot oven (190°C/375°F, Gas Mark 5) for 15 to 20 minutes or until risen and golden brown. Cool on a wire rack.

Brush the cakes with the jam, then roll in coconut to coat on all sides. Top each with a cherry half.

Makes 15 to 16

Chocolate Butter Kisses

METRIC	IMPERIAL
75 g unsalted butter	3 oz unsalted butter
75 g caster sugar	3 oz caster sugar
100 g plain flour	4 oz plain flour
2 tablespoons cocoa powder	2 tablespoons cocoa powder
1 teaspoon baking powder	1 teaspoon baking powder
pinch of salt	pinch of salt
100 g seeded raisins, chopped	4 oz seeded raisins, chopped
25 g walnuts, chopped	1 oz walnuts, chopped
1 tablespoon milk	1 tablespoon milk
½ quantity Chocolate Buttercream*	½ quantity Chocolate Buttercream*
sifted icing sugar	sifted icing sugar

Cream the butter with the sugar until light and fluffy. Sift the flour, cocoa powder, baking powder and salt into the bowl and work into the creamed mixture. Add the raisins, walnuts and milk and mix well.

Place teaspoonfuls of the mixture, well spaced apart, on greased baking sheets. Bake in a preheated moderately hot oven (190°C/375°F, Gas Mark 5) for 20 minutes. Leave to cool on the baking sheets for 2 minutes, then transfer to a wire rack to cool completely.

When the biscuits are cold, sandwich them together in pairs with buttercream. Sprinkle with icing sugar.

Makes 12

Cooling and storing biscuits

Unless a recipe directs you to do otherwise, remove biscuits from baking sheets as soon as they are taken from the oven. Use a fish slice or wide spatula, and transfer the biscuits to a wire rack, arranging them so they do not touch each other, to cool. They will probably be soft, but will firm up as they cool. If left to cool on the baking sheet, the biscuits will continue to cook in the heat from the baking sheet, and may well stick to it.

Bars and cake-like squares, on the other hand, are usually left to cool in the tin in which they were baked. They may be cut into bars, etc. before or after cooling.

To keep biscuits fresh, store them in an airtight metal container. Bars or squares can be wrapped in aluminium foil for storage, or left in their baking tin and covered tightly with foil.

Preserves

When the greengrocer's prices are
reasonable, or there is a glut in your garden,
and fruits and vegetables are at their best,
it is time to get the jars ready for preserving.
What a delight for the cook to bring forth
on a cold winter's night the fruits of her
summer's labours. An array of beautiful
bottled fruits and vegetables, jams, jellies,
chutneys and pickles can be very rewarding.
Just imagine what satisfaction there will
be in presenting a host or hostess a gaily
wrapped jar of your very own preserves.
Many bazaars, summer fêtes and church
functions will appreciate your appetizing
concoctions, too.

Apricot Jam

METRIC	IMPERIAL
2 kg apricots, halved	4 lb apricots, halved
450 ml water	¾ pint water
3 tablespoons lemon juice	3 tablespoons lemon juice
2 kg preserving or granulated sugar	4 lb preserving or granulated sugar

Stone the apricots, reserving a few of the stones. Remove the kernels and blanch in boiling water for 2 minutes. Drain and slip off the skins.

Place the apricots in a large preserving pan or saucepan with the water, lemon juice and kernels. Bring to the boil and simmer until the fruit is soft.

Add the sugar and stir until dissolved. Boil until setting point is reached (see page 156). Pour into hot clean jars. Cover, label and store in a cool dry place.

Makes about 3 kg/6½ lb

VARIATIONS

Strawberry jam: Make as above using 1.5 kg/3 lb strawberries. Simmer with the lemon juice, omitting the water, until the fruit is soft but not mushy. Stir in 1.5 kg/3 lb sugar until dissolved, then boil until setting point is reached (see page 156). Allow the jam to cool for 20 minutes before potting, to prevent the fruit rising in the jam. Makes about 2.25 kg/5 lb

Peach and Pear Jam

METRIC	IMPERIAL
1 kg peaches, stoned and chopped	2 lb peaches, stoned and chopped
1 kg pears, chopped	2 lb pears, chopped
juice of 3 lemons	juice of 3 lemons
pith of 2 lemons	pith of 2 lemons
2 kg preserving or granulated sugar	4 lb preserving or granulated sugar

Crack a few of the peach stones and remove the kernels. Blanch the kernels in boiling water for a few minutes, then cool under cold water and slip off the skins. Place the kernels in a large preserving pan or saucepan with the peaches, pears and lemon juice. Tie the lemon pith in a muslin bag and add to the pan.

Bring to the boil and simmer until the fruit is very tender. Add the sugar and stir until dissolved. Continue boiling until setting point (see page 156).

Skim the jam and remove the muslin bag, squeezing it against the side of the pan. Pour into hot clean jars. Cover, label and store in a cool dry place.

Makes about 3 kg/6 lb

Pectin

Pectin is an almost flavourless substance which is found in most fruit, although some fruits contain a lot more than others. The correct amount of pectin in jams, jellies and marmalades is what ensures a good set. Fruits which are high in pectin are: tart green cooking apples, crab apples, currants, green gooseberries, lemons, limes and bitter oranges. Fruits which contain a moderate amount of pectin are dessert apples, cranberries, damsons, grapes, loganberries and quinces. Fruits which are low in pectin are: bananas, bilberries, blackberries, tart red cherries, underripe figs, melons, plums, greengages and raspberries. Fruits which have little or no pectin are: apricots, sweet ripe cherries, elderberries, ripe figs, nectarines, peaches, pears, pineapple, ripe raspberries, rhubarb and strawberries.

If you are not sure whether the jam you are making contains enough pectin, test the cooked fruit or pulp as follows: place 1 teaspoon fruit in a cup and add 1 tablespoon methylated spirits. Leave for 1 minute. If at the end of this time a firm clot has formed, there is plenty of pectin. A softer clot that breaks easily into smaller clots indicates a moderate amount of pectin, and a very soft clot that breaks into many smaller clots even when the cup is moved means a poor pectin content.

There are several ways to add pectin to jams and jellies. One is to use commercial pectin which is available in liquid or powder form. Another is to combine two fruits to make the jam or jelly, choosing one fruit that is high in pectin. A third way is to add a fruit juice that is high in pectin such as apple or redcurrant in place of water. Finally, the rinds of citrus fruit, tied in muslin, may be added to the fruit.

Tomato Jam

METRIC	IMPERIAL
1 kg firm tomatoes, skinned and quartered	2 lb firm tomatoes, skinned and quartered
1 kg preserving or granulated sugar	2 lb preserving or granulated sugar
4 tablespoons lemon juice	4 tablespoons lemon juice

Place the tomatoes in a saucepan, sprinkle over the sugar and leave overnight.

The next day, heat gently, stirring to dissolve the sugar. Add the lemon juice and bring to the boil. Boil until setting point is reached (see page 156).

Allow to cool for 5 minutes before pouring into clean hot jars. Cover, label and store in a cool dry place.

Makes about 2 kg/4 lb

Preserves

Lemon Curd

METRIC	IMPERIAL
grated rind and juice of 4 lemons	grated rind and juice of 4 lemons
500 g granulated sugar	1 lb granulated sugar
5 eggs, beaten	5 eggs, beaten
100 g butter, cut into small pieces	4 oz butter, cut into small pieces

Place all the ingredients in a heatproof bowl placed over a saucepan of simmering water. Cook, stirring occasionally, until the mixture begins to thicken.

Pour into hot clean jars. Cover immediately, label and store in a cool dry place.

Makes about 1 kg/2 lb

Rose Hip Jelly

If you would like to spice this jelly, add 6 cloves and a small cinnamon stick to the hips at the beginning of the cooking time.

METRIC	IMPERIAL
1 kg rose hips	2 lb rose hips
1 kg apples, chopped	2 lb apples, chopped
1.2 litres water	2 pints water
juice of 1 lemon	juice of 1 lemon
preserving or granulated sugar	preserving or granulated sugar

Place the rose hips and apples in separate pans and add half the water to each. Add the lemon juice to the hips. Bring to the boil and simmer until the fruits are soft and pulpy.

Pour the juice and pulp from both pans into a jelly bag and allow to drain. Do not press the fruit through the bag; let it drain through unaided into a clean bowl.

Test for pectin (see page 152). Measure the juice and pour back into the pan. Add 500 g/1 lb sugar for each 600 ml/1 pint of juice. Bring slowly to the boil, stirring to dissolve the sugar. Boil until setting point has been reached (see page 156).

Skim the jelly, then pour into hot clean jars. Cover, label and store in a cool dry place.

VARIATION

Grapefruit jelly: Make as above, using 3 grapefruit and 4 lemons, chopped, instead of the rose hips and apples. Cook them together, omitting the lemon juice. Increase the water to 2.25 litres/4 pints and simmer for about 2 hours or until the peel is soft. After draining through the jelly bag, stir in about 1.5 kg/3 lb sugar, and boil until setting point is reached. Skim, then pour into hot clean jars. Cover, label and store in a cool dry place.

Mincemeat

The alcohol may be omitted, but this will reduce the keeping time from about 1 year to 2 to 3 weeks.

METRIC	IMPERIAL
500 g firm cooking apples, peeled, cored and finely chopped (prepared weight)	1 lb firm cooking apples, peeled, cored and finely chopped (prepared weight)
225 g shredded suet	8 oz shredded suet
350 g seeded raisins	12 oz seeded raisins
225 g sultanas	8 oz sultanas
225 g currants	8 oz currants
225 g chopped mixed candied peel	8 oz chopped mixed candied peel
350 g soft brown sugar	12 oz soft brown sugar
grated rind and juice of 1 lemon	grated rind and juice of 1 lemon
grated rind and juice of 1 orange	grated rind and juice of 1 orange
$\frac{1}{2}$ teaspoon mixed spice	$\frac{1}{2}$ teaspoon mixed spice
$\frac{1}{4}$ teaspoon grated nutmeg	$\frac{1}{4}$ teaspoon grated nutmeg
150 ml brandy or whisky	$\frac{1}{4}$ pint brandy or whisky

Place all the ingredients except half the brandy or whisky in a large bowl and mix together thoroughly. Pack loosely into clean dry jars and spoon the remaining alcohol over the tops. Cover, label and store in a cool dry place.

Makes about 2.25 kg/5 lb

Rhubarb and Orange Butter

METRIC	IMPERIAL
4 oranges	4 oranges
2 kg rhubarb, chopped	4 lb rhubarb, chopped
granulated sugar	granulated sugar

Peel the oranges thinly, taking only the rind and none of the white pith. Cut the oranges in half and squeeze out the juice. Place the juice and rind in a large saucepan with the rhubarb. Add enough water to cover the fruit. Bring to the boil and simmer until the rhubarb is very tender.

Rub the mixture through a fine sieve and weigh the purée. For each 500 g/1 lb purée, allow 225 g/8 oz sugar.

Retain the purée to the pan and bring to the boil. Cook, until the purée is beginning to thicken. Add the sugar and stir until it dissolves, then continue boiling until no extra liquid remains, stirring occasionally.

Pour into hot clean jars. Cover, label and store in a cool dry place.

Apple Mint Butter

METRIC	IMPERIAL
1.5 kg cooking apples, peeled, cored and sliced	3 lb cooking apples, peeled, cored and sliced
600 ml water	1 pint water
1.5 kg granulated sugar	3 lb granulated sugar
3 tablespoons lemon juice	3 tablespoons lemon juice
1 tablespoon malt vinegar	1 tablespoon malt vinegar
50 g fresh mint, chopped	2 oz fresh mint, chopped

Place the apples and water in a large saucepan and cook gently, covered, until the apples are soft and pulpy. Stir in the sugar until dissolved. Add the lemon juice and bring to the boil. Boil, stirring frequently, until thick. To test if the butter is thick enough, spoon a little on to a saucer and cool. A skin should form on the surface which wrinkles when pushed with a finger.

Stir in the vinegar and mint. Pour into hot clean jars. Cover, label and store in a cool dry place.

Makes about 2.25 kg/5lb

Spiced Blackberry Jelly

Try serving this jelly with cold meat as well as on the tea table.

METRIC	IMPERIAL
1 kg blackberries	2 lb blackberries
500 g cooking apples, chopped	1 lb cooking apples, chopped
600 ml water	1 pint water
4 cloves	4 cloves
1 small cinnamon stick	1 small cinnamon stick
preserving or granulated sugar	preserving or granulated sugar
wine vinegar	wine vinegar

Place the blackberries, apples and water in a large preserving pan or saucepan. Tie the spices in a muslin bag and add to the pan. Bring to the boil, then simmer until the fruit is tender.

Mash the fruit, then pour the juice and pulp into a jelly bag and allow to drain. Do not press the fruit through the bag; let it drain through unaided into a clean bowl.

Test for pectin (see page 152). Measure the juice and pour back into the pan. Add 500 g/1 lb sugar and 2 tablespoons vinegar for each 600 ml/1 pint of juice. Bring slowly to the boil, stirring to dissolve the sugar. Boil until setting point has been reached (see page 156). Skim the jelly, then pour into hot clean jars. Cover, label and store in a cool dry place.

Three Fruit Marmalade

The total weight of the three fruits should be about 1.5 kg/3 lb.

METRIC	IMPERIAL
2 grapefruit, halved	2 grapefruit, halved
4 lemons, halved	4 lemons, halved
2 sweet oranges, halved	2 sweet oranges, halved
3.6 litres water	6 pints water
3 kg preserving or granulated sugar	6 lb preserving or granulated sugar

Squeeze the juice from the fruit into a large preserving pan or saucepan. Reserve the pips. Cut as much of the white pith from the rinds as possible. Tie the pips and pith in a muslin bag and add to the pan. Cut the rind into thin matchstick strips and add to the pan with the water. Bring to the boil and simmer for about 2 hours or until the rind is tender. Remove the muslin bag, squeezing out all the liquid.

Add the sugar and stir until dissolved. Boil until setting point has been reached (see page 156). Skim the marmalade. Allow it to cool slightly, then pour into hot clean jars. Cover, label and store in a cool dry place.

Makes about 5 kg/10 lb

VARIATIONS
Seville orange marmalade: Make as above, using 1.5 kg/3 lb Seville oranges instead of the three fruits, and adding the juice of 2 lemons with the water.
Chunky dark marmalade: Make as for Seville orange marmalade, but cut the orange rind into chunks instead of matchstick strips. Add 1 tablespoon black treacle with the sugar.
Brandied orange marmalade: Make as above, using 1.5 kg/3 lb sweet oranges instead of the three fruits, and adding the juice of 2 lemons with the water. Stir in 2 tablespoons brandy just before setting point is reached.
Cidered orange marmalade: Make as above, using 750 g/1½ lb Seville oranges instead of the three fruits, and adding the juice of 2 lemons. Reduce the water to 600 ml/1 pint and add 1.5 litres/2½ pints dry cider. Reduce the sugar to 1.5 kg/3 lb. Makes about 2.25 kg/5 lb

---

Making herb vinegar
A bottle of herb vinegar would make a delightful gift, particularly if you make it yourself. Lightly bruise a long spray of tarragon or basil, or crush a clove of garlic, and add to a bottle of red or white wine vinegar. Cover and leave for 3 days, then strain the vinegar and return it to the bottle. It will be delightfully flavoured and will enhance all salad dressings, sauces and marinades in which it is used.

Mint Jelly

This piquant jelly is perfect with roast lamb.

METRIC	IMPERIAL
1.5 kg green apples, quartered	3 lb green apples, quartered
600 ml water	1 pint water
small bunch of fresh mint	small bunch of fresh mint
750 ml white malt vinegar	1¼ pints white malt vinegar
preserving or granulated sugar	preserving or granulated sugar
3 tablespoons finely chopped fresh mint	3 tablespoons finely chopped fresh mint
green food colouring	green food colouring

Place the apples, water and bunch of mint in a large preserving pan or saucepan. Bring to the boil, then simmer until the apples are soft and pulpy. Stir in the vinegar and boil for a further 5 minutes.

Pour the apple mixture into a jelly bag and allow to drain. Do not press the fruit through the bag; let it drain through unaided into a clean bowl.

Test for pectin (see page 152). Measure the juice and pour back into the pan. Add 500 g/1 lb sugar for each 600 ml/1 pint of juice. Bring slowly to the boil, stirring to dissolve the sugar. Stir in the mint and a few drops of food colouring. Boil until setting point has been reached (see page 156). Skim the jelly, then pour into hot clean jars. Cover, label and store in a cool dry place.

Tomato Chutney

METRIC	IMPERIAL
3 kg ripe tomatoes, skinned and chopped	6 lb ripe tomatoes, skinned and chopped
2 onions, finely chopped	2 onions, finely chopped
600 ml spiced vinegar (see recipe for Pickled Onions, page 156)	1 pint spiced vinegar (see recipe for Pickled Onions, page 156)
2 teaspoons paprika	2 teaspoons paprika
¼ teaspoon cayenne	¼ teaspoon cayenne
1 tablespoon salt	1 tablespoon salt
350 g granulated sugar	12 oz granulated sugar

Place the tomatoes and onions in a large enamel or stainless steel pan. Bring to a simmer and cook, stirring occasionally, until thick and pulpy. Stir in half the vinegar, the paprika, cayenne and salt and bring to the boil. Simmer until thickened.

Add the remaining vinegar and the sugar and stir until the sugar has dissolved. Simmer, stirring from time to time, until thick.

Pour into hot clean jars. Cover, label and store in a cool dry place.

Makes about 2 kg/4 lb

Apple and Banana Chutney

The flavour of a chutney depends largely on long, gentle cooking and then a keeping period to allow the flavour to mellow.

METRIC	IMPERIAL
2 kg apples, peeled, cored and finely chopped	4 lb apples, peeled, cored and finely chopped
12 bananas, thinly sliced	12 bananas, thinly sliced
500 g onions, finely chopped	1 lb onions, finely chopped
225 g seeded raisins	8 oz seeded raisins
1 tablespoon salt	1 tablespoon salt
1 teaspoon ground ginger	1 teaspoon ground ginger
1 teaspoon ground cinnamon	1 teaspoon ground cinnamon
1 teaspoon dry mustard	1 teaspoon dry mustard
1 tablespoon curry powder	1 tablespoon curry powder
1.2 litres malt vinegar	2 pints malt vinegar
500 g granulated sugar	1 lb granulated sugar

Place the apples, bananas, onions, raisins, salt, spices, mustard, curry powder and half the vinegar in a large enamel or stainless steel pan. Bring to the boil and simmer for 30 minutes.

Add the remaining vinegar and sugar and stir until the sugar has dissolved. Bring back to the boil and summer, stirring occasionally, until thickened.

Pour into hot clean jars. Leave to cool completely, then cover, label and store in a cool dry place.

Makes about 5 kg/10 lb

Pickled Mushrooms

METRIC	IMPERIAL
500 g button mushrooms	1 lb button mushrooms
1 mace blade	1 mace blade
6 white peppercorns	6 white peppercorns
1 teaspoon salt	1 teaspoon salt
1 cm piece root ginger, peeled	½ inch piece root ginger, peeled
½ small onion	½ small onion
white vinegar	white vinegar

Place the mushrooms, mace, peppercorns, salt, ginger and onion in a saucepan and add enough vinegar just to cover the mushrooms. Bring to the boil, then cover and simmer until the mushrooms are beginning to shrink.

Pack the mushrooms into clean hot jars. Strain the vinegar and pour back into the pan. Bring back to the boil, then pour over the mushrooms. Cover and label. Store in a cool dry place.

Make 500 g/1 lb

Mixed Vegetable Mustard Pickle

METRIC	IMPERIAL
350 g dried red kidney beans, soaked overnight	12 oz dried red kidney beans, soaked overnight
4 red peppers, seeded and cut into pieces	4 red peppers, seeded and cut into pieces
1 medium cauliflower, broken into florets	1 medium cauliflower, broken into florets
500 g French beans, cut into 5 cm pieces	1 lb French beans, cut into 2 inch pieces
salt	salt
1 × 400 g can sweetcorn kernels, drained	1 × 14 oz can sweetcorn kernels, drained
1.2 litres cider vinegar	2 pints cider vinegar
175 g soft brown sugar	6 oz soft brown sugar
3 tablespoons mustard seed	3 tablespoons mustard seed
5 tablespoons dry mustard	5 tablespoons dry mustard
1 teaspoon turmeric	1 teaspoon turmeric

Drain the kidney beans and place in a large saucepan. Cover with fresh cold water. Bring to the boil and boil for 10 minutes, then reduce the heat and simmer for 1 to 1½ hours or until tender. Drain well.

Blanch the red peppers, cauliflower and French beans in boiling salted water for 5 minutes. Drain and mix with the kidney beans and corn.

Place the vinegar, sugar, mustard seed, mustard and turmeric in a large saucepan and bring to the boil, stirring to dissolve the sugar. Add the vegetables and simmer gently for 5 minutes.

Cool slightly, then ladle into hot clean jars. Cover, label and store in a cool dry place.

Makes 1.75 kg/3½ lb

Testing jams

There are three ways of testing a jam, jelly or marmalade to see if it has reached setting point.
1) The temperature test: Place a sugar thermometer in hot water. When setting point is near, stir the jam and place the thermometer in the centre of the pan but not touching the bottom. The temperature should read 104 to 106°C/220 to 222°F for setting point.
2) The flake test: Dip a wooden spoon into the jam and spoon up about 1 teaspoonful of the mixture. Holding the spoon over the pan, allow the hot jam to cool slightly. If setting point has been reached, the jam will not run off the spoon but will drop off cleanly in clots or flakes.
3) The wrinkle test: Remove the pan of jam from the heat. Spoon about 1 teaspoonful of jam on to a cold saucer and leave to cool for a few minutes. Push the jam gently with your finger; setting point has been reached if the surface has set and wrinkles.

Pickled Pears

METRIC	IMPERIAL
1 kg firm dessert pears, peeled, cored and quartered	2 lb firm dessert pears, peeled, cored and quartered
450 ml cider vinegar	¾ pint cider vinegar
300 ml water	½ pint water
500 g sugar	1 lb sugar
1 cinnamon stick	1 cinnamon stick
10 cloves	10 cloves
small piece of root ginger, bruised	small piece of root ginger, bruised

Place the pears in a large saucepan and cover with boiling water. Simmer gently for 10 minutes or until just tender. Drain and return to the pan.

Place the remaining ingredients in another large saucepan and bring to the boil. Simmer for 5 minutes. Add the pears and continue simmering until the pears are transparent.

Remove the pears with a slotted spoon and pack into clean hot jars. Pour over the boiling syrup, cover and label. Store in a cool dry place for at least 1 month before serving.

Pickled Onions

Many vegetables may be pickled in the same ways as onions. Try cauliflower florets, sliced courgettes (add ¼ teaspoon dill seeds to each 300 ml/½ pint jar), sliced cucumbers, gherkins or red cabbage (don't make a brine, just layer with salt and rinse after overnight salting).

METRIC	IMPERIAL
500 g pickling onions	1 lb pickling onions
225 g salt	8 oz salt
2.25 litres water	4 pints water
Spiced vinegar:	*Spiced vinegar:*
5 cm cinnamon stick	2 inch cinnamon stick
12 cloves	12 cloves
4 mace blades	4 mace blades
15 allspice berries	15 allspice berries
8 peppercorns	8 peppercorns
1.2 litres malt vinegar	2 pints malt vinegar

First make the vinegar. Add the spices to the bottle of vinegar, cover and leave for 6 to 8 weeks, shaking the bottle occasionally. Strain before using.

Alternatively, if time is short, pour the vinegar into a heatproof bowl placed over a saucepan of cold water. Cover the bowl with a plate, then bring the water to the boil. Remove from the heat and add the spices to the vinegar. Cover again and leave to steep for about 2 hours. Strain before using.

Peel the onions, using a stainless steel knife to

prevent discoloration. Place the onions in a bowl. Dissolve the salt in the water, then pour this brine over the onions just to cover them. (Make more brine if necessary.) Place a plate on top of the onions so they remain immersed. Leave for 24 to 36 hours.

Drain the onions and pack them into clean jars. Cover with the cold spiced vinegar, seal and label. Store in a cool dry place for 3 months before serving.

VARIATIONS

For a hotter pickle: Use the following spices to flavour the vinegar: 2 tablespoons mustard seeds, 24 cloves, 24 black peppercorns, 2 tablespoons ground allspice berries and 2 tablespoons dried chillies. If liked, add 1 crushed garlic clove.

Mixed vegetable pickle: use only 225 g/8 oz pickling onions and add 1 cauliflower, broken into florets, 1 cucumber, cut into 1 cm/½ inch dice, and 500 g/1 lb French beans, cut into 2.5 cm/1 inch pieces. Layer the vegetables in a bowl, sprinkling each layer with salt. Cover and leave for 48 hours. Rinse and drain well, then pack loosely into clean jars, arranging the vegetables attractively. Cover with cold spiced vinegar, seal and label. Store in a cool dry place.

Tomato Ketchup

METRIC	IMPERIAL
2 kg ripe tomatoes, sliced	4 lb ripe tomatoes, sliced
salt	salt
150 ml white malt	¼ pint white malt
1 garlic clove, crushed	1 garlic clove, crushed
1 small mace blade	1 small mace blade
1½ teaspoons white peppercorns	1½ teaspoons white peppercorns
1½ teaspoons allspice berries	1½ teaspoons allspice berries
2.5 cm piece root ginger, bruised	1 inch piece root ginger, bruised
1 bay leaf	1 bay leaf
150 ml white malt vinegar	¼ pint whit malt vinegar
granulated sugar	granulated sugar

Place the tomatoes in layers in a large bowl, sprinkling each layer with salt. Cover and leave overnight.

The next day, tip the tomatoes into a large enamel or stainless steel pan and add the onion, garlic, spices and bay leaf. Simmer gently, stirring occasionally, until thick and pulpy.

Sieve the tomato mixture and return to the rinsed-out pan. Add the vinegar and sugar to taste. Bring to the boil, stirring to dissolve the sugar, and simmer until beginning to thicken. Stir frequently.

Pour into hot clean bottles and cover immediately. Place the bottles in a deep saucepan and pour in simmering water to come up to the necks. Simmer for 30 minutes. Remove the bottles from the water and leave to cool before labelling.

Herbs and herb vinegars
Herb vinegars and oils add subtle flavours to salad dressings and other foods. To make them, pack freshly gathered leaves of basil, chervil, chives, lemon thyme, marjoram, mint, parsley, rosemary, sage, tarragon, or thyme, or a mixture of herbs into a glass jar and fill up with red or white wine vinegar, distilled white vinegar, cider vinegar or oil. Cork tightly and leave for at least 2 weeks or until the vinegar or oil is flavoured. Strain into another bottle and cork tightly again. Use within 3–4 months.

*

To dry herbs, gather them on a dry day and choose young, small sprigs. Small-leaved herbs such as thyme should be rinsed and drained well. When dry, tie them into small bundles, wrap in muslin to protect them from dust, and hang in a warm place to dry. Large-leaved herbs should be stripped from their stems, tied in muslin and then dipped into boiling water for 1 minute. Drain, spread out on a wire rack covered with muslin and dry out in a cool oven (43–54°C/110–130°F, Gas Mark ¼), with the oven door slightly open, for about 1 hour, then crush and store in tightly stoppered jars.

Sweetcorn Relish

If preferred, the vegetables may be minced instead of finely chopped.

METRIC	IMPERIAL
10 large sweetcorn cobs	10 large sweetcorn cobs
1 small cabbage, finely chopped	1 small cabbage, finely chopped
2 onions, finely chopped	2 onions, finely chopped
2 green peppers, cored, seeded and finely	2 green peppers, cored, seeded and finely
2 red chilli peppers, seeded and finely chopped	2 red chilli peppers, seeded and finely chopped
½ teaspoon celery salt	½ teaspoon celery salt
1 teaspoon dry mustard	1 teaspoon dry mustard
¼ teaspoon turmeric	¼ teaspoon turmeric
2 teaspoons salt	2 teaspoons salt
600 ml white malt vinegar	1 pint white malt vinegar

Cook the corn in boiling water for 5 minutes. Drain and cool, then scrape off the kernels. Place the kernels in a clean large saucepan and add the remaining ingredients. Bring to the boil and simmer for 15 to 20 minutes or until the vegetables are tender.

Pour into hot clean jars. Cover, label and store in a cool dry place.

Makes about 2.25 kg/5 lb

Spiced Orange Slices

METRIC	IMPERIAL
6 oranges	6 oranges
450 ml white malt vinegar	¾ pint white malt vinegar
500 g granulated sugar	1 lb granulated sugar
10 cm cinnamon stick	4 inch cinnamon stick
8 cloves	8 cloves
4 mace blades	4 mace blades

Place the oranges in a saucepan and cover with water. Bring to the boil, then cover and simmer until the orange rind is tender (test with a fork). Drain the oranges, reserving the water, and cool. Thinly slice the oranges.

Place the vinegar in a clean large saucepan with the sugar and 150 ml/¼ pint of the reserved orange water. Tie the spices in a muslin bag and add to the pan. Bring to the boil, stirring to dissolve the sugar, and simmer for 5 to 10 minutes.

Add the orange slices. Return to the boil, then simmer for 30 minutes. Pour the mixture into a bowl, cover and leave for 24 hours.

The next day, drain the oranges, reserving the vinegar mixture, and pack them into clean hot jars. Discard the spice bag from the vinegar mixture and pour it into a saucepan. Bring to the boil and boil until beginning to thicken. Pour over the orange slices. Leave to cool, then cover and label. Store for at least 6 weeks before serving.

Pickling walnuts

Gather the walnuts before the end of June, before the shells begin to form at the end opposite the stalk. Wearing rubber gloves to protect your hands from stains, prick the nuts with a needle or silver fork. Discard any nuts in which a shell can be felt. Make a brine with 225 g/8 oz salt dissolved in 2.4 litres/4 pints water, add the nuts and leave to soak for 5 days. Make up a fresh brine, add the drained nuts and soak for a further 7 days. Drain and spread out to dry until the nuts have turned black all over. Pack into jars and cover with spiced vinegar. Use after about 4 weeks.

*

Salting beans

Salting is still a popular method for preserving beans. Choose young, fresh beans and top and tail or string them if necessary. Cut runner beans into large chunks, but leave French beans whole. Layer beans and salt, using 500 g/1 lb salt to each 1.5 kg/3 lb beans, in an earthenware crock or large glass jar. Begin and end with salt, and press each layer down firmly. Leave about 4 days or until the beans shrink, then fill up the jar again with more beans and salt. Cover with moisture-proof covering and use within 1 year.

To use, wash the beans well, then soak in warm water for 2 hours before cooking in the usual way.

Here are the times and temperatures for bottling fruits by the methods described opposite.

FRUIT	METHOD 1	METHOD 2	METHOD 3	METHOD 4	METHOD 5
Apples, slices	74°C/165°F for 10 minutes	74°C/165°F for 2 minutes	1 minute	not recommended	30–40 minutes
Apricots	82°C/180°F for 15 minutes	82°C/180°F for 10 minutes	1 minute	not recommended	40–50 minutes
Berries (including gooseberries & currants	74°C/165°F for 10 minutes	74°C/165°F for 2 minutes	1 minute	44–55 minutes	30–40 minutes
Cherries, stoned	82°C/180°F for 15 minutes	82°C/180°F for 10 minutes	1 minute	55–70 minutes	40–50 minutes
Citrus fruits, segments	82°C/180°F for 15 minutes	81°C/180°F for 10 minutes	1 minute	not recommended	40–50 minutes
Pears, halved	88°C/190°F for 30 minutes	88°C/190°F for 40 minutes	5 minutes	not recommended	60–70 minutes
Plums, dark	82°C/180°F for 15 minutes	82°C/180°F for 10 minutes	1 minute	not recommended	40–50 minutes
Tomatoes, whole	88°C/190°F for 30 minutes	88°C/190°F for 40 minutes	5 minutes	not recommended	60–70 minutes
Tomatoes, halved or quartered	88°C/190°F for 40 minutes	88°C/190°F for 50 minutes	15 minutes	not recommended	70–80 minutes

Times given are for 500 g–1 kg/1–2 lb bottles. Allow an extra 5 minutes (10 minutes for method 5) if using 1.5–2 kg/3–4 lb bottles.

Preserves

Bottling fruit by:	Preparation	Method	Aftercare
1. Slow water bath	Pour cold syrup or water into bottles of fruit, almost filling and covering fruit, then adjust clips or put on screw tops loosely. Stand in deep pan on false bottom, not touching sides or other bottles, and cover pan.	Heat water slowly until after 1 hour it reaches 54°C/130°F. After further 30 minutes, specified temperature should be reached and maintained for required time.	Lift out jars onto heat-proof surface. Tighten screwtops but leave clip tops. Cool for 24 hours, then **test seal**: remove screw or clip tops, then grip lids and lift bottles. Lids should stay firm. Label and store.
2. Quick water bath	Pour hot syrup or water (60°C/140°F) into warmed bottles of fruit, then proceed as for slow water bath.	Fill pan with warm water (38°C/100°F) and heat to 88°C/190°F in 25–30 minutes. Maintain for required time.	As slow water bath.
3. Pressure cooker	Pour 2.5 cm/1 inch water into cooker, add rack and bring to the boil. Pour boiling syrup or water into warmed bottles of fruit. Put on lids and tops, then loosen screwtops a quarter turn. Stand on rack, not touching other bottles or sides of cooker. Cover pan, with vent open.	Heat till steam escapes, then close vent and bring pressure to 2.25 kg/5 lb. Reduce heat and maintain pressure for required time.	Remove cooker from heat, cool 10 minutes and open. Then proceed as for slow water bath.
4. Slow oven (130°C/250°F, Gas Mark ½)	Stand bottles, not touching each other, on cardboard or baking sheet lined with four thicknesses of newspaper. Fill with fruit only and do not cover.	Put into preheated oven and heat for required time.	Remove from oven, one at a time, and fill with boiling syrup or water. Cover. Cool for 24 hours, then test seal as for slow water bath.
5. Moderate oven (150°C/300°F, Gas Mark 2)	Pour boiling syrup or water into warmed bottles of fruit. Cover bottles but do not add screw or clip tops. Proceed as for slow oven.	As for slow oven.	Remove from oven, one at a time, and add screw or clip tops. Cool for 24 hours, then test seal as for slow water bath.

The recent popularity of cocktails indicates
that more people are drinking for the fun
of it, and enjoying new flavours.
Non-alcoholic drinks can also be fun and
offer a colourful alternative to the more
traditional sherries and spirits. All age
groups can enjoy creations like Grenadine
Grape Fizz, Fruit Punch and Creamy
Applenut Drink, or you can add your
favourite 'tipple' to suit. These new 'fun'
drinks add a sparkle to a special occasion
and can create an instant party as soon as
they appear.

Fruit Punch

METRIC	IMPERIAL
4 cooking apples, peeled, cored and sliced	4 cooking apples, peeled, cored and sliced
4 tablespoons honey	4 tablespoons honey
6 cloves	6 cloves
2 cinnamon sticks	2 cinnamon sticks
600 ml water	1 pint water
600 ml pineapple juice	1 pint pineapple juice
600 ml orange juice	1 pint orange juice
600 ml soda water	1 pint soda water
To garnish:	*To garnish:*
seedless grapes	seedless grapes
fresh mint leaves	fresh mint leaves

Place the apples, honey, spices and water in a large saucepan and simmer gently until the apples are very soft. Strain, pressing the apple pulp through the sieve. Cool and chill.

Mix the apple liquid with the fruit juices and soda water in a large punch bowl. Add seedless grapes, mint leaves and ice.

Serves 12 to 14

Ginger Punch

This may be served hot or cold.

METRIC	IMPERIAL
1.2 litres pineapple juice	2 pints pineapple juice
1.8 litres ginger ale or ginger beer	3 pints ginger ale or ginger beer
For hot punch:	*For hot punch:*
2–3 tablespoons chopped preserved ginger	2–3 tablespoons chopped preserved ginger
pinch of ground ginger	pinch of ground ginger
few glacé cherries	few glacé cherries
For cold punch:	*For cold punch:*
strawberries	strawberries
cucumber slices	cucumber slices

For a hot punch, place the pineapple juice and ginger ale or beer in a saucepan and heat until just below boiling point. Pour into a large heatproof bowl and stir in the preserved and ground gingers and cherries. Serve hot.

For a cold punch, place the pineapple juice and ginger ale or beer in a punch bowl with crushed ice and float strawberries and cucumber slices on top.

Serves 16 to 20

> ### Serving a hot punch
> Serve a hot punch straight into heatproof glasses, or even mugs, from the pan (a preserving pan is ideal).

Hot Spiced Cider Cup

METRIC	IMPERIAL
4 small cooking apples	4 small cooking apples
20 cloves	20 cloves
2 tablespoons demerara sugar	2 tablespoons demerara sugar
1 orange, sliced	1 orange, sliced
2 cinnamon sticks	2 cinnamon sticks
3.6 litres dry cider	6 pints dry cider
3 tablespoons dark rum	3 tablespoons dark rum

Stud each apple with five cloves. Place in a large preserving pan or saucepan with the sugar, orange slices and cinnamon. Just cover with cider and bring to the boil. Simmer for 5 minutes.

Remove the cinnamon sticks and add the remaining cider and the rum. Bring to the boil. Serve hot.

Serves 24

Tea Punch

METRIC	IMPERIAL
600 ml strong tea, strained	1 pint strong tea, strained
300 ml peach or apricot nectar	½ pint peach or apricot nectar
1.2 litres orange juice	2 pints orange juice
2 teaspoons orange bitters	2 teaspoons orange bitters
2 large bottles dry ginger ale	2 large bottles dry ginger ale
orange slices to garnish	orange slices to garnish

Mix together the tea, nectar, orange juice and bitters in a punch bowl. Add ice, then stir in the ginger ale. Garnish with orange slices.

Serves 15

Mulled Lager

METRIC	IMPERIAL
1.8 litres lager	3 pints lager
1 cinnamon stick	1 cinnamon stick
3–4 cloves	3–4 cloves
pinch of ground ginger	pinch of ground ginger
1 tablespoon sugar	1 tablespoon sugar
120–250 ml brandy	4–8 fl oz brandy

Heat the lager with the spices and sugar until almost boiling. Stir in the brandy and serve hot.

Serves 8 to 10

Drinks

Cider Orange Punch

This is an attractive summer punch.

METRIC	IMPERIAL
750 ml orange juice	1¼ pints orange juice
1 litre cider	1¾ pints cider
600 ml water	1 pint water
ice cubes	ice cubes
cucumber and orange slices to garnish	cucumber and orange slices to garnish

Place the orange juice, cider and water in a glass punch bowl and stir well. Add ice cubes and float cucumber and orange slices on the surface.

Serves 10

Cold punches

For a party, whether in winter or summer, a punch is an easy and attractive way to entertain your guests. In the warmer weather, a light refreshing punch is perfect for sipping through the day into the evening, and the punch bowl can be decorated with lovely flowers and fruits. If you don't have a punch bowl, punches can also be served in tall glass jugs or – if you're outdoors and you want something unbreakable – even a new, scrupulously clean plastic washing up bowl or bucket. For chilling a punch, it is best to use a large block of ice instead of small cubes which will melt more quickly and dilute the punch.

Grape Cup

METRIC	IMPERIAL
600 ml white grape juice	1 pint white grape juice
juice of 2 lemons	juice of 2 lemons
300 ml unsweetened pineapple juice	½ pint unsweetened pineapple juice
1 large bottle dry ginger ale	1 large bottle dry ginger ale
seedless green grapes to garnish	seedless green grapes to garnish

Mix together the grape juice, lemon juice, pineapple juice and ginger ale in a punch bowl. Add ice and garnish with grapes.

Serves 8 to 10

Tomato Juice Cocktail

METRIC	IMPERIAL
120–175 ml tomato juice	4–6 fl oz tomato juice
juice of ½ lemon	juice of ½ lemon
dash of Worcestershire sauce	dash of Worcestershire sauce
pepper	pepper
lemon slice to garnish	lemon slice to garnish

Place the tomato and lemon juices, Worcestershire sauce and pepper to taste in a screwtop jar or jug with a lid and add crushed ice. Shake well together, then strain into a glass. Add a lemon slice and serve.

Serves 1

Tropical Fruit Cup

METRIC	IMPERIAL
600 ml pineapple juice	1 pint pineapple juice
150 ml lemon juice	¼ pint lemon juice
½ bottle orange squash	½ bottle orange squash
500 g mixed fruit (pears, peaches, apricots, apples, bananas, etc.), chopped	1 lb mixed fruit (pears, peaches, apricots, apples, bananas, etc.), chopped
2 large bottles lemonade	2 large bottles lemonade
2 large bottles dry ginger ale	2 large bottles dry ginger ale

Mix together the pineapple and lemon juices, squash and fruit in a large punch bowl. Just before serving, stir in the lemonade and ginger ale, and add ice.

Serves about 18

Creamy Applenut Drink

METRIC	IMPERIAL
300 ml unsweetened apple juice	½ pint unsweetened apple juice
1 tablespoon honey	1 tablespoon honey
4 tablespoons vanilla ice cream	4 tablespoons vanilla ice cream
300 ml sweet cider	½ pint sweet cider
To decorate:	*To decorate:*
finely chopped nuts	finely chopped nuts
grated nutmeg	grated nutmeg

Place the apple juice and honey in a large screwtop jar or jug with a lid and add crushed ice. Shake well, then strain into tall glasses. Add a spoonful of ice cream to each glass and top up with cider, stirring with a long-handled spoon. Sprinkle nuts and nutmeg on top.

Serves 4

Citrus Cup

This is a refreshing non-alcoholic punch, full of vitamin C. A blender or processor will be needed.

METRIC	IMPERIAL
1 grapefruit	1 grapefruit
3 oranges	3 oranges
1 lemon	1 lemon
300 ml tonic water	½ pint tonic water
caster sugar to taste	caster sugar to taste
fresh mint sprigs to garnish	fresh mint sprigs to garnish

Thinly pare the rind from half the grapefruit and place it in the blender goblet or processor. Peel the grapefruit, removing all the white pith. Separate the segments and place in the blender goblet or processor.

Repeat this process with the oranges and lemon, adding the rind from 1½ oranges and ½ lemon.

Pour in the tonic water. Blend on maximum speed for 30 seconds. Strain into a jug and sweeten to taste. Chill before serving, garnished with mint.

Serves 4

Fruity Tea Cup

METRIC	IMPERIAL
25 g tea leaves	1 oz tea leaves
600 ml warm water	1 pint warm water
600 ml sparkling apple juice	1 pint sparkling apple juice
600 ml grape juice	1 pint grape juice
600 ml ginger ale	1 pint ginger ale
4 tablespoons lime juice cordial	4 tablespoons lime juice cordial
4 tablespoons clear honey	4 tablespoons clear honey
12 lemon slices	12 lemon slices
12 cocktail cherries	12 cocktail cherries
ice cubes	ice cubes

Mix the tea with the water and leave to infuse overnight. The next day, strain the tea liquid.

Place the tea in a large jug or punch bowl and add the fruit juices, ginger ale, lime juice cordial and honey. Stir well.

Spear a lemon slice and a cherry on 12 wooden cocktail sticks and add to the punch with ice cubes. Serve immediately.

Serves 12

VARIATION

Make as above, using 1.2 litres/2 pints each fragrant China tea and orange juice, 600 ml/1 pint each apple juice and grape juice, and 1½ teaspoons angostura bitters. Garnish with orange slices and mint sprigs.

Pink Lemonade

METRIC	IMPERIAL
juice of 4 lemons	juice of 4 lemons
120 ml raspberry syrup	4 fl oz raspberry syrup
2 large bottles lemonade	2 large bottles lemonade
raspberries (optional)	raspberries (optional)

Mix together the lemon juice, raspberry syrup and lemonade. Pour into tall glasses and add ice cubes. Garnish each serving with raspberries, if liked.

Serves 8

Iced Tomato Cocktail

An ideal drink when on a diet.

METRIC	IMPERIAL
300 ml tomato juice	½ pint tomato juice
300 ml plain yogurt	½ pint plain yogurt
½ teaspoon Worcestershire sauce	½ teaspoon Worcestershire sauce
1 teaspoon lemon juice	1 teaspoon lemon juice
1 teaspoon celery salt	1 teaspoon celery salt
pepper	pepper
fresh mint sprigs	fresh mint sprigs

Whisk together the tomato juice, yogurt, Worcestershire sauce, lemon juice, celery salt and pepper to taste. Chill well before serving, garnished with mint.

Serves 4

Chocoffee

METRIC	IMPERIAL
1 heaped teaspoon cocoa powder	1 heaped teaspoon cocoa powder
1 teaspoon instant coffee powder	1 teaspoon instant coffee powder
1 tablespoon caster sugar	1 tablespoon caster sugar
300 ml milk	½ pint milk
1 tablespoon vanilla ice cream	1 tablespoon vanilla ice cream
ground cinnamon	ground cinnamon

Mix the cocoa, instant coffee and sugar to a paste with a little of the milk. Add the rest of the milk and whisk vigorously. Alternatively, whirl all the ingredients in a blender or food processor.

Pour into a glass and top with the ice cream and a sprinkling of cinnamon.

Serves 1

Tips for serving drinks
Be sure all glasses are scrupulously clean. Chill glasses by refrigerating them.

To frost the rims, wet with lightly forked egg white and dip into caster or icing sugar (or wet with lemon or lime juice and dip into salt, depending on the drink being served).

Tall drinks and those which are to be stirred or shaken are best chilled with crushed ice, rather than ice cubes. To crush ice, place it in a polythene bag and bang with a rolling pin.

To give a drink a subtle lemon or lime flavour, rub the lemon or lime over the rim of the glass, then shave off a strip of peel (without any white pith), twist over the glass to release the zest or oil and add the peel to the glass.

Decorate drinks with orange or other fruit: cut slices about 5 mm/¼ inch thick, slit the slices and hang on the rim of the glass. Other simple decorations for drinks, depending on the recipe, are stuffed green olives, cocktail onions, maraschino cherries, fresh pineapple chunks or spears, mint or other fresh herb sprigs, celery or cucumber sticks, and even fresh flowers!

Honey Egg Nog

METRIC	IMPERIAL
300 ml hot milk	½ pint hot milk
2 tablespoons clear honey	2 tablespoons clear honey
1 egg	1 egg
2 tablespoons sweet sherry	2 tablespoons sweet sherry
¼ teaspoon grated nutmeg	¼ teaspoon grated nutmeg
¼ teaspoon ground cloves	¼ teaspoon ground cloves

Place all the ingredients in a blender goblet or food processor and blend for 10 seconds. Alternatively, whisk together until well mixed and frothy. Serve immediately.

Serves 2

Mint Cooler

METRIC	IMPERIAL
100 g granulated sugar	4 oz granulated sugar
120 ml water	4 fl oz water
handful of fresh mint leaves	handful of fresh mint leaves
juice of 4 lemons	juice of 4 lemons
600 ml unsweetened pineapple juice	1 pint unsweetened pineapple juice
soda water	soda water

Place the sugar and water in a saucepan and bring to the boil, stirring to dissolve the sugar. Remove from the heat and cool.

Add the mint leaves to the syrup and crush with the back of a wooden spoon. Leave to infuse overnight.

The next day, strain the mint-flavoured syrup. Add the lemon and pineapple juices and stir well. Pour into glasses and add crushed ice and soda water to taste.

Serves 6

Banana Milk Shake

METRIC	IMPERIAL
3 ripe bananas, chopped	3 ripe bananas, chopped
900 ml milk	1½ pints milk
4 rounded tablespoons vanilla ice cream	4 rounded tablespoons vanilla ice cream

Place all the ingredients in a blender goblet or food processor and blend for 1 minute or until well mixed.

Alternatively, if you don't have a blender or food processor, mash the bananas and gradually whisk in the milk. Allow the ice cream to soften, then add to the banana mixture. Whisk vigorously until the milk shake is thick and frothy. Serve immediately.

Serves 4

VARIATION
Strawberry milk shake: Make as above, using 500 g/1 lb strawberries instead of the bananas, and adding 50 g/2 oz caster sugar and 1 teaspoon vanilla essence. Without a blender or processor, first sieve the strawberries. If liked, top the milk shake with whipped cream and a few sliced strawberries.

Tiger Shake

This nourishing drink would make a quick snack meal.

METRIC	IMPERIAL
1 ripe banana, mashed	1 ripe banana, mashed
2 teaspoons malt extract	2 teaspoons malt extract
2 teaspoons honey	2 teaspoons honey
1 egg, beaten	1 egg, beaten
600 ml milk, chilled	1 pint milk, chilled

Mix together the banana, malt extract and honey. Beat in the egg, then gradually whisk in the milk. Serve in tall glasses.

Serves 2 to 4

Grenadine Grape Fizz

METRIC	IMPERIAL
300 ml grape juice	½ pint grape juice
1 tablespoon grenadine syrup	1 tablespoon grenadine syrup
1 egg white	1 egg white
soda water	soda water

Place the grape juice, grenadine and egg white in a screwtop jar or jug with a lid and add cru'hed ice. Shake vigorously, then strain into two tall glasses. Fill with soda water and serve.

Serves 2

Orange Juice Fizz

If fresh pineapple is not in season, use wedges of unpeeled orange to garnish.

METRIC	IMPERIAL
1.2 litres orange juice	2 pints orange juice
1 large bottle lemonade	1 large bottle lemonade
fingers of fresh pineapple	fingers of fresh pineapple

Mix together the orange juice and lemonade and pour into tall glasses. Add ice cubes and a finger of pineapple to each glass.

Serves 10

Summer Quencher

METRIC	IMPERIAL
1 large cucumber, peeled and chopped	1 large cucumber, peeled and chopped
1 avocado, peeled and stoned	1 avocado, peeled and stoned
5 tablespoons chopped parsley	5 tablespoons chopped parsley
juice of 1 large lemon	juice of 1 large lemon
1 tablespoon oil	1 tablespoon oil
To garnish:	*To garnish:*
lemon slices	lemon slices
cucumber peel	cucumber peel

Place all the ingredients in the blender goblet and add crushed ice. Blend until well mixed and the ice has melted.

Strain into glasses and garnish with lemon slices and cucumber peel.

Serves 4

Fresh Lemon Drink

METRIC	IMPERIAL
3 large lemons, cut into 1 cm cubes	3 large lemons, cut into ½ inch cubes
100 g granulated sugar	4 oz granulated sugar
1.2 litres boiling water	2 pints boiling water
fresh mint sprigs	fresh mint sprigs
lemon slices to garnish	lemon slices to garnish

Place the lemons and sugar in a large stoneware jug and pour in the boiling water. Leave to infuse for 20 minutes, then strain.

Allow to cool, then serve cold poured over ice cubes, garnished with mint sprigs and lemon slices.

Serves 6 to 8

Peach Froth

METRIC	IMPERIAL
250 ml peach nectar	8 fl oz peach nectar
175 ml milk	6 fl oz milk
1 teaspoon honey	1 teaspoon honey
1 egg white	1 egg white
grated nutmeg	grated nutmeg

Place the peach nectar, milk, honey and egg white in a mixing bowl and whisk vigorously until light and frothy. Alternatively, use a blender.

Pour into glasses and sprinkle over a little nutmeg.

Serves 2

Citrus Fizz

METRIC	IMPERIAL
1 tablespoon lime cordial	1 tablespoon lime cordial
4 mint sprigs	4 mint sprigs
juice of ½ lemon	juice of ½ lemon
6 tablespoons orange juice	6 tablespoons orange juice
2 dashes of orange bitters	2 dashes of orange bitters
ginger ale	ginger ale
orange slice to garnish	orange slice to garnish

Place the lime cordial and mint sprigs in a tall glass and crush well with a long-handled spoon. Add the lemon and orange juices and orange bitters and stir well. Add an ice cube and fill the glass with ginger ale. Garnish with an orange slice.

Serves 1

DRINKS

Name of cocktail	Main ingredients	Other ingredients	Method	Glass&Garnish
Americano	1¼ oz Campari 1¼ oz sweet vermouth	soda	Mix with ice, then strain and add soda and ice	highball
Black Russian	1½ oz vodka ¾ oz Tia Maria		Shake with ice, then strain and add ice	highball
Bloody Mary	1½ oz vodka	3 oz tomato juice 1 teaspoon lemon juice few drops of Worcestershire and Tabasco sauces	Shake with ice, strain and season to taste with salt and pepper	sour
Brandy Alexander	1½ oz brandy 1 oz dark creme de cacao	1 oz double cream	Shake with ice and strain	champagne saucer
Bullshot	1½ oz vodka	4 oz beef stock dash of Worcestershire sauce	Mix and add ice	highball, with lemon twist
Daiquiri	2 oz white rum	1 oz lime juice 1 teaspoon sugar syrup*	Shake with ice, strain and add ice	cocktail
Gibson	2½ oz gin few drops of dry vermouth		Stir	cocktail, with cocktail onion
Gimlet	2 oz gin	2 teaspoons lime juice cordial	Shake with ice, strain and add ice	highball
Grasshopper	1 oz green creme de menthe 1 oz white creme de cacao	1 oz double cream	Shake with ice, then strain	champagne saucer
Harvey Wallbanger	1 oz vodka 2 teaspoons Galliano	orange juice	Put vodka in glass, add ice and fill with orange juice, then float Galliano on top	highball
Maiden's Prayer	¾ oz gin ¼ oz Cointreau	1 teaspoon lemon juice 1 teaspoon orange juice	Shake with ice, strain and add ice	cocktail
Manhattan	2½ oz rye or other whisky 1 oz sweet vermouth		Stir	cocktail, with maraschino cherry
Marguerita	2 oz tequila 2 teaspoons Cointreau	1 tablespoon lime juice	Shake with ice, then strain	cocktail, frosted with lime juice and salt**
Martini	2 oz gin 1 teaspoon dry vermouth (more or less)		Stir	cocktail, with stuffed olive
Mint Julep	2 oz bourbon	1 oz lemon juice 1 oz sugar syrup* crushed mint sprigs	Blend for 20 seconds with crushed ice	highball, with maraschino cherry and mint sprig
Old-fashioned	2½ oz bourbon or any whisky	few drops of sugar syrup* few dashed of angostura bitters	Stir	old-fashioned, with orange slice, lemon twist or maraschino cherry
Pink Lady	2 oz gin	1 oz lemon juice 1 oz sugar syrup* ½ oz double cream few drops of grenadine	Shake with ice, strain and add ice	cocktail
Rusty Nail	1 oz Scotch 1 oz Drambuie		Mix and stir in ice	highball
Scorpion	2 oz white rum 1 oz brandy	2 oz orange juice 2 tablespoons lemon juice 2 teaspoons almond essence	Blend with crushed ice for 15 seconds, then strain and add ice	collins, with orange slice
Tom Collins	2 oz gin	1½ oz lemon juice 1½ teaspoons sugar syrup* soda	Stir, then add ice and soda	collins, with maraschino cherry

* Sugar syrup is made by dissolving 225 g/8 oz sugar in 120 ml/4 fl oz hot water and cooling.   ** see page 165
Glasses: Cocktail holds 3½ oz and has triangular-shaped bowl; Brandy holds 3 oz and has rounded sides; Sour holds 5 oz and is shaped like red wine glass; Old-fashioned holds 6–8 oz and is squat with straight sides; Highball holds 8 oz and is taller than Old-fashioned but same shape; Collins holds 10–14 oz and is taller than Highball but same shape; Champagne Saucer holds 8 oz.

Basic Recipes

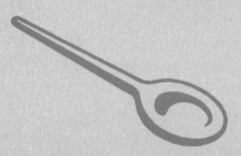

This chapter will be a tremendous help to
all cooks because, at your fingertips, you
will find the basic recipes you'll need to
prepare the dishes in this book, and in
other cookery books. How simple it is to refer
to sauces, stocks, batters, icings, stuffings,
pastries and salad dressings. Where these
basic recipes are used elsewhere in this
book, the recipe title is followed by
an asterisk.

Flaky Pastry

This pastry uses the same proportions of fat to flour as rough puff pastry, but it is made by a different method. It is excellent hot or cold.

METRIC	IMPERIAL
225 g plain flour	8 oz plain flour
pinch of salt	pinch of salt
175 g mixed butter and lard	6 oz mixed butter and lard
1 teaspoon lemon juice	1 teaspoon lemon juice
cold water (see method)	cold water (see method)

Sift the flour and salt into a bowl. Cream the butter and lard together until softened, then divide into four equal portions. Rub one portion into the flour until the mixture resembles fine crumbs. Add the lemon juice and just enough cold water to bind to a soft but not sticky dough.

Roll out the dough on a floured surface to a 38 × 18 cm/15 × 7 inch rectangle. Mark the rectangle across into three equal portions. Flake a second portion of fat over the top two-thirds of the dough rectangle leaving a 1 cm/$\frac{1}{2}$ inch border clear. Fold the bottom third up over the fat, then fold the top third down over that. Seal the edges with a rolling pin and turn the dough so that the folds are to the sides.

Repeat the rolling out, flaking with fat and folding twice more, then roll out and fold again, without adding any fat. Chill until firm before using.

Makes a 225 g/8 oz quantity

Puff Pastry

Because this pastry is so time-consuming to make the frozen variety is often used. This recipe is equivalent to 450 g/1 lb frozen pastry.

METRIC	IMPERIAL
225 g plain flour	8 oz plain flour
pinch of salt	pinch of salt
cold water (see method)	cold water (see method)
225 g butter	8 oz butter

Sift the flour and salt into a bowl. Add enough water to mix to a pliable dough. Roll out the dough on a floured surface to a 30 × 20 cm/12 × 8 inch rectangle.

Place the block of butter in the centre of the dough rectangle. Fold the dough up and down over the butter, then turn so that the folds are to the sides. Seal the edges, then roll out again into a rectangle.

Fold, turn and roll out six more times, chilling for about 15 minutes between each process. Use as required.

Makes a 225 g/8 oz quantity

Shortcrust Pastry

METRIC	IMPERIAL
175 g plain or wholemeal flour	6 oz plain or wholemeal flour
pinch of salt	pinch of salt
40 g butter or margarine	1$\frac{1}{2}$ oz butter or margarine
40 g lard	1$\frac{1}{2}$ oz lard
2–3 tablespoons water	2–3 tablespoons water

Sift the flour and salt into a bowl. Rub in the fats until the mixture resembles fine crumbs. Add enough water to bind the ingredients, then knead lightly to make a firm dough. Use as required.

This quantity of dough will line a 20 cm/8 inch flan tin.

Makes a 175 g/6 oz quantity

VARIATIONS
To make a 225 g/8 oz quantity, use 225 g/8 oz flour and 100 g/4 oz fat.
Rich shortcrust: Increase the butter or margarine to 65 g/2$\frac{1}{2}$ oz and the lard to 50 g/2 oz, and add 1 egg yolk. Decrease the water accordingly.
Sweet shortcrust: Increase the butter or margarine to 100 g/4 oz and omit the lard. Add 2 tablespoons caster sugar and 1 egg yolk. Decrease the water accordingly.
Cheese shortcrust: Add a pinch of dry mustard and one of cayenne pepper, if liked, with the salt. Stir in 50 to 75 g/2 to 3 oz grated cheese before adding the water. If liked, add 1 egg yolk and decrease the water accordingly.
Herb shortcrust: Add $\frac{1}{2}$ teaspoon dried mixed herbs to the rubbed-in mixture (either Shortcrust or Rich Shortcrust).

Hot Water Crust Pastry

Do not let the finished pastry cool; it should be used while it is warm, soft and pliable. It can be moulded around a tin or mould, or used to line a tin.

METRIC	IMPERIAL
100 g fat, preferably lard	4 oz fat, preferably lard
150 ml water	$\frac{1}{4}$ pint water
350 g plain flour	12 oz plain flour
good pinch of salt	good pinch of salt
1 egg yolk (optional)	1 egg yolk (optional)

Place the fat and water in a saucepan and heat until the fat has melted. Sift the flour and salt into a bowl and add the warm fat mixture. Knead lightly, then knead in the egg yolk, if used. (The egg yolk makes the pastry crisper, and gives it a better colour.) Use as required.

Makes a 350 g/12 oz quantity

Basic Recipes

Choux Pastry

METRIC	IMPERIAL
150 ml water	¼ pint water
50 g butter	2 oz butter
pinch of salt	pinch of salt
65 g plain flour, sifted	2½ oz plain flour, sifted
2 eggs, beaten	2 eggs, beaten

Put the water, butter and salt in a saucepan and bring to the boil, stirring to melt the butter. Remove from the heat and quickly beat in the flour all at once. Continue beating until the mixture draws away from the sides of the pan. Leave to cool slightly, then gradually beat in the eggs until the dough is smooth and glossy. Use as required.

Makes a 65 g/2½ oz quantity

Using suet pastry

To line a pudding basin with suet pastry, roll out the dough to a round 5 mm/¼ inch thick and 10 cm/4 inches larger all round than the top of the basin. Cut one-quarter out of the round.

Lift the remaining three-quarters of the dough round into the basin, centre it and ease in so that the cut edges overlap. Dampen the cut edges and press them together to seal. Press the dough evenly against the side of the basin. Trim off any dough hanging over the rim.

Place the filling in the basin, then fold over the edge of the pastry lining on top of the filling. Brush this pastry rim with water.

Gather the reserved one-quarter of dough into a ball and roll out into a round to fit the top of the basin. Lay over the filling and press the edges of the pastry together to seal.

Suet Crust Pastry

A pudding, either sweet or savoury, made with this pastry can be baked or steamed.

METRIC	IMPERIAL
225 g self-raising flour	8 oz self-raising flour
pinch of salt	pinch of salt
100 g shredded suet	4 oz shredded suet
cold water (see method)	cold water (see method)

Sift the flour and salt into a bowl and stir in the suet. Add just enough cold water to bind to a soft but not sticky dough. Use as required.

Note: Plain flour sifted with 1 tablespoon baking powder may be used instead of self-raising flour.

Makes a 225 g/8 oz quantity

Rough Puff Pastry

This is the simplest of the rich, flaky-textured pastries. The proportion of fat to flour is higher than that for shortcrust, and the fat is rolled into the dough rather than being rubbed in.

METRIC	IMPERIAL
225 g plain flour	8 oz plain flour
pinch of salt	pinch of salt
175 g butter or margarine and lard, mixed	6 oz butter or margarine and lard, mixed
1 teaspoon lemon juice	1 teaspoon lemon juice
cold water (see method)	cold water (see method)

Sift the flour and salt into a bowl. Cut the fat into 2 cm/¾ inch cubes and add to the bowl. Toss until the cubes are coated with flour.

Add the lemon juice and just enough cold water to bind into a dough, without breaking up the lumps of fat. Turn out on to a floured surface and roll out into a rectangle about 1 cm/½ inch thick. Fold up the bottom third, then fold down the top third. Seal the edges with the rolling pin, then turn the dough so the folds are to the sides.

Repeat the rolling out, folding and turning three or four times until no streaks of fat are visible in the dough. Chill until firm before using.

Makes a 225 g/8 oz quantity

French Flan Pastry

The pastry is usually made on a flat surface rather than in a bowl, and is richer and sweeter than Rich or Sweet Shortcrust Pastry.

METRIC	IMPERIAL
100 g plain flour	4 oz plain flour
pinch of salt	pinch of salt
50 g butter, softened	2 oz butter, softened
2 egg yolks	2 egg yolks
50 g caster sugar	2 oz caster sugar

Sift the flour and salt on to a flat surface. Make a well in the centre and put in the butter, egg yolks and sugar. Using the fingertips of one hand, work the ingredients in the well together to make a paste, then gradually draw in the flour. Knead lightly to a smooth dough.

Cover and chill for 20 minutes before using.

Makes a 100 g/4 oz quantity

VARIATION
To make a 175 g/6 oz quantity, use 175 g/6 oz flour and 75 g/3 oz butter with the same number of egg yolks and the same amount of sugar.

Crumb Crust

METRIC	IMPERIAL
225 digestive biscuits, finely crushed	8 oz digestive biscuits, finely crushed
100 g butter, melted	4 oz butter, melted

Mix together the biscuit crumbs and butter. Press evenly over the bottom and up the sides of a greased 20 cm/8 inch flan dish. Chill until firm.

Makes a 20 cm/8 inch crust

VARIATION
Chocolate crumb crust: Make as above, using plain chocolate digestive biscuits.

Cornflake Flan Case

METRIC	IMPERIAL
50 g butter	2 oz butter
50 g caster sugar	2 oz caster sugar
1 tablespoon golden syrup	1 tablespoon golden syrup
75 g cornflakes, roughly crushed	3 oz cornflakes, roughly crushed

Place the butter, sugar and syrup in a saucepan and heat until smooth and melted. Remove from the heat and fold in the cornflakes.

Press firmly over the bottom and up the sides of a 20 cm/8 inch flan tin. Chill until set.

Makes a 20 cm/8 inch crust

Yeast Pizza Dough

METRIC	IMPERIAL
¼ teaspoon caster sugar	¼ teaspoon caster sugar
150 ml lukewarm water	¼ pint lukewarm water
1 teaspoon dried yeast	1 teaspoon dried yeast
225 g plain flour	8 oz plain flour
1 teaspoon salt	1 teaspoon salt
25 g butter or lard, softened, or 2 tablespoons olive oil	1 oz butter or lard, softened, or 2 tablespoons olive oil

Dissolve the sugar in the water, then sprinkle the yeast on top. Leave in a warm place until frothy.

Sift the flour and salt into a bowl. Add the yeast liquid and butter, lard or oil and mix to a soft dough. Cover and leave to rise in a warm place for about 45 minutes or until doubled in size.

Knock back the dough, then use as required.

Making pastry
When making pastry, with the exception of choux and hot water crust, have all equipment and ingredients cool, and work in a kitchen that isn't hot with other baking or cooking. Your hands should be cool, too.

Pancake Batter

METRIC	IMPERIAL
100 g plain flour	4 oz plain flour
¼ teaspoon salt	¼ teaspoon salt
1 egg, beaten	1 egg, beaten
300 ml milk	½ pint milk
1 teaspoon oil	1 teaspoon oil

Sift the flour and salt into a bowl. Make a well in the centre and add the egg and half the milk. Beat vigorously with a wooden spoon until thick and creamy, then gradually beat in the remaining milk and the oil until smooth. Pour into a jug for easy pouring and use as required.

To make pancakes, lightly oil a 25 cm/10 inch pancake or frying pan and heat it. Pour a little batter into the pan and tilt so that the bottom is covered in a thin layer. Cook over high heat until the underside is golden brown, then flip or turn over the pancake and cook the other side. Slide the pancake out of the pan and keep warm while you cook the remaining pancakes in the same way.

This quantity of batter should make 12 pancakes

VARIATION
To make a coating batter for food that is to be deep fried quickly, use only 150 ml/¼ pint milk. If liked the egg may be separated: beat the egg yolk with the flour and milk, and fold in the stiffly whisked white just before using the batter. This lighter batter is particularly good for coating shellfish, fruit and vegetables.

Labelling and recording food for freezing
When preparing food for the freezer, be sure to label every package and to add the date of freezing. It is also useful to note the date by which the frozen food should be eaten. Without these notations you would find it almost impossible to identify the frozen shapes in your freezer. Use moisture proof labels or pens so your details stay on the package rather than falling off into the freezer or rubbing away.

If you are really organised, keep a log book in which you can enter all the items you have frozen and the dates by which they should be eaten.

Beef Stock

METRIC	IMPERIAL
1 kg shin or neck of beef or beef bones, chopped	2 lb shin or neck of beef or beef bones, chopped
2 carrots, sliced	2 carrots, sliced
1 onion, quartered	1 onion, quartered
1 leek, chopped	1 leek, chopped
1 celery stick, sliced	1 celery stick, sliced
1 bouquet garni	1 bouquet garni
6 black peppercorns	6 black peppercorns
salt	salt

Place the beef in a saucepan and cover with cold water (about 2 litres/3½ pints). Add the remaining ingredients with salt to taste and bring to the boil. Skim off any scum that rises to the surface, then cover and simmer gently for about 2 hours, adding more water if the level drops to below that of the beef.

Strain the stock and allow to cool. Skim off any fat from the surface and use immediately, or keep in the refrigerator or freezer.

VARIATIONS

Poultry stock: Make as above, using a chicken, duck or turkey carcass instead of beef bones.

Ham stock: Make as above, using a ham (knuckle or shank) bone instead of beef bones.

White stock: Make as above, using blanched veal bones instead of beef bones.

Brown Sauce

To give a good flavour to this sauce, add 1 to 2 tablespoons of the meat jelly that forms under the dripping from a roasted joint.

METRIC	IMPERIAL
25 g butter or dripping	1 oz butter or dripping
25 g flour	1 oz flour
300 ml beef stock	½ pint beef stock
salt and pepper	salt and pepper

Melt the butter or dripping in a saucepan. Stir in the flour and cook for 2 to 3 minutes or until the mixture turns golden brown. Gradually stir in the stock. Bring to the boil, stirring, and simmer until thickened.

Season to taste with salt and pepper and use as required.

Makes 300 ml/½ pint

VARIATIONS

Sherry sauce: Add to the finished sauce 1 finely chopped small onion or shallot, 2 teaspoons chopped parsley, 3 tablespoons dry sherry and 1 tablespoon lemon juice. Simmer for 10 minutes, then add 1 table-spoon of meat juices from the roasted or grilled meat with which you are serving the sauce.

Red wine sauce: Add to the finished sauce 2 teaspoons finely chopped onion or shallot, 2 teaspoons chopped parsley, 1 teaspoon chopped fresh tarragon and 4 tablespoons red wine. Simmer for 10 minutes.

Cavalier sauce: Add to the finished sauce 1 tablespoon tomato purée, 2 teaspoons tarragon vinegar and 1 teaspoon French mustard. Simmer for 2 minutes, then stir in 1 tablespoon chutney, 2 teaspoons chopped gherkins and 2 teaspoons chopped capers. Serve with pasta as well as meat and poultry dishes.

Court Bouillon

This is basically a fish stock and is used for poaching fish as well as for forming the basis for fish soups and sauces. It is cooked for only a short time because longer cooking would release the gelatine from the bones, making the stock sticky. If you want to reduce the stock by boiling, strain it first.

METRIC	IMPERIAL
500–750 g fish trimmings (bones, skin, head, etc.)	1–1½ lb fish trimmings (bones, skin, head, etc.)
1 onion, sliced	1 onion, sliced
1 carrot, sliced	1 carrot, sliced
1 small celery stick	1 small celery stick
1 bouquet garni	1 bouquet garni
1 teaspoon salt	1 teaspoon salt
10 peppercorns	10 peppercorns
about 1.8 litres water	about 3 pints water
120 ml dry white wine, or 1 tablespoon white wine vinegar	4 fl oz dry white wine, or 1 tablespoon white wine vinegar

Place all the ingredients in a saucepan, adding just enough water to cover the fish trimmings, and bring to the boil. Skim off the scum that rises to the surface. Simmer for 20 to 30 minutes.

Strain the stock through a fine-meshed sieve and use as required.

Homemade stock

Cooked or uncooked meat and poultry bones may be used on their own with vegetables and herbs, but the stock will be improved if meat trimmings or giblets are added.

Vegetables such as turnips and parsnips have a strong flavour, so they should be added in small quantities, if at all. Do not use potatoes as they'll make the stock cloudy.

Store homemade stock in the refrigerator or freezer. If kept in the fridge, boil it up every 2 days to prevent it becoming sour. For freezing, boil stock until well reduced to concentrate the flavour.

Basic White Sauce

The quantities given below are for a pouring sauce. For a thicker result, to use as a coating sauce, increase the butter and flour to 50 g/2 oz each.

METRIC	IMPERIAL
25 g butter	1 oz butter
25 g flour	1 oz flour
300 ml milk (or half milk and half cooking liquid from the fish or vegetable with which the sauce is to be served)	½ pint milk (or half milk and half cooking liquid from the fish or vegetable with which the sauce is to be served)
salt and pepper	salt and pepper
pinch of grated nutmeg (optional)	pinch of grated nutmeg (optional)

Melt the butter in a heavy-based saucepan. Do not allow the butter to brown. Add the flour and stir well to mix with the butter. Cook for 1 minute.

Remove the pan from the heat and gradually stir in the milk. If the sauce becomes lumpy, whisk with a balloon or rotary whisk. When all the milk has been incorporated, return the pan to the heat and bring to the boil, stirring constantly. Simmer until thickened.

Season to taste with salt, pepper and the nutmeg, if used. Use as required.

Makes 300 ml/½ pint

VARIATIONS

Anchovy sauce: Make the basic white sauce using half fish cooking liquid. Stir in 1 to 2 teaspoons anchovy essence and 1 teaspoon lemon juice. Serve with fish.

Béchamel sauce: Place the milk in a saucepan with 1 slice of onion, 1 slice of carrot, 1 small celery stick, 1 bay leaf, 3 black peppercorns and a mace blade, if available. Bring almost to boiling point, then cover and remove from the heat. Leave to infuse for 20 minutes. Strain the milk and use to make the sauce as above.

Caper sauce: Stir 1 tablespoon chopped capers and 1 teaspoon caper liquid into the basic white sauce. Serve with lamb, pork or oily fish.

Cheese sauce: Season the basic white sauce with 1 teaspoon French mustard, then stir in 50 to 75 g/ 2 to 3 oz grated cheese until melted and smooth. Serve with vegetables, fish, chicken or pasta.

Egg sauce: Add 2 chopped hard-boiled eggs and 1 tablespoon chopped parsley or chives to the basic white sauce. Serve with fish or chicken.

Mustard sauce: Stir ½ teaspoon dry mustard, 2 teaspoons lemon juice or white wine vinegar and ½ teaspoon caster sugar into the basic white sauce. Alternatively, just stir in 2 tablespoons of continental mustard. Serve with fish.

Parsley sauce: Add 2 tablespoons chopped parsley to the basic white sauce. Serve with ham, fish, chicken or vegetables.

Shrimp sauce: Substitute cayenne pepper for the nutmeg, and add 50 g/2 oz chopped cooked peeled prawns to the basic white sauce. Heat through gently. Serve with white fish.

Soured cream sauce: Add 4 tablespoons soured cream to the basic white sauce. Serve with veal, chicken, fish or vegetables.

Onion Sauce

Serve this sauce with roast lamb, or try it poured over hard-boiled eggs for a quick supper dish.

METRIC	IMPERIAL
2 large onions, chopped	2 large onions, chopped
salt and pepper	salt and pepper
40 g butter	1½ oz butter
40 g flour	1½ oz flour
300 ml milk	½ pint milk

Place the onions in a saucepan and cover with water. Season to taste with salt and pepper. Bring to the boil and simmer until tender.

Drain the onions, reserving 150 ml/¼ pint of the cooking liquid.

Melt the butter in the cleaned saucepan. Stir in the flour and cook for 2 minutes, then gradually stir in the milk and reserved onion cooking liquid. Bring to the boil, stirring, and simmer until thickened. Stir in the onions and taste and adjust the seasoning. Serve hot.

Makes 450 ml/¾ pint

Chestnut Stuffing

METRIC	IMPERIAL
3 streaky bacon rashers, rinded and chopped	3 streaky bacon rashers, rinded and chopped
100 g fresh breadcrumbs	4 oz fresh breadcrumbs
1 tablespoon chopped parsley	1 tablespoon chopped parsley
1 × 225 g can unsweetened chestnut purée	1 × 8 oz can unsweetened chestnut purée
25 g butter, melted	1 oz butter, melted
1 egg, beaten	1 egg, beaten
salt and pepper	salt and pepper

Fry the bacon in a frying pan until golden brown and crisp. Drain on paper towels, then mix with the remaining ingredients, adding salt and pepper to taste. Use as required.

Enough for a 5 kg/10 lb turkey

Making stuffings
A good stuffing helps keep the shape of the joint or bird during roasting and prevents it drying out.

A stuffing should not be too wet or it will be sloppy, nor too dry or it will crumble. Follow the recipe carefully. Don't pack in a stuffing too tightly because during roasting, the stuffing absorbs juices from the meat and expands. If you have made too much, roll the surplus into small balls and cook round the joint or bird.

Sausagemeat and Celery Stuffing

METRIC	IMPERIAL
25 g butter	1 oz butter
1 onion, chopped	1 onion, chopped
2 celery sticks, diced	2 celery sticks, diced
500 g pork sausagemeat	1 lb pork sausagemeat
1 tablespoon chopped parsley	1 tablespoon chopped parsley
1 teaspoon dried mixed herbs	1 teaspoon dried mixed herbs
25 g fresh breadcrumbs	1 oz fresh breadcrumbs
salt and pepper	salt and pepper

Melt the butter in a frying pan. Add the onion and celery and fry until softened. Drain the vegetables on paper towels, then add to the remaining stuffing ingredients, with salt and pepper to taste. Mix well and use as required.

Enough for a 5 kg/10 lb turkey

Sage and Onion Stuffing

Use this to stuff a chicken or boned pork joint.

METRIC	IMPERIAL
2–3 large onions, chopped	2–3 large onions, chopped
salt and pepper	salt and pepper
75 g fresh breadcrumbs	3 oz fresh breadcrumbs
$\frac{1}{2}$ teaspoon dried sage	$\frac{1}{2}$ teaspoon dried sage
50 g shredded suet	2 oz shredded suet
1 egg, beaten	1 egg, beaten

Place the onions in a saucepan and cover with water. Season to taste with salt and pepper. Bring to the boil and simmer for 10 minutes. Drain, reserving the cooking liquid.

Mix the onions with the breadcrumbs, sage, suet and salt and pepper to taste. Bind with the egg. If the mixture is too dry, add a little of the onion cooking liquid. Use as required.

Tomato Sauce

This sauce is made with canned tomatoes which have a lot of flavour. Vary the herbs according to use: for a pizza or pasta dish, use oregano or dried Italian seasoning; to serve with cauliflower or other cooked vegetables, use basil, thyme or dried mixed herbs.

METRIC	IMPERIAL
2 tablespoons oil	2 tablespoons oil
1 large onion, finely chopped	1 large onion, finely chopped
1 garlic clove, crushed (optional)	1 garlic clove, crushed (optional)
1 × 400 g can tomatoes	1 × 14 oz can tomatoes
1 teaspoon caster sugar	1 teaspoon caster sugar
1 tablespoon tomato purée	1 tablespoon tomato purée
$\frac{1}{4}$ teaspoon dried herbs	$\frac{1}{4}$ teaspoon dried herbs
salt and pepper	salt and pepper

Heat the oil in a saucepan. Add the onion and garlic, if used, and fry until softened. Stir in the tomatoes with their juice and break them up with the spoon. Add the remaining ingredients, with salt and pepper to taste, and simmer, stirring occasionally, until the sauce is thick.

Taste and adjust the seasoning, and use as required.

Barbecue Sauce

METRIC	IMPERIAL
1 tablespoon oil	1 tablespoon oil
2 onions, chopped	2 onions, chopped
1 streaky bacon rasher, rinded and chopped	1 streaky bacon rasher, rinded and chopped
1 tablespoon tomato purée	1 tablespoon tomato purée
300 ml dry cider	$\frac{1}{2}$ pint dry cider
50 g demerara sugar	2 oz demerara sugar
1 tablespoon Worcestershire sauce	1 tablespoon Worcestershire sauce
1 tablespoon sweet pickle	1 tablespoon sweet pickle
salt and pepper	salt and pepper
1 teaspoon arrowroot	1 teaspoon arrowroot
2 tablespoons water	2 tablespoons water

Heat the oil in a saucepan. Add the onions and bacon and fry until the onions are softened. Stir in the tomato purée, cider, sugar, Worcestershire sauce, pickle and salt and pepper to taste and bring to the boil. Simmer for 20 minutes.

Blend the arrowroot with the water and add to the pan. Simmer, stirring, until thickened. Taste and adjust the seasoning before serving.

Makes about 300 ml/$\frac{1}{2}$ pint

Bread Sauce

METRIC	IMPERIAL
1 onion	1 onion
3 cloves	3 cloves
600 ml milk	1 pint milk
4 black peppercorns	4 black peppercorns
salt	salt
25 g butter	1 oz butter
100 g fresh white breadcrumbs	4 oz fresh white breadcrumbs

Stud the onion with the cloves. Put into a saucepan and add the milk, peppercorns and salt to taste. Heat until the milk is almost boiling, then cover and remove from the heat. Leave to infuse for 30 minutes.

Remove the onion and peppercorns. Add the butter and breadcrumbs and mix well. Cook gently for 15 minutes, stirring occasionally. Serve hot.

Makes 600 ml/1 pint

Horseradish Sauce

This creamy sauce is the perfect accompaniment to roast beef, and is far superior to the bought variety.

METRIC	IMPERIAL
150 ml double cream	$\frac{1}{4}$ pint double cream
150 ml single cream	$\frac{1}{4}$ pint single cream
1 tablespoon lemon juice	1 tablespoon lemon juice
3–4 tablespoons grated fresh horseradish	3–4 tablespoons grated fresh horseradish
1 tablespoon caster sugar	1 tablespoon caster sugar
salt and pepper	salt and pepper

Whip the double cream until thick, then gradually beat in the single cream and lemon juice. Fold in the horseradish and sugar and season to taste with salt and pepper.

Makes about 250 ml/8 fl oz

Apple Sauce

Serve this sauce with roast pork or sausages.

METRIC	IMPERIAL
500 g apples, peeled, cored and sliced	1 lb apples, peeled, cored and sliced
2–3 tablespoons water	2–3 tablespoons water
25 g butter	1 oz butter
sugar to taste	sugar to taste

Place the apples and water in a saucepan. Cover and cook gently until soft. Uncover the pan and beat until the apples are smooth. Continue cooking gently until thickened.

Cranberry Sauce

Fresh or frozen cranberries may be used.

METRIC	IMPERIAL
175 g sugar	6 oz sugar
150 ml water	$\frac{1}{4}$ pint water
225 g cranberries	8 oz cranberries
2 tablespoons sherry (optional)	2 tablespoons sherry (optional)

Dissolve the sugar in the water in a saucepan. Add the cranberries and simmer for about 10 minutes or until the fruit is just soft. Remove from the heat and allow to cool.

If used, stir in the sherry before serving.

Makes about 600 ml/1 pint

Cumberland Sauce

METRIC	IMPERIAL
1 orange	1 orange
1 lemon	1 lemon
4 tablespoons redcurrant jelly	4 tablespoons redcurrant jelly
$\frac{1}{4}$ teaspoon dry mustard	$\frac{1}{4}$ teaspoon dry mustard
pinch of ground ginger	pinch of ground ginger
salt and pepper	salt and pepper

Pare half the rind from the orange and lemon and cut into very thin shreds. Blanch in boiling water for 5 minutes. Drain and dry on paper towels.

Squeeze the juice from the orange and lemon and place in a saucepan with the redcurrant jelly, mustard, ginger and salt and pepper to taste. Heat until the jelly has melted, stirring occasionally. Stir in the shreds of rind and serve.

Makes about 150 ml/$\frac{1}{4}$ pint

Making Yorkshire pudding

Yorkshire puddings are simply made from basic Pancake Batter*. Grease individual muffin tins and heat them in a preheated hot oven (220°C/425°F, Gas Mark 7) for 5 minutes. Divide the batter between the tins, filling them half full. Return to the oven and bake for 20 to 30 minutes or until the puddings are well risen, crisp and golden. Serve immediately.

Wrapping food for the freezer

If food for the freezer is not adequately wrapped it may be exposed to the very cold air which could cause it to spoil. This spoilage, called freezer burn, is caused by moisture and juices being lost from the food, and appears as brown or greyish-white patches on the food's surface. Freezer burn will not make the food uneatable (just cut off the affected parts after thawing) but it is wasteful.

To ensure that freezer burn does not occur, and that the food you put into the freezer will be in prime condition when you want to eat it, it must be well wrapped in freezerproof wrappings and containers. Freezer foil is an exellent wrapping as it can be moulded around awkwardly-shaped food. The lighter foil, called kitchen foil, can also be used provided it is in double thickness. Polythene, or cling film, is good too, especially as it is self-sealing. But be sure to use the heavy-duty freezerproof variety.

Bags made of heavy-gauge polythene and foil-lined freezer bags are convenient to use. Ordinary polythene bags will do, but they will puncture more easily than those specially designed for freezing. Boil-in-bags are designed to go straight from the freezer into boiling water, so they are good for foods that need to be reheated.

Containers can be polythene, rigid plastic, foil, waxed cartons or your own cooking pots such as casserole dishes (remember, though, that they will be out of action while they are in the freezer).

All packages should be airtight before freezing. Containers that have suction, clip-on or screw-top lids are easy to seal, and solid foods that are wrapped in foil or polythene are no problem. But bags must have all air excluded. Do this by squeezing out the air with your hands, working from the bottom of the bag to the top, or by sucking the air out with a drinking straw.

Seal all packages with wire closures or ties, freezer tape, or a heat sealing unit or iron, then label before freezing.

Mayonnaise

For a more economical mayonnaise, up to half the oil used may be corn oil.

METRIC	IMPERIAL
2 egg yolks	2 egg yolks
$\frac{1}{4}$ teaspoon caster sugar	$\frac{1}{4}$ teaspoon caster sugar
$\frac{1}{2}$ teaspoon French mustard	$\frac{1}{2}$ teaspoon French mustard
salt and pepper	salt and pepper
150 ml olive oil	$\frac{1}{4}$ pint olive oil
1 tablespoon wine vinegar or lemon juice	1 tablespoon wine vinegar or lemon juice

Place the egg yolks, sugar, mustard and salt and pepper to taste in a bowl and mix well together with a wooden spoon. Very gradually trickle in the oil, beating constantly.

When the mixture thickens, stir in a little of the vinegar or lemon juice, then continue beating in the oil. After about half the oil has been added, the remainder may be poured in more quickly.

Stir in the remaining vinegar or lemon juice, and taste and adjust the seasoning.

Makes 150 ml/$\frac{1}{4}$ pint

VARIATIONS
Tartare sauce: Add the following to the finished mayonnaise: 2 teaspoons finely chopped capers, 2 teaspoons finely chopped gherkins, 1 teaspoon finely chopped shallots, 2 tablespoons finely chopped parsley, and more mustard and lemon juice to taste.
Green mayonnaise: Add chopped mixed fresh herbs to the finished mayonnaise. Tint a pale green with food colouring.

Hollandaise Sauce

This delicate sauce is served warm, not hot, with fish, chicken, asparagus, artichokes or broccoli. Do not allow it to cool as it will separate. It is not difficult to make if you remember to add the butter slowly, and keep the bowl of sauce from getting too hot.

METRIC	IMPERIAL
2 egg yolks	2 egg yolks
about 1 tablespoon lemon juice	about 1 tablespoon lemon juice
100 g unsalted butter, cut into small pieces	4 oz unsalted butter, cut into small pieces
salt	salt

Place the egg yolks and lemon juice in a heatproof bowl placed over a saucepan of simmering water. Do not let the bottom of the bowl touch the water. Beat until the mixture begins to thicken.

Add the butter, one piece at a time, allowing each piece to melt before adding the next. If the sauce gives any sign of 'scrambling', remove the bowl from the pan and stir in 1 teaspoon of cold water.

Continue adding the butter as before, and replace the bowl over the hot water, adding more cold water when required.

When all the butter has been incorporated, add salt and more lemon juice to taste. Serve immediately.

Makes about 150 ml/$\frac{1}{4}$ pint

VARIATION
Mousseline sauce: Add 4 to 6 tablespoons single cream to the finished hollandaise sauce, with more salt and lemon juice to taste. Gently reheat the sauce over the hot water and serve warm or cold.

Soured Cream Dressing

To vary this dressing, one or more of the following may be added: 50 g/2 oz chopped walnuts, 2 teaspoons tomato purée, 1 teaspoon made mustard, 1 tablespoon chopped chives, 2 teaspoons grated horseradish, or ¼ cucumber, peeled and grated.

METRIC	IMPERIAL
150 ml soured cream	¼ pint soured cream
1 tablespoon milk	1 tablespoon milk
1 tablespoon lemon juice	1 tablespoon lemon juice
1 teaspoon icing sugar	1 teaspoon icing sugar
salt and pepper	salt and pepper

Whisk or blend together the soured cream, milk, lemon juice and sugar. Season to taste with salt and pepper. Leave in a cool place for 15 minutes before serving.

Makes about 175 ml/6 fl oz

Yogurt Dressing

If liked, add one of the following to the dressing with the seasoning: 3 tablespoons finely chopped watercress, 2 teaspoons curry powder, 1 teaspoon Worcestershire sauce, 1 tablespoon tomato purée.

METRIC	IMPERIAL
150 ml plain yogurt	¼ pint plain yogurt
2 tablespoons single cream	2 tablespoons single cream
1 tablespoon lemon juice	1 tablespoon lemon juice
1 teaspoon icing sugar	1 teaspoon icing sugar
salt and pepper	salt and pepper

Whisk or blend together the yogurt, cream, lemon juice and sugar. Season to taste with salt and pepper. Leave in a cool place for 15 to 20 minutes before serving.

Makes about 175 ml/6 fl oz

French Dressing

METRIC	IMPERIAL
6 tablespoons oil	6 tablespoons oil
2 tablespoons wine or cider vinegar or lemon juice	2 tablespoons wine or cider vinegar or lemon juice
pinch of dry mustard	pinch of dry mustard
salt and pepper	salt and pepper

Place the ingredients, with salt and pepper to taste, in a screwtop jar and shake until well combined.

Makes 120 ml/4 fl oz

VARIATIONS
Add 1 crushed garlic clove. Or, for a less pronounced garlic flavour, add a halved garlic clove and leave to infuse for 30 minutes before removing.
Add 1 or 2 tablespoons chopped fresh herbs.

Piquant Tomato Dressing

METRIC	IMPERIAL
6 tablespoons tomato juice	6 tablespoons tomato juice
2 tablespoons lemon juice	2 tablespoons lemon juice
1–2 teaspoons Worcestershire sauce	1–2 teaspoons Worcestershire sauce
1 tablespoon chopped fresh herbs (parsley, chives or mint)	1 tablespoon chopped fresh herbs (parsley, chives or mint)
salt and pepper	salt and pepper

Place all the ingredients, with salt and pepper to taste, in a small bowl and mix well together.

Makes about 120 ml/4 fl oz

Minted Fruit Juice Dressing

METRIC	IMPERIAL
150 ml orange or grapefruit juice	¼ pint orange or grapefruit juice
1–2 teaspoons chopped fresh mint	1–2 teaspoons chopped fresh mint
salt and pepper	salt and pepper

Mix together the ingredients, seasoning to taste with salt and pepper.

Makes 150 ml/¼ pint

Dressings for dieters
The simplest and most refreshing salad dressing is made by squeezing fresh lemon juice over salad greens, add chopped fresh herbs as available and season to taste.
   Many mayonnaise-based salad dressings can be made less rich and calorific by using plain yogurt or sieved cottage cheese in place of some or all of the mayonnaise. Sieved cottage cheese, mixed with lemon juice and seasoning, is a piquant dressing, which is also delicious spooned into hot baked jacket potatoes (less fattening than soured cream).

Basic Recipes

Butterscotch Sauce

METRIC	IMPERIAL
50 g butter	2 oz butter
100 g soft brown sugar	4 oz soft brown sugar
pinch of salt	pinch of salt
150 ml evaporated milk	¼ pint evaporated milk

Place the butter, sugar and salt in a heavy-based saucepan and heat, stirring, until smooth and the sugar just begins to caramelize. Stir in the evaporated milk until well combined.

Serve hot, or allow to cool, stirring occasionally.

Makes about 250 ml/8 fl oz

Custard

Make this dessert sauce in a heatproof bowl placed over a pan of simmering water, or in the top of a double boiler. If it is cooked over direct heat it is very likely to curdle. A homemade custard is delicious and also very nutritious.

METRIC	IMPERIAL
3 egg yolks	3 egg yolks
1 tablespoon caster sugar	1 tablespoon caster sugar
300 ml milk	½ pint milk
¼ teaspoon vanilla essence	¼ teaspoon vanilla essence

Place the egg yolks and sugar in a heatproof bowl and whisk together until well blended.

Heat the milk in a saucepan until it is almost boiling. Gradually whisk the milk into the egg yolk mixture. Place the bowl over a pan of simmering water and stir until the custard thickens enough to coat the back of a wooden spoon in a creamy film.

Stir in the vanilla essence. Taste and add more caster sugar if liked. Strain and serve warm, or pour into a cold bowl and allow to cool, stirring occasionally to prevent a skin forming.

Makes about 300 ml/½ pint

VARIATIONS
Coffee custard: Mix 2 teaspoons instant coffee powder with the egg yolks and sugar.
Sherry custard: Replace 3 tablespoons of the milk with sweet sherry, adding the sherry to the finished custard.
Orange custard: Replace 3 tablespoons of the milk with orange juice, adding the juice to the finished custard. For an even stronger orange flavour, add the grated rind of 1 large orange to the milk before it is heated. Strain before adding the milk to the egg yolks.

Evaporated and condensed milk
Evaporated milk is fresh milk from which about 60% of the water has been removed. If chilled, it will whip like cream, for which it is an economical alternative. Condensed milk is evaporated milk with sugar added.

Chocolate Fudge Sauce

Top vanilla ice cream with this rich sauce, a dollop of whipped cream and chopped toasted almonds.

METRIC	IMPERIAL
50 g plain chocolate	2 oz plain chocolate
120 ml sweetened condensed milk	4 fl oz sweetened condensed milk
4 tablespoons water	4 tablespoons water
25 g butter	1 oz butter

Place the chocolate and condensed milk in a heatproof bowl over a saucepan of simmering water and heat, stirring, until the chocolate has melted. Beat in the water and butter until the sauce is smooth. Serve hot.

Makes about 250 ml/8 fl oz

Chocolate Sauce

METRIC	IMPERIAL
175 g plain chocolate	6 oz plain chocolate
150 ml water	¼ pint water
100 g caster sugar	4 oz caster sugar

Place the chocolate and 2 tablespoons of the water in a heavy-based saucepan. Heat gently, stirring, until melted and smooth. Add the remaining water and the sugar and mix well. Bring to the boil and simmer for 10 minutes. Serve hot or cold.

Makes about 175 ml/6 fl oz

VARIATIONS
Mocha sauce: Add 1 teaspoon instant coffee powder to the chocolate when it is melted.
Quick chocolate caramel sauce: Melt 3 Mars bars with 4 tablespoons milk in a heatproof bowl over a pan of simmering water.
Milk chocolate sauce: Mix 1 tablespoon each cornflour, cocoa powder and caster sugar with a little of 300 ml/½ pint milk to make a paste. Warm the remaining milk with 15 g/½ oz butter until almost boiling, then stir into the cocoa mixture. Pour back into the saucepan and bring to the boil, stirring. Simmer until thickened. Stir in ¼ teaspoon vanilla essence, and add more sugar if desired. Serve warm.

Fruit Sauce

Serve this with ice cream or steamed puddings.

METRIC	IMPERIAL
225 g soft fruit (strawberries, raspberries, etc.)	8 oz soft fruit (strawberries, raspberries, etc.)
juice of 1 orange	juice of 1 orange
50 g caster sugar	2 oz caster sugar

Purée the fruit in a blender or food processor and strain out the seeds. Alternatively, sieve the fruit. Stir in the orange juice and sugar until the sugar has dissolved, then chill for at least 1 hour before serving.

Makes about 250 ml/8 fl oz

Honey Sauce

This is delicious with hot or cold desserts.

METRIC	IMPERIAL
120 ml clear honey	4 fl oz clear honey
120 ml single cream	4 fl oz single cream
2 tablespoons whisky (optional)	2 tablespoons whisky (optional)

Place all the ingredients in a heatproof bowl over a saucepan of simmering water and stir until piping hot and well mixed. Serve hot, or allow to cool and store in a covered container in the refrigerator.

Makes about 250 ml/8 fl oz

Brandy Butter

This hard sauce is traditionally served with Christmas pudding and hot mince pies, but it is equally delicious with baked apples and other hot puddings.

METRIC	IMPERIAL
100 g unsalted butter	4 oz unsalted butter
100 g caster sugar	4 oz caster sugar
3 tablespoons brandy	3 tablespoons brandy

Cream the butter until softened. Gradually beat in the sugar until the mixture is light and fluffy. Beat in the brandy. Chill until firm.

Serves 4 to 6

VARIATION
Cumberland rum butter: Make as above, using soft brown sugar instead of caster sugar and rum instead of brandy. Beat 2 teaspoons grated lemon rind into the butter and sugar mixture before the rum.

Storing cakes
Iced cakes are best stored in an airtight container that is large enough to hold the cake without it touching the sides or top. A cake covered or filled with whipped cream should be eaten the day it is made. Otherwise, store overnight in the fridge.

Royal iced and decorated cakes should be covered lightly with tissue paper.

Chantilly Cream

Use this sweetened, vanilla-flavoured cream to fill cakes or pastries, or serve it with fruit desserts.

METRIC	IMPERIAL
300 ml double cream	$\frac{1}{2}$ pint double cream
1 teaspoon vanilla essence	1 teaspoon vanilla essence
1 tablespoon icing sugar	1 tablespoon icing sugar
2 tablespoons milk	2 tablespoons milk

Whip or blend all the ingredients together until thick.

Makes about 300 ml/$\frac{1}{2}$ pint

Vanilla Buttercream

METRIC	IMPERIAL
75 g unsalted butter	3 oz unsalted butter
175 g icing sugar, sifted	6 oz icing sugar, sifted
$\frac{1}{4}$ teaspoon vanilla essence	$\frac{1}{4}$ teaspoon vanilla essence
1–2 teaspoons warm water	1–2 teaspoons warm water

Cream the butter until softened, then gradually beat in the sugar. Add the vanilla essence and enough warm water to make a smooth, pliable texture.

Enough to cover the top and sides of an 18 cm/7 inch sandwich cake, or to fill and cover the top

VARIATIONS
Chocolate buttercream: Replace 25 g/1 oz of the sugar with cocoa or chocolate powder.
Orange or lemon buttercream: Cream the butter with the grated rind of 1 small orange or $\frac{1}{2}$ lemon. Use orange or lemon juice instead of water.
Coffee buttercream: Add 2 teaspoons instant coffee powder with the sugar. Omit the vanilla essence, if preferred.
Mocha buttercream: Add 1 teaspoon instant coffee powder and 1 tablespoon cocoa or chocolate powder with the sugar. Omit the vanilla essence.
Walnut buttercream: Add 2 tablespoons finely chopped walnuts to the finished vanilla, chocolate, coffee or mocha buttercream.

Royal Icing

METRIC	IMPERIAL
3 egg whites	3 egg whites
750 g icing sugar, sifted	1½ lb icing sugar, sifted
1½ teaspoons lemon juice	1½ teaspoons lemon juice
2 teaspoons glycerine	2 teaspoons glycerine

Place the egg whites in a bowl and beat lightly. Add half the icing sugar and beat for 5 to 10 minutes or until smooth, glossy and white. Beat in the lemon juice and glycerine, then gradually beat in the remaining sugar, adding enough to make a stiff icing that will form peaks.

Use as required, keeping any unused icing for decorations covered with a damp cloth.

Enough to cover the top and sides of a 20 cm/8 inch square or 23 cm/9 inch round cake

Almond Paste

METRIC	IMPERIAL
450 g ground almonds	1 lb ground almonds
225 g caster sugar	8 oz caster sugar
225 g icing sugar, sifted	8 oz icing sugar, sifted
1½ teaspoons lemon juice	1½ teaspoons lemon juice
few drops of almond essence	few drops of almond essence
1 egg	1 egg
1 egg yolk	1 egg yolk

Mix together the almonds and sugars in a bowl. Combine the lemon juice, almond essence, egg and egg yolk and add to the almond mixture. Mix to a stiff paste.

Turn out on to a board dusted with icing sugar and knead until smooth.

This quantity will cover the top and sides of a 20 cm/8 inch square or 23 cm/9 inch round cake.

Makes 1 kg/2 lb

American Frosting

METRIC	IMPERIAL
450 g sugar	1 lb sugar
150 ml water	¼ pint water
2 egg whites	2 egg whites

Dissolve the sugar in the water in a heavy-based saucepan. Bring to the boil and boil the syrup until it reaches 118°C/240°F on a sugar thermometer. Remove from the heat.

Whisk the egg whites until stiff. Gradually whisk in the sugar syrup and continue whisking until the frosting stiffens and holds its shape. Use immediately.

Enough to cover the top and sides of a 20 cm/8 inch sandwich cake

Glacé Icing

METRIC	IMPERIAL
100 g icing sugar	4 oz icing sugar
water (see method)	water (see method)
few drops of vanilla essence	few drops of vanilla essence

Sift the icing sugar into a bowl. Stir in just enough water to make a spreading consistency. Stir in the vanilla essence.

Use the icing at once as it sets quickly.

Enough to coat the top of an 18 cm/7 inch cake

VARIATIONS

Lemon or orange glacé icing: Use lemon or orange juice instead of water, and add a few drops of yellow or orange food colouring, if liked.
Coffee glacé icing: Sift 2 teaspoons instant coffee powder with the sugar.
Chocolate glacé icing: Sift 1 tablespoon cocoa with the sugar and mix with black coffee.
Peppermint glacé icing: Add a few drops of peppermint oil to the basic mixture.

Chocolate Fudge Frosting

METRIC	IMPERIAL
50 g plain chocolate	2 oz plain chocolate
6 tablespoons milk	6 tablespoons milk
100 g sugar	4 oz sugar
pinch of salt	pinch of salt
1 tablespoon golden syrup	1 tablespoon golden syrup
15 g butter, melted	½ oz butter, melted
few drops of vanilla essence	few drops of vanilla essence

Place the chocolate and milk in a heavy-based saucepan and heat until the chocolate has melted. Stir in the sugar, salt and syrup and stir until the sugar has dissolved. Bring to the boil and boil until the mixture reaches 115°C/238°F on a sugar thermometer. Remove from the heat and beat in the butter and vanilla essence. Allow to cool until the frosting is thick enough to coat the back of a spoon, then use as required.

Enough to cover the top of a 20 cm/8 inch cake

Special Occasion Menus

Menu for Four

Avocado with grapefruit
(page 20)
★
Stuffed chicken cutlets
(page 38)

Boiled new potatoes

Petits pois
★
Profiteroles
(page 108)

SEVERAL HOURS BEFORE: Make profiteroles but do not fill until just before serving. Prepare chicken and vegetables for cooking. Prepare avocado.

Cook chicken and vegetables while eating avocado.

Menu for Six

Creamed vegetable herb soup
(page 13)

Wholemeal bread
(page 128)
★
Beef olives with horseradish
(page 48)

Country-style beans
(page 90)

Green salad
★
Rich raspberry soufflé
(page 116)

NIGHT BEFORE: Make soufflé (decorate just before serving). Bake bread.

SEVERAL HOURS BEFORE: Make soup to reheat just before serving. Prepare salad and dressing but keep separate. Prepare beef and leave to cook.

Cook beans while eating soup.

Christmas Menu for Four/Six

Pâté stuffed eggs
(page 22)
★
Roast stuffed turkey
(page 41)

Bread sauce
(page 176)

Cranberry sauce
(page176)

Roast potatoes
(page 89)

Moulded sprouts
(page 90)

Waldorf salad
(page 96)
★
Christmas pudding
(page 103)
with Brandy butter
(page 180)

MONTHS BEFORE: Make pudding.

NIGHT BEFORE: Make brandy butter, cranberry sauce and stuffings for turkey. Make waldorf salad and chill.

SEVERAL HOURS BEFORE: Stuff turkey and put to roast. Steam pudding. Prepare potatoes for roasting and add to turkey. Prepare sprouts and cook. Prepare eggs. Make bread sauce just before serving eggs.

Menu for Four/Six

French pork pâté
(page 18)

Rosemary bread
(page 126)
★
Colonial goose
(page 54)

Scalloped potatoes
(page 88)

Courgettes (steamed or fried in butter)
★
Oranges in caramel sauce
(page 112)
with Brandy snaps
(page 147)

DAY BEFORE: Make pâté. Bake bread. Make brandy snaps but do not fill with cream until just before serving.

SEVERAL HOURS BEFORE: Prepare oranges and chill. Prepare courgettes for cooking. Make lamb and leave to cook. Make potatoes and put into oven with lamb to cook.

Cook courgettes while eating pâté.

To Appeal to Children

Tuna and cheese pizza (page 76)

Deep sea cakes (page 73)

Macaroni with frankfurters (page 81)

Cheese double deckers (page 84)

Baked bean salad (page 95)

Baked bananas (page 105)

Strawberry yogurt lollies (page 121)

Gingerbread (page 138)

Honey chocolate biscuits (page 144)

Chocolate crackles (page 146)

Cocktail Party Ideas

Devilled dip with raw vegetables
(page 23)

Piquant cheese spread with savoury biscuits
(page 23)

Cheese dip with crisps
(page 23)

Cheese straws
(page 20)

Recipes for dips and spread serve 4–6, so increase quantities according to the number of guests. Make ahead of time, cover and chill.

Buffet Ideas

Chicken drumsticks en croûte
(page 40)

Glazed ham
(page 61)

Brawn
(page 67)

Sage and onion quiche
(page 75)

Egg and bacon pie
(page 75)

Boston baked beans
(page 88)

Mixed bean salad
(page 94)

Nutty apple coleslaw
(page 97)

Rum babas
(page 109)

Strawberry almond shortcake
(page 112)

Lemon refrigerator cheesecake
(page 111)

Quiche, pie, shortcake and cheesecake will serve 4–6 each, so make two of each as necessary. Double recipes for salads if required.

Warm Weather Menus

Menu for Four

Tuna and cucumber cocktail
(page 23)
or
Prawn and cream cheese pâté
(page 18)
★
Grilled marinated steak
(page 50)

Mandarin rice salad
(page 97)
★
Strawberries Cordon Bleu
(page 111)

NIGHT BEFORE: Marinate the steak.

SEVERAL HOURS BEFORE: Prepare cocktail or pâté, rice salad and strawberries. Cover all and chill.

Cook steak while eating cocktail or pâté.

Menu for Four

Corn on the cob
(page 121)
★
Barbecued pork chops
(page 60)

Boiled new potatoes with mint

Mixed salad
★
Gooseberry ice cream
(page 120)
with Coconut macaroons
(page 148)

DAY BEFORE: Make ice cream.

SEVERAL HOURS BEFORE: Marinate chops. Prepare corn and potatoes for cooking. Prepare salad and dressing, but keep separately.

Cook corn just before eating. Cook chops and potatoes while eating corn.

Menu for Six

Salmon mousse
(page 19)
or
Minted pea soup
(page 13)
★
Spring lamb casserole
(page 55)

Broccoli or French beans
★
Summer pudding
(page 111)

NIGHT BEFORE: Make mousse and chill, or (if liked) make soup and reheat just before serving. Make pudding.

SEVERAL HOURS BEFORE: Prepare vegetables for cooking. Make casserole and leave to cook.

Cook vegetables while eating mousse or soup.

Picnic ideas

Stuffed sausage loaves (page 78)

Cornish pasties (page 78)

Tomato herb quiche (page 74)

Egg and potato salad loaf (page 96)

Tuna and grapefruit cake (page 33)

Cheddar scotch eggs (page 78)

Honey spice cake (page 135)

Brownies (page 144)

Flapjacks (page 147)

Cold Weather Menus

Menu for Four

Cream of mushroom soup
(page 14)

*

Baked apple mackerel
(page 32)

Broad or green beans

*

Cheese with Oatmeal biscuits
(page 148)

Fresh fruit

SEVERAL HOURS BEFORE: Make soup to reheat just before serving. Prepare vegetables for cooking. Make mackerel and leave to cook.

Cook vegetables while eating soup.

Menu for Four

Sardine lemons
(page 20)

*

Sausage and kidney casserole
(page 63)

Mashed potatoes

Red cabbage with apple
(page 88)

*

Guards' pudding
(page 100)

SEVERAL HOURS BEFORE: Prepare vegetables for cooking. Make lemons and chill. Make pudding and put to steam. Make casserole and leave to cook.

Cook vegetables while eating lemons.

Menu for Six

Herring salad
(page 19)

*

Beef cooked in beer
(page 46)

Glazed carrots
(page 90)

Jacket baked potatoes

*

Orange baked apples
(page 102)

or

Spiced apple raisin crumble
(page 104)

SEVERAL HOURS BEFORE: Make salad and chill. Make beef stew and leave to cook. Scrub potatoes and put to cook with stew after 30 minutes. Prepare carrots and apples for cooking.

Put apples to bake when serving salad, or prepare crumble just before serving salad.

Menu for Four/Six

French onion soup
(page 12)

*

Roast chicken with sweet and sour stuffing
(page 37)

Sugared turnips
(page 91)

Brussels sprouts

*

Banana cream syllabub
(page 110)

NIGHT BEFORE: If liked, make soup to reheat just before serving.

SEVERAL HOURS BEFORE: Prepare vegetables for cooking. Stuff chicken and put to cook. Prepare syllabub and chill.

Cook vegetables while eating soup.

INDEX

INDEX